Grammar and Writing 4

Student Edition

First Edition

MW01044961

Mary Hake

Christie Curtis

Houghton Mifflin Harcourt Publishers, Inc.

Grammar and Writing 4

First Edition

Student Edition

Copyright © 2014 by Houghton Mifflin Harcourt Publishing Company and Mary E. Hake and Christie Curtis

This edition is based on the work titled *Grammar and Writing 4* © 2012 by Mary E. Hake and Christie Curtis and originally published by Hake Publishing.

Printed in the U.S.A.

ISBN 978-0-544-04420-3

12   2266   22 21 20

4500810673   B C D E F G

Contents

54m

Introduction

Welcome to a language arts program created for easy reading and instruction. Behind this program is a team of dedicated teachers who care about your success and want to present incremental teaching material in a simple format.

This program consists of a series of **daily lessons**, **review sets**, and **tests** that are carefully sequenced to develop a variety of skills and concepts. We include lessons on capitalization, punctuation, parts of speech, sentence structure, spelling rules, correct word usage, and dictionary skills with a focus on improving your writing.

To increase your understanding, you will learn to diagram sentences. Diagramming a sentence, like doing a puzzle, exercises your brain and helps you to see the structure of the sentence and the function of its parts. Knowing how to diagram an English sentence will make your future study of foreign languages much easier. It will also help you with correct word usage and punctuation as you write.

Because of the incremental nature of this program, **it is essential that the lessons be taught in order, that all review sets are completed, and that no lessons are skipped.**

In addition to the daily lessons, the program includes a series of **writing lessons**. These are designed to guide you through the process of composing a complete essay. Also included are weekly **dictations** for practice in spelling and punctuation. You will also be asked to keep a journal; the program contains suggested **journal topics**.

MONDAY—Find your weekly dictation in the appendix and copy it to practice for your Friday test.

TUESDAY, WEDNESDAY, THURSDAY—Find your journal topic in the appendix and begin writing.

FRIDAY—Look over your dictation to prepare for your dictation test.

Mastery of the English language is one of the most valuable tools you can possess. It is our hope that this program provides you with a strong foundation not only for future language arts studies but also for a lifetime of satisfying and successful writing.

Best wishes!

The Sentence: Two Parts

> **Dictation or Journal Entry**
> **Vocabulary:**
> *Bare* means "without covering or clothing." Some trees are *bare* in winter.
>
> A *bear* is a large animal with thick fur and a short tail. The hungry *bear* roared. *Bear* also means "to hold up, support, or carry." Mules often *bear* heavy loads for people.

A **sentence** is a group of words, ~~that~~ and expresses a complete thought. which contains a subject and a predicate

The word groups below do *not* express a complete thought.

>   A polar bear.
>
>   Can swim.
>
>   Giant pandas.
>
>   Need bamboo for food.

The word groups above are not sentences. However, we can combine them to make the following complete sentences:

>   A polar bear can swim.
>
>   Giant pandas need bamboo for food.

Two Parts of a Sentence   A sentence has **two parts:** (1) the subject and (2) the predicate. Both parts are necessary to make a complete sentence.

Subject   The **subject** of a sentence tells whom or what the sentence is about. Subjects are underlined below.

>   <u>A polar bear</u> can swim.
>
>   <u>Giant pandas</u> need bamboo for food.

Predicate   The **predicate** of a sentence tells what the subject does or is. Predicates are underlined below.

>   A polar bear <u>can swim</u>.
>
>   Giant pandas <u>need bamboo for food</u>.

Example 1   (a) Write the subject of this sentence:

>   My sister saw a black bear in the forest.

(b) Write the predicate of this sentence:

Two bear cubs slept in their den.

Solution (a) We write, **"My sister,"** for it is the subject of the sentence; it tells *who* saw a black bear in the forest.

(b) We write, **"slept in their den,"** for it is the predicate of the sentence; it tells what the two bear cubs *did*.

Example 2 Rewrite the sentences below. Then, draw a vertical line between the subject and the predicate of each sentence.

Most grizzly bears live in national parks.

The picture showed a large polar bear.

That brown bear is hunting for berries.

Solution We rewrite the sentences and draw vertical lines between the subjects and predicates:

Most grizzly bears | live in national parks.

The picture | showed a large polar bear.

That brown bear | is hunting for berries.

Practice For a and b, write the subject of the sentence.
a. Mammals have hair.

b. A sow feeds milk to her cubs.

For c and d, write the predicate of the sentence.
c. Baby mammals drink milk from their mothers.

d. An angry bear bares its teeth.

Rewrite sentences e and f, drawing a vertical line between the subject and the predicate of each sentence.
e. A female bear is a sow.

f. Tyrell and his brother have seen pandas in China.

For g and h, replace the blank with *bear* or *bare*.
g. She had no shoes; her feet were _____.

h. A _____ has a stumpy tail.

Review Set 1 Choose the correct word to complete sentences 1–6.

1. A (bare, bear) is a mammal.

2. (*Bare, bear*) means "without covering or clothing."

3. A complete sentence has (twelve, two) main parts.

4. The (subject, predicate) of the sentence tells whom or what the sentence is about.

5. The (subject, predicate) of the sentence tells what the subject does, is, or is like.

6. A (subject, sentence) is a word group that expresses a complete thought.

Write the subject of sentences 7–10.

7. A male bear is a boar.

8. Hair keeps a mammal warm and dry.

9. Deep snow blankets the meadow.

10. Winter wind howls through redwoods.

Write the predicate of sentences 11–14.

11. Cubs must learn about danger.

12. A cozy den protects the cubs.

13. Black bears hibernate until spring.

14. The sloth bear eats termites.

Rewrite sentences 15–20, drawing a vertical line between the subject and the predicate of each sentence.

15. A rainbow trout escaped from the grizzly!

16. Some male grizzly bears stand eight feet tall.

17. You might see a spectacled bear in South America.

18. Playful bear cubs wrestle.

19. Omnivores eat both plants and animals.

20. Bears are omnivores. *Stopped here 9/28/2021*

Four Types of Sentences

Dictation or Journal Entry
Vocabulary:
To *pause* is to stop for a short time. Let us *pause* to smell the roses. A *pause* is a brief stop or delay. After a *pause*, he continued speaking.

Paws are the feet of an animal having nails for claws. My dog digs with his front *paws*.

A group of words that expresses a complete thought is called a sentence. A capital letter begins each sentence. There are **four types of sentences.**

Declarative
tells

A **declarative sentence** makes a statement and ends with a period.

> We followed animal footprints.
>
> I found rabbit and skunk tracks.
>
> A skunk is the size of a small cat.

Interrogative
question
?

An **interrogative sentence** asks a question and ends with a question mark.

> Did you follow the animal footprints?
>
> Have you seen rabbit or skunk tracks?
>
> How big is a skunk?

Imperative
command

An **imperative sentence** expresses a command or a request and ends with a period.

> Follow the animal footprints.
>
> Find some rabbit tracks.
>
> Look for the skunk.

Exclamatory
surprise
strong emotion

An **exclamatory sentence** shows excitement or strong feeling and ends with an exclamation point.

> Hooray!
>
> I found it!
>
> Watch out for that skunk!

Example For a–d, write whether the sentence is declarative, interrogative, imperative, or exclamatory.

(a) Where is Yellowstone National Park?

(b) *Paws* and *pause* sound alike.

(c) Draw a porcupine.

(d) It stinks!

Solution (a) This is an **interrogative** sentence because it asks a question and ends with a question mark.

(b) This sentence makes a statement and ends with a period. It is **declarative.**

(c) This sentence commands you to do something, and it ends with a period. Therefore, it is **imperative.**

(d) This sentence ends with an exclamation point and shows strong feeling. We recognize the **exclamatory** sentence.

Practice For a–d, write whether the sentence is declarative, interrogative, imperative, or exclamatory.

a. Where are skunks found?

b. I know!

c. Skunks live in forests, meadows, and towns.

d. Find Yellowstone National Park on the map.

For e and f, replace each blank with *paws* or *pause*.

e. A bear's _____ made prints in the sand.

f. The hikers _____ to examine animal tracks.

Review Set 2 Choose the correct word to complete sentences 1–12.

Numbers in parentheses indicate the number of the lesson in which the concept was introduced.

1. A (bear, bare) might (bear, bare) its teeth when angry.
(1)

2. A dog has four (pause, paws).
(2)

3. A(n) (declarative, interrogative) sentence makes a
(2) statement.

4. A(n) (declarative, interrogative) sentence asks a question.
(2)

5. An (interrogative, imperative) sentence expresses a
(2) command or request.

6. A(n) (declarative, exclamatory) sentence shows strong
(2) feeling.

7. Declarative and imperative sentences end with a (period,
(2) question mark).

8. The (subject, predicate) of a sentence tells whom or what
(1) the sentence is about.

9. The (subject, predicate) of the sentence tells what the
(1) subject does or is.

10. A sentence begins with a (lower case, capital) letter.
(2)

11. An interrogative sentence ends with a (period, question
(2) mark).

12. An exclamatory sentence ends with a(n) (question mark,
(2) exclamation point).

For 13–16, write whether the sentence is declarative,
interrogative, exclamatory, or imperative.

13. Wow, the polar bear is huge!
(2)

14. Who is Laura Ingalls Wilder?
(2)

15. The grizzly bear stood eight feet tall and weighed a
(2) thousand pounds.

16. Sketch a grizzly bear.
(2)

17. Write the subject of this sentence: Porcupines sleep during
(1) the day.

18. Write the predicate of this sentence: Porcupines look for
(1) food at night.

Rewrite sentences 19 and 20, drawing a vertical line between the subject and the predicate.

19. Porcupine quills are sharp.
(1)

20. Ms. Prickle likes porcupines.
(1)

Simple Subjects • Simple Predicates

Dictation or Journal Entry

Vocabulary:

A *predator* is an animal that lives by killing and eating other animals. Hawks, lions, and wolves are *predators*.

Prey is any animal hunted or killed for food. Mice and other small mammals are the *prey* of owls.

We have learned that a sentence has two main parts: (1) the subject and (2) the predicate. The subject is the part that tells whom or what the sentence is about. The predicate is the part that tells something about the subject. The sentences below have been divided into their two main parts—subjects and predicates.

COMPLETE SUBJECT	COMPLETE PREDICATE
An unselfish person	helps others.
Ms. Prickle	talked about porcupines.
A noisy rooster	crows at dawn.
Animals	are interesting.

The complete (whole) subject or predicate may be a single word or many words. However, a subject or predicate of many words always has one main part that we call the *simple subject* or *simple predicate*.

Simple Subject   The main word or words in a sentence that tell *who* or *what* is doing or being something is called the **simple subject.** In the sentence below, *uncle* is the simple subject, because it tells *who* frightens the chickens.

My bearded *uncle* | frightens the chickens.

In the sentences below, we have italicized the simple subjects.

An unselfish *person* | helps others.

Ms. Prickle | talked about porcupines.

A noisy *rooster* | crows at dawn.

Animals | are interesting.

Example 1 Write the simple subject from this sentence:

A good soccer player practices every day.

Solution Who or what practices every day? A good soccer player does, so **player** is the simple subject. (The word "soccer" tells what kind of player.)

Simple Predicate The **simple predicate** is the verb. A **verb** expresses action or being. In the sentence below, "pecked" is the simple predicate, because it tells what a hen did.

A black and white hen <u>pecked</u> my bearded uncle.

We have underlined the simple predicates of the sentences below.

ACTION: An unselfish *person* <u>helps</u> others.

ACTION: *Ms. Prickle* <u>talked</u> about porcupines.

ACTION: A noisy *rooster* <u>crows</u> at dawn.

BEING: *Animals* <u>are</u> interesting.

Notice that sometimes the simple predicate contains more than one word, as in these sentences:

A *thief* <u>has stolen</u> the key!   ~~thief~~   ~~has stolen~~

Dad <u>will be looking</u> for me.

I <u>should have called</u> him.

Example 2 Write the simple predicate of the sentence below.

A good soccer player practices every day.

Solution We examine the sentence and discover that the player "practices." Therefore, **practices** is the simple predicate.

Practice For a–c, write the simple subject of each sentence.
  a. Most reptiles lay hard-shelled eggs.

  b. A brown lizard rested in the sun.

  c. Crocodiles are the largest reptiles.

For d–f, write the simple predicate of each sentence.
  d. Most reptiles lay hard-shelled eggs.

  e. A brown lizard rested in the sun.

f. Crocodiles are the largest reptiles.

For g and h, replace each blank with *predator* or *prey*.

g. The mouse was in danger, for a _____ was nearby.

h. The hungry wolf smelled the scent of its _____.

Review Set 3

*Numbers in parentheses indicate the number of the lesson in which the concept was introduced.

Choose the correct word to complete sentences 1–10.

1. The main word in a sentence that tells whom or what the
(3) sentence is about is called the simple (subject, predicate).

2. The simple (subject, predicate) of a sentence tells whom
(3) or what the sentence is about.

3. The simple (subject, predicate) is the verb.
(3)

4. A (verb, subject) expresses action or being.
(3)

5. A complete sentence has two parts—a (subject, verb) and
(1) a predicate.

6. A (bare, bear) is a large animal.
(1)

7. A (predator, prey) hunts other animals for food.
(3)

8. (Predator, Prey) is hunted by another animal.
(3)

9. After a (pause, paws), the music began again.
(2)

10. The cat held a ball of yarn in its (pause, paws).
(2)

Write the simple subject of sentences 11 and 12.

11. The fierce leopard was purring like a house cat.
(3)

12. The tiger is the largest member of the cat family.
(3)

Write the simple predicate of sentences 13 and 14.

13. The fierce leopard was purring like a house cat.
(3)   Hint: was _____

14. The tiger is the largest member of the cat family.
(3)

For sentences 15–18, write whether the sentence is declarative, interrogative, imperative, or exclamatory.

15. Describe a snow leopard.
(2)

16. Does it have spots?
(2)

17. Its paws are padded for warmth.
(2)

18. It has a beautiful coat!
(2)

Rewrite sentences 19 and 20, drawing a vertical line between the subject and the predicate of each sentence.

19. Cats stalk their prey.
(1)

20. Some predators hunt at night.
(1)

Reversed Subject and Predicate • Split Predicate

Reversed Subject and Predicate

In most sentences, the subject of the sentence comes first, and the predicate follows.

(subject) | (predicate)

The *bats* | will fly at sundown.

However, sometimes the order of the subject and predicate is reversed so that the predicate comes before the subject as in the sentences below:

(predicate)   (subject)

There go | the *bats*.

Up the street came | a tall white *horse*.

Example 1 Write the simple subject and the simple predicate of this sentence:

At the bottom of the sea lies an old ship.

Solution We remember that sometimes the predicate comes before the subject. The simple subject of this sentence is **ship.** What does the ship do? It "lies." The simple predicate is **lies.** Do not be confused by the word "sea." It is not the subject. "At the bottom of the sea" tells where the ship lies.

Split Predicate

In interrogative sentences, we usually find parts of the predicate split by the subject as in this sentence:

Did *you* mail the letter?

In the sentence above, the simple subject is *you*, and the simple predicate is did mail.

Example 2 Write the simple predicate of this sentence:

Has Rex found his bone?

Solution The subject is *Rex*. The simple predicate is **has found**.

Practice For a and b, replace the blank with *mane* or *main*.

   a. The _____ road through town is busy.

   b. The lion shook his _____.

Write the simple subject of sentences c and d.

   c. There are colorful macaws in the rainforest.

   d. Deep in the jungle lives a gorilla.

Write the simple predicate of sentences e and f.

   e. Have you seen Rex's bone? Hint: Have _____

   f. Did Rex dig that hole? Hint: Did _____

More Practice See "More Practice Lesson 4" in the Student Workbook.

Review Set 4 Choose the correct word to complete sentences 1–10.

*Numbers in parentheses indicate the number of the lesson in which the concept was introduced.

   1. The main word in a sentence that tells what the subject
   (3) does or is is called the simple (subject, predicate).

   2. The simple (subject, predicate) of a sentence tells whom
   (3) or what the sentence is about.

   3. The simple predicate is the (subject, verb).
   (3)

   4. A verb expresses (action, anger) or being.
   (3)

   5. A complete (verb, sentence) has two parts—a subject and
   (1) a predicate.

   6. The much-loved stuffed animal had (bear, bare) spots
   (1) where its fur was worn.

   7. A small fish might be a shark's (predator, prey).
   (3)

   8. The (mane, main) water pipe broke, flooding the area.
   (4)

   9. Cats often (paws, pause) before pouncing on their prey.
   (2)

   10. Dirty (paws, pause) leave marks on the floor.
   (2)

For 11 and 12, write the simple subject of each sentence.

11. Do llamas eat plants?
(3, 4)

12. High in the oak tree sits a baby squirrel.
(3, 4)

For 13 and 14, write the simple predicate of each sentence.

13. Does Rex bury his bones? Hint: Does _____
(3, 4)

14. From beneath the bridge flew two small bats.
(3, 4)

For sentences 15–18, write whether the sentence is declarative, interrogative, imperative, or exclamatory.

15. Drink plenty of water.
(2)

16. Have you ever seen a llama?
(2)

17. An ostrich cannot fly.
(2)

18. Wow, that ostrich runs fast!
(2)

Rewrite sentences 19 and 20, drawing a vertical line between the subject and the predicate of each sentence.

19. The male ostrich dug a hole as a nest.
(1)

20. The female ostrich is laying eggs.
(1)

LESSON 5

Complete Sentence or Sentence Fragment

Dictation or Journal Entry

Vocabulary:

A *horse* is a four-legged mammal with hoofs and a long mane and tail. Roy rode his *horse* to town.

Hoarse means "sounding deep and unclear." She has a *hoarse* voice because of her illness.

Complete Sentences

A **complete sentence** expresses a complete thought. It has both a subject and a predicate. The following are **complete sentences**.

Alex had a sly grin.

Who ate my sandwich?

Please tell me.

Notice that the sentence above, "Please tell me," does not appear to have a subject. It is an imperative sentence, a command. The subject *you* is understood.

(You) please tell me.

Fragments

A piece of a sentence is called a **fragment.** When a sentence fragment fails to tell us who or what is doing the action, it is missing the subject. The following sentence fragments are missing subjects.

Washes the dog. (who?)

Whistled in the dark. (who or what?)

If we identify the subject (who or what is doing the action), and we do not know what it is doing, the expression is missing a verb. The sentence fragments below are missing verbs.

The largest reptiles on earth. (do what? are what?)

The villain in the story. (does what?)

If the subject or verb is missing, we identify the expression as a **fragment.** Other errors that result in fragments are leaving out punctuation marks or using the *to* form and *ing* form of the verb.

FRAGMENTS	COMPLETE SENTENCES
A man trimming trees.	A man trims trees.
	A man trimming trees found a bird's nest.
Dennis to play checkers.	Ben asked Dennis to play checkers.
	Dennis wanted to play checkers.

Example Tell whether each of the following is a complete sentence or a sentence fragment.

(a) Rex digs.

(b) A garter snake shedding its skin.

(c) Snakes shed their skin.

(d) To fear rattlesnakes.

Solution (a) **Complete sentence.**

(b) This expression is missing part of the verb, so it is a **sentence fragment.** [Corrected: A garter snake is shedding its skin. (or) I saw a garter snake shedding its skin.]

(c) **Complete sentence.**

(d) This expression uses the *to* form of the verb, and it lacks a subject. It is not a complete thought. It is a **sentence fragment.** [Corrected: Dogs learn to fear rattlesnakes. (or) Should we fear rattlesnakes?]

Practice For a–d, write whether each word group is a sentence fragment or a complete sentence.

  a. Crocodiles have long, narrow snouts.

  b. Resting on the sunny riverbank.

  c. To measure the length of a crocodile.

  d. Crocodiles can grow bigger than alligators.

For e and f, replace each blank with *horse* or *hoarse*.

e. A black _____ galloped through town.

f. Your voice sounds _____ today.

More Practice Write whether each word group is a complete sentence or a sentence fragment.

1. Sitting on a bale of hay.

2. Elle dreams about horses.

3. She needs a saddle.

4. A black Morgan horse with white socks.

5. To gallop through the fields.

6. Friends riding together.

Review Set 5 Choose the correct word to complete sentences 1–10.

*Numbers in parentheses indicate the number of the lesson in which the concept was introduced.

1. A complete sentence has both a subject and a (fragment,
*(1,5) predicate).

2. A piece of a sentence is called a sentence (fragment,
(5) reptile).

3. The simple (subject, predicate) expresses action or being.
(3)

4. If a sentence fragment fails to tell who or what is doing
(5) the action, it is missing the (subject, predicate).

5. If a sentence fails to tell what the subject is or is doing, it
(5) is missing a (subject, predicate).

6. After her cold, Jill's voice was (horse, hoarse).
(5)

7. Have you ever ridden a (horse, hoarse)?
(5)

8. The lion's (main, mane) was tangled.
(4)

9. Coyotes are (prey, predators), for they kill and eat other
(3) animals.

10. Let us (paws, pause) to rest before we hike up the hill.
(2)

For 11 and 12, write whether the word group is a complete sentence or a sentence fragment.

11. Sarah laughed.
(5)

12. Waves slapping the shore.
(5)

Write the simple subject of sentences 13 and 14.

13. Do gorillas have thumbs?
(3, 4)

14. Along came an elephant.
(3, 4)

Write the simple predicate of sentences 15 and 16.

15. Do gorillas have thumbs? Hint: Do _____
(3, 4)

16. Along came an elephant.
(3, 4)

For sentences 17–19, write whether the sentence is declarative, interrogative, imperative, or exclamatory.

17. The giraffe is so tall!
(2)

18. Look at the zebras.
(2)

19. Have you seen a wombat?
(2)

20. Rewrite the following sentence, drawing a vertical line
(1) between the subject and the predicate:

Wombats live in Australia and Tasmania.

LESSON 6

Correcting a Sentence Fragment

> **Dictation or Journal Entry**
> **Vocabulary:**
> A *tail* is the hindmost part of an animal's body. My dog wags his *tail* when he sees me.
>
> A *tale* is a story. She told a *tale* about hunting snakes in Africa.

We have learned that a complete sentence expresses a complete thought and that it has both a subject and a predicate. On the other hand, a **sentence fragment** is a piece of a sentence that is missing a subject, predicate, or proper punctuation mark.

Correcting Fragments   We can correct sentence fragments by adding subjects, verbs, and punctuation marks.

Example 1   Correct this sentence fragment: Barked loudly.

Solution   There is more than one right answer. We add a subject to tell who or what barked.

> ### *Dogs* <u>barked</u> loudly.

> ### *Seals* <u>barked</u> loudly.

Example 2   Correct this sentence fragment: The wooden stairs.

Solution   There are different ways to correct this sentence fragment. We can add an action verb telling what the wooden stairs do.

> ### The wooden *stairs* <u>creak</u>.

We can also add a being verb to tell what the wooden stairs are.

> ### The wooden *stairs* <u>are</u> old.

Practice   For a–d, rewrite and correct each sentence fragment, making a complete sentence. There is more than one correct answer.

    a. Found a lizard in my shoe.

    b. An enormous raccoon.

    c. My new friend.

    d. Was scratching its ear.

For e and f, replace each blank with *tail* or *tale*.

  e. The brown horse had a black mane and _____.

  f. Have you heard the _____ of the boa that escaped from the zoo?

More Practice For 1–5, correct each sentence fragment, making a complete sentence. There is more than one correct answer.

  1. A skinny coyote.

  2. Two jackrabbits.

  3. To wax the car.

  4. Played the drums.

  5. Might live in that burrow.

Review Set 6 Choose the correct word to complete sentences 1–8.

  1. The dog barked until it became (horse, hoarse).
  (5)

  2. The tourists drove on the (main, mane) street through town.
  (4)

  3. Sometimes a small bird is the (predator, prey) of a cat.
  (3)

  4. Some cats have six toes on their (paws, pause).
  (2)

  5. Mules can (bare, bear) heavy loads on mountain trails.
  (1)

  6. An (exclamatory, interrogative) sentence ends with a question mark.
  (2)

  7. The simple (subject, predicate) of a sentence is the verb.
  (3)

  8. An (exclamatory, interrogative) sentence ends with an exclamation point.
  (2)

For 9–11, write whether the word group is a complete sentence or a sentence fragment.

  9. Riding my bicycle.
  (5)

  10. Wombats are marsupials.
  (5)

11. A baby wombat in its mother's pouch.
(5)

For 12 and 13, rewrite and correct each sentence fragment, making a complete sentence. There is more than one correct answer.

12. To hike the mountain trail.
(6)

13. My favorite animal.
(6)

Write the simple subject of sentences 14 and 15.

14. At the top of that tree sits an eagle.
(3, 4)

15. Do wombats eat hamburgers?
(3, 4)

Write the simple predicate of sentences 16 and 17.

16. At the top of that tree sits an eagle.
(3, 4)

17. Do wombats eat hamburgers? Hint: Do _____
(3, 4)

For sentences 18 and 19, write whether the sentence is declarative, interrogative, imperative, or exclamatory.

18. I can read music.
(2)

19. Sing with me.
(2)

20. Rewrite the following sentence, drawing a vertical line
(1) between the subject and the predicate:

A magnificent unicorn flaps its wings.

Action Verbs

Dictation or Journal Entry
Vocabulary:
It's means "it is." *It's* windy in the city.
Its means "belonging to it." The bear bared *its* teeth.

Action Verbs   A sentence is made up of a subject and a verb. The verb tells what the subject is or does. An **action verb** describes what the subject does or did. *Mixed* is an action verb in the sentence below. It tells what "Nate" did.

Nate <u>mixed</u> the pancake batter.

Sometimes a sentence has more than one action verb. In the sentence below, *crows* and *chases* are two action verbs telling what "my rooster" does.

My rooster <u>crows</u> early and <u>chases</u> the hens.

Example   Identify each action verb in these sentences.

(a) Josh brushes the horses and cleans their stall.

(b) Ken kept his promises.

(c) The lamb tripped on a stone and fell.

Solution   (a) The action verbs **brushes** and **cleans** tell what "Josh" does.

(b) The action verb **kept** tells what "Ken" did.

(c) The action verbs **tripped** and **fell** tell what the "lamb" did.

Practice   Write each action verb in sentences a–c.

a. The lizard lost its tail but escaped.

b. Later, it grows a new tail.

c. The chameleon shoots out its tongue and catches insects.

For d and e, replace each blank with *it's* or *its*.

d. That lizard has lost _____ tail.

e. I wonder if _____ sad.

Review Set 7 Choose the correct word to complete sentences 1–5.

1. A rabbit wiggles (it's, its) nose.
(7)

2. That poor dog has fleas from head to (tale, tail).
(6)

3. Clydesdales are one type of (hoarse, horse).
(5)

4. A donkey, too, has a (main, mane).
(4)

5. (It's, Its) a sunny day.
(7)

Write each action verb in sentences 6–8.

6. A chameleon changes its body color.
(7)

7. A chameleon matches its surroundings.
(7)

8. Its large eyes bulge and look in all directions.
(7)

For 9 and 10, write whether the word group is a complete sentence or a sentence fragment.

9. A harmless garter snake.
(5)

10. Giving birth to live babies.
(5)

For 11 and 12, rewrite and correct each sentence fragment, making a complete sentence. There is more than one correct answer.

11. A poisonous snake.
(6)

12. To meet a rattlesnake.
(6)

Write the simple subject of sentences 13 and 14.

13. Do tortoises live here?
(3, 4)

14. On that flat rock rests an enormous turtle.
(3, 4)

Write the simple predicate of sentences 15 and 16.

15. Do tortoises live here? Hint: Do _____
(3, 4)

16. On that flat rock rests an enormous turtle.
(3, 4)

For sentences 17–19, write whether the sentence is declarative, interrogative, imperative, or exclamatory.

17. Wow, that sea turtle is huge!
(2)

18. Did it lay many eggs?
(2)

19. Sea turtles have flat shells and flippers for swimming.
(2)

20. Rewrite the following sentence, drawing a vertical line
(1) between the subject and the predicate:

A snake smells with its long, forked tongue.

LESSON 8

Capitalizing Proper Nouns

> **Dictation or Journal Entry:**
>
> **Vocabulary:**
>
> *Their* means "belonging to them." Snakes shed *their* skin.
>
> *There* means "at or in that place." Stay *there*.

Proper Nouns

A noun is a name word—a person, place, or thing. A noun may be common or proper. A *common noun* does not name a specific person, place, or thing. A **proper noun** does name a specific person, place, or thing and requires a capital letter.

Common noun—cat; **Proper noun—Spats**

We capitalize every proper noun.

COMMON NOUN	PROPER NOUN
city	Boston
state	Massachusetts
day	Monday
month	June
girl	Amelia Rivas
character	Peter Rabbit

Common Nouns Within Proper Nouns

When a common noun such as "lake," "river," "mountain," "street," or "school" is a part of a proper noun, we capitalize it, as in the examples below.

COMMON NOUN	PROPER NOUN
street	Main Street
school	Gidley Elementary School
ocean	Pacific Ocean
family	Hahn Family
river	Mississippi River

Small Words Within Proper Nouns

When the following small words are parts of a proper noun, we do not capitalize them unless they are the first or last word:

a, an, and, at, but, by, for, from,

if, in, into, of, on, the, to, with

Notice the examples below.

The Wizard of Oz
"The Tortoise and the Hare"
Sea of Galilee
On the Banks of Plum Creek
"America the Beautiful"

Example   Capitalize letters in these sentences as needed.

    (a) The story is about swans named louis and serena.

    (b) Have you read *trumpet of the swan?*

    (c) The davis family lived near lake michigan.

    (d) Many americans came from other countries.

Solution   (a) We capitalize **Louis** and **Serena** because they are specific swans.

    (b) **Trumpet** and **Swan** are capitalized because they are words of a book title. We do not capitalize the small words *of* and *the.*

    (c) **Davis Family** is a specific family and needs capital letters. Also, **Lake Michigan** is a specific lake.

    (d) **Americans** is capitalized because it is a group of people from a specific country.

Practice   Rewrite sentences a–e, capitalizing each proper noun.

    a. Does andrew attend cleminson elementary school?

    b. fannie sue named her goat burpy.

    c. dan read the story "jack and the beanstalk."

    d. They live in temple city.

    e. Where is the golden gate bridge?

For f and g, replace each blank with *their* or *there.*

    f. I left my key _____ on the desk.

    g. They brought _____ lunches with them.

More Practice   See "More Practice Lesson 8" in the Student Workbook.

Review Set 8   Choose the correct word to complete sentences 1–5.

    1. Please wait (there, their) for me.
    (8)

    2. (Its, It's) fun to watch the monkeys.
    (7)

    3. A (tale, tail) helps an animal to balance.
    (6)

4. A quarter (horse, hoarse) runs fast for a short distance.
(5)

5. A hungry dolphin searches for (predator, prey).
(3)

Write and capitalize each proper noun in sentences 6–8.

6. Do any bears live in india?
(8)

7. frances hodgson burnett wrote *the secret garden*.
(8)

8. Elephants from africa have larger ears than those from india.
(8)

9. Write each action verb in this sentence:
(7)
Rex sneaks in and licks icing from the cake.

For 10 and 11, write whether the word group is a complete sentence or a sentence fragment.

10. Listening to her dolphin calf.
(5)

11. A mother dolphin protects her calf.
(5)

For 12 and 13, rewrite and correct each sentence fragment, making a complete sentence. There is more than one correct answer.

12. Splashing dolphins.
(6)

13. A crab on the beach.
(6)

Write the simple subject of sentences 14 and 15.

14. The elephant's trunk held two gallons of water!
(3)

15. Up the tree ran three squirrels.
(3)

Write the simple predicate of sentences 16 and 17.

16. The elephant's trunk held two gallons of water!
(3)

17. Up the tree ran three squirrels.
(3, 4)

For sentences 18 and 19, write whether the sentence is declarative, interrogative, imperative, or exclamatory.

18. Name three different kinds of bears.
(2)

19. What do deer eat in winter?
(2)

20. Rewrite the following sentence, drawing a vertical line
(1) between the subject part and the predicate part:

A tiger claims its own territory.

Present Tense of Verbs

> **Dictation or Journal Entry**
>
> **Vocabulary:**
>
> A *fir* is a type of evergreen tree of the pine family. They decorated a *fir* tree for Christmas.
>
> *Fur* is the hairy coat of certain animals. The white rabbit had soft, thick *fur*.

Verbs tell us not only what action is occurring but also when it is occurring. The form of a verb, or the **verb tense,** changes to show when the action takes place. Three simple verb tenses are present, past, and future. In this lesson, we will talk about the present tense.

Present Tense

The **present tense** refers to action that is happening now. We add an *s* when the subject is singular, except when the pronoun is *I* or *you*.

PLURAL SUBJECTS AND PRONOUNS *I* AND *YOU*	SINGULAR SUBJECTS
Lions <u>roar</u>.	The lion <u>roars</u>.
Dogs <u>bark</u>.	A dog <u>barks</u>.
I <u>wink</u>.	She <u>winks</u>.
We <u>rest</u>.	He <u>rests</u>.
They <u>laugh</u>.	Joe <u>laughs</u>.
You <u>sing</u>.	Ana <u>sings</u>.
Jen and Ken <u>talk</u>.	Grandpa <u>talks</u>.

When a verb ends in *s, x, z, ch,* or *sh,* we add *es* when the subject is singular.

PLURAL SUBJECTS AND PRONOUNS *I* AND *YOU*	SINGULAR SUBJECTS
You <u>rush</u>.	She <u>rushes</u>.
Bees <u>buzz</u>.	A bee <u>buzzes</u>.
We <u>munch</u>.	He <u>munches</u>.
Snakes <u>hiss</u>.	A snake <u>hisses</u>.
I <u>fix</u> lunch.	Rob <u>fixes</u> lunch.

When a verb ends in a consonant and a *y*, we change the *y* to *i* and add *es* for the singular form.

PLURAL SUBJECTS AND PRONOUNS *I* AND *YOU*	SINGULAR SUBJECTS
I <u>dry</u> the wet dog.	He <u>dries</u> the wet dog.
They <u>empty</u> the box.	Lily <u>empties</u> the box.

Example Replace each blank with the singular present tense form of the verb.

(a) You <u>reply</u>. She _____.

(b) Bats <u>fly</u>. A bat _____.

(c) People <u>cry</u>. A person _____.

(d) Sodas <u>fizz</u>. One soda _____.

(e) They <u>guess</u>. He _____.

Solution (a) **replies** (Since the verb ends in *y*, we change the *y* to *i* and add *es*.)

(b) **flies** (Since the verb ends in *y*, we change the *y* to *i* and add *es*.)

(c) **cries** (Since the verb ends in *y*, we change the *y* to *i* and add *es*.)

(d) **fizzes** (The verb ends in *z*, so we add *es*.)

(e) **guesses** (The verb ends in *s*, so we add *es*.)

Practice For a and b, replace each blank with *fir* or *fur*.

a. Some animals have _____.

b. They planted _____ trees.

For c–f, replace each blank with the singular present tense form of the underlined verb.

c. Jan and Van <u>wash</u>. Tim _____.

d. Meg and Jon <u>wish</u>. Quan _____.

e. They <u>reply</u>. One man _____.

f. People <u>try</u>. She _____.

Review Set 9 Choose the correct word to complete sentences 1–5.

1. Sometimes, I brush my cat's thick (fir, fur).
(9)

2. The students closed (there, their) books.
(8)

3. A giraffe lifts (its, it's) head toward the sky.
(7)

4. Mr. Chu read the (tail, tale) to the children.
(6)

5. Your voice may become (horse, hoarse) with too much
(5) use.

6. Write and capitalize each proper noun from the following
(8) sentence:

Last august, molly saw a white-tailed deer in canada.

For 7 and 8, replace the blank with the singular present tense form of the underlined verb.

7. Bullfrogs <u>catch</u> flies. One bullfrog _____ flies.
(9)

8. Two kittens <u>cry</u>. One kitten _____.
(9)

9. Write each action verb in this sentence:
(7)
A toad hears a noise and leaps into the pond.

For 10 and 11, write whether the word group is a complete sentence or a sentence fragment.

10. Waterbirds, such as ducks and gulls.
(5)

11. Do gulls make nests on cliffs?
(5)

For 12 and 13, rewrite and correct each sentence fragment, making a complete sentence. There is more than one correct answer.

12. A raven in the treetop.
(6)

13. Picking bushels of cherries.
(6)

Write the simple subject of sentences 14 and 15.

14. Do tigers live in North America?
(3, 4)

15. High overhead soars an eagle.
(3, 4)

Write the simple predicate of sentences 16 and 17.

16. Do tigers live in North America? Hint: Do _____
(3, 4)

17. High overhead soars an eagle.
(3, 4)

For sentences 18 and 19, write whether the sentence is declarative, interrogative, imperative, or exclamatory.

18. Wow, its wings are powerful!
(2)

19. Eagles use the same nest year after year.
(2)

20. Rewrite the following sentence, drawing a vertical line
(1)   between the subject and the predicate:

Four plump pigeons landed on our picnic table.

LESSON 10

Past Tense of Regular Verbs

> **Dictation or Journal Entry**
>
> **Vocabulary:**
> *Who's* means "who is." *Who's* there?
>
> *Whose* means "belonging to whom or which." *Whose* book is this? I know an animal *whose* fur changes color.

We remember that verbs tell us not only what action is occurring but also when it is occurring. The form of a verb, or the verb tense, changes in order to show when the action takes place. Three simple verb tenses are present, past, and future.

In this lesson, we will talk about the past tense of regular verbs. There are many irregular verb forms that we will learn later.

Past Tense The **past tense** shows action that has already occurred. To form the past tense of regular verbs, we add *ed*.

roar—roared

bark—barked

When a one-syllable verb ends in a single consonant, we double the consonant and add *ed*.

clip—clipped

pat—patted

When a verb ends in *e*, we drop the *e* and add *ed*.

bake—baked

love—loved

When the verb ends in *y*, we change the *y* to *i* and add *ed*.

cry—cried

reply—replied

Example 1 Write the past tense form of each verb.

(a) slip   (b) dare   (c) try

(d) tap   (e) hurry   (f) live

Solution (a) **slipped** (Because this is a one-syllable verb ending in a consonant, we double the consonant and add *ed*.)

Grammar and Writing 4   **35**   **Student Edition**
Lesson 10

(b) **dared** (The verb ends in *e*, so we drop the *e* and add *ed*.)

(c) **tried** (The verb ends in *y*, so we change the *y* to *i* and add *ed*.)

(d) **tapped** (Since this is a short verb ending in a consonant, we double the consonant and add *ed*.)

(e) **hurried** (The verb ends in *y*, so we change the *y* to *i* and add *ed*.)

(f) **lived** (The verb ends in *e*, so we drop the *e* and add *ed*.)

Errors to Avoid Do not use the present tense form for the past tense.

NO:	Yesterday, Jake <u>calls</u> me.
YES:	Yesterday, Jake <u>called</u> me.
NO:	Last night, I <u>work</u> late.
YES:	Last night, I <u>worked</u> late.
NO:	A week ago, she <u>rakes</u> the leaves.
YES:	A week ago, she <u>raked</u> the leaves.

Do not shift from past to present in the same phrase.

NO:	He <u>washed</u> everything but <u>dries</u> nothing.
YES:	He <u>washed</u> everything but <u>dried</u> nothing.
NO:	A robin <u>chirped</u> and <u>flaps</u> its wings.
YES:	A robin <u>chirped</u> and <u>flapped</u> its wings.

Example 2 Choose the correct form of the verb to complete each sentence.

(a) Josh cleaned the sink and (mops, mopped) the floor.

(b) Last week, I (slip, slipped) on a banana peel.

Solution (a) Josh cleaned the sink and **mopped** the floor.

(b) Last week, I **slipped** on a banana peel.

Practice For a and b, replace each blank with *who's* or *whose*.

a. _____ coming with me?

b. _____ backpack is this?

For c–j, write the past tense form of each verb.

c. clap   **d.** worry   **e.** hug   **f.** trace

g. dry   **h.** hike   **i.** tip   **j.** step

For k and l, choose the correct verb form.

k. Yesterday, my cat (walks, walked) to the park.

l. The cat stalked a tennis ball and (swallows, swallowed) it whole.

Review Set 10

Choose the correct word to complete sentences 1–5.

1. I do not know (who's, whose) car that is.
(10)

2. Douglas (fur, fir) trees are popular at Christmastime.
(9)

3. Place your backpacks over (there, their).
(8)

4. (It's, Its) hot outside.
(7)

5. A lizard can lose its (tale, tail).
(6)

6. Write and capitalize each proper noun from the following sentence:
(8)

Did yin yu fly from memphis, tennessee, to sacramento, california?

For 7 and 8, replace the blank with the singular present tense form of the underlined verb.

7. Cats <u>hiss</u>. My cat _____.
(9)

8. Two cooks <u>fry</u> eggs. One cook _____ eggs.
(9)

9. Write each action verb in this sentence:
(7)
Squirrels hunt, gather, and bury acorns.

For 10 and 11, write whether the word group is a complete sentence or a sentence fragment.

10. A mammal with a pouch for its young.
(5)

11. The koala is a marsupial.
(5)

12. Rewrite and correct the following sentence fragment,
(6) making a complete sentence. There is more than one
correct answer.

Defend themselves with sharp claws.

Write the simple subject of sentences 13 and 14.

13. Do koalas live in trees?
(3, 4)

14. Here comes a kangaroo!
(3, 4)

Write the simple predicate of sentences 15 and 16.

15. Do koalas live in trees? Hint: Do _____
(3, 4)

16. Here comes a kangaroo!
(3, 4)

For sentences 17 and 18, choose the correct verb form.

17. My friend called and (chats, chatted) for a while.
(10)

18. Yesterday, she (picks, picked) oranges.
(10)

19. For a and b, write the past tense form of the verb.
(10) (a) clip   (b) try

20. Rewrite the following sentence, drawing a vertical line
(1) between the subject and the predicate:

The baby koala crawls into its mother's pouch.

Concrete, Abstract, and Collective Nouns

> **Dictation or Journal Entry**
> **Vocabulary:**
> *You're* means "you are." *You're* a good student.
> *Your* means "belonging to you." I like *your* idea.

We know that a noun is a word for a person, place, or thing. We group nouns into these classes: common, proper, concrete, abstract, and collective.

We have learned the difference between common and proper nouns. In this lesson, we will learn the difference between concrete and abstract nouns. We will also learn to recognize collective nouns.

Concrete Nouns

A **concrete noun** names a person, place, or thing that can be seen or touched. It may be either common or proper.

CONCRETE COMMON NOUNS	CONCRETE PROPER NOUNS
mountain	Mount Baldy
doctor	Dr. Green
state	Georgia

Abstract Nouns

An **abstract noun** names something that cannot be seen or touched. It names something that you can only think about. An abstract noun can be common or proper as well.

ABSTRACT COMMON NOUNS	ABSTRACT PROPER NOUNS
religion	Judaism
holiday	Thanksgiving Day
nationality	Irish
language	Spanish
day	Friday

Example 1

Tell whether each noun is concrete or abstract.

(a) Christianity   (b) wisdom

(c) Indian Ocean   (d) tooth

(e) hope   (f) truth

Solution (a) **abstract** (Christianity is a religion.)

(b) **abstract** (We can only *think* about wisdom.)

(c) **concrete**   (d) **concrete**

(e) **abstract**   (f) **abstract**

Collective Nouns A **collective noun** names a collection of persons, places, animals, or things. We list a few examples below.

PERSONS: team, crew, class, army, family, chorus

ANIMALS: flock, herd, school (fish), litter

PLACES: Africa, Asia, Europe, Central America

THINGS: batch, bunch, assortment, collection

Example 2 Write the collective noun from each sentence.

(a) A pod of dolphins played near our ship.

(b) This herd belongs to that tribe.

(c) I live in the United States.

(d) Eva baked a batch of muffins.

Solution (a) **pod**   (b) **herd, tribe**

(c) **United States**   (d) **batch**

Practice For a and b, replace each blank with *you're* or *your*.

a. Please open _____ book.

b. Please come when _____ ready.

For c–f, tell whether each noun is abstract or concrete.

c. bird   **d.** peace

e. faith   **f.** horse

For g and h, write the collective noun that you find in each sentence.

g. With this bushel of peaches, I shall make jam.

h. Rex found a colony of red ants near his water dish.

For 1–12, tell whether each noun is abstract or concrete.

1. happiness   2. apple   3. forest   4. fear

5. lion   6. sadness   7. joy   8. bone

9. plum   10. beak   11. toe   12. hope

Write each collective noun that you find in sentences 13–15.

13. Abe has started a rock collection.

14. A fleet of ships passed a school of fish.

15. This assortment of sandwiches might attract that swarm of bees!

Review Set 11

Choose the correct word to complete sentences 1–5.

1. (Who's, Whose) pounding on the door?
(10)

2. Huskies have two layers of (fur, fir).
(9)

3. (Their, There) are ants in my lunch bag!
(8)

4. Will that dog ever stop (it's, its) barking?
(7)

5. Nan told an amazing (tail, tale) about a swan.
(6)

6. Write and capitalize each proper noun from the following
(8)   sentence:

A ship named misty sits in san francisco bay.

For 7 and 8, replace the blank with the singular present tense form of the underlined verb.

7. Two princesses <u>kiss</u> frogs. One princess _____
(9)   a frog.

8. Some birds <u>fly</u> south. One bird _____ south.
(9)

Write each action verb in sentences 9 and 10.

9. Rex disturbs the ants and then yelps when they bite
(7)   him.

10. In the past, horses plowed the land, pulled carriages, and
(7)   hauled heavy loads.

For 11 and 12, write whether the word group is a complete sentence or a sentence fragment.

11. Known as the giants of the deep.
(5)

12. A blue whale can be one hundred feet long.
(5)

13. Rewrite and correct the following sentence fragment, making a complete sentence. There is more than one correct answer.
(6)

Spends its entire life in the sea.

14. For a and b, write whether the noun is concrete or abstract.
(11)

(a) whale   (b) foolishness

15. Write each collective noun that you find in this sentence:
(11)
The road crew watched a gaggle of geese in flight.

Write the simple subject of sentences 16 and 17.

16. With their gills, fish breathe underwater.
(3)

17. Did Rex eat my muffin?
(3, 4)

Write the simple predicate of sentences 18 and 19.

18. With their gills, fish breathe underwater.
(3)

19. Did Rex eat my muffin? Hint: Did _____
(3, 4)

For sentences 20 and 21, choose the correct verb form.

20. Long ago, wild animals (roam, roamed) this valley.
(10)

21. Nate picked cherries and (bakes, baked) them in a pie.
(10)

22. For a and b, write the past tense form of the verb.
(10)
(a) pit   (b) fry

For 23 and 24, write whether the sentence is declarative, interrogative, imperative, or exclamatory.

23. A whale is not a fish.
(2)

24. Do whales have scales?
(2)

25. Rewrite the following sentence, drawing a vertical line
(1) between the subject and the predicate:

A whale's tail moves up and down.

LESSON 12

Helping Verbs

Dictation or Journal Entry

Vocabulary:
Canine means "of or like a dog." Rex shows his *canine* loyalty by guarding the house.

Feline means "belonging to the cat family; catlike." She walks with *feline* grace, not making a sound.

Helping Verbs We know that every predicate contains a verb. Sometimes, the verb is more than one word in the sentence. The main verb may have one or more **helping verbs.** The main verb shows the action; the helping verbs do not show action, but they help to form the verb tense.

Rex <u>might have eaten</u> my muffin.

In the sentence above, "eaten" is the main verb, and "might" and "have" are helping verbs. "Might have eaten" is called a verb phrase.

Memorize these common helping verbs:

is, am, are, was, were, be, being, been,

has, have, had, may, might, must,

can, could, do, does, did,

shall, will, should, would

Example In the following sentences, write the entire verb phrase and circle each helping verb:

(a) Elle should have been guarding my muffin.

(b) She might have saved it.

(c) Instead, she has been watching television.

(d) I shall bake another muffin.

Solution (a) (should)(have)(been) guarding (*Should, have,* and *been* are helping verbs for the main verb "guarding.")

(b) (might)(have) saved

(c) (has)(been) watching

(d) (shall) bake

a. Study the helping verbs listed in this lesson. Memorize them one line at a time. Practice saying them *in order* (perhaps to your teacher or a friend). Then, write as many as you can from memory.

For sentences b–e, write the entire verb phrase and circle each helping verb.

b. Kim must have been planting corn today.

c. She should have called me.

d. I could have helped her.

e. Next year, I shall offer my help.

For f and g, replace each blank with *canine* or *feline.*

f. Dogs are _____ animals.

g. Cats are _____ animals.

More Practice See "More Practice Lesson 12" in the Student Workbook.

Review Set 12 Choose the correct word to complete sentences 1–7.

1. (Your, You're) the author of this short story!
(11)

2. (Who's, Whose) keys are these?
(10)

3. The (fir, fur) trees were covered with snow.
(9)

4. The students picked up (their, there) trash.
(8)

5. (Its, It's) a laughing hyena!
(7)

6. He jumped when a gorilla (taps, tapped) on his window.
(10)

7. Write and capitalize each proper noun from the following
(8) sentence: My friend alba goes to durfee school on star street.

For 8 and 9, replace the blank with the singular present tense form of the underlined verb.

8. All the students <u>try</u> hard. One student _____ hard.
(9)

9. Two cars <u>miss</u> the turn. A car _____ the turn.
(9)

10. Write each action verb in this sentence: We paddled our
(7) canoe alongside a crocodile.

11. From memory, write the common helping verbs listed in
(12) this lesson.

For sentences 12 and 13, write the entire verb phrase, circling each helping verb.

12. Next week, we shall be practicing for the spelling bee.
(12)

13. You should have seen that crocodile's teeth!
(12)

For 14 and 15, write whether the word group is a complete sentence or a sentence fragment.

14. Watering the tomato plants and the corn.
(5)

15. Kenny fed the chickens.
(5)

16. Rewrite and correct the following sentence fragment,
(6) making a complete sentence: My favorite activities.

17. For a–d, write whether the noun is concrete or abstract.
(11)
   (a) paw   (b) wisdom   (c) idea   (d) bear

18. Write each collective noun that you find in this sentence:
(11) A pod of whales surprised the rowing team.

Write the simple subject of sentences 19 and 20.

19. The large male wolf avoided people.
(3)

20. Away ran the wolf.
(3, 4)

Write the simple predicate of sentences 21 and 22.

21. The large male wolf avoided people.
(3)

22. Away ran the wolf.
(3, 4)

23. For a–d, write the past tense form of the verb.
(10)
   (a) jog   (b) rely   (c) mop   (d) dry

24. Write whether the following sentence is declarative,
$^{(2)}$ interrogative, imperative, or exclamatory: That weasel is
eating my lunch!

25. Rewrite the following sentence, drawing a vertical line
$^{(1)}$ between the subject and the predicate:

My cousin in Florida has planted a grove of citrus trees.

Singular, Plural, Compound, and Possessive Nouns

Dictation or Journal Entry

Vocabulary:

Offensive means "irritating, attacking, angering, or causing displeasure." Skunks can make an *offensive* odor.

Defensive means "protective; resisting attack." To keep out critters, he built a *defensive* wall around his garden.

Singular or Plural

Nouns are either singular or plural. A **singular noun** names only one person, place, or thing. A **plural noun** names more than one person, place, or thing.

SINGULAR NOUNS	PLURAL NOUNS
eagle	eagles
perch	perches
cliff	cliffs
nest	nests

Example 1   Tell whether each noun is singular or plural.

(a) fox   (b) wishes   (c) clips

(d) mole   (e) stories   (f) monkey

Solution   (a) **singular**   (b) **plural**   (c) **plural**

(d) **singular**   (e) **plural**   (f) **singular**

Compound

A noun made up of two or more words is a **compound noun.** Sometimes, we write a compound noun as one word:

softball, storybook, hummingbird

Often, we write compound nouns as two words:

elementary school, post office, gopher snake

Other compound nouns are hyphenated:

sister-in-law, hand-me-down, show-off

There is no pattern for knowing whether to spell a compound noun as one word, two separate words, or one hyphenated word. We must use the dictionary.

Example 2   Write the compound nouns from this list:

        encyclopedia   eyebrow

        take-off   dictionary

Solution   The compound nouns from the list above are **eyebrow** and **take-off.**

Possessive   A **possessive noun** tells "who" or "what" owns something. Possessive nouns can be either singular or plural. The possessive form of a noun has an apostrophe and an *s* added to it.

    a *kangaroo's* pouch   the *tree's* branches
    a *circus's* tent   the *dog's* name
    somebody's shoe   a *fish's* tail
    nobody's business   a *bull's* horns

Usually only an apostrophe is added to plural nouns when they end with the letter *s*.

    two *elephants'* trunks   some *girls'* bicycles
    the *horses'* saddles   the *nurses'* help
    the *Curtises'* rooster   several *farmers'* crops

Example 3   Write the possessive noun from each sentence.

(a) I might make a card for Father's Day.

(b) What are your parents' names?

(c) Lucy's bicycle has a flat tire.

(d) My friend's words encourage me.

Solution   (a) **Father's**   (b) **parents'**   (c) **Lucy's**   (d) **friend's**

Practice   For a–d, write whether each noun is singular or plural.

    a. cherries   **b.** rectangle

    c. Venus   **d.** sons

    e. Write each compound noun from this list:
    son-in-law   soccer ball
    snowman   alligator

For f and g, write the possessive noun from each sentence.

f. A reptile's skin has scales.

g. Have you read those scientists' journals?

For h and i, replace each blank with *offensive* or *defensive*.

h. At midnight, the fighting cats made a(n) _____ noise.

i. A(n) _____ player blocks the other team from scoring points in the game.

More Practice See "Funny Fill-in #1" in the Student Workbook. Have fun!

Review Set 13 Choose the correct word to complete sentences 1–7.

1. Cats and tigers are (feline, canine) animals.
(12)

2. (You're, Your) short story had a surprise ending.
(11)

3. I wonder (who's, whose) lunch that is.
(10)

4. Rex's (fir, fur) was muddy.
(9)

5. (Bear, Bare) heads need hats in cold weather.
(1)

6. Madison removed her mittens and (rubs, rubbed) her cold fingers.
(10)

7. *Paws* is a (singular, plural) noun.
(13)

8. Write and capitalize each proper noun from the following sentence: Last monday, my friend james rode his bicycle from mount baldy to the pacific ocean.
(8)

9. Replace the blank with the singular present tense form of the underlined verb: Two squirrels <u>hurry</u>. One squirrel _____.
(9)

10. Write each action verb in the following sentence: Rex jumps fences, chases squirrels, and digs holes.
(7)

11. From memory, write the common helping verbs listed in Lesson 12.
(12)

12. Write the entire verb phrase, circling each helping verb in
(12) this sentence: Rex has been barking all day.

13. Write whether the following word group is a complete
(5) sentence or a sentence fragment: Dolphins eat fish and
squid.

14. Write each compound noun from this list:
(13)
look-alike   timber wolf
amphibian   timetable

15. Write the possessive noun from this sentence: A vulture's
(13) bill is slightly hooked.

16. Rewrite and correct the following sentence fragment,
(6) making a complete sentence: To pick berries near the creek.

17. For a–d, write whether the noun is concrete or abstract.
(11) (a) vulture   (b) justice   (c) mercy   (d) fur

18. Write each collective noun that you find in this sentence:
(11) This crop of corn is ready to harvest.

Write the simple subject of sentences 19 and 20.

19. There are magnificent, fragrant roses in the garden.
(3, 4)

20. Has Dad been trimming trees?
(3, 4)

Write the simple predicate of sentences 21 and 22.

21. There are magnificent, fragrant roses in the garden.
(3, 4)

22. Has Dad been trimming trees?
(3, 4)

23. For a–d, write the past tense form of the verb.
(10) (a) trim   (b) worry   (c) scrub   (d) reply

24. Write whether the following sentence is declarative,
(2) interrogative, imperative, or exclamatory: Why do beavers
build dams?

25. Rewrite the following sentence, drawing a vertical line
(1) between the subject and the predicate:

A swarm of beetles have been eating the plants.

Future Tense

Dictation or Journal Entry

Vocabulary:

Foul means "extremely offensive to the senses" or "very dirty." Rotten potatoes create a *foul* odor.

Fowl are chickens, turkeys, ducks, geese, pheasants, or grouse. Hungry pioneers hunted *fowl* to eat.

The **future tense** refers to action that has not yet occurred. The future tense is usually formed with the helping verbs *shall* or *will*. With the pronouns *I* and *we*, the use of *shall* is preferable in formal writing.

He *will* sing.	We *shall* sing.
They *will* play.	I *shall* play.
You *will* help.	We *shall* help.
Ana *will* come.	She and I *shall* come.
Ben *will* leave.	He and I *shall* leave.
Ben and Ana *will* talk.	We *shall* talk.

Example 1 Complete the future tense verb form by replacing each blank with *will* or *shall*, as you would do in formal writing.

(a) Tony _____ play a drum in the parade.

(b) Sophia and I _____ march with the band.

(c) It _____ rain tomorrow.

(d) I _____ carry my umbrella.

Solution (a) Tony **will** play a drum in the parade.

(b) Sophia and I **shall** march with the band.

(c) It **will** rain tomorrow.

(d) I **shall** carry my umbrella.

Errors to Avoid Do not use the present for the future tense.

NO: Tomorrow I <u>bake</u> muffins.
YES: Tomorrow I <u>shall bake</u> muffins.

NO: We <u>race</u> next Friday.
YES: We <u>shall race</u> next Friday.

NO: Next week he <u>plays</u> his clarinet.
YES: Next week he <u>will play</u> his clarinet.

Example 2 Identify the following underlined verbs as present, past, or future:

(a) Grandpa <u>fixes</u> things.

(b) He <u>will repair</u> the flat tire.

(c) Elva <u>called</u> him.

Solution (a) **present**   (b) **future**   (c) **past**

Example 3 Write the correct form of the verb.

(a) The band (past of *perform*) yesterday.

(b) Kate (future of *fill*) Rex's water dish.

(c) A miner (present of *search*) for diamonds.

(d) Rex (past of *bury*) his bones.

Solution (a) The band **performed** yesterday.

(b) Kate **will fill** Rex's water dish.

(c) A miner **searches** for diamonds.

(d) Rex **buried** his bones.

Practice For sentences a–d, tell whether the underlined verb is present, past, or future tense.

a. Many students <u>enjoy</u> the outdoors.

b. We <u>shall plan</u> a trip.

c. <u>Will</u> you <u>call</u> me later?

d. Noah <u>asked</u> for a ride.

For e–g, write the correct form of the verb.

e. Oscar (past of *hurry*) home.

f. He (future of *prove*) his case.

g. The bear (present of *growl*) angrily.

For h–k, replace each blank with *will* or *shall*, as you would do in formal writing, in order to complete the future tense form of the verb.

h. That little fir tree _____ grow tall.

i. I _____ eat green vegetables.

j. They _____ help me.

k. We _____ listen carefully.

For l and m, replace each blank with *foul* or *fowl*.

l. Skunks defend themselves with a _____ odor.

m. The _____ on their farm included peacocks and turkeys.

Review Set 14

Choose the correct word to complete sentences 1–8.

1. The (offensive, defensive) neighbor enters others' homes
(13) without knocking.

2. A lion is a member of the (canine, feline) family.
(12)

3. The teacher thinks that (you're, your) polite.
(11)

4. (Whose, Who's) ready to play soccer?
(10)

5. Please place your books (there, their) on the shelf.
(8)

6. The male crickets rubbed (there, their) wings together
(8, 10) and (chirps, chirped).

7. We (will, shall) hear crickets chirping after dark.
(14)

8. *Walrus* is a (singular, plural) noun.
(13)

9. Write and capitalize each proper noun from the following
(8) sentence: Llamas carry heavy loads near the andes
mountains in south america.

10. Replace the blank with the singular present tense form of
(9) the underlined verb: Some groomers <u>brush</u> horses. One
groomer _____ horses.

11. Write each action verb in the following sentence: A crab
(7) catches food and defends itself with its claws.

12. From memory, write the common helping verbs listed in
(12) Lesson 12.

13. In the following sentence, write the entire verb phrase,
(12) circling each helping verb: That llama has been traveling
for days without water.

14. In the following sentence, write whether the underlined
(10, 14) verb phrase is present, past, or future tense: A bright red
macaw <u>screamed</u>.

15. Write whether the following word group is a complete
(5) sentence or a sentence fragment: With a sharp bill as
strong as a vice.

16. Write each compound noun from this list:
(13)
wolverine   sea horse

predator   sunburn

17. Write the possessive noun from this sentence: An
(13) ostrich's wings are small.

18. Rewrite and correct the following sentence fragment,
(6) making it a complete sentence: To eat more fruits and
vegetables.

19. For a–d, write whether the noun is concrete or abstract.
(11)
(a) mane   (b) courage   (c) prey   (d) hope

20. Write each collective noun that you find in this sentence:
(11) Has the herd of llamas moved to higher ground?

21. Write the simple subject of the following sentence: May I
(3, 4) help you?

22. Write the simple predicate of the following sentence:
(3, 4) May I help you?

23. For a–d, write the past tense form of the verb.
(10)
(a) dip   (b) marry   (c) rub   (d) bury

24. Write whether the following sentence is declarative,
interrogative, imperative, or exclamatory: People make
blankets and clothing from llamas' wool.

25. Rewrite the following sentence, drawing a vertical line
between the subject and the predicate:

The weary black llama sat down in the shade.

Capitalization: Sentence, Pronoun *I*, Poetry

Dictation or Journal Entry

Vocabulary:

Vertebrate means "having a backbone or spinal column." A *vertebrate* animal has a skeleton of bone or cartilage and a brain enclosed in a skull. *Vertebrates* include fish, reptiles, amphibians, mammals, and birds.

Invertebrate means "having no backbone; not vertebrate." The jellyfish is an *invertebrate*.

There are many reasons why words are capitalized. Because proper nouns name a specific person, place, or thing, they need to be capitalized. We also remember that a common noun linked with a proper noun requires a capital letter. Therefore, the word "ocean" is capitalized in "Pacific Ocean."

However, little words such as *a*, *of*, *the*, *an*, and *in* are not capitalized when they are part of a proper noun (as in the United States of America, the Gulf of Mexico, and John the Baptist).

Now, we will learn more about capitalization.

First Word of Every Sentence

The **first word of every sentence** requires a capital letter.

Macaws make homes in rainforests.

They scream and bite in captivity.

With powerful bills, they break open nuts.

The Pronoun *I*

The **pronoun *I*** is always capitalized, no matter where it is placed in the sentence.

I shall learn which words to capitalize.

Shall I use a capital letter here?

Rules, I am told, help us with our writing.

First Word in a Line of Poetry

The **first words of each line in most poetry** are usually capitalized.* For example, Robert Louis Stevenson begins "Nest Eggs" this way:

Here in the fork
The brown nest is seated;
For little blue eggs
The mother keeps heated.

The poem ends like this:

> They shall go flying
> With musical speeches
> High overhead in the
> Tops of the beeches.
>
> In spite of our wisdom
> And sensible talking,
> We on our feet must go
> Plodding and walking.

* However, for effect, some poets purposely do not capitalize first words of their lines of poetry.

Example Add capital letters wherever needed.

(a) May i read you a poem?

(b) look at that bright red macaw!

(c) Ogden Nash capitalizes the first word of each line of his poem "The Shrew":

> strange as it seems, the smallest mammal
> is the shrew, and not the camel.
> and that is all I ever knew,
> or wish to know, about the shrew.

Solution (a) We capitalize the pronoun *I* in this sentence.

(b) Since the first word in every sentence must be capitalized, we write, "Look at that bright red macaw!"

(c) We write,
> **S**trange as it seems, the smallest mammal
> **I**s the shrew, and not the camel.
> **A**nd that is all I ever knew,
> **O**r wish to know, about the shrew.

Practice Write each word that should be capitalized in a and b.

a. in june, i shall move to alaska.

b. Ogden Nash capitalized the first word of each line in his poem "The Duck," which goes like this:
> behold the duck.
> it does not cluck.
> a cluck it lacks.
> it quacks.

For c and d, replace each blank with *vertebrate* or *invertebrate*.

    c. Jellyfish, sponges, starfish, coral, worms, crabs, spiders, and insects are _____ animals.

    d. The horse is a _____ .

More Practice   See "More Practice Lesson 15" in the Student Workbook.

Review Set 15   Choose the correct word(s) to complete sentences 1–8.

   1. Turkeys are the most commonly eaten (foul, fowl) at
   (14) Thanksgiving.

   2. The (offensive, defensive) mother duck protected her
   (13) ducklings.

   3. (Canines, Felines) make useful guard animals and police
   (12) helpers.

   4. Did (you're, your) teacher grade the test?
   (11)

   5. Too much running on asphalt can injure a dog's (paws,
   (2) pause).

   6. Randy and Candy pulled weeds and (work, worked) in
   (10) their garden today.

   7. I (will, shall) pull weeds over (there, their) tomorrow.
   (8, 14)

   8. *Vertebrates* is a (singular, plural) noun.
   (13)

   9. Rewrite the following sentence, adding capital letters as
   (8, 15) needed: the bay of bengal lies east of india.

  10. Replace the blank with the singular present tense form of
   (9) the underlined verb: Mules <u>carry</u> supplies. A mule
   _____ supplies.

  11. Write each action verb in the following sentence: A tiny
   (7) spider monkey swings by its tail and leaps from branch to
   branch.

  12. From the following list, write the word that is *not* a
   (12) helping verb: is, am, are, was, where, be, being, been.

13. In the following sentence, write whether the underlined
(9, 10, 14) verb phrase is present, past, or future tense: Monkeys <u>will</u>
<u>hide</u> from other animals.

14. Write whether the following word group is a complete
(5) sentence or a sentence fragment: Llamas' wool for clothing,
blankets, and ropes.

15. Write each compound noun from this list:
(13)

horseshoe   vertebrate

invertebrate   doorbell

16. Write each possessive noun from this sentence: Some of
(13) Ogden Nash's poems talk about animals' differences.

17. Rewrite and correct the following sentence fragment,
(6) making a complete sentence: To ride a donkey.

18. For a–d, write whether the noun is concrete or abstract.
(11)   (a) dream   (b) raccoon   (c) prey   (d) gentleness

19. Write the collective noun in this sentence: A band of
(11) monkeys lives there.

20. Write the simple subject of the following sentence: Are
(3, 4) those monkeys friendly?

21. Write the simple predicate of the following sentence: Are
(3, 4) those monkeys friendly?

22. Rewrite the following lines of poetry, adding capital
(15) letters as needed:

hey diddle diddle,

the cat and the fiddle.

the cow jumped over the moon...

23. For a–d, write the past tense form of the verb.
(10)   (a) tug   (b) skip   (c) shop   (d) bully

24. Write whether the following sentence is declarative,
(2) interrogative, imperative, or exclamatory: Tell me about
yourself.

25. Rewrite the following sentence, drawing a vertical line
₍₁₎ between the subject and the predicate:

An old tom turkey struts through the pen.

LESSON 16

Irregular Plural Nouns, Part 1

Plural Nouns **We never form a plural with an apostrophe.** In most cases, we make a singular noun plural by adding an *s*.

SINGULAR	PLURAL
frog	frogs, NOT frog's
habit	habits

Irregular Forms Some nouns have irregular plural forms. We must learn these. We add *es* to a singular noun ending in the following letters: *s, sh, ch, x, z.*

SINGULAR	PLURAL
Moses	Moseses
boss	bosses
bush	bushes
bench	benches
fox	foxes
López	Lópezes
buzz	buzzes

We change *y* to *i* and add *es* when a singular noun ends in a consonant plus *y*.

SINGULAR	PLURAL
butterfly	butterflies
baby	babies
party	parties
dairy	dairies

Note: Not all words that end in *y* are irregular. We add an *s* when a singular noun ends with *ay, ey, oy* or *uy*.

SINGULAR	PLURAL
day	days
key	keys
boy	boys
guy	guys

Example For a–h, write the plural form of each singular noun.

(a) habitat   (b) porch   (c) box   (d) toy

(e) dish   (f) way   (g) sky   (h) supply

Solution (a) **habitats** (regular)   (b) **porches** (ends in *ch*)

(c) **boxes** (ends in *x*)   (d) **toys** (ends in *oy*)

(e) **dishes** (ends in *sh*)   (f) **ways** (ends in *ay*)

(g) **skies** (ends in consonant plus *y*)

(h) **supplies** (ends in consonant plus *y*)

Practice For a and b, replace each blank with *habit* or *habitat*.

a. Gert is trying to break the _____ of chewing her pencil.

b. Cactus often grows well in a desert _____.

For c–j, write the plural form of each singular noun.

c. tax   **d.** puppy   **e.** donkey   **f.** brush

g. Gómez   **h.** berry   **i.** tray   **j.** wrench

Review Set 16 Choose the correct word(s) to complete sentences 1–10.

1. Canines are (vertebrates, invertebrates) because they have
(15) a backbone.

2. Spoiled milk has a (fowl, foul) odor.
(14)

3. The (offensive, defensive) basketball player guarded the
(13) shooter well.

4. Some (canines, felines) bark loudly.
(12)

5. Someone needs to brush that tangled (mane, main).
(4)

6. Josh and Nate picked apples and (trap, trapped) fruit flies
(10) this morning.

7. Annabelle and I (will, shall) be (there, their) soon.
(8, 14)

8. We (never, sometimes, always) form a plural with an
(16) apostrophe.

9. *Frog* is a(n) (concrete, abstract) noun.
(11)

10. *Toothbrush* is a (compound, possessive, collective) noun.
(11, 13)

11. Rewrite the following sentence, adding capital letters as
(8, 15) needed: yes, i think john lives near the delaware river in
new jersey.

12. Replace the blank with the singular present tense form of
(9) the underlined verb: Two people <u>wax</u> cars. One person
_____ cars.

13. Write each action verb in the following sentence: Elle works
(7) hard in school and helps other students.

14. From the following list, write the word that is *not* a
(12) helping verb: has, have, had, may, might, mutt, can,
could.

15. In the following sentence, write the entire verb phrase,
(12) circling each helping verb: Mr. Buldorf has been limping
since the accident.

16. In the following sentence, write whether the underlined
(10, 14) verb is present, past, or future tense: He <u>visited</u> the doctor
on Tuesday.

17. Write whether the following word group is a complete
(5) sentence or a sentence fragment: Some insects are
helpful.

18. Rewrite and correct the following sentence fragment,
(6) making a complete sentence: With a five-dollar bill.

19. Write the simple subject of the following sentence: Kurt's
(3) sister paints colorful macaws.

20. Write the simple predicate of the following sentence:
(3, 4) Does Kurt's sister paint colorful pandas?

21. Rewrite the following lines of poetry, adding capital
(15) letters as needed:

birds of a feather
flock together...

22. Write the past tense form of the verb *try*.
(10)

23. Write whether the following sentence is declarative,
(2) interrogative, imperative, or exclamatory: Do you speak
Spanish?

24. For a–d, write the plural of each noun.
(16)
(a) key   (b) pony   (c) lunch   (d) cherry

25. Rewrite the following sentence, drawing a vertical line
(1) between the subject and the predicate:

Some helpful insects eat harmful insects.

Irregular Plural Nouns, Part 2

Dictation or Journal Entry:

Vocabulary:

Knew is the past tense of the verb *know*. Max *knew* how to raise fowl, for he lived on a farm.

New means "having existed only a short time." Annabelle's *new* shoes hurt her feet.

We continue our study of plural nouns.

Irregular Forms Some singular nouns change completely in their plural forms.

SINGULAR	PLURAL
woman	women
man	men
person	people
tooth	teeth
foot	feet

Other nouns are the same in their singular and plural forms.

SINGULAR	PLURAL
moose	moose
deer	deer
cod	cod

Dictionary When we are uncertain, we use a dictionary to check plural forms. If the plural form of the noun is regular (only add *s* to the singular noun), then the dictionary will not list it. Sometimes the dictionary will list two plural forms for a noun. The first one listed is the preferred one. (Example: cactus *n.*, *pl.* cacti, cactuses)

Example 1 Write the plural form of each of the following singular nouns. Use a dictionary if you are in doubt.

(a) mouse   (b) ox   (c) child   (d) sheep

Solution   (a) **mice** (irregular form)   (b) **oxen** (irregular form)

(c) **children** (irregular form)

(d) We check the dictionary and find that the plural of *sheep* is **sheep.**

Nouns Ending in *f*, *ff*, *fe* For most nouns ending in *f, ff,* and *fe,* we add *s* to form the plural.

SINGULAR	PLURAL
cuff	cuffs
gulf	gulfs
safe	safes

However, for some nouns ending in *f* and *fe,* we change the *f* to *v* and add *es.*

SINGULAR	PLURAL
life	lives
calf	calves
wolf	wolves

Nouns Ending in *o* We usually add *s* to form the plurals of nouns ending in *o,* especially if they are musical terms.

SINGULAR	PLURAL
auto	autos
solo	solos
piano	pianos
alto	altos
soprano	sopranos
banjo	banjos

However, the following are important exceptions:

SINGULAR	PLURAL
echo	echoes
hero	heroes
tomato	tomatoes
potato	potatoes
mosquito	mosquitoes

(There are many more!)

Because there are many more exceptions, we must check the dictionary to be sure of the correct spelling.

Example 2 Write the plural form of each of the following singular nouns. Use a dictionary if you are in doubt.

(a) puff   (b) piano   (c) hero   (d) half

Solution (a) **puffs** (word ending in *ff*)

(b) **pianos** (musical term ending in *o*)

(c) We notice that the word *hero* is in the list of exceptions to words ending in *o*. We check the dictionary and find that the plural of *hero* is **heroes.**

(d) We check the dictionary and find that the plural of *half* is **halves.**

Practice For a–i, write the plural form of each singular noun. Use the dictionary if you are in doubt.

    a. cliff   **b.** tomato   **c.** chief

    d. knife   **e.** salmon   **f.** tooth

    g. goose   **h.** cello   **i.** zoo

For j and k, replace each blank with *knew* or *new*.

    j. I _____ you could do it.

    k. Sam made a _____ friend.

More Practice Write the plural of each noun.

1. cross	**2.** bunch	**3.** boy	**4.** lunch
5. bush	**6.** boss	**7.** cherry	**8.** bay
9. sheep	**10.** man	**11.** lady	**12.** woman
13. person	**14.** mouse	**15.** gentleman	**16.** bluff
17. leaf	**18.** loaf	**19.** alto	**20.** potato

Review Set 17 Choose the correct word(s) to complete sentences 1–8.

    1. Brushing your teeth is a good (habit, habitat).
    (10)

    2. (Vertebrates, Invertebrates) have no backbone.
    (15)

    3. Chickens and ducks are types of (foul, fowl).
    (14)

    4. The (defensive, offensive) noise hurts our ears.
    (13)

    5. Kittens belong to the (canine, feline) family.
    (12, 6)

6. Amelia and she sat in the shade and (sips, siped, sipped)
(8, 10) (there, their) lemonade.

7. We never form a (plural, possessive) noun with an
(16) apostrophe.

8. The word *pelican's* is (compound, abstract, collective,
(11, 13) possessive).

9. Rewrite the following sentence, adding capital letters as
(8, 15) needed: every sunday, quan jogs along main street.

10. Replace the blank with the singular present tense form of
(9) the underlined verb: Two children <u>reply</u>. One child
_____.

11. Write each action verb in the following sentence: Rex yawns
(7) stretches, and scratches his ear.

12. From the following list, write the word that is *not* a
(12) helping verb: can, could, do, does, dip, shall, will,
should, would.

13. In the following sentence, write the entire verb phrase,
(12) circling each helping verb: Have you seen my other shoe?

14. In the following sentence, write whether the underlined
(10, 14) verb phrase is present, past, or future tense: Tony <u>waded</u>
into the river.

15. Write whether the following word group is a complete
(5) sentence or a sentence fragment: Tiny hummingbirds suck
liquid from flowers.

16. Rewrite and correct the following sentence fragment,
(6) making a complete sentence: One day after school.

17. Write each collective noun that you find in this sentence:
(11) Rex disturbed a colony of red ants.

18. Write the simple subject of the following sentence: May I
(3, 4) have some lemonade?

19. For the following sentence, write the correct form of the
(14) verb: We (future of *paint*) the fence together.

20. Write the simple predicate of the following sentence:
(3, 4) May I have some lemonade?

21. Rewrite the following lines of poetry, adding capital
(15) letters as needed:

wind in the trees,
wind in my hair,
mud on my knees,
but i haven't a care.

22. Write the past tense form of the verb *clap*.
(10)

23. Write whether the following sentence is declarative,
(2) interrogative, imperative, or exclamatory: Some people
prefer cold weather.

24. For a–d, write the plural of each noun.
(16, 17) (a) piano   (b) ranch   (c) life   (d) child

25. Rewrite the following sentence, drawing a vertical line
(1) between the subject and the predicate:

My friend's mother plays ragtime music on the piano.

LESSON 18

Irregular Verbs, Part 1: *Be, Have,* and *Do*

> **Dictation or Journal Entry**
>
> **Vocabulary:**
>
> *Nocturnal* means "active at night." The raccoon is a *nocturnal* animal, searching for food at night.
>
> A *marsupial* is a type of mammal, the female of which has an abdominal pouch for carrying her young after birth. The kangaroo is a *marsupial.*

Three of the most frequently used verbs in the English language are *be, have,* and *do.* The tenses of these verbs are irregular; they do not fit the pattern of the regular verbs. Therefore, we must memorize them.

Points of View Verb forms often change according to three points of view:

(1) First person, the speaker—*I* or *we*

(2) Second person, the person or thing spoken to—*you*

(3) Third person, the person or thing spoken of—*he, she, it, they,* and singular or plural nouns

Below are charts showing the verb forms of *be, have,* and *do.*

Be

	PRESENT		PAST	
	SINGULAR	PLURAL	SINGULAR	PLURAL
1ST PERSON	I <u>am</u>	we <u>are</u>	I <u>was</u>	we <u>were</u>
2ND PERSON	you <u>are</u>	you <u>are</u>	you <u>were</u>	you <u>were</u>
3RD PERSON	he <u>is</u>	they <u>are</u>	he <u>was</u>	they <u>were</u>

Have

	PRESENT		PAST	
	SINGULAR	PLURAL	SINGULAR	PLURAL
1ST PERSON	I <u>have</u>	we <u>have</u>	I <u>had</u>	we <u>had</u>
2ND PERSON	you <u>have</u>	you <u>have</u>	you <u>had</u>	you <u>had</u>
3RD PERSON	he <u>has</u>	they <u>have</u>	he <u>had</u>	they <u>had</u>

Do

	PRESENT		PAST	
	SINGULAR	PLURAL	SINGULAR	PLURAL
1ST PERSON	I <u>do</u>	we <u>do</u>	I <u>did</u>	we <u>did</u>
2ND PERSON	you <u>do</u>	you <u>do</u>	you <u>did</u>	you <u>did</u>
3RD PERSON	he <u>does</u>	they <u>do</u>	he <u>did</u>	they <u>did</u>

Example Complete each sentence with the correct form of the verb.

  (a) He (present of *have*) brown hair.

  (b) You (present of *be*) so helpful!

  (c) We (past of *be*) on time.

  (d) I (past of *do*) my homework last night.

  (e) Nan (present of *do*) chores each day.

  (f) They (past of *have*) an old car.

Solution (a) He **has** brown hair.

  (b) You **are** so helpful!

  (c) We **were** on time.

  (d) I **did** my homework last night.

  (e) Nan **does** chores each day.

  (f) They **had** an old car.

Practice Write the correct verb form to complete sentences a–f.

  a. Classical and jazz (present of *be*) types of music.

  b. Rex (present of *have*) floppy ears.

  c. Ana (present of *do*) fifty push-ups daily.

  d. Ben (past of *have*) apples and cheese for lunch.

  e. We (past of *be*) watching the monkeys.

  f. I (past of *do*) my best.

For g and h, replace each blank with *nocturnal* or *marsupial*.

  g. Bats come out only at night, so they are _____.

  h. The pouched wallaby is a _____.

More Practice

1. For a–d, choose the correct present tense form of the verb *be*.

   (a) I (am, are, is) (b) You (am, are, is)

   (c) He (am, are, is) (d) They (am, are, is)

2. For a–d, choose the correct present tense form of the verb *have*.

   (a) I (have, has) (b) You (have, has)

   (c) She (have, has) (d) We (have, has)

3. For a–d, choose the correct present tense form of the verb *do*.

   (a) I (do, does) (b) You (do, does)

   (c) It (do, does) (d) They (do, does)

4. For a–d, choose the correct past tense form of the verb *be*.

   (a) I (was, were) (b) You (was, were)

   (c) He (was, were) (d) They (was, were)

For 5–16, choose the correct verb form for each sentence.

5. James (do, does) the work.

6. He (have, has) red hair.

7. Mr. Flores (were, was) my teacher last year.

8. (Are, Is) you coming?

9. They (was, were) late.

10. Mea and Kurt (is, are) cousins.

11. (Was, Were) you worried?

12. (Was, Were) your brother with you?

13. Josh (have, has) a tree frog.

14. (Do, Does) Nate like frogs?

15. I (are, is, am) studying marsupials.

16. Elle (do, did) my chores for me.

Review Set 18

Choose the correct word(s) to complete sentences 1–7.

1. I (new, knew) a raccoon had been there.
   (17)

2. My backyard is a safe (habit, habitat) for the raccoon family.
   (16)

3. A vertebrate has a backbone or (marble, spinal) column.
(15)

4. A (fowl, foul) odor seeped from the trash can.
(14)

5. (Your, You're) learning fast.
(11)

6. Elle and her grandmother (was, were) still working when
(18) I arrived.

7. (Its, It's) snowing up (their, there) on the mountain.
(7, 8)

8. Rewrite the following sentence, adding capital letters as
(8, 15) needed: this may, i would like to sail to orcus island.

For 9 and 10, replace the blank with the singular present
tense form of the underlined verb.

9. Some men <u>wash</u> dishes. One man _____ dishes.
(9)

10. Children <u>dry</u> dishes. A child _____ dishes.
(9)

11. Write each action verb in the following sentence: Jake writes
(7) songs and plays the guitar.

12. From the following list, write the word that is *not* a
(12) helping verb: do, does, did, shall, fill, should, would.

13. In the following sentence, write the entire verb phrase,
(12) circling each helping verb: Teo might have fed the dog.

14. In the following sentence, write whether the underlined
(9, 14) verb phrase is present, past, or future tense: Officer
Gómez <u>has</u> a canine helper.

15. Write whether the following word group is a complete
(5) sentence or a sentence fragment: Taking great leaps with
their long, thin legs and large wings.

16. Write the possessive noun from this sentence: The fish
(13) found itself inside a pelican's beak.

17. Rewrite and correct the following sentence fragment,
(6) making a complete sentence: A red-headed woodpecker
in the oak tree.

18. Write each collective noun that you find in this sentence:
(11) A herd of elephants thundered through the village.

19. Write the simple subject of the following sentence: Then,
(3, 4) along came a giraffe.

20. For the following sentence, write the correct form of the
(18) verb: We (past of *be*) surprised.

21. Write the simple predicate of the following sentence:
(3, 4) Then, along came a giraffe.

22. Write the past tense form of the verb *drop*.
(10)

23. Write whether the following sentence is declarative,
(2) interrogative, imperative, or exclamatory: Watch out for
that snake!

24. For a–d, write the plural of each noun.
(16, 17) (a) church   (b) sheep   (c) potato   (d) thief

25. Rewrite the following sentence, drawing a vertical line
(1) between the subject and the predicate:

The pelican scoops up fish with its large beak.

Four Principal Parts of Verbs

Dictation or Journal Entry

Vocabulary:

A *spider* is an invertebrate with a body divided into two parts, four pairs of legs, and several pairs of spinnerets that spin threads for making webs and cocoons. The *spider* trapped a flying insect in its web.

An *insect* is an invertebrate with three pairs of legs and a body divided into three parts, and in the adult, usually two pairs of wings. Ants, flies, grasshoppers, and beetles are *insects*.

Four Principal Parts
Every verb has **four** basic forms, or **principal parts.** In order to form all the tenses of each verb, we need to learn these principal parts: the verb (present tense), the present participle, the past tense, and the past participle.

(1) Present Tense
The first principal part is the singular verb in its **present tense** form, which is used to express *present time*, something that is *true at all times*, and *future time*:

play   learn   wish   hope

(2) Present Participle
The second principal part, used to express continuing action, is preceded by a form of the *be* helping verb. The **present participle** is formed by adding *ing* to the singular verb:

(is) playing   (are) learning   (is) wishing   (are) hoping

(3) Past Tense
The third principal part of a verb, used to express *past time*, is the **past tense,** which we form by adding *ed* to most verbs.

played   learned   wished   hoped

(4) Past Participle
The fourth principal part of a verb, used to express completed action, is the **past participle.** It is preceded by a form of the *have* helping verb. With regular verbs, the past and the past participle are the same.

PAST	PAST PARTICIPLE
played	(have) played
learned	(has) learned
wished	(have) wished
hoped	(has) hoped

Example Complete the chart by writing the second, third, and fourth "principal parts" (present participle, past tense, and past participle) of each verb.

VERB	PRESENT PARTICIPLE	PAST TENSE	PAST PARTICIPLE
help	(is) helping	helped	(has) helped
(a) look	_____	_____	_____
(b) climb	_____	_____	_____
(c) try	_____	_____	_____
(d) watch	_____	_____	_____
(e) ask	_____	_____	_____

Solution

VERB	PRESENT PARTICIPLE	PAST TENSE	PAST PARTICIPLE
(a) look	**(is) looking**	**looked**	**(has) looked**
(b) climb	**(is) climbing**	**climbed**	**(has) climbed**
(c) try	**(is) trying**	**tried**	**(has) tried**
(d) watch	**(is) watching**	**watched**	**(has) watched**
(e) ask	**(is) asking**	**asked**	**(has) asked**

Practice For a–d, complete the chart by writing the second, third, and fourth "principal parts" (present participle, past tense, and past participle) of each verb.

VERB	PRESENT PARTICIPLE	PAST TENSE	PAST PARTICIPLE
a. act	_____	_____	_____
b. want	_____	_____	_____
c. walk	_____	_____	_____
d. work	_____	_____	_____

For e and f, replace each blank with *spider* or *insect*.

  e. A(n) _____ has six legs.

  f. A(n) _____ has eight legs.

Choose the correct word(s) to complete sentences 1–9.

  1. At night, noctural animals are usually (awake, asleep).
  (18)

  2. I have a (knew, new) friend from Japan.
  (17)

  3. Finishing your homework is a good (habitat, habit).
  (16)

  4. A human being is a(n) (vertebrate, invertebrate).
  (15)

  5. The police officer had a (canine, feline) helper.
  (12)

  6. Tira (do, does) yard work for her aunt.
  (18)

  7. (Its, It's) fun for Tira to work out (their, there) in the
  (7, 8) yard.

  8. Rex (have, has) dark brown eyes.
  (18)

  9. The (present, past) participle of the verb *fix* is *(has)*
  (19) *fixed.*

  10. Rewrite the following sentence, adding capital letters as
  (8, 15) needed: are there whales in the caspian sea?

  11. Replace the blank below with the singular present tense
  (9) form of the underlined verb.

  Students <u>try</u>. A student _____.

  12. From the following list, write the word that is *not* a
  (12) helping verb: is, am, far, was, were, be, being, been.

  13. In the following sentence, write the entire verb phrase,
  (12) circling each helping verb: Have you been stung by a
  jellyfish?

  14. In the following sentence, write whether the underlined
  (9, 14) verb phrase is present, past, or future tense: Jellyfish <u>have</u>
  no bones.

15. Write whether the following word group is a complete sentence or a sentence fragment: Starfish eat clams and oysters.
_(5)_

16. Write each compound noun from this list:
_(13)_

chimpanzee   sunlight

weekday   dictionary

17. For a–d, write whether the noun is concrete or abstract.
_(11)_ (a) shark   (b) joy   (c) sorrow   (d) knee

18. Write the simple subject of the following sentence: Has
_(3, 4)_ Clark been flying?

19. For the following sentence, write the correct form of the
_(18)_ verb: Rex (present of *have*) fleas.

20. Write the simple predicate of the following sentence: Has
_(3, 4)_ Clark been flying?

21. Rewrite the following lines of poetry, adding capital
_(15)_ letters as needed:

a nickel, a nickel!
let's buy a pickle.

22. For the verb *fix*, write the (a) present participle, (b) past
_(19)_ tense, and (c) past participle.

23. Write whether the following sentence is declarative,
_(2)_ interrogative, imperative, or exclamatory: Salmon are
born in freshwater streams.

24. For a–d, write the plural of each noun.
_(16, 17)_ (a) berry   (b) monkey   (c) half   (d) tomato

25. Rewrite the following sentence, drawing a vertical line
_(1)_ between the subject and the predicate:

A lobster's strong claw pinched my finger.

LESSON 20

Simple Prepositions, Part 1

Dictation or Journal Entry

Vocabulary:

Mist is tiny droplets of water in the air. The *mist* from the waterfall made my hair and clothes damp.

Missed is the past tense of the verb *miss*. I *missed* the bus because I arrived late.

Prepositions **Prepositions** are words belonging to the part of speech that shows the relationship between a noun or pronoun and another word. Notice how a preposition (italicized) shows the spatial relationship between a bug and the straw:

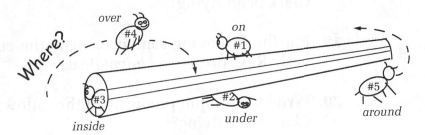

Bug #1 is *on* the straw. Bug #2 is *under* the straw. Bug #3 is *inside* the straw. Bug #4 is jumping *over* the straw. Bug #5 is walking *around* the straw.

Prepositions also show time relationships:

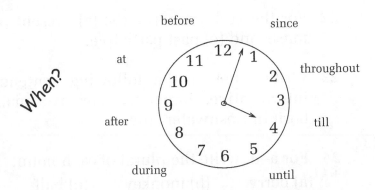

I sneezed *before* lunch, *at* lunch, *during* lunch, *throughout* lunch, *after* lunch, and *until* midnight. I've been sneezing *since* yesterday!

Besides showing spatial and time relationships, prepositions also show abstract (thought or idea) relationships. The prepositions listed below can show abstract relationships.

concerning	except	like	regarding
considering	excepting	of	save
despite	for	opposite	unto

Simple Prepositions

Some prepositions are single words; others are groups of words such as *across from, along with, apart from, by means of,* etc. In this lesson, we will learn to recognize single-word prepositions, **simple prepositions,** which we list alphabetically here. To help you memorize these, we list them in four columns.

1	2	3	4
aboard	*beside*	*inside*	*since*
about	*besides*	*into*	*through*
above	*between*	*like*	*throughout*
across	*beyond*	*near*	*till*
after	*but*	*of*	*to*
against	*by*	*off*	*toward*
along	*concerning*	*on*	*under*
alongside	*considering*	*onto*	*underneath*
amid	*despite*	*opposite*	*until*
among	*down*	*out*	*unto*
around	*during*	*outside*	*up*
at	*except*	*over*	*upon*
before	*excepting*	*past*	*via*
behind	*for*	*regarding*	*with*
below	*from*	*round*	*within*
beneath	*in*	*save*	*without*

Simple prepositions are underlined in the sentences below. Notice how they show the relationship between "went" and "fence."

The cat went <u>under</u> the fence.

The cat went <u>over</u> the fence.

A person, place, or thing always follows a preposition. We call this word the **object of the preposition.** In the first sentence, we see that *fence* is the object of the preposition *under.* In the second sentence, *fence* is the object of the preposition *over.* We will practice this concept in a later lesson.

Example Underline each preposition in sentences a–c.

(a) People aboard that train arrived at the station before noon.

(b) Children in this town and throughout the world know the importance of fresh air.

(c) Rex ran alongside the trolley, from Main Street to Lemon Drive.

Solution (a) People **aboard** that train arrived **at** the station **before** noon.

(b) Children **in** this town and **throughout** the world know the importance **of** fresh air.

(c) Rex ran **alongside** the trolley, **from** Main Street **to** Lemon Drive.

Practice a. Memorize the first column of prepositions. Study the column for a moment, then cover it, and say the prepositions to yourself or to a friend. Repeat this until you can say all the prepositions in the first column.

b. Now, follow the instructions for Practice "a" to memorize the second column of prepositions, and say them to yourself or to a friend.

c. Have a "preposition contest" with yourself or with a friend to see how many prepositions you can write in one minute.

For d–f, list all the prepositions that you find in each sentence.

d. At the store, I bought eggs for breakfast.

e. Young salmon swim from freshwater streams to the ocean.

f. Mature salmon swam up the stream against the current.

For g and h, replace each blank with *missed* or *mist*.

g. Martin waters the ferns with a fine _____.

h. I have _____ you since you moved away.

More Practice For 1 and 2, replace each blank with the missing preposition from your alphabetical list of simple prepositions in this lesson (columns 1 and 2).

1. aboard, about, _____, across, _____, against, along, alongside, amid, among, _____, at, _____, behind, _____, beneath

2. beside, besides, _____, beyond, _____, by, concerning, considering, despite, _____, during, except, _____, for, _____, in

Write each preposition that you find in sentences 3–8.

3. Looking for fun, my pet tortoise crawls under our fence and down the street.

4. He looks along the ground for food and hides from cats and dogs.

5. Sometimes, he wanders around the pond at the park.

6. Opposite the park is his favorite restaurant.

7. During lunch, someone might share some lettuce with him.

8. He prefers lettuce without mustard on it.

Review Set 20 Choose the correct word(s) to complete sentences 1–9.

1. The black widow (insect, spider) spins an unusual web.
(19)

2. A (nocturnal, marsupial) mother carries her baby in an abdominal pouch.
(18)

3. Rex (knew, new) that he was in trouble.
(17)

4. The zoo tried to create a natural (habit, habitat) for the elephants.
(16)

5. (It's, Its) a tiger!
(7)

6. I (am, is, are) taller than she.
(18)

7. A moose left (its, it's) footprints (their, there) in the snow.
(7, 8)

8. Daisy (do, does) puzzles on rainy days.
(18)

9. The (present, past) participle of the verb *fix* is *(has) fixed.*
(19)

10. Rewrite the following sentence, adding capital letters as needed: today, i shall pick some california oranges.
(8, 15)

11. Replace the blank below with the singular present tense form of the underlined verb.
(9)

Gabe and Ben <u>mix</u> paint. Ana _____ paint.

12. Write each action verb in the following sentence: Miss
(7) Ling lost her keys, forgot her lunch, and arrived late.

13. From the following list, write the word that is *not* a
(12) helping verb: has, have, mad, may, might, must, can.

14. In the following sentence, write the entire verb phrase,
(12) circling each helping verb: Mary has been harvesting
corn this week.

15. Write each preposition that you find in the following
(20) sentence: Herds of giraffes live on the grasslands in
Africa.

16. Replace each blank below with a preposition from the
(20) alphabetical list (column 1) provided in this lesson.

aboard, about, above, _____, _____,
against, along, _____, amid, _____, around,
at, before, behind, _____, beneath

17. Write the compound possessive noun from the following
(13) sentence: The newspaper's front page was missing.

18. Rewrite and correct the following sentence fragment,
(6) making a complete sentence: Wearing sunglasses and a
crazy hat.

19. Write each collective noun that you find in this sentence:
(11) A new shipment of dog food should arrive tomorrow.

20. Write the simple subject of the following sentence: Do
(3, 4) giraffes have sharp eyesight?

21. For the following sentence, write the correct form of the
(18) verb: Rex (past tense of *have*) fleas.

22. Write the simple predicate of the following sentence: Do
(3, 4) giraffes have sharp eyesight?

23. For the verb *answer*, write the (a) present participle, (b) past
(19) tense, and (c) past participle.

24. For a–d, write the plural of each noun.
(16, 17)
(a) ostrich   (b) butterfly   (c) discovery   (d) fox

25. Rewrite the following sentence, drawing a vertical line
(1) between the subject and the predicate:

A huge black beetle made its home in my shoe.

LESSON 21

Simple Prepositions, Part 2

Dictation or Journal Entry

Vocabulary:

Deficient means "lacking something important; incomplete." His diet is *deficient* in vitamins, for he does not eat green vegetables.

Sufficient means "enough, as much as is needed." One blanket provided *sufficient* warmth.

In this lesson, we continue to practice memorizing prepositions and identifying them in a sentence.

We will focus on memorizing the third and fourth columns of simple prepositions:

3	4
inside	*since*
into	*through*
like	*throughout*
near	*till*
of	*to*
off	*toward*
on	*under*
onto	*underneath*
opposite	*until*
out	*unto*
outside	*up*
over	*upon*
past	*via*
regarding	*with*
round	*within*
save	*without*

Practice **a.** Memorize preposition column #3. Study the column for a moment, then cover it, and say the prepositions to yourself or to a friend. Repeat this until you can say all the prepositions in the third column.

b. Now, follow the Practice "a" instructions to memorize column #4 so that you can say this list of prepositions to yourself or to a friend.

c. Have a "preposition contest" with yourself or with a friend to see how many prepositions you can write in one minute.

Write each preposition that you find in sentences d–f.

d. During the winter, weasels may grow a white coat for camouflage in snow.

e. Underneath an oak tree sits a squirrel with a pile of acorns.

f. Since sunrise, three young squirrels have been leaping from limb to limb.

For g and h, replace each blank with *deficient* or *sufficient*.

g. With _____ water, those trees will grow tall.

h. The plants died because their soil was _____ in nutrients.

More Practice For 1 and 2, replace each blank with the missing preposition from your alphabetical list of simple prepositions in this lesson (columns 3 and 4).

1. inside, into, like, _____, of, _____, on, onto, opposite, _____, outside, over, _____, regarding, _____, save

2. since, through, _____, till, _____, toward, under, _____, until, _____, up, upon, via, _____, within, without

For 3–14, write whether each word is a noun, verb, or preposition. Write "N" for noun, "V" for verb, or "P" for preposition.

3. says   **4.** forest   **5.** upon   **6.** went

7. with   **8.** bird   **9.** ran   **10.** until

11. bush   **12.** into   **13.** eat   **14.** car

Review Set 21 Choose the correct word(s) to complete sentences 1–9.

1. I (mist, missed) you while you were away.
(20)

2. An ant is a(n) (spider, insect).
(19)

3. Because they hunt during the night, owls are (marsupial nocturnal).
(18)

4. I need (knew, new) socks, for my old ones have holes.
(17)

5. Bob had a cold, and his voice sounded (horse, hoarse).
(5)

6. Mea (have, has) longer hair than I.
(18)

7. (Its, It's) quiet (their, there) in the forest.
(7, 8)

8. Juan (do, does) his chores before school.
(18)

9. The (present, past) participle of the verb *pause* is *(has)*
(19) *paused*.

10. Rewrite the following sentence, adding capital letters as
(8, 15) needed: in may, i shall visit the lincoln park zoo in chicago.

11. Replace the blank below with the singular present tense
(9) form of the underlined verb.

They <u>copy</u> the dictation. Josh _____ the dictation.

12. Write each action verb in the following sentence: The
(7) saltwater turtle dug a hole on the shore, laid her eggs, and swam away.

13. From the following list, write the word that is *not* a
(12) helping verb: may, might, rust, can, could, do, does, did.

14. In the following sentence, write the entire verb phrase,
(12) circling each helping verb: Some turtles can live nearly one hundred years.

15. In the following sentence, write whether the underlined
(9, 14) verb is present, past, or future tense: Some Galapagos turtles <u>weigh</u> nearly two hundred pounds.

16. Write whether the following word group is a complete
(5) sentence or a sentence fragment: Red-footed tortoises in South American rainforests.

17. Write each preposition that you find in the following
(20, 21) sentence: At the zoo on Saturday, I walked among the monkey cages with my cousin Nate.

18. Replace each blank below with a preposition from the
(20, 21) alphabetical list (column 3) provided in this lesson.

inside, _____, like, near, of, _____, on, onto,
opposite, _____, _____, over, past, regarding,
_____, save

19. Write the compound, possessive noun from the following
(13) sentence: I see a hummingbird's nest in that tree!

20. Rewrite and correct the following sentence fragment,
(6) making a complete sentence: In the hot, dry desert.

21. For a–d, write whether the noun is concrete or abstract.
(11)
(a) frog   (b) strength   (c) skill   (d) fowl

22. Write each collective noun that you find in this sentence:
(11) A crow swoops over a flock of doves.

23. Write the simple subject of the following sentence:
(3, 4) Do flamingos have webbed feet?

24. For the following sentence, write the correct form of the
(18) verb: The chickens (past tense of *be*) scratching.

25. Write the simple predicate of the following sentence:
(3, 4) Do flamingos have webbed feet?

26. Rewrite the following lines of poetry, adding capital
(15) letters as needed:

there came a great spider
and sat down beside her,…

27. Write the present participle of the verb *laugh*.
(19) Hint: (is) _____

28. Write whether the following sentence is declarative,
(2) interrogative, imperative, or exclamatory: Ouch, I
touched the cactus!

29. For a–d, write the plural of each noun.
(16, 17)
(a) inch   (b) colony   (c) day   (d) wolf

30. Rewrite the following sentence, drawing a vertical line
(1) between the subject and the predicate:

Long-legged flamingos wade through deep water.

LESSON 22

Irregular Plural Nouns, Part 3

Dictation or Journal Entry
Vocabulary:
A *root* is the lower part of a plant that grows downward to anchor the plant in the soil. That weed had a very long *root*.

A *route* is a way for travel. We shall take the overland *route*.

We continue our study of irregular plural nouns. In this lesson, we shall learn the plural forms of compound nouns and nouns ending in *ful*.

Compound Nouns   We make the main part plural in a compound noun.

SINGULAR	PLURAL
sister-in-law	*sisters*-in-law
commander in chief	*commanders* in chief
officer of the law	*officers* of the law
justice of the peace	*justices* of the peace
king of England	*kings* of England

Nouns Ending in *ful*   We form the plurals of nouns ending in *ful* by adding an *s* at the end of the word.

SINGULAR	PLURAL
cupful	cupfuls
spoonful	spoonfuls

Example   Write the plural form of each of the following singular nouns. Use a dictionary if you are in doubt.

(a) handful   (b) sister of the bride   (c) brother-in-law

Solution   (a) **handfuls** (word ending in *ful*)

(b) **sisters of the bride** (compound noun)

(c) **brothers-in-law** (compound noun)

Practice   For a–d, write the plural form of the singular noun.

a. son-in-law   **b.** chief of staff

c. bucketful   **d.** mouthful

For e and f, replace the blank with *root* or *route*.

e. A _____ is a way to go somewhere.

f. A _____ is a part of a plant.

Review Set 22 Choose the correct word(s) to complete sentences 1–9.

1. I shall cook plenty of rice so that there will be (sufficient, deficient) food for all.
(21)

2. Teo waters the ferns with a fine (mist, missed).
(20)

3. Wasps may hunt black widow (insects, spiders).
(19)

4. The kangaroo is a(n) (invertebrate, marsupial).
(18)

5. The dog wagged (it's, its) tail.
(7)

6. Kim and Jim (is, am, are) twins.
(18)

7. Kim and Jim watched (their, there) cat sharpen (its, it's) claws on Miss Ng's chair.
(7, 8)

8. Emma (do, does) her homework by herself.
(18)

9. The (present, past) participle of the verb *listen* is *(is) listening.*
(19)

10. Rewrite the following sentence, adding capital letters as needed: perhaps i can see mars and venus through this telescope.
(8, 15)

11. Replace the blank below with the singular present tense form of the underlined verb.
(9)
Banks <u>cash</u> checks. A bank _____ checks.

12. Write each action verb in the following sentence: The leopard sneaks through the jungle and hunts for prey.
(7)

13. From the following list, write the word that is *not* a helping verb: do, does, did, shall, will, should, wood.
(12)

14. In the following sentence, write the entire verb phrase, circling each helping verb: That armadillo might be digging for insects.
(12)

15. In the following sentence, write whether the underlined verb is present, past, or future tense: Two rabbits <u>hopped</u> across the playground.
(10, 14)

16. Write whether the following word group is a complete sentence or a sentence fragment: Pigeons live all over the world.
(5)

17. Write each preposition that you find in the following sentence: Many birds migrate to warmer places in winter.
(20, 21)

18. From the following list, write the word that is *not* a preposition: aboard, about, above, across, ant, against, along, alongside, amid, among, around, at, before, behind.
(20, 21)

19. Write the compound, possessive noun from the following sentence: Did you hear the seabird's cry?
(13)

20. Rewrite and correct the following sentence fragment, making a complete sentence:
(6)

Swatting flies with their tails.

21. For a–d, write whether the noun is concrete or abstract.
(11)

(a) fur   (b) tale   (c) honesty   (d) tail

22. Write each collective noun that you find in this sentence: I paused when I saw the pack of wolves.
(11)

23. Write the simple subject of the following sentence: From high in the tree came the hoot of an owl.
(3, 4)

24. For the following sentence, write the correct form of the verb: Mr. Flores (present of *have*) two dogs.
(18)

25. Write the simple predicate of the following sentence: From high in the tree came the hoot of an owl.
(3, 4)

26. Rewrite the following lines of poetry, adding capital letters as needed:
(15)

when the owl hoots,
the mouse scoots.

27. Write the past participle of the verb *miss*.
(19) Hint: (has) _____

28. Write whether the following sentence is declarative, interrogative, imperative, or exclamatory:
(2)

Unlike monkeys, apes have no tails.

29. For a–d, write the plural of each noun.
(17, 22) (a) calf   (b) son of Abraham   (c) spoonful   (d) sheep

30. Rewrite the following sentence, drawing a vertical line
(1) between the subject and the predicate:

A big red hen with black tail feathers guards her fluffy chicks.

Complete Sentence or Run-on Sentence?

Dictation or Journal Entry

Vocabulary:

Anterior means "at or toward the front or head." *Anterior* feelers help to guide the centipede.

Posterior means "at or toward the back." Some of the centipede's *posterior* legs were stuck in mud, but its front legs were free.

Run-on Sentences

A sentence is complete only if it expresses a complete thought.

Here are two complete sentences:

> Owls live in woodlands. They hunt at night.

Two or more complete thoughts written or spoken as one sentence without proper punctuation or connecting words is called a **run-on sentence,** as shown below.

> Owls live in woodlands they hunt at night. (Run-on)

Sometimes a comma is used where there should be a period:

> Owls live in woodlands, they hunt at night. (Run-on)

We may join sentences with the words *and, or, so,* or *but.* However, if we omit the joining words or punctuation between sentences, we have a run-on sentence.

> RUN-ON SENTENCE:
> Ana caught one fish Ben caught two Daisy caught ten.

> COMPLETE SENTENCE:
> Ana caught one fish, and Ben caught two, but Daisy caught ten.

Example Tell whether each of the following is a complete sentence or a run-on sentence.

(a) Owls have brown feathers they live in trees.

(b) They catch prey such as mice and small birds.

(c) Owls fly quietly they hoot loudly.

(d) High in the oak, an owl was hooting.

Solution (a) This expression is two complete thoughts without punctuation. Therefore, it is a **run-on sentence.** (Corrected: Owls have brown feathers. They live in trees.)

(b) **complete sentence**

(c) This is two complete thoughts without connecting words or punctuation, so it is a **run-on sentence.** (Corrected: Owls fly quietly, but they hoot loudly.)

(d) **complete sentence**

Practice For a–d, write whether each word group is a complete sentence or a run-on sentence.

    a. The woodpecker hammers into tree trunks it licks up insects with its long tongue.

    b. Long-tailed chickadees peck insects off leaves.

    c. Flycatchers snap up passing insects.

    d. Two finches argued they would not share the seeds.

For e and f, replace each blank with *anterior* or *posterior*.

    e. Many animals have a _____ tail.

    f. _____ parts of an animal are at its front or head.

More Practice Write whether each word group is a complete sentence or a run-on sentence.

    1. I can't open the cage its door is locked.

    2. Can you open it?

    3. I found a key let's try it.

    4. Don't let the parrots out!

    5. They're too loud I can't hear you.

    6. Please do not open the cage.

Review Set 23 Choose the correct word(s) to complete sentences 1–9.

    1. Carrots are a (route, root) vegetable.
    (22)

2. (Deficient, Sufficient) in vitamin C, the sailors developed
(21) a disease called scurvy.

3. The tourist (mist, missed) the train.
(20)

4. Known for their buzzing, flies are an annoying (spider,
(19) insect).

5. Please place your coats over (their, there).
(8)

6. Frogs (was, were) croaking a funny song.
(18)

7. Monkeys like the jungle climate, but (its, it's) too hot
(7, 8) (their, there) for me.

8. (Do, Does) a manatee have gills?
(18)

9. *(Has) missed* is the (present, past) participle of the verb
(19) *miss*.

10. Rewrite the following sentence, adding capital letters as
(8, 15) needed: on monday, i received a postcard from hampton,
virginia.

11. Replace the blank below with the singular present tense
(9) form of the underlined verb.

Chefs <u>mash</u> potatoes. Rob _____ potatoes.

12. Write each action verb in the following sentence: My cousin
(7) drew a lizard, signed the drawing, and framed it.

For sentences 13 and 14, write the entire verb phrase, circling
each helping verb.

13. Has Max been telling tall tales?
(12)

14. Can you outrun an ostrich?
(12)

15. In the following sentence, write whether the underlined
(14) verb phrase is present, past, or future tense:

I <u>shall show</u> you a rare butterfly.

16. Write whether the following word group is a complete
(5, 23) sentence, a sentence fragment, or a run-on sentence:

A powerful mother brown bear with her two cubs.

17. Write each preposition that you find in the following
(20, 21) sentence:

In a forest of South America, an ocelot hunts at night.

18. From the following list, write the word that is *not* a
(20, 21) preposition:

beside, besides, between, beyond, but, buy, concerning,
considering, despite, down, during, except.

19. Write the compound, possessive noun from the following
(13) sentence:

The wildcat's striped coat helps it to hide in the forest.

20. Rewrite and correct the following sentence fragment,
(6) making a complete sentence:

To eat ants and termites.

21. For a–d, write whether the noun is concrete or abstract.
(11)
(a) mane   (b) paws   (c) courage   (d) habit

22. Write each collective noun that you find in this sentence:
(11)
A herd of cattle grazed in the pasture.

23. Write the simple subject of the following sentence:
(3, 4)
Did the groomer brush the pony?

24. For the following sentence, write the correct form of the
(18) verb:

Miss Kim whistles as she (present of *do*) her chores.

25. Write the simple predicate of the following sentence:
(3, 4)
Did the groomer brush the pony?

26. Rewrite the following lines of poetry, adding capital
(15) letters as needed:

sleep tight
eat right
test bright

27. Write the present participle of the verb *hunt*.
(19) Hint: (is) _____

28. Write whether the following sentence is declarative,
(2) interrogative, imperative, or exclamatory:

What is that kitten's name?

29. For a–d, write the plural of each noun.
(17, 22) (a) deer   (b) leader of the pack   (c) forkful   (d) shelf

30. Rewrite the following sentence, drawing a vertical line
(1) between the subject and the predicate:

Two fennec foxes with big ears trotted across the hot
sand.

LESSON	**Correcting a Run-on Sentence**
24	

> **Dictation or Journal Entry**
>
> **Vocabulary:**
>
> *Horizontal* means "level, extending from left to right like the horizon, where the sky seems to meet earth or sea." When I lie down, I am in a *horizontal* position.
>
> *Vertical* means "extending up and down; upright." When I stand, I am in a *vertical* position.

We have learned that two or more complete thoughts written or spoken as one sentence without proper punctuation or connecting words is called a **run-on sentence.**

Correcting Run-ons
We correct run-on sentences by adding punctuation or connecting words, and by removing unnecessary words.

Example
Correct this run-on sentence:

Eden has a goat she feeds it grain.

Solution
We see that the run-on sentence above has two subjects and two predicates, or two complete thoughts.

subject | predicate   subject | predicate
Eden | has a goat   she | feeds it grain

We may add a period and capital letter to make two complete sentences.

Eden has a goat. She feeds it grain.

Or, we may add a comma and a connecting word to make a complete compound sentence. We shall learn more about compound sentences in a later lesson.

Eden has a goat, and she feeds it grain.

Practice
For a–d, rewrite and correct each run-on sentence. There is more than one correct answer.

a. My cousins grow oranges they also raise chickens.

b. Manny felt restless he went for a walk.

c. Plant eaters have grinding teeth meat eaters have more pointed teeth.

d. Some whales have no teeth they trap food like a sieve.

For e and f, replace each blank with *vertical* or *horizontal*.

    e. In most homes, the floors are _____.

    f. In most homes, the walls are _____.

More Practice For 1–4, correct each run-on sentence. There is more than one correct answer.

    1. It's sunny let's go outside.

    2. I need exercise I'll put on my shoes.

    3. Please come with me I enjoy your company.

    4. Birds are chirping they like the weather.

Review Set 24 Choose the correct word(s) to complete sentences 1–9.

    1. The (anterior, posterior) of an animal is near its tail.
    (23)

    2. (Route, Root) 66, an old road, passes through eight states.
    (22)

    3. Plants need (deficient, sufficient) light to live.
    (21)

    4. At the shore, breaking waves created a (mist, missed).
    (20)

    5. Brushing one's teeth twice a day is a good (habitat, habit).
    (16)

    6. Beavers (is, are) rodents.
    (18)

    7. Mr. and Mrs. Yu noticed that (there, their) bird had
    (7,8) injured (its, it's) left wing.

    8. (Has, Have) the cows come home?
    (18)

    9. *(Is) sneezing* is the (present, past) participle of the verb
    (19) *sneeze.*

    10. Rewrite the following sentence, adding capital letters as
    (8, 15) needed: we drove along pacific coast highway to newport
    beach.

    11. Replace the blank below with the singular present tense
    (9) form of the underlined verb.

    Students <u>identify</u> insects. A student _____ insects.

12. Write each action verb in the following sentence: My
(7) kitten runs through the house, jumps onto the sofa, and
climbs up the curtains.

For sentences 13 and 14, write the entire verb phrase, circling
each helping verb.

13. Should I send Kitcat outside?
(12)

14. Kitcat has been scratching furniture.
(12)

15. In the following sentence, write whether the underlined
(9, 14) verb is present, past, or future tense: Cats <u>stalk</u> their prey.

16. Write whether the following word group is a complete
(5, 23) sentence, a sentence fragment, or a run-on sentence:

Wildcats live alone they hunt at night.

17. Write each preposition that you find in the following
(20, 21) sentence: On Tuesday, Max found a beehive in his
chimney.

18. From the following list, write the word that is *not* a
(20, 21) preposition: inside, into, light, near, of, off, on, onto,
opposite, out, outside, over, past, regarding, round.

19. Write the proper, possessive noun from the following
(13) sentence: The students like Ms. Ng's habit of smiling at
them.

20. Rewrite and correct the following run-on sentence (there
(24) is more than one correct answer): Today is Saturday I shall
bathe the dog.

21. For a–d, write whether the noun is concrete or abstract.
(11)
(a) strength   (b) forgiveness   (c) insect   (d) spider

22. Write each collective noun that you find in this sentence:
(11) The committee will plan a safari.

23. Write the simple subject of the following sentence: There
(3, 4) were ants on my lunch!

24. For the following sentence, write the correct form of the
(18) verb: They (past tense of *be*) fair.

25. Write the simple predicate of the following sentence:
(3, 4) There were ants on my lunch!

26. Rewrite the following lines of poetry, adding capital
(15) letters as needed:

all things bright and beautiful,
all creatures great and small,...

27. Write the past participle of the verb *hunt.*
(19) Hint: (has) _____

28. Write whether the following sentence is declarative,
(2) interrogative, imperative, or exclamatory: Please do not
bring your python to school.

29. For a–d, write the plural of each noun.
(16, 22) (a) story   (b) brother-in-law   (c) fistful   (d) moss

30. Rewrite the following sentence, drawing a vertical line
(1) between the subject and the predicate:

Lions may attack crocodiles on the riverbank.

Capitalization: Titles

Dictation or Journal Entry

Vocabulary:

Mourning is grieving; feeling or expressing sorrow. Ray was *mourning* after his brother's death.

Morning is the first part of the day, beginning at midnight or dawn and ending at noon. Ray awoke early this *morning*.

We have learned to capitalize proper nouns, common nouns when they are a part of proper nouns, the pronoun *I*, the first word of every sentence, and the first word in every line of most poetry. We have also learned that little words like *of*, *and*, and *an* are not capitalized when part of a proper noun.

Titles   Titles require special capitalization. In titles, we capitalize the following:

1. The first and last words of a title

2. All verbs (action or being words)

3. All other words in the title except certain short words

4. A preposition with five or more letters (such as *outside, underneath, between,* etc.)

Look at the examples below.

Eight Cousins

The Adventures of Sherlock Holmes

"The Ugly Duckling"

Unless located first or last in the title, words like *a, an, and, the, but, or, for, nor,* and prepositions with four letters or fewer do not need a capital letter.

Animals Around the World

"The Lion and the Mouse"

Peter and the Wolf

The Indian in the Cupboard

Example   Provide capital letters as needed in the following titles.

(a) "the city mouse and the country mouse"

(b) "the journey of a day"

(c) *the silver chair*

(d) "oh, suzanna"

Solution   (a) "**The City Mouse and the Country Mouse**" is a story. We capitalize the first and last words in a story title and all other words except the little words *and* and *the*.

(b) "**The Journey of a Day**" is also a story. The little words *of* and *a* are not capitalized. The first and last words as well as the important words need a capital letter.

(c) *The Silver Chair* is a book title. We capitalize the first, the last, and the important words.

(d) "**Oh, Suzanna**" is a song title. We capitalize the first and last words.

Practice   Rewrite titles a–d, adding capital letters as needed.

a. *the call of the wild*

b. *the road to oz*

c. *the wonderful wizard of oz*

d. "down by the old mill stream"

For e and f, replace each blank with *morning* or *mourning*.

e. Someone who feels sad might be _____.

f. The sun rises in the _____.

More   See "More Practice Lesson 25" in the Student Workbook.
Practice

Review Set   Choose the correct word to complete sentences 1–9.
25
1. Most trees stand in a (horizontal, vertical) position.
(24)

2. I see the (anterior, posterior) side of your teeth when you
(23) smile.

3. The tree's (routes, roots) grew deep in the earth.
(22)

4. We need (sufficient, deficient) vitamin D for bone
(21) health.

5. An ant can be a pesty (spider, insect).
(19)

6. The two main parts of a sentence are the subject and the
(1) (predator, predicate).

7. (There, Their) is a cat chasing (it's, its) tail!
(7, 8)

8. Emma (do, does) sit-ups to strengthen her muscles.
(18)

9. *(Has) mourned* is the (present, past) participle of the verb
(19) *mourn.*

10. Rewrite the following sentence, adding capital letters as
(8, 15) needed: the gobi desert has freezing winters.

11. Replace the blank below with the singular present tense
(9) form of the underlined verb.

Birds <u>fly</u> south. A bird _____ south.

12. Write each action verb in the following sentence:
(7) The weasel stood tall, sniffed the air, then chased a vole
into its borrow.

13. In the following sentence, write the entire verb phrase,
(12) circling each helping verb:

Has the weasel caught any voles?

14. Write the following song title, using correct
(25) capitalization: "pop goes the weasel"

15. In the following sentence, write whether the underlined
(14) verb phrase is present, past, or future tense: I <u>shall see</u>
you in the morning.

16. Write whether the following word group is a complete
(5, 23) sentence, a sentence fragment, or a run-on sentence:

Dormice may hibernate for many months.

17. Write each preposition that you find in the following
(20, 21) sentence: Sea mammals live near the surface of the water.

18. From the following list, write the word that is *not* a
(20, 21) preposition: save, since, through, throughout, till, toot,
toward, under.

19. Write the proper, possessive noun from the following
(13) sentence: From Oscar's sailboat, we saw whales, dolphins, and seals.

20. Rewrite and correct the run-on sentence below. There is
(24) more than one correct answer.

Otters have no blubber for warmth instead they have thick fur.

21. For a–d, write whether the noun is concrete or abstract.
(11)
(a) otter   (b) adventure   (c) ocean   (d) fear

22. Write each collective noun that you find in this sentence:
(11) A school of polliwogs hid under the lily pad.

23. Write the simple subject of the following sentence: Is the
(3, 4) walrus a type of seal?

24. For the following sentence, write the correct form of the
(18) verb: We (past of *be*) neighbors in Montana.

25. Write the simple predicate of the following sentence: Is
(3, 4) the walrus a type of seal?

26. Rewrite the following lines of poetry (song words),
(15) adding capital letters as needed:

all around the cobbler's bench
the monkey chased the weasel ...

27. Write the present participle of the verb *mourn*.
(19) Hint: *(is)* _____

28. Write whether the following sentence is declarative,
(2) interrogative, imperative, or exclamatory: Watch out for
the tiger snake!

29. For a–d, write the plural of each noun.
(17, 22)
(a) tubful   (b) friend of Jacob   (c) princess   (d) sky

30. Rewrite the following sentence, drawing a vertical line
(1) between the subject and the predicate:

A flock of finches nested in the outback.

LESSON 26

Capitalization: Outlines and Quotations

> **Dictation or Journal Entry**
>
> **Vocabulary:**
>
> A *male* is a boy or man. A *male* chicken is a rooster.
>
> A *female* is a girl or woman. A *female* chicken is a hen.
>
> *Mail* is letters and packages sent or received by a postal system. I found a surprise package in today's *mail*.

We have learned to capitalize proper nouns, common nouns when they are a part of proper nouns, the pronoun *I*, the first word of every sentence, and the first word in every line of most poetry. We have learned that little words like *of*, *and*, and *an* are not capitalized when part of a proper noun and that titles require special capitalization.

In this lesson, we shall learn the correct capitalization of outlines and quotations.

Outlines We can organize written material by outlining. **Outlines** require capital letters for the Roman numerals and for the letters of the first major topics. We also capitalize the first letter of the first word in each line of an outline.

> I. Sea mammals
>   A. Whales
>   B. Seals
>   C. Dolphins
>   D. Otters
>
> II. Types of seals
>   A. True seals
>   B. Sea lions
>   C. Walruses

Quotations We capitalize the first word of a dialogue **quotation,** as shown below.

> Ava asked, "Can you swim?"
>
> Lily replied, "No, I cannot."

Example Provide capital letters as needed.

(a) i. kinds of turtles
    a. freshwater turtles
    b. saltwater turtles
    c. tortoises

(b) Lola explained, "red-eared sliders live in ponds."

Solution (a) We remember that outlines require capital letters for their Roman numerals, major topics, and first words.

    I. Kinds of turtles
      A. Freshwater turtles
      B. Saltwater turtles
      C. Tortoises

(b) We use a capital *r* in "**R**ed-eared sliders live in ponds."

Practice Rewrite a–c, using correct capitalization.

a. i. facts about tortoises
    a. what they eat
    b. where they live

b. ava said, "when i was ten, i learned to swim."

c. then she explained, "my canoe tipped over on a deep lake."

For d–f, replace each blank with the correct vocabulary word from this lesson.

d. James's _____ goes to a post office box.

e. A _____ horse, or stallion, might father a foal, or baby horse.

f. The _____ horse, or mare, gave birth to a foal.

More Practice See "More Practice Lesson 26" in the Student Workbook.

Review Set 26 Choose the correct word to complete sentences 1–9.

1. Roosters crow in the (mourning, morning).
(25)

2. We tied the hammock from tree to tree in a (vertical, horizontal) position.
(24)

3. The hamstring muscles are on the back side or (posterior,
(23) anterior) part of the leg.

4. This train takes the southern (route, root) across the
(22) country.

5. Owls are (marsupial, nocturnal) birds.
(18)

6. The word *safety* is a(n) (abstract, concrete) noun.
(11)

7. Some students think (its, it's) too cold in (there, their)
(7, 8) classroom.

8. Emma (have, has) strong muscles because she exercises
(18) daily.

9. *(Is) missing* is the (present, past) participle of the verb
(19) *miss.*

10. Rewrite the following sentence, adding capital letters as
(8, 15) needed: andrew said, "interesting animals live in the
grasslands of africa."

11. Replace the blank below with the singular present tense
(9) form of the underlined verb.

Cats <u>hiss</u>. A cat _____.

12. Write the action verb in the following sentence:
(7)
Wildebeests trek across the vast African grasslands.

13. In the following sentence, write the entire verb phrase,
(12) circling each helping verb:

You should have heard the hyenas!

14. Using correct capitalization, write the following song
(25) title: "the friendly beasts"

15. In the following sentence, write whether the underlined
(10, 14) verb phrase is present, past, or future tense: The lion
<u>roared</u>.

16. Write whether the following word group is a complete
(5, 23) sentence, a sentence fragment, or a run-on sentence:

Male lions defending the pride, or group of lions.

17. Write the three prepositions that you find in the following sentence: During the day, cheetahs attack prey with a short burst of speed.
    (20, 21)

18. From the following list, write the word that is *not* a preposition: underneath, until, unto, up, upon, vulture, with, within, without.
    (20, 21)

19. Write the proper, possessive noun from the following sentence:
    (13)

    Africa's large grasslands are called savannas.

20. Rewrite and correct the run-on sentence below. There is more than one correct answer.
    (24)

    Meerkats live in the savannas they like the sun.

21. Rewrite the following sentence fragment, making a complete sentence:
    (6)

    To roam the savannas with wildebeests.

22. Write the compound noun that you find in this sentence:
    (13)

    Herds of antelope graze in the grasslands.

23. Write the simple subject of the following sentence:
    (3, 4)

    Behind a clump of golden grass lies a leopard.

24. For the following sentence, write the correct form of the verb: They (present of *be*) neighbors now.
    (18)

25. Write the simple predicate of the following sentence:
    (3, 4)

    Behind a clump of golden grass lies a leopard.

26. Rewrite the following outline, adding capital letters as needed:
    (26)

    i. grassland cats
        a. lion
        b. leopard
        c. cheetah

27. Write the past participle of the verb *mourn*.
    (19) Hint: *(has)* _____

28. Write whether the following sentence is declarative,
(2) interrogative, imperative, or exclamatory: Can Kitcat
roar?

29. For a–d, write the plural of each noun.
(16, 22) (a) baby   (b) pocketful   (c) son-in-law   (d) mouse

30. Rewrite the following sentence, drawing a vertical line
(1) between the subject and the predicate:

The pride of lions shared their prey.

Dictionary Information About a Word, Part 1

Dictation or Journal Entry

Vocabulary:

To *wail* is to make a mournful sound expressing grief or pain. A lost or frightened child might *wail*.

A *whale* is a large mammal with a fish-like body, horizontal tail fins, and flippers. We saw a blue *whale* on our ocean voyage.

Definitions   A dictionary's main function is to provide word meanings. Because a single word may have many meanings, we carefully read all its definitions.

Parts of Speech   Usually, an italicized abbreviation indicates the part of speech of the word being defined. A dictionary's front or back matter explains its abbreviations, like the ones below.

n.	noun	*v.*	verb
adj.	adjective	*adv.*	adverb
pron.	pronoun	*prep.*	preposition
conj.	conjunction	*interj.*	interjection
v.t.	transitive verb	*v.i.*	intransitive verb

Spelling   The bold-faced word that begins a dictionary entry gives the accepted spelling. If there are two or more accepted spellings, these are given as well. The dictionary also provides the spelling of irregular plurals, principal parts of verbs, comparative or superlative forms of adjectives, and other grammatical changes in word forms.

Syllable Division   The bold-faced dictionary entry shows syllable division by a dot or by a space.

con·ceal   con ceal

Pronunciation   Using a fixed symbol for each of the common English sounds, the pronunciation guide re-spells the entry word with accent marks to show which syllables are spoken with more stress than the others. A heavier mark indicates the heaviest accent, or stress on the syllable; a lighter mark indicates a lighter accent.

met·a·mor·pho·sis   met´ə môr´ fə sis

Example   Use a dictionary to complete the following.

(a) Write two different definitions for the word *molt.*

(b) Write the part of speech indicated by the dictionary for the word *hibernation.*

(c) Write two accepted spellings for the plural of *fish.*

(d) Rewrite the word *invertebrate* showing its syllable division.

(e) Rewrite the word *negate* showing its pronunciation, including accent marks.

Solution   (a) Answers will vary. **1. to shed hair, feathers, skin, or shell. 2. that which is shed by molting.**

(b) **noun**   (c) **fish, fishes**

(d) **in·ver·te·brate**   (e) **ni gāt´**

Practice   Use a dictionary to answer a–e.

a. Write two different meanings for the word *fly.*

b. The word *habit* is what part of speech?

c. Write two accepted spellings for the plural of *cactus.*

d. Rewrite the word *marsupial* showing its syllable division.

e. Rewrite the word *marrow* showing its pronunciation.

For f and g, replace each blank with *wail* or *whale.*

f. A _____ is a sea mammal.

g. A _____ is a mournful sound.

Review Set 27   Choose the correct word to complete sentences 1–9.

1. A (male, female) horse is called a stallion.
(26)

2. There is a time of (morning, mourning) when a loved one dies.
(25)

3. People walk in a (vertical, horizontal) position.
(24)

4. The chest and abdominals are on the front or (posterior,
(23) anterior) side of the body.

5. (Root, Route) 66 is a famous highway crossing the United
(22) States.

6. The word *whale* is a(n) (abstract, concrete) noun.
(11)

7. Uh-oh, (their, there) is a viper showing (it's, its) fangs!
(7, 8)

8. This fly trap (do, does) its job.
(18)

9. *(Has) trapped* is the (present, past) participle of the verb
(19) *trap.*

10. Rewrite the following sentence, adding capital letters as
(15, 26) needed: ava said, "on thursday, i was in buffalo, new
york."

11. Replace the blank below with the singular present tense
(9) form of the underlined verb.

Eggs <u>hatch</u>. An egg _____.

12. Write each action verb in the following sentence:
(7)
The boa rolls itself into a ball and hides its head among
its coils.

13. In the following sentence, write the entire verb phrase,
(12) circling each helping verb:

That anaconda might have come from Brazil.

14. Write the following story title, using correct
(25) capitalization: "the rattlesnake at mount wilson"

15. In the following sentence, write whether the underlined
(14) verb phrase is present, past, or future tense: Watch out!
That viper <u>will bite</u>!

16. Write whether the following word group is a complete
(5, 23) sentence, a sentence fragment, or a run-on sentence:

Cobras are deaf they cannot dance to music.

17. Write the two prepositions that you find in the following sentence:
(20, 21)

That cobra is swaying to the movement of the flute.

18. Use a dictionary: (a) The word *insect* is what part of speech? (b) Write its pronunciation.
(27)

19. Write the possessive noun from the following sentence:
(13)

The cobra's hood can frighten enemies.

20. Rewrite and correct the run-on sentence below. There is more than one correct answer.
(24)

The snake opened its mouth I saw fangs.

21. Rewrite the sentence fragment below, making a complete sentence. There is more than one correct answer.
(6)

A king cobra lying in the sun.

22. Write the collective noun that you find in this sentence:
(11)

Ava rests in a hammock in the oak grove.

23. Write the simple subject of the following sentence:
(3, 4)

Through the grove slithers a snake.

24. For the following sentence, write the correct form of the verb: The garter snake (present of *have*) three light stripes along its body.
(18)

25. Write the simple predicate of the following sentence:
(3, 4)

Through the grove slithers a snake.

26. Rewrite the following outline, adding capital letters as needed:
(26)

   i. venomous snakes
     a. front-fanged snakes
     b. rear-fanged snakes

27. Write the present participle of the verb *wail*.
(19)

28. Write whether the following sentence is declarative, interrogative, imperative, or exclamatory: The garter snake is harmless.
(2)

29. For a–c, write the plural of each noun.
(16, 17, 22)

(a) city   (b) bird of prey   (c) knife

30. Rewrite the following sentence, drawing a vertical line
(1) between the subject and the predicate:

Some rattlesnakes hide in rocky places.

Spelling Rules: Silent Letters
k, g, w, t, d, and *c*

> **Dictation or Journal Entry**
>
> **Vocabulary:**
>
> To *preen* (of birds) means "to clean and smooth (feathers) with the beak." The peacock on the lawn *preens* itself.
>
> To *molt* is to shed hair, feathers, skin, or shell that will be replaced by new growth. A bird loses many feathers as it *molts.*

Why Are Some Letters Silent? The English language contains many words that are spelled differently than they are pronounced. There are several reasons for this.

As the language changed and grew through the centuries, the way people pronounced a word often changed, yet the way the word was spelled remained the same.

Some early scholars insisted on applying Latin rules of spelling to English words. (Because English borrowed the Latin alphabet, this idea was logical.)

More words were borrowed from other languages, and their foreign spellings were kept.

In the midst of this, the printing press appeared. It helped to "freeze" the spelling of all these words, no matter how irregular. Most English words are spelled today just as they were in the 1500s. As a result, there are many words that contain letters that we no longer (or never did) pronounce.

The Letter *k* A silent *k* at the beginning of a word is always followed by an *n*.

> knit   knock   knee   know

The Letter *g* A silent *g* may also be followed by an *n* at the beginning or the end of a word.

> gnaw   gnat   reign   campaign

The Letter *w* A silent *w* can come before the letter *r*.

> wrinkle   write   wren   wreath

Sometimes the silent *w* comes before the letter *h*.

> whole   who   whose

Other silent *w*'s appear in the words *answer, sword,* and *two.*

The Letter _t_ A silent _t_ can follow the letter _s_.

rustle   castle   listen   fasten

A silent _t_ can also come before the letters _ch_.

watch   match   sketch   ditch

Not all words that end with the "ch" sound have a silent _t_ (_much_, _rich_, _attach_, _such_, _sandwich_, etc.). When in doubt, check the dictionary.

Other silent _t_'s appear in words borrowed from the French, such as _ballet_, _depot_, _debut_, and others.

The Letter _d_ The letters _ge_ usually follow a silent _d_.

ju**dge**   do**dge**   bri**dge**   e**dge**   ba**dge**

We also find silent _d_'s in these words:

a**d**just   We**d**nesday   han**d**some

The Letter _c_ A silent _c_ can follow the letter _s_.

scent   **s**cience   **s**cene   **s**cissors

Example Rewrite these words and circle each silent letter.

(a) badger   (b) answer   (c) pitch

(d) kneel   (e) gnaw   (f) wrong

Solution (a) ba**d**ger   (b) ans**w**er   (c) pi**t**ch

(d) **k**neel   (e) **g**naw   (f) **w**rong

Practice Rewrite words a–h, circling each silent letter.

a. sign   **b.** wrench   **c.** gnu   **d.** itch

e. knife   **f.** fudge   **g.** scenery   **h.** whistle

For i and j, replace each blank with _preen_ or _molt_.

i. Birds often _____, taking care of their feathers.

j. A snake might _____, leaving its old skin behind.

Review Set 28 Choose the correct word to complete sentences 1–9.

1. The upset child made a loud (whale, wail).
(27)

2. A (male, female) horse is called a mare.
(26)

3. We shall start our hike in the (morning, mourning).
(25)

4. We usually lay rugs in a (horizontal, vertical) position on
(24) the floor.

5. Rex bites the ear of my teddy (bare, bear).
(1)

6. The word *whales* is a (plural, possessive) noun.
(15)

7. (It's, Its) common for kittens to chase (their, there) tails.
(7, 8)

8. Abe and Kim (is, was, were) drawing pictures.
(18)

9. *(Is) roaring* is the (present, past) participle of the verb
(19) *roar.*

10. Rewrite the following sentence, adding capital letters as
(15, 26) needed: dan said, "my father and i saw snakes in india."

11. Replace the blank below with the singular present tense
(9) form of the underlined verb.

Josh and Nate <u>fish</u>. Elle _____.

12. Write each action verb in the following sentence:
(7)
Rex looks before he leaps.

13. In the following sentence, write the entire verb phrase,
(12) circling each helping verb:

The mouse must have entered my room through that
hole!

14. Write the following story title, using correct
(25) capitalization: "the scarecrow of oz"

15. In the following sentence, write whether the underlined
(10, 14) verb is present, past, or future tense: The sleepy child
<u>wailed</u>.

16. Write whether the following word group is a complete
(5, 23) sentence, a sentence fragment, or a run-on sentence:

Woodpeckers hammering on the roof.

17. Write the three prepositions that you find in the
(20, 21) following sentence:

In cold weather, leaves fall from trees, and birds fly to
warmer places.

18. Use a dictionary: (a) The word *beak* is what part of
(27) speech? (b) Write its pronunciation.

19. Rewrite the following words, circling each silent letter:
(28)
(a) kneel   (b) design   (c) hatch

20. Rewrite and correct the run-on sentence below. There is
(24) more than one correct answer.

Male eagle owls make loud hoots have you heard them?

21. Rewrite the following sentence fragment, making a
(6) complete sentence:

To keep their nests out of sight.

22. Write the compound noun that you find in this sentence:
(13)
Tropical rainforests are wonderful bird habitats.

23. Write the simple subject of the following sentence:
(3, 4)
Do parrots spread seeds?

24. For the following sentence, write the correct form of the
(18) verb: Macaws (past of *be*) nesting in that leafy tree.

25. Write the simple predicate of the following sentence:
(3, 4)
Do parrots spread seeds?

26. Rewrite the following lines of poetry, adding capital
(15) letters as needed:

sparrow, robin, wren, and bat—
if only I had wings like that!

27. Write the past participle of the verb *wail*.
(19)

28. Write whether the following sentence is declarative,
(2) interrogative, imperative, or exclamatory:

The kookaburra, a giant kingfisher, rarely eats fish!

29. For a–c, write the plural of each noun.
(16, 17, 22)

(a) solo   (b) pailful   (c) canary

30. Rewrite the following sentence, drawing a vertical line
(1)   between the subject and the predicate:

A flock of green parrots landed in the fruit tree.

Spelling Rules: Silent Letters *p, b, l, u, h, n,* and *gh*

Dictation or Journal Entry

Vocabulary:

A *cow* is a mature female of the cattle family, or of some other large mammal, as the elephant, whale, or seal. A mother seal is a *cow.*

A *bull* is a mature male of the cattle family, or of certain other large animals, as the elephant, moose, whale, or seal. We call a mature male elephant a *bull.*

The Letter *p*   The Greek language is a source of many words that contain a silent *p*. The silent *p* occurs only before the letters *n, s,* and *t.*

pneumonia   **p**salm   **p**sychology   **p**terodactyl

Other words with a silent *p* include *recei**p**t, cu**p**board,* and *cor**p**s.*

The Letter *b*   Many words contain the letter *m* followed by a silent *b.*

com**b**   clim**b**   lam**b**

Other silent *b*'s are found in the words *de**b**t, dou**b**t,* and *su**b**tle.*

The Letter *l*   Many words that contain a silent *l* follow a similar pattern: an *l* followed by a consonant that makes the *l* difficult to pronounce.

chalk   talk   walk   yolk   folk

palm   calm   would   could   should

calf (calves)   half (halves)

Other silent *l*'s are found in the words *colonel* and *salmon.*

The Letter *u*   A silent *u* usually follows the letter *g*. It reminds us to pronounce the *g* with a "hard" sound (*g*) rather than a "soft" sound (*j*), at either the beginning or the end of the word.

guard   guess   guide   plague

The Letter *h*   A silent *h* usually follows *c, r,* or *g,* as in these words:

school   ache   rhombus

aghast   ghost   rheumatism

An initial *h* can also be silent, as in the words *honor, hour,* and *heir.*

The Letter _n_ Sometimes the letter _m_ is followed by a silent _n_, as in these words:

column   condemn   hymn   solemn

The Letters _gh_ The letter combination _gh_ is always silent when it comes before the letter _t_.

bright   daughter   light   taught

right   bought   eight   thought

A _gh_ at the end of a word can be silent as well:

sleigh   though   through   high

weigh   bough   dough   sigh

Example Rewrite these words, circling silent letter(s).

(a) guard   (b) would   (c) walk   (d) thumb

(e) limb   (f) ache   (g) ought   (h) column

(i) should   (j) debt   (k) corps   (l) dough

Solution (a) g**u**ard   (b) wou**l**d   (c) wa**l**k   (d) thum**b**

(e) lim**b**   (f) ac**h**e   (g) ou**gh**t   (h) colum**n**

(i) shou**l**d   (j) de**b**t   (k) cor**ps**   (l) dou**gh**

Practice Rewrite words a–h, circling silent letter(s).

a. psalm   **b.** dumb   **c.** could   **d.** guest

e. hour   **f.** tight   **g.** hymn   **h.** sigh

For i and j, replace each blank with _cow_ or _bull_.

i. A _____ is a male.

j. A _____ is a female.

Review Set 29 Choose the correct word to complete sentences 1–9.

1. When a bird (preens, molts), it loses feathers.
(28)

2. People take boats out into the ocean to watch (wails,
(27) whales).

3. One type of bull is a (male, female) bovine.
(26)

4. The widow who was (morning, mourning) wore black.
(25)

5. There was a brief (paws, pause) before the song ended.
(2)

6. The word *spider* is a(n) (abstract, concrete) noun.
(11)

7. (Their, There) is a porcupine rattling (it's, its) quills.
(7, 8)

8. Alex (do, does, did) his homework last night.
(10, 18)

9. *(Has) done* is the (present, past) participle of the verb
(19) *do.*

10. Rewrite the following sentence, adding capital letters as
(26) needed: mea asked, "has anyone seen rex?"

11. Replace the blank below with the singular present tense
(9) form of the underlined verb.

Eagles <u>fly</u> high. An eagle _____ high.

12. Write each action verb in the following sentence:
(7)
Some birds soar and glide, while others hover in one place.

13. In the following sentence, write the entire verb phrase,
(12) circling each helping verb:

That little ostrich might have hatched only yesterday.

14. Using correct capitalization, write the following song
(25) title: "the farmer in the dell"

15. In the following sentence, write whether the underlined
(14) verb is present, past, or future tense: We <u>shall count</u>
hummingbirds.

16. Write whether the following word group is a complete
(5, 23) sentence, a sentence fragment, or a run-on sentence:

Some birds do not fly at all.

17. Write the four prepositions that you find in the following
^(20, 21) sentence:

After sunset, the owl flew from tree to tree around the lake.

18. Use a dictionary: (a) The word *puffin* is what part of
⁽²⁷⁾ speech? (b) Show its syllable division.

19. Rewrite the following words, circling silent letter(s).
^(28, 29) (a) limb   (b) light   (c) knob

20. Rewrite and correct the run-on sentence below. There is
⁽²⁴⁾ more than one correct answer.

Most birds bathe and preen daily some take dust baths.

21. Rewrite the sentence fragment below, making a complete
⁽⁶⁾ sentence. There is more than one correct answer.

The tail feathers of a peacock.

22. Write the collective noun that you find in this sentence:
⁽¹¹⁾ A family of redstarts nests in that tree hole.

23. Write the simple subject of the following sentence:
^(3, 4) Have the geese flown south?

24. For the following sentence, write the correct form of the
⁽¹⁸⁾ verb: This woodpecker (present of *have*) a red head.

25. Write the simple predicate of the following sentence:
^(3, 4) Have the geese flown south?

26. Rewrite the following outline, adding capital letters as
⁽²⁶⁾ needed:

    i. unusual nests
       a. oriole's nest
       b. warbler's nest

27. For the verb *do*, write the (a) present participle, (b) past
⁽¹⁹⁾ tense, and (c) past participle.

28. Write whether the following sentence is declarative,
⁽²⁾ interrogative, imperative, or exclamatory: Watch the cow with her calf.

29. For a–c, write the plural of each noun.
(16, 17) (a) family   (b) child   (c) goose

30. Rewrite the following sentence, drawing a vertical line
(1)   between the subject and the predicate:

Many different birds live near my home.

Dictionary Information About a Word, Part 2

Dictation or Journal Entry

Vocabulary:

A *buck* is an adult male deer, antelope, sheep, goat, kangaroo, or rabbit. The *buck* raised his antlers and looked at me.

A *doe* is an adult female deer, antelope, kangaroo, sheep, goat, or rabbit. A *doe* led her fawn into the meadow.

We have learned that dictionaries give the following information about a word: definitions, parts of speech, spelling, syllable division, and pronunciation. In this lesson, we shall see that dictionaries also provide etymologies, field labels, synonyms, and antonyms.

Etymologies

Etymologies are word histories showing the word's original language and meaning. Usually, the dictionary's front pages explain abbreviations used to indicate the languages from which words come. The symbol < or the abbreviation *fr.* may mean "from." See examples below.

DICTIONARY ABBREVIATION	MEANING
< F	from French
< Heb-Aram	from Hebrew-Aramaic
fr. OE	from Old English
< Gr	from Classical Greek
< Heb	from Hebrew
fr. L	from Latin

Field Labels

Some dictionary words are not part of our general vocabulary but have to do with a special subject, area, or usage. These words may have **field labels**, such as the ones below.

SUBJECT LABELS

Med. (medicine)	*Chem.* (chemistry)
Zool. (zoology)	*Music*
Baseball	*Comput.* (computer science)

AREA LABELS

Netherl. (Netherlandic)	*Scotland*
Northwest U.S.	*NGmc* (North Germanic)

USAGE LABELS

Dialect	Slang	Rare
Informal	Old-fashioned	Literary
Archaic	Obsolete	Vulgar

Synonyms and Antonyms At the end of an entry, a dictionary may list **synonyms** (SYN, words of similar meaning) and/or **antonyms** (ANT, words of opposite meaning).

Example Use a dictionary to complete the following.

(a) The word *antenna* comes from what language?

(b) Write the field label given to the word *andante*.

(c) Write a synonym of the word *tardy*.

Solution (a) **Latin** (b) *Music* (c) **late**

Practice Use a dictionary to answer a–c.

a. Write the origin of the word *mandible*.

b. Write the field label given to the word *stolon*.

c. Write a synonym of the word *tranquil*.

For d and e, replace each blank with *buck* or *doe*.

d. An adult female deer is a _____.

e. An adult male deer is a _____.

Review Set 30 Choose the correct word to complete sentences 1–8.

1. Another type of (cow, bull) is a mature male elephant.
(29)

2. A bird (molts, preens) itself daily.
(28)

3. We heard the (whale, wail) of a siren.
(27)

4. A birthday card came in the (mail, male).
(26)

5. The owl, a night (prey, predator), is looking for small rodents.
(3)

6. The word *cow's* is a (plural, possessive) noun.
(13)

7. A(n) (posterior, anterior, etymology) shows a word's
(30) original language and meaning.

8. Synonyms are words of (similar, opposite) meaning.
(30)

9. Write the past tense form of the verb *clip.*
(10)

10. Rewrite the following sentence, adding capital letters as
(26) needed: emily asked, "how do snake eggs hatch?"

11. Replace the blank below with the singular present tense
(9) form of the underlined verb.

Eggs <u>hatch</u>. An egg _____ .

12. Write each action verb in the following sentence:
(7)

Male monitor lizards stand on their hind legs and wrestle
with each other.

13. In the following sentence, write the entire verb phrase,
(12) circling each helping verb:

Geckos can cling to smooth surfaces, even glass.

14. Write the following book title, using correct
(25) capitalization: *lizards of southeast asia*

15. In the following sentence, write whether the underlined
(10, 14) verb is present, past, or future tense: The mother
crocodile <u>gathered</u> her babies in her mouth.

16. Write whether the following word group is a complete
(5, 23) sentence, a sentence fragment, or a run-on sentence:

The female alligator builds a nest of mud and grass she
lays up to eighty eggs.

17. Write the two prepositions that you find in the following
(20, 21) sentence:

The saltwater crocodile of Southeast Asia builds her nest
near water.

18. Use a dictionary: (a) The word *amnion* is what part of
(27, 30) speech? (b) Write its pronunciation. (c) Write its etymology.

19. Rewrite the following words, circling silent letter(s):
(28, 29) (a) hour   (b) talk   (c) ridge

20. Rewrite and correct the run-on sentence below. There is
(24) more than one correct answer.

A marine turtle might lay two hundred eggs they hatch six to ten weeks later.

21. Rewrite the sentence fragment below, making a complete
(6) sentence. There is more than one correct answer.

The crocodile guarding her offspring against predators.

22. Write the compound noun that you find in this sentence:
(13) The iguana relaxed when I closed its eyelids.

23. Write the simple subject of the following sentence:
(3, 4) Beneath the water lies a crocodile.

24. For the following sentence, write the correct form of the
(14) verb:

We (future of *study*) reptiles next.

25. Write the simple predicate of the following sentence:
(3, 4) Beneath the water lies a crocodile.

26. For the verb *try*, write the (a) present participle, (b) past
(19) tense, and (c) past participle.

27. Write whether the following sentence is declarative,
(2) interrogative, imperative, or exclamatory: Will a mongoose attack a cobra?

28. Rewrite the rhyme, adding capital letters as needed:
(15)
lizard, snake, or crocodile—
which of these will make you smile?

29. For a–c, write the plural of each noun.
(17, 22) (a) monkey   (b) life   (c) branch

30. Rewrite the following sentence, drawing a vertical line
(1) between the subject and the predicate:

The female alligator covers her nest with her body.

LESSON
31

Linking Verbs

Dictation or Journal Entry

Vocabulary:

A *boar* is an adult male pig or hog. The thick, bristly skin of the *boar* was caked with mud.

A *sow* is an adult female pig. That *sow* has eight piglets.

Linking Verbs

A **linking verb** "links" the subject of a sentence to the rest of the predicate. It does not show action, and it is not "helping" an action verb. Its purpose is to connect a name or description to the subject.

Early <u>is</u> a horse.

In the sentence above, *is* links "Early" with "horse." The word *horse* names Early's species (kind of animal).

Early <u>is</u> reliable.

In the sentence above, *is* links "Early" with "reliable." The word *reliable* describes Early.

Watch Out!

We must carefully examine our sentences. Some verbs can be used as either linking or action verbs, as shown in the two sentences below.

Kim <u>looks</u> happy today. (*Looks* is a linking verb. It links "Kim" with "happy.")

Kim <u>looks</u> at the sky. (*Looks* is an action verb, not a linking verb. Kim is doing something.)

Common Linking Verbs

Common linking verbs include all of the forms of the verb "to be."

is, am, are, was, were, be, being, been

The following are also common linking verbs. Memorize these:

look, feel, taste, smell, sound

seem, appear, grow, become

remain, stay

Identifying Linking Verbs

To tell whether a verb is a linking verb, we replace it with a form of the verb "to be"—*is, am, are, was, were, be, being, been*, as in the example below.

Kim *feels* hopeful.

We replace *feels* with *is*:

Kim *is* hopeful.

Because the sentence still makes sense, we know that *feels* is a linking verb in this sentence. Now, let us examine the word *feels* in the sentence below.

Kim *feels* the cool breeze.

We replace *feels* with *is*:

Kim *is* the cool breeze.

The sentence no longer makes sense, so we know that *feels* is not a linking verb in this sentence.

Example Identify and write the linking verb, if any, in each sentence.
(a) Roy was a cowhand.

(b) Early seemed tired.

(c) The cattle grew restless.

(d) The job proved difficult.

(e) Roy looks at the herd.

Solution (a) The linking verb *was* links "Roy" to "cowhand."

(b) The verb *seemed* links "Early" to "tired."

(c) The verb *grew* links "cattle" to "restless."

(d) The verb *proved* links "job" to "difficult."

(e) We replace the verb *looks* with *is* : Roy *is* at the herd. The sentence no longer makes sense, so we know that the word *looks* is not a linking verb in this sentence. There are **no linking verbs** in this sentence.

Practice **a.** Study the linking verbs (including the forms of the verb "to be") listed in this lesson. Memorize them line by line. Then say them to your teacher or to a friend.

b. Have a "linking verb contest" with yourself or with a partner. Write as many as you can from memory in one minute.

Write the linking verbs, if any, from sentences c–j.

c. Man O' War was a racehorse.

d. He became famous long ago.

e. Tom's horse appears nervous.

f. Big Red remained strong in the race.

g. The race seemed easy for him.

h. The violin music sounds mournful.

i. We smelled fresh bread.

j. The bread smelled delicious.

For k and l, replace each blank with *boar* or *sow*.

k. The _____ nursed her piglets.

l. A _____ might be the father of piglets.

More Practice

Write each linking verb from sentences 1–8.

1. The rules seemed fair.

2. After the fifth mile, I grew weary.

3. Ms. Vong stayed cheerful all day.

4. Throughout the contest, we felt confident.

5. Mea appeared surprised when her brother tasted the fish bait.

6. Fish bait tastes terrible.

7. The bait smells fishy.

8. We remained calm through the storm.

For 9–14, tell whether each verb is action or linking.

9. Roy <u>smells</u> the rose.

10. The rose <u>smells</u> sweet.

11. She <u>sounds</u> the alarm.

12. Her voice <u>sounds</u> hoarse.

13. He <u>tastes</u> the chili.

14. The chili <u>tastes</u> spicy.

Choose the correct word to complete sentences 1–8.

1. Some adult male animals, like deer, are called (does, bucks).
(30)

2. Some mature females are called (cows, bucks).
(29)

3. When a snake (preens, molts), its old skin falls off.
(28)

4. An orca is a black and white (wail, whale).
(27)

5. We found the city hall on the town's (main, mane) street.
(4)

6. The word *truth* is a(n) (concrete, abstract) noun.
(11)

7. A linking (noun, verb) links the subject of a sentence to the rest of the predicate.
(31)

8. Antonyms are words of (similar, opposite) meaning.
(30)

9. Write the past tense form of the verb *trot.*
(10)

10. Rewrite the following sentence, adding capital letters as needed:
(26)

mr. yu said, "we rode arabian horses in texas."

11. Replace the blank below with the singular present tense form of the underlined verb.
(9)

People <u>harness</u> horses. Roy _____ a horse.

12. Write each action verb in the following sentence:
(7)

Early jumped the fence and trotted through the field.

13. In the following sentence, write the entire verb phrase, circling each helping verb:
(12)

She might have broken a fence post.

14. Write the following song title, using correct capitalization: "i ride an old paint"
(25)

15. Write the linking verb in the following sentence:
(31)

Early grew curious.

16. Write whether the following word group is a complete sentence, a sentence fragment, or a run-on sentence:

(5, 23)

The mare's ears pointed forward.

17. Write the two prepositions that you find in the following sentence:

(20, 21)

Early rolls on her back in the pasture.

18. Use a dictionary: (a) The word *foal* is what part of speech? (b) Write its pronunciation. (c) Write its etymology.

(27, 30)

19. Rewrite the following words, circling silent letter(s):

(28, 29)

    (a) whom   (b) neigh   (c) walk

20. Rewrite and correct the run-on sentence below. There is more than one correct answer.

(24)

Roy rides Early his brother rides a stallion.

21. Rewrite the sentence fragment below, making a complete sentence. There is more than one correct answer.

(6)

Swishing their tails at flies.

22. Write the collective noun that you find in this sentence:

(11)

Early nibbles the bouquet of roses.

23. Write the simple subject of the following sentence:

(3, 4)

Into the stable trots Early.

24. For the following sentence, write the correct form of the verb:

(9)

Roy (present of *fry*) bacon.

25. Write the simple predicate of the following sentence:

(3, 4)

Into the stable trots Early.

26. For the verb *hurry*, write the (a) present participle, (b) past tense, and (c) past participle.

(19)

27. Write whether the following sentence is declarative,
(2) interrogative, imperative, or exclamatory:

Here comes Big Red!

28. Rewrite the outline below, adding capital letters as
(26) needed:

    i. main groups of horses
       a. ponies
       b. light horses
       c. heavy horses

29. For a–c, write the plural of each noun.
(17, 22) (a) pony   (b) sister-in-law   (c) jockey

30. Rewrite the following sentence, drawing a vertical line
(1) between the subject and the predicate:

Mounted police may patrol the streets.

Diagramming Simple Subjects and Simple Predicates

We have learned to find the simple subject and simple predicate of a sentence. Now, we will learn how to **diagram** our sentence according to this pattern:

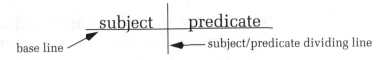

The subject and predicate sit on a horizontal "base line" and are separated by a vertical line that passes through the base line. Below is a **simple subject and simple predicate diagram** of this sentence:

Early trotted into the stable.

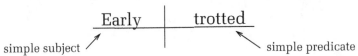

As you can see above, we place the simple subject on the left and the simple predicate on the right. We separate the two with a vertical line.

Example 1 Diagram the simple subject and simple predicate of the following sentence:

A bee buzzes near Early's ear.

Solution The "who or what" (subject) of the sentence is "bee." The action word connected with "bee" (predicate) is "buzzes."

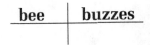

Example 2 Diagram the simple subject and simple predicate of the following sentence:

Early is a gentle horse.

Solution   We refer to the list of helping verbs and linking verbs in the previous lessons. "Is" is a linking verb in this sentence. We ask ourselves, "Who or what *is*?" The answer is the subject, Early.

Early	is

Example 3   Diagram the simple subject and simple predicate of this sentence:

Early's tail has been swishing.

Solution   We recall our list of helping verbs and see that the verb phrase <u>has been swishing</u> is the simple predicate telling what *tail* (subject) has been doing.

tail	has been swishing

Practice   Diagram the simple subject and the simple predicate of sentences a–d.

a. A big green apple fell from the tree.

b. The fruit appears juicy.

c. Later, I shall eat it.

d. Shall I share it with you?

For e and f, replace each blank with *herd* or *heard*.

e. We _____ coyotes howling.

f. A _____ of sheep grazed in the meadow.

Review Set 32   Choose the correct word to complete sentences 1–8.

1. A male pig is a (boar, sow).
(31)

2. The fawn's mother is a (buck, doe).
(30)

3. Mature females of several types of animals are called
(29) (bulls, cows).

4. The parakeets (molted, preened) themselves, smoothing
(28) their feathers.

5. The baby (whaled, wailed) for its mother.
(27)

6. The word *horses* is a (plural, possessive) noun.
(13)

7. In a sentence diagram, the subject goes on the (left, right).
(32)

8. In a sentence diagram, the predicate goes on the (left, right).
(32)

9. Write the past tense form of the verb *tap*.
(10)

10. Rewrite the following sentence, adding capital letters as needed:
(26)

miss ortiz said, "horses are herbivores."

11. Replace the blank below with the singular present tense form of the underlined verb.
(9)

They <u>mash</u> turnips. He _____ turnips.

12. Write each action verb in the following sentence:
(7)

Dark clouds cover the sky and hide the sun.

13. In the following sentence, write the entire verb phrase, circling each helping verb:
(12)

Wind has been whistling through the pines.

14. Write the following story title, using correct capitalization: "chased by a bear"
(25)

15. Write the linking verb in the following sentence:
(31) Children feel safe around Early.

16. Write whether the following word group is a complete sentence, a sentence fragment, or a run-on sentence:
(5, 23)

Watching the rodeo.

17. Write the two prepositions that you find in the following sentence:
(20, 21)

Within seconds, the steer had a rope around its neck.

18. Use a dictionary: (a) The word *femur* is what part of speech? (b) Write its pronunciation. (c) Write its etymology.
(27, 30)

19. Rewrite the following words, circling silent letter(s):
(28, 29)
    (a) guard   (b) who   (c) high

20. Rewrite and correct the run-on sentence below. There is
(24) more than one correct answer.

    Roy can identify his cattle they have been branded.

21. From memory, write the linking verbs listed in Lesson
(31) 31.

22. Write the compound noun that you find in this sentence:
(13)

    Six cowhands work on Roy's ranch.

23. For the following sentence, write the correct form of the
(10) verb:

    I (past of *fry*) the squash.

24. For the verb *worry*, write the (a) present participle, (b)
(10) past tense, and (c) past participle.

25. Write whether the following sentence is declarative,
(2) interrogative, imperative, or exclamatory:

    Give Early an apple.

26. Rewrite the following lines of poetry, adding capital
(15) letters as needed:

    some horses act wild,
    but dear Early is mild.

27. For a–c, write the plural of each noun.
(17, 22)
    (a) fox   (b) Monday   (c) fly

Diagram the simple subject and simple predicate of sentences 28–30. See hints below.

28. There go the horses!
(32)

29. The pony with the white muzzle seems frisky.
(32)

30. Can that cowhand rope a steer?
(32)

    28.   29.   30.

LESSON 33

Spelling Rules: Suffixes, Part 1

> **Dictation or Journal Entry**
> **Vocabulary:**
> *Cheap* means "low in price." I found some *cheap* pens at the art supply store.
>
> To *cheep* is to chirp or peep, as a young bird. Finches and sparrows began to *cheep* at dawn.

In this lesson, we will learn rules for adding suffixes.

Words Ending in *y* A final *y* usually changes to *i* when suffixes (except for the suffix *-ing*) are added:

$$\text{rely} + \text{able} = \text{reliable}$$
$$\text{fly} + \text{er} = \text{flier}$$
$$\text{try} + \text{ed} = \text{tried}$$
$$\text{duty} + \text{ful} = \text{dutiful}$$
$$\text{hurry} + \text{es} = \text{hurries}$$
$$\text{worry} + \text{some} = \text{worrisome}$$
$$\text{steady} + \text{ly} = \text{steadily}$$
$$\text{muddy} + \text{est} = \text{muddiest}$$
$$\text{glory} + \text{ous} = \text{glorious}$$
$$\text{happy} + \text{ness} = \text{happiness}$$

but: relying, flying, trying, hurrying, worrying, steadying, glorying

When preceded by a vowel, the final *y* does not change to *i* when a suffix is added.

$$\text{stay} + \text{ing} = \text{staying}$$
$$\text{toy} + \text{ed} = \text{toyed}$$
$$\text{enjoy} + \text{able} = \text{enjoyable}$$
$$\text{gray} + \text{est} = \text{grayest}$$

Exceptions Important exceptions include the following:

$$\text{lay} + \text{ed} = \text{laid}$$
$$\text{pay} + \text{ed} = \text{paid}$$
$$\text{say} + \text{ed} = \text{said}$$
$$\text{day} + \text{ly} = \text{daily}$$

Example 1 Add suffixes to these words ending in *y*.

(a) play + ed = _____

(b) funny + er = _____

(c) crazy + ness = _____

(d) pity + ful = _____

(e) merry + ly = _____

Solution (a) play + ed = **played** (The *y* is preceded by a vowel, so it does not change to an *i*.)

(b) funny + er = **funnier** (The final *y* usually changes to *i* when suffixes are added.)

(c) crazy + ness = **craziness**

(d) pity + ful = **pitiful**

(e) merry + ly = **merrily**

Words Ending in a Silent *e* We usually drop the silent *e* before adding a suffix beginning with a vowel (including the suffix *-y*).

fame + ous = famous

wire + y = wiry

wave + y = wavy

come + ing = coming

love + able = lovable

blue + ish = bluish

sense + ible = sensible

However, we keep the final *e* when we add a suffix beginning with a consonant.

encourage + ment = encouragement

like + ness = likeness

tire + less = tireless

rare + ly = rarely

shame + ful = shameful

Exceptions   Exceptions to the silent *e* rules include the following words:

$$\text{judge} + \text{ment} = \text{judgment}$$
$$\text{argue} + \text{ment} = \text{argument}$$
$$\text{wise} + \text{dom} = \text{wisdom}$$
$$\text{gentle} + \text{ly} = \text{gently}$$
$$\text{true} + \text{ly} = \text{truly}$$

Also, when adding *-ous* or *-able* to a word ending in *ge* or *ce*, we keep the final *e* to indicate the soft sound of the *c* (as in *celery*) or *g* (as in *giant*).

$$\text{manage} + \text{able} = \text{manageable}$$
$$\text{trace} + \text{able} = \text{traceable}$$
$$\text{change} + \text{able} = \text{changeable}$$
$$\text{outrage} + \text{ous} = \text{outrageous}$$
$$\text{courage} + \text{ous} = \text{courageous}$$

Example 2   Add suffixes to these words ending in a silent *e*.

(a) believe + able = _____

(b) please + ing = _____

(c) come + ing = _____

(d) safe + ly = _____

(e) brave + ly = _____

(f) manage + able = _____

(g) gentle + ly = _____

Solution   (a) believe + able = **believable** (We usually drop the silent *e* when the suffix begins with a vowel.)

(b) please + ing = **pleasing**

(c) come + ing = **coming**

(d) safe + ly = **safely** (We usually keep the final *e* when the suffix begins with a consonant.)

(e) brave + ly = **bravely**

(f) manage + able = **manageable** (We keep the silent *e* after the *g* to retain the soft *g* sound.)

(g) gentle + ly = **gently** (This is an exception to the rule.)

Practice Add suffixes to words a–k.

a. plenty + ful = _____

b. happy + ness = _____

c. cheery + est = _____

d. gloomy + ly = _____

e. bite + ing = _____

f. plate + ful = _____

g. drive + er = _____

h. live + ly = _____

i. change + able = _____

j. skate + ing = _____

k. clue + less = _____

For l and m, replace each blank with *cheap* or *cheep.*

l. Birds _____.

m. _____ means "inexpensive."

Review Set 33 Choose the correct word to complete sentences 1–6.

1. We (herd, heard) the choir singing.
(32)

2. The (boar, sow) gave birth to eight piglets.
(31)

3. The huge (buck, doe) had enormous antlers.
(30)

4. A male moose is called a (cow, bull).
(29)

5. The pig has a curly (tale, tail).
(6)

6. The word *happiness* is a(n) (concrete, abstract) noun.
(11)

7. Add suffixes to the following words ending in *y*:
(33)

(a) rely + able   (b) lay + ing

8. Add suffixes to the following words ending in a silent *e*:
(33)

(a) live + ing   (b) peace + ful

9. Write the past tense form of the verb *reply*.
(10)

10. Rewrite the following sentence, adding capital letters as
(26) needed:

mrs. green replied, "yes, i am ready for the race."

11. Replace the blank below with the singular present tense
(9) form of the underlined verb.

They <u>brush</u> dogs. Amy _____ dogs.

12. Write each action verb in the following sentence:
(7)

Week-old puppies only sleep and nurse.

13. In the following sentence, write the entire verb phrase,
(12) circling each helping verb:

Their eyes will open soon.

14. Write the following story title using correct capitalization:
(25) "anna and the lost poodle"

15. Write the linking verb in the following sentence:
(31)

Rex remains loyal to his master.

16. Write whether the following word group is a complete
(5, 23) sentence, a sentence fragment, or a run-on sentence:

Dogs are excellent smellers they also hear more sounds
than we do.

17. Write the two prepositions that you find in the following
(20, 21) sentence:

A pack of wild canines came into town.

18. Use a dictionary: (a) The word *dingo* is what part of
(27, 30) speech? (b) Write its pronunciation. (c) Write its
etymology.

19. Rewrite the following words, circling silent letter(s):
(28, 29)

    (a) talk   (b) resign   (c) knot

20. Rewrite and correct the run-on sentence below. There is
(24) more than one correct answer.

Dogs hear more sounds than we do they are also excellent smellers.

21. From memory, write the linking verbs listed in Lesson
(31) 31.

22. Write the collective noun that you find in this sentence:
(11)

Nate's class cheered when he found his lost dog.

23. For the following sentence, write the correct form of the
(10) verb:

Annabelle (past of *grin*) at the poodle.

24. For the verb *carry*, write the (a) present participle, (b)
(19) past tense, and (c) past participle.

25. Write whether the following sentence is declarative,
(2) interrogative, imperative, or exclamatory:

Where might you see a dingo?

26. Rewrite the following outline, adding capital letters as
(26) needed:

    i. types of dogs
      a. herding dogs
      b. guard dogs
      c. hounds
      d. terriers

27. For a–c, write the plural of each noun.
(16, 17, 22)

    (a) tax   (b) man   (c) puppy

Diagram the simple subject and simple predicate of sentences 28–30.

28. There goes a chihuahua!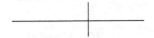
(32)

29. That collie seems obedient.
(32)

30. Does your dog herd sheep?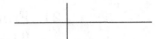
(32)

LESSON 34

Spelling Rules: Suffixes, Part 2

Doubling Final Consonants

When a one-syllable word ends with a single consonant preceded by a single vowel, we double the final consonant before adding a suffix that begins with a vowel.

$$trap + ed = trapped$$
$$win + er = winner$$
$$drip + ing = dripping$$
$$big + est = biggest$$
$$fun + y = funny$$

Exceptions include the words *sew* (sewing), *bow* (bowed), and *tax* (taxing).

When a word of two or more syllables ends with a single consonant preceded by a single vowel, we double the final consonant if the word is accented (stressed) on the last syllable.

$$forget + ing = forgetting$$
$$expel + ed = expelled$$
$$admit + ed = admitted$$

Do Not Double

We **do not** double the final consonant of any of the words described above (words ending with a single consonant preceded by a single vowel) when adding a suffix that begins with a consonant.

$$mad + ly = madly$$
$$spot + less = spotless$$
$$sad + ness = sadness$$

We **do not** double the final consonant if it is preceded by two vowels or another consonant:

$$rain + ed = rained$$
$$warm + ly = warmly$$
$$broad + est = broadest$$
$$dish + ful = dishful$$

Example Add suffixes to these words.

(a) chop + ing = _____

(b) submit + ed = _____

(c) glad + ly = _____

(d) pain + less = _____

(e) luck + y = _____

Solution (a) chop + ing = **chopping** (We double the final consonant when we add a suffix beginning with a vowel.)

(b) submit + ed = **submitted** (When a two-syllable word is accented on the final syllable, we double the final consonant if it is preceded by a single vowel.)

(c) glad + ly = **gladly** (When the suffix begins with a consonant, we do not double the final consonant before adding the suffix.)

(d) pain + less = **painless** (A final consonant preceded by two vowels is not doubled.)

(e) luck + y = **lucky** (A final consonant preceded by another consonant is not doubled.)

Practice Add suffixes to words a–e.

a. drop + ed = _____

b. stop + ing = _____

c. bad + ly = _____

d. regret + ed = _____

e. flat + ness = _____

For f and g, replace each blank with *pollen* or *stamen*.

f. _____ in the air sometimes makes me sneeze, for it is fine and powdery.

g. The _____ of a flower bears pollen.

Choose the correct word to complete sentences 1–6.

1. Chicks may (cheap, cheep) for grain.
(33)

2. A (herd, heard) of bison blocked the road.
(32)

3. (Kittens, Boars) have thick, bristly skin.
(31)

4. The (doe, buck) carried her baby in her pouch.
(30)

5. The family chose a (fir, fur) for their Christmas tree.
(9)

6. The word *puppy's* is a (plural, possessive) noun.
(13)

7. Add suffixes to the following words:
(33)

(a) fry + ed   (b) come + ing

8. Add suffixes to the following words:
(34)

(a) sit + ing   (b) mad + ly

9. Write the past tense form of the verb *tip.*
(10)

10. Rewrite the following sentence, adding capital letters as
(26) needed:

melody said, "my dog's name is penny."

11. Replace the blank below with the singular present tense
(9) form of the underlined verb.

Boys <u>rush</u> out. David _____ out.

12. Write each action verb in the following sentence:
(7)

Rex sniffs the air and listens.

13. In the following sentence, write the entire verb phrase,
(12) circling each helping verb:

A skunk has been digging in the rose garden.

14. Write the following story title, using correct capitalization:
(25) "the bravest dog of all"

15. Write the linking verb in the following sentence:
(31)

Rex looks silly in that raincoat.

16. Write whether the following word group is a complete
(5, 23) sentence, a sentence fragment, or a run-on sentence:

Two frisky border collies, good sheep herders.

17. Write the two prepositions that you find in the following
(20, 21) sentence:

Border collies herd livestock through the pasture and into
the barn.

18. Use a dictionary: (a) The word *distaff* is what part of
(27, 30) speech? (b) Write its pronunciation. (c) Write its
etymology.

19. Rewrite the following words, circling silent letter(s):
(28, 29)
    (a) wrong   (b) right   (c) hymn

20. Rewrite and correct the sentence fragment below, making
(6) a complete sentence. There is more than one correct
answer.

Poacher, the meanest dog in town.

21. From memory, write the linking verbs listed in Lesson
(31) 31.

22. Write the compound noun that you find in this sentence:
(13)
Poacher belongs in his doghouse.

23. For the following sentence, write the correct form of the
(9, 19) verb:

Rex (present of *howl*) at night.

24. For the verb *bury*, write the (a) present participle, (b) past
(19) tense, and (c) past participle.

25. Write whether the following sentence is declarative,
(2) interrogative, imperative, or exclamatory:

My dog is loyal and obedient.

26. Rewrite the following lines of poetry, adding capital
(15) letters as needed:

> my dog rex sleeps in a chair.
> at dinnertime, he won't be there.
> under the table is where he'll wait,
> begging for something from my plate.

27. For a–c, write the plural of each noun.
(17, 22) (a) duty   (b) tooth   (c) tax

Diagram the simple subject and simple predicate of sentences
28–30.

28. Into the chair jumps Rex.
(32)

29. The dog in the chair looks sleepy.
(32)

30. Will Rex wake at dinnertime?
(32)

LESSON 35

Spelling Rules: *ie* or *ei*

> **Dictation or Journal Entry**
> **Vocabulary:**
> A *creek* is a small stream. We found tadpoles in the *creek*.
> To *creak* is to make a squeaking sound. The old wooden stairs *creak* beneath my feet.

To determine whether to use *ie* or *ei* to make the long *e* sound in a word, we recall this rhyme:

Use *i* before *e*

Except after *c*

Or when sounded like *ay*

As in *neighbor* and *weigh*.

USE *i* BEFORE *e*:

bel*ie*ve	f*ie*ld	sh*ie*ld	br*ie*f	v*ie*w
ch*ie*f	pr*ie*st	n*ie*ce	rel*ie*ve	ach*ie*ve

EXCEPT AFTER *c*:

c*ei*ling	rec*ei*pt	dec*ei*t
dec*ei*ve	conc*ei*ve	perc*ei*ve

OR WHEN SOUNDED LIKE *ay*:

n*ei*ghbor	w*ei*gh	fr*ei*ght	r*ei*gn

Exceptions In *Grammar and Writing 5*, we shall learn exceptions to this rule.

Example Write the words that are spelled correctly.

(a) peice, piece   (b) beleive, believe

(c) cieling, ceiling   (d) receive, recieve

(e) nieghbor, neighbor   (f) wiegh, weigh

Solution (a) **piece** (Use *i* before *e*)   (b) **believe**

(c) **ceiling** (Except after *c*)   (d) **receive**

(e) **neighbor** (Or when sounded as *ay*)

(f) **weigh**

Grammar and Writing 4   **154**   **Student Edition**
Lesson 35

Practice For a–f, write the words that are spelled correctly.

   a. achieve, acheive   **b.** yeild, yield

   c. recieve, receive   **d.** deciet, deceit

   e. freight, frieght   **f.** riegn, reign

   For g and h, replace each blank with *creek* or *creak.*

   g. Sometimes floorboards _____ when we walk on them.

   h. My clothes were soaked after I fell into the _____ .

Review Set 35 Choose the correct word to complete sentences 1–6.

   1. We find (prey, pollen) on the stamen of a flower.
   (34)

   2. (*Cheap, Cheep*) means "low in price."
   (33)

   3. Neighbors (herd, heard) the church bells ring.
   (32)

   4. Mature female pigs are called (boars, sows).
   (31)

   5. (Who's, Whose) that knocking at the door?
   (10)

   6. The word *poodle* is a(n) (abstract, concrete) noun.
   (11)

   7. Add suffixes to the following words:
   (33)
     (a) scare + y   (b) fly + er

   8. Add suffixes to the following words:
   (34)
     (a) hop + ed   (b) cold + est

   9. For a and b, write the word that is spelled correctly.
   (35)
     (a) receive, recieve   (b) believe, beleive

   10. Rewrite the following sentence, adding capital letters as
   (26)   needed:

       miss ng said, "my niece doesn't have any pets."

   11. Replace the blank below with the singular present tense
   (9)   form of the underlined verb.

       People <u>relax</u>. He _____ .

12. Write each action verb in the following sentence:
(7)

The kitten yawned and closed its eyes.

13. In the following sentence, write the entire verb phrase,
(12) circling each helping verb:

The thief had been deceiving people for years.

14. Write the following story title, using correct
(25) capitalization: "the lion and the mouse"

15. Write the linking verb in the following sentence:
(31)

The thief's words proved false.

16. Write whether the following word group is a complete
(5, 23) sentence, a sentence fragment, or a run-on sentence:

Believe me.

17. Write the three prepositions that you find in the
(20, 21) following sentence:

Spats swatted at my shoe, dashed across the kitchen, and
ducked under a chair.

18. Use a dictionary: (a) The word *virtue* is what part of
(27, 30) speech? (b) Write its pronunciation. (c) Write its
etymology.

19. Rewrite the following words, circling silent letter(s):
(28, 29)

(a) bomb   (b) listen   (c) know

20. Rewrite and correct the run-on sentence below. There is
(24) more than one correct answer.

Persian cats have long fur the hairs are silky and fine.

21. From the following list, write the word that is *not* a
(31) linking verb: is, am, car, was, were, be, being, been.

22. Write the collective noun that you find in this sentence:
(11)

A flock of geese honked overhead.

23. For the following sentence, write the correct form of the
(18) verb:

I (future of *call*) you later.

24. For the verb *smile*, write the (a) present participle, (b)
(19) past tense, and (c) past participle.

25. Write whether the following sentence is declarative,
(2) interrogative, imperative, or exclamatory:

Persian cats molt in warm weather.

26. Rewrite the following poem, adding capital letters as
(15) needed:

use *i* before *e*
except after *c*
or when sounded like *ay*
as in *neighbor* and *weigh*.

27. For a–c, write the plural of each noun.
(17, 22) (a) branch   (b) son-in-law   (c) berry

Diagram the simple subject and simple predicate of sentences
28–30.

28. Out go the mice.
(32)

29. The baker's voice sounds stern.
(32)

30. Have the mice eaten many muffins?
(32)

LESSON 36

Phrases and Clauses

Dictation or Journal Entry
Vocabulary:
Mature means "having reached full growth or development." The *mature* oak trees survived the storm.

Immature means "not having reached full growth or development." Sometimes *immature* people are selfish.

Phrases   A **phrase** is a group of words that functions as a single unit in a sentence. A phrase may contain nouns and verbs, but it does not have both a subject and a predicate. Below are some phrases.

> above the clouds
>
> in the wild
>
> may have flown
>
> during the winter
>
> might have matured

Clauses   A **clause** is a group of words with a subject and a predicate. In the clauses below, we have italicized the simple subjects and underlined the simple predicates.

> before the *egg* <u>hatches</u>
>
> as *you* <u>said</u>
>
> but *they* <u>will mature</u>
>
> for the *duck* <u>flies</u> south
>
> (*you*) <u>Look</u> up!

Example 1   Tell whether each group of words is a phrase or a clause.

(a) when I was young

(b) inside the cave

(c) along the edge of the creek

(d) before he came

Solution   (a) This group of words is a **clause.** It has both a subject (I) and a predicate (was).

(b) This group of words is a **phrase.** It does not have a subject or predicate.

Grammar and Writing 4   **158**   **Student Edition** Lesson 36

(c) This is a **phrase.** It has no subject or predicate.

(d) This is a **clause.** Its subject is *he*; its predicate is <u>came</u>.

Every complete sentence has at least one clause. Some sentences have more than one clause. We have italicized the simple subjects and underlined the simple predicates in each clause of the sentence below. Notice that it contains three clauses (three subject and predicate combinations).

The *sun* <u>had set</u>, and *clouds* <u>covered</u> the moon, so *Nan* <u>used</u> her flashlight.

Below, we have diagrammed the simple subjects and simple predicates of each clause from the sentence above.

(1) The sun had set,

sun	had set

(2) and clouds covered the moon,

clouds	covered

(2) so Nan used her flashlight.

Nan	used

Example 2 Diagram the simple subjects and simple predicates of the clauses in this sentence:

The canary sang until the cat came.

Solution We examine the sentence and find that there are two clauses:

1. The *canary* <u>sang</u>

2. until the *cat* <u>came</u>

We diagram the first clause:

canary	sang

We diagram the second clause:

cat	came

Practice For a–d, tell whether the group of words is a phrase or a clause.

a. since the ducks flew south

b. regarding the eagles' habitat

c. then they can come home

d. after watching the falcon

Diagram each simple subject and simple predicate in clauses e–g.

e. before the race began

f. for they eat insects

g. but the grouse was hiding

For h and i, replace each blank with *mature* or *immature*.

h. _____ students are usually polite.

i. _____ trees might blow down in the wind.

Review Set 36
Choose the correct word to complete sentences 1–6.

1. We found frogs near the (creak, creek).
(35)

2. Pollen is found on the (posterior, stamen) of a flower.
(34)

3. Newly hatched birds (cheap, cheep) loudly for food.
(33)

4. A border collie guides the (heard, herd) of sheep.
(32)

5. Black Beauty is a well-known (hoarse, horse).
(5)

6. The word *eagles* is a (plural, possessive) noun.
(13)

7. Add suffixes to the following words:
(33)
(a) merry + ly   (b) fly + ing

8. Add suffixes to the following words:
(34)
(a) big + er   (b) bad + ly

9. For a and b, write the word that is spelled correctly.
(35)
(a) view, veiw   (b) beleif, belief

10. Rewrite the following sentence, adding capital letters as needed:
(26)

daisy asked, "can emus fly?"

11. Replace the blank below with the singular present tense form of the underlined verb.
(9)

Children <u>march</u>. A child _____.

12. Write whether the following word group is a phrase or a
(36) clause: if you see a bobcat

13. In the following sentence, write the entire verb phrase,
(12) circling each helping verb:

Finches must have built those nests.

14. Rewrite the following song title, using correct
(25) capitalization: "getting to know you"

15. Write the linking verb in the following sentence:
(31)
The ugly duckling became a swan.

16. Write whether the following word group is a complete
(5, 23) sentence, a sentence fragment, or a run-on sentence:

There are many species of ducks they nest near water or
in tree holes.

17. Write the two prepositions that you find in the following
(20, 21) sentence:

Mallards paddled across the lake and waddled onto the
shore.

18. Use a dictionary: (a) The word *tern* is what part of
(27, 30) speech? (b) Write its pronunciation. (c) Write its
etymology.

19. Rewrite the following words, circling silent letter(s):
(28, 29)
(a) scene   (b) honor   (c) kneel

20. Rewrite and correct the following sentence fragment,
(6) making a complete sentence:

to explore the Arctic in summer

21. From the following list, write the word that is *not* a
(31) linking verb: look, feel, taste, smell, hear, seem, appear.

22. Write the two compound nouns that you find in this
(13) sentence:

Shorebirds found insects and seeds in the grasslands.

23. For the following sentence, write the correct form of the verb:

(14)

We (future of *see*) each other soon.

24. For the verb *believe*, write the (a) present participle, (b) past tense, and (c) past participle.

(19)

25. Write whether the following sentence is declarative, interrogative, imperative, or exclamatory:

(2)

Where is Antarctica?

26. Rewrite the following outline, adding capital letters as needed:

(26)

i. two main types of ducks
   a. dabbling ducks
   b. diving ducks

27. For a–c, write the plural of each noun.

(17, 22)

(a) lunch   (b) colony   (c) police chief

28. Diagram the simple subject and simple predicate of each clause in the following sentence:

(36)

If the puffin would stand still, I could sketch it.

Diagram the simple subject and simple predicate of sentences 29–30.

29. Here come the seagulls.

(32)

30. Draw a puffin.

(32)

Diagramming a Direct Object

Dictation or Journal Entry

Vocabulary:

A *larva* is an early, usually wormlike, form of an insect. The caterpillar is the *larva* of a butterfly.

A *pupa* is an insect in the stage of development between larva and adult. The larva becomes a *pupa* before it becomes a butterfly.

Finding the Direct Object

A **direct object** follows an *action verb* and tells who or what receives the action.

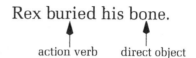

Rex buried his bone.

action verb   direct object

We can answer these three questions to find the direct object of a sentence:

1. What is the verb in the sentence?

2. Is it an *action verb*?

3. Who or what receives the action? (direct object)

We will follow the steps above to find the direct object of this sentence:

Rex chases cats.

QUESTION 1: What is the verb?
ANSWER: The verb is "chases."

QUESTION 2: Is it an *action verb*?
ANSWER: Yes.

QUESTION 3: Who or what receives the action?
ANSWER: *Cats* are "chased."

Therefore, "cats" is the direct object.

Example 1

Follow the procedure above to find the direct object of this sentence:

A hummingbird sips nectar.

Solution

We answer the questions as follows:

QUESTION 1: What is the verb?
ANSWER: The verb is "sips."

QUESTION 2: Is it an *action verb*?
ANSWER: Yes.

QUESTION 3:   Who or what receives the action?
ANSWER: The *nectar* is "sipped."

Therefore, **nectar** is the direct object.

Example 2   Answer the three questions above to find the direct object of this sentence:

The condor is a bird of prey.

Solution   We answer the questions as follows:

QUESTION 1:   What is the verb?
ANSWER: The verb is "is."

QUESTION 2:   Is it an *action verb*?
ANSWER: No. "Is" is a linking verb.

Therefore, this sentence has **no direct object.**

Diagramming the Direct Object   Below is a diagram of the simple subject, simple predicate, and direct object of this sentence:

Rex chases cats.

Rex	chases	cats
(subject)	(verb)	(direct object)

Notice that a vertical line after the action verb indicates a direct object.

Example 3   Diagram the simple subject, simple predicate, and direct object of this sentence:

A hummingbird sips nectar.

hummingbird	sips	nectar
(subject)	(verb)	(direct object)

Practice   For a–c, write the direct object, if there is one, in each sentence.

a. Nate flies kites.

b. The hummingbird's nest is tiny.

c. The swan is calling its mate.

Diagram the simple subject, simple predicate, and direct object of sentences d and e.

d. Alba asked questions.

e. We were playing checkers.

For f and g, replace each blank with *larva* or *pupa*.

f. The larva becomes a _____ before the insect is mature.

g. A caterpillar is the _____ of a butterfly.

Review Set 37

Choose the correct word to complete sentences 1–6.

1. A(n) (mature, immature) student does homework.
(36)

2. The floorboards (creek, creak) when stepped upon.
(35)

3. (Pollen, Pupa) acts as a fertilizer in plant production.
(34)

4. Many items at the yard sale were (cheep, cheap).
(33)

5. (You're, Your) smile made me happy.
(11)

6. The word *greed* is a(n) (abstract, concrete) noun.
(11)

7. Add suffixes to the following words:
(33)
   (a) bury + ed   (b) scare + y

8. Add suffixes to the following words:
(34)
   (a) sun + y   (b) stop + ing

9. For a and b, write the word that is spelled correctly.
(35)
   (a) grief, greif   (b) recieve, receive

10. Rewrite the following sentence, adding capital letters as needed:
(26)

molly replied, "no, emus cannot fly."

11. Replace the blank below with the singular present tense form of the underlined verb.
(9)

Goats <u>munch</u> oats. A goat _____ oats.

12. Write whether the following word group is a phrase or a
(36) clause: with a very loose tooth

13. In the following sentence, write the entire verb phrase,
(12) circling each helping verb:

Rex might have dug that hole.

14. Write the following poem title, using correct
(25) capitalization: "the crow and the pitcher"

15. Write the linking verb in the following sentence:
(31)
David grew stronger.

16. Write whether the following word group is a complete
(5, 23) sentence, a sentence fragment, or a run-on sentence:

Eagles soar above mountain tops.

17. Write each preposition that you find in the following
(20, 21) sentence:

Boil a pound of noodles in water for ten minutes.

18. Use a dictionary: (a) The word *novice* is what part of speech?
(27,30) (b) Write its pronunciation. (c) Write its etymology.

19. Rewrite the following words, circling silent letter(s):
(28, 29)
(a) who   (b) sign   (c) light

20. Rewrite and correct the run-on sentence below. There is
(24) more than one correct answer.

Rex chewed Dad's shoe he also ate my homework.

21. From the following list, write the word that is *not* a
(31) linking verb: sound, seem, appear, growl, remain, stay.

22. Write the collective noun that you find in this sentence:
(11)
A swarm of flies attacked my sandwich.

23. For the following sentence, write the correct form of the
(18) verb:

We (past of *sip*) ice water.

24. For the verb *sip*, write the (a) present participle, (b) past
(19) tense, and (c) past participle.

25. Write whether the following sentence is declarative,
(2) interrogative, imperative, or exclamatory:

Wow, that sunset is colorful!

26. Rewrite the following lines of poetry, adding capital
(15) letters as needed:

the porcupine
is a friend of mine.

27. For a–c, write the plural of each noun.
(17, 22)
(a) torch   (b) library   (c) spoonful

28. Diagram the simple subject and simple predicate of each
(36) clause in the following sentence:

Throughout the day, you have been working, but I have
been playing today.

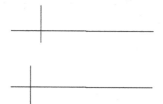

Diagram the simple subject, simple predicate, and direct
object of sentences 29–30.

29. Lisa is writing stories.
(32, 37)

30. Did you feed Rex?
(32, 37)

LESSON 38

Capitalization: People Titles, Family Words, and School Subjects

Dictation or Journal Entry

Vocabulary:
Metamorphosis is the process by which certain animals change their form as they develop from an immature form to an adult. By *metamorphosis*, a tadpole becomes a frog.

Pollination is the transfer of pollen from flower to flower, allowing plants to reproduce. Plants depend on bees, butterflies, and other insects to help with *pollination*.

We have learned that proper nouns require capital letters and that common nouns are capitalized when they are a part of a proper noun. We also capitalize parts of an outline, the first word of a sentence, the first word of every line of poetry, the pronoun *I*, the first word in a direct quotation, and the important words in titles. Now, we will add more rules for capitalization.

Titles Used with Names of People

Titles used with names of people require a capital letter. Often, these are abbreviations. We capitalize initials because they stand for names of people.

> Mr. and Mrs. David Campos
> Dr. Richard M. Curtis
> General George S. Patton
> Aunt Em
> Grandma Moses

Family Words

When **family words** such as *father, mother, grandmother,* or *grandfather* are used instead of a person's name, these words are capitalized. However, they are not capitalized when words such as *my, your, his, our,* or *their* are used before them.

> Did you stir the soup, *Dad*?
> I asked *my dad* if he had stirred the soup.

> Andrew wants to see *Grandma*.
> Andrew wants to see *his grandma*.

School Subjects

When the name of a school subject comes from a proper noun, it is capitalized. Otherwise, it is not.

> English   math
> Latin   biology
> Spanish   language arts

Example Correct the following sentences by adding capital letters.

    (a) Is dr. kim s. wang in her office?

    (b) please help grandfather to pick apples.

    (c) my favorite classes are math and english.

Solution (a) We capitalize **Dr.** because it is a title used with the name of a person. We capitalize **Kim S. Wang** because it is a proper noun, and the letter *S* is an initial.

    (b) We capitalize **Please** because it is the first word of the sentence. *Grandfather* requires a capital because it is used instead of a person's name.

    (c) **My** is the first word of the sentence. **English** comes from a proper noun, so we capitalize it.

Practice Add capital letters where they are needed in sentences a–d.

    a. are you taking french this year?

    b. i think dad needs a haircut.

    c. the dentist's name is dr. will u. brush.

    d. my aunt and uncle grow pumpkins.

For e and f, replace each blank with *metamorphosis* or *pollination.*

    e. By _____, an egg becomes a larva, which becomes a pupa, which becomes a butterfly.

    f. Plants reproduce by _____.

More Practice See "More Practice Lesson 38" in the Student Workbook.

Review Set 38 Choose the correct word to complete sentences 1–6.

    1. A (larva, pollen) is an immature form of an insect.
    (37)

    2. A larva becomes a (stamen, pupa) before it becomes a butterfly.
    (37)

    3. A (creek, creak) is easier to cross than a river.
    (35)

    4. The (stamen, pupa) is the pollen-bearing organ of a flower.
    (34)

5. Our dog, Rex, is the (canine, feline) member of our
(12) family.

6. The word *boss's* is a (plural, possessive) noun.
(13)

7. Add suffixes to the following words:
(33) (a) sunny + er   (b) fame + ous

8. Add suffixes to the following words:
(34) (a) sad + ly   (b) begin + ing

9. For a and b, write the word that is spelled correctly.
(35) (a) weigh, wiegh   (b) niece, neice

10. Rewrite the following sentence, adding capital letters as
(26) needed:

miss yu asked, "do toads have warts?"

11. Replace the blank below with the singular present tense
(9) form of the underlined verb.

Wet socks <u>dry</u>. A wet sock _____.

12. Write whether the following word group is a phrase or a
(36) clause: when lightning strikes

13. In the following sentence, write the entire verb phrase,
(12) circling each helping verb:

You should have seen that platypus!

14. Write the following sentence, using correct
(38) capitalization: yes, mom is taking a chinese class.

15. Write the linking verb in the following sentence:
(31)
That lion looks ferocious.

16. Write whether the following word group is a complete
(5, 23) sentence, a sentence fragment, or a run-on sentence:

A word meaning "famous."

17. Write each preposition that you find in the following
(20, 21) sentence:

Crocodiles swam alongside our boat until dusk.

18. Use a dictionary: (a) The word *addax* is what part of speech? (b) Write its pronunciation. (c) Write its etymology.
(27,30)

19. Rewrite the following words, circling silent letter(s):
(28, 29)

(a) half   (b) caught   (c) comb

20. Rewrite and correct the sentence fragment below, making a complete sentence. There is more than one correct answer.
(6)

Fishing from the bridge.

21. From the following list, write the word that is *not* a linking verb: is, am, are, was, were, be, bead, been.
(31)

22. Write the compound noun that you find in this sentence:
(13)

Will Rex bring me the newspaper?

23. For the following sentence, write the correct form of the verb:
(18)

Rex (past of *rip*) the newspaper.

24. For the verb *rip*, write the (a) present participle, (b) past tense, and (c) past participle.
(10, 19)

25. Write whether the following sentence is declarative, interrogative, imperative, or exclamatory:
(2)

Try again.

26. Rewrite the following outline, adding capital letters as needed:
(26)

i. birds of australia
  a. laughing kookaburra
  b. rainbow lorikeets

27. For a–c, write the plural of each noun.
(17, 22)

(a) body   (b) birthday   (c) reptile egg

28. Diagram the simple subject and simple predicate of each clause in the following sentence:
(36)

While Nam trimmed the bushes, I swept the porch.

Diagram the simple subject, simple predicate, and direct object of sentences 29–30.

29. Have you written stories?
(32, 37)

30. The cat must have caught a mouse.
(32, 37)

Descriptive Adjectives

Dictation or Journal Entry
Vocabulary:
A *flea* is an insect that feeds on the blood of warm-blooded animals. A *flea* has strong legs for leaping and sharp mouth parts for biting.

To *flee* is to run away swiftly. Squirrels often *flee* when they see us.

An adjective is a word that describes a person, place, or thing. There are many different kinds of adjectives. They tell "which one," "what kind," "how many," or "whose."

Descriptive Adjectives In this lesson, we will examine **descriptive adjectives**, which describe a person, place, or thing. Sometimes, they answer the question "What kind?" Descriptive adjectives are italicized below.

long tail

hoarse voice

huge, hungry bear

Often, descriptive adjectives precede the person, place, or thing, as in the sentences below.

Mature apples fall.

Dark clouds bring *heavy* rain.

Sometimes, descriptive adjectives follow the noun or pronoun, as in the example below.

Sid, *kind* but *firm,* trains horses.

Some descriptive adjectives end in suffixes like these:

-able	*lovable, breakable, washable, believable*
-al	*natural, unusual, global, factual*
-ful	*joyful, helpful, peaceful, thankful*
-ible	*terrible, edible, possible, invisible*
-ive	*aggressive, active, creative, expensive*
-less	*painless, fearless, useless, careless*
-ous	*enormous, dangerous, famous, curious*
-y	*breezy, funny, wordy, wormy, cheery*

Example 1   Write each descriptive adjective in sentences a–c.

(a) Aggressive animals make poor pets.

(b) Sensible people avoid poisonous snakes.

(c) The trail, steep and rocky, goes nowhere.

Solution   (a) **Aggressive** (describes "animals"), **poor** (describes "pets")

(b) **Sensible** (describes "people"), **poisonous** (describes "snakes")

(c) **steep, rocky** (describes "trail")

Improving Our Writing   Descriptive adjectives help us to draw pictures using words. They make our writing clearer, more exact, and more interesting. For example, fur can be *long, short, thick, fuzzy, spotted, striped, fluffy, sleek, shiny, curly, muddy, tangled, smooth, black, brown, white, gray, orange,* or *red*. An animal's ears can be *silky, pointed, floppy,* or *furry*. When we write, we can use descriptive adjectives to create more detailed pictures.

Example 2   Replace each blank with a descriptive adjective to add more detail to the word "puppies" in this sentence:

The mother dog has _____, _____ puppies.

Solution   Our answers will vary. Here are some possibilities: ***tiny, wiggly, cute, playful, active, sleepy, friendly, healthy,*** and ***lively.***

Practice   Write each descriptive adjective in sentences a–c.

a. The cat, young and frisky, might scratch you.

b. Ripe apples make tasty pies.

c. Anna chooses delicious, healthful snacks.

For d–f, write two descriptive adjectives to describe each noun.

d. chair   **e.** story   **f.** cloud

For g and h, replace each blank with *flea* or *flee*.

ear   *feet*

   g. A thief might try to _____ from the police.

   h. I might have _____ bites on my ankles.

More Practice See "Funny Fill-in #2" in the Student Workbook. Have fun!

Review Set 39 Choose the correct word to complete sentences 1–6.

   1. (Mourning, Metamorphosis, Molt) is the process by
   (38) which certain animals change their form as they mature.

   2. A (larva, preen, molt) is an immature insect.
   (37)

   3. A butterfly is the (immature, stamen, mature) form of a
   (36) caterpillar.

   4. A (creek, creak, herd) provides a healthy environment for
   (35) tadpoles to mature into frogs.

   5. Fish swim by moving their (tales, tails, manes).
   (6)

   6. The word *mood* is a(n) (abstract, concrete) noun.
   (11)

   7. Add suffixes to the following words:
   (33) (a) say + ed   (b) pity + ful

   8. Add suffixes to the following words:
   (34) (a) swat + ed   (b) warm + er

   9. For a and b, write the word that is spelled correctly.
   (35) (a) nieghbor, neighbor   (b) veiw, view

   10. Write each descriptive adjective from the following
   (39) sentence:

   An enormous paw with sharp claws swatted me.

   11. Replace the blank below with the singular present tense
   (9) form of the underlined verb.

   Boats <u>reach</u> the shore. A boat _____ the shore.

   12. Write whether the following word group is a phrase or a
   (36) clause: down the street from the post office

13. In the following sentence, write the entire verb phrase, (12) circling each helping verb:

Has Rex been sleeping all day?

14. Rewrite the following book title, using correct (25) capitalization: *the fox and the grapes*

15. Write the linking verb in the following sentence:
(31)
Rex remains loyal to his master.

16. Write whether the following word group is a complete (5, 23) sentence, a sentence fragment, or a run-on sentence:

Some reptile eggs have soft shells others have hard shells.

17. Write each preposition that you find in the following (20, 21) sentence:

Underneath the table, Rex snoozed until dinnertime.

18. Use a dictionary: (a) The word *edible* is what part of (27, 30) speech? (b) Write its pronunciation. (c) Write its etymology.

19. Rewrite the following words, circling silent letter(s):
(28, 29)
(a) two   (b) guard   (c) kneel

20. Rewrite and correct the run-on sentence below. There is (24) more than one correct answer.

Some reptile eggs have soft shells others have hard shells.

21. From the following list, write the word that is *not* a (31) linking verb: look, feel, taste, smell, pound, seem, appear.

22. Write the collective noun that you find in this sentence:
(11)
A pack of dogs ran the other way.

23. For the following sentence, write the correct form of the (14) verb:

We (future of *sing*) "Happy Birthday" to Kim.

24. For the verb *trot*, write the (a) present participle, (b) past (19) tense, and (c) past participle.

25. In the sentence below, replace each blank with a descriptive adjective to add more detail to the word "boots." There are many possible answers.

(39)

The soldier wore _____, _____ boots.

26. Rewrite the following lines of poetry, adding capital letters as needed:

(15)

he closed the gate,
but it was too late.

27. For a–c, write the plural of each noun.

(17, 22)

(a) armadillo   (b) fly   (c) leader of the pack

28. Diagram the simple subject and simple predicate of each clause in the following sentence:

(36)

Nate slices cheese while Josh toasts bread.

Diagram the simple subject, simple predicate, and direct object of sentences 29–30.

29. Grandma has been swatting flies.

(32, 37)

30. Have flies been bothering Grandma?

(32, 37)

29.

30.

The Limiting Adjective •
Diagramming Adjectives

Dictation or Journal Entry

Vocabulary:

A *colt* is a male horse under four years old. The *colt* pranced alongside his mother.

A *filly* is a young female horse. That *filly* will be tall when she is mature.

Limiting adjectives help to define, or "limit," a noun or pronoun. They tell "which one," "what kind," "how many," or "whose." There are six categories of limiting adjectives. They include articles, demonstrative adjectives, numbers, possessive pronouns, possessive nouns, and indefinites.

Articles   Articles are the most commonly used adjectives, and they are also the shortest—***a***, ***an***, and ***the***.

a rock	*the* rock
a pony	*the* pony
an ape	*the* ape
an egg	*the* egg

We use *a* before words beginning with a consonant sound, and *an* before words beginning with a vowel sound. It is the sound and not the spelling that determines whether we use *a* or *an*:

an hour	*a* hen
an umbrella	*a* uniform
an R-rating	*a* rat
an x-ray	*a* xylophone

Demonstrative Adjectives   WHICH ONE?

this street	*that* town
these hills	*those* trees

Numbers   HOW MANY?

three ships	*twelve* inches	*one* fish
twenty-four hours	*fifteen* pages	*forty* years

Possessive Pronouns	WHOSE?		
	her pencil	*its* hoof	*my* friend
	our land	*their* shoes	*your* help

Possessive Nouns	WHOSE?		
	Abe's glove	*Rosa's* plan	*turtle's* egg
	Liz's idea	*Tio's* hat	*Omar's* chin

Indefinites	HOW MANY?		
	some sheep	*few* bugs	*many* cars
	several mice	*no* coins	*any* money

Example 1 Write each limiting adjective that you find in these sentences.

(a) Where did those turtles lay their eggs?

(b) That turtle laid its eggs on the beach.

(c) Many turtles were hatching on one nest.

(d) A turtle stepped on Amelia's foot.

Solution (a) **those, their**   (b) **That, its, the**

(c) **Many, one**   (d) **A, Amelia's**

Diagramming Adjectives We diagram adjectives by placing them on a slanted line beneath the noun or pronoun they describe, or "limit."

Amelia's (possessive adjective) *baby* (descriptive adjective) turtle can swim.

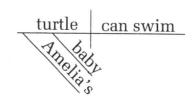

In this sentence, *Amelia's* and *baby* tell "whose" and "what kind" of turtle, so we attach them to the word "turtle."

Example 2 Diagram this sentence:

Those tiny turtles must reach the water.

Solution We see that the adjectives *those* and *tiny* describe "turtles," and the adjective *the* describes "water," so we diagram the sentence like this:

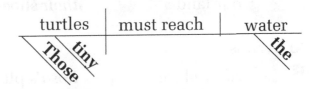

Practice For a and b, replace each blank with *colt* or *filly*.

    a. The _____ shook her mane and snorted.

    b. The _____ swished his tail and looked at me.

Write each limiting adjective that you find in sentences c–f.

    c. Noah's father has written several songs.

    d. He wrote one song about the moon.

    e. That singer lost his voice.

    f. Some music hurts my ears.

    g. Diagram this sentence: Tina plays a shiny trumpet.

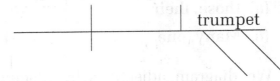

More Practice See "More Practice Lesson 40" in the Student Workbook.

Review Set 40 Choose the correct word to complete sentences 1–6.

    1. The dog provided a home for many (flees, fleas, wails).
    (39)

    2. Bees transfer pollen from flower to flower during
    (38) (pollination, metamorphosis, mourning).

    3. Cocoons are a protective covering for the (pollination,
    (37) stamen, pupa).

    4. Puppies display such (mature, cheep, immature)
    (36) behavior as digging up plants and jumping on people.

5. Carrots, turnips, and beets are (route, root, stamen)
(22) vegetables.

6. The word *Larrys* is a (possessive, plural) noun.
(13)

7. Add suffixes to the following words:
(33)
    (a) lazy + ness   (b) pay + ed

8. Add suffixes to the following words:
(34)
    (a) pour + ing   (b) mop + ed

9. For a and b, write the word that is spelled correctly.
(35)
    (a) reciept, receipt   (b) priest, preist

10. Write each descriptive adjective from the following
(39) sentence:

Red blossoms attract colorful hummingbirds.

11. Replace the blank below with the singular present tense
(9) form of the underlined verb.

Pets <u>rely</u> on you. A pet _____ on you.

12. Write whether the following word group is a phrase or a
(36) clause: if the bear smells food

13. In the following sentence, write the entire verb phrase,
(12) circling each helping verb:

Should Omar have disturbed the bees?

14. Rewrite the following sentence, using correct capitalization:
(38)
yes, mr. cruz teaches the spanish class.

15. Write the linking verb in the following sentence:
(31)
That piglet seems nervous without its mother.

16. Write whether the following word group is a complete
(5, 23) sentence, a sentence fragment, or a run-on sentence:

Anteaters have no teeth.

17. Write each preposition that you find in the following
^(20, 21) sentence:

Behind a bush, Omar hides from the bees.

18. Use a dictionary: (a) The word *mortal* is what part of
^(27,30) speech? (b) Write its pronunciation. (c) Write its
etymology.

19. Rewrite the following words, circling silent letter(s):
^(28, 29)
(a) honest   (b) sign   (c) listen

20. Rewrite and correct the following sentence fragment,
⁽⁶⁾ making a complete sentence:

Hiding from the bees.

21. From the following list, write the word that is *not* a
⁽³¹⁾ linking verb:

seem, hide, grow, become, remain, stay.

22. Write the three limiting adjectives from the following
⁽⁴⁰⁾ sentence:

That evening, Rex buried his two bones.

23. For the following sentence, write the correct form of the
⁽¹⁰⁾ verb:

I (past of *reply*) yesterday.

24. For the verb *reply*, write the (a) present participle, (b) past
⁽¹⁹⁾ tense, and (c) past participle.

25. Replace each blank with a descriptive adjective to add
⁽³⁹⁾ more detail to the word "parrot" in the sentence below.
There are many possible answers.

A(n) _____, _____ parrot lands on a branch.

26. Rewrite the following sentence, adding capital letters as
⁽²⁶⁾ needed:

mr. brown asked, "have you read *the horse and his boy*?"

27. For a–c, write the plural of each noun.
^(17, 22)
(a) Friday   (b) peach   (c) hairbrush

28. Diagram the simple subject and simple predicate of each
(36) clause in the following sentence:

While bees are buzzing, Omar is hiding.

Diagram each word of sentences 29–30.

29. Mr. Hake can juggle three balls.
(37, 40)

30. Can you juggle three balls?
(37, 40)

29.

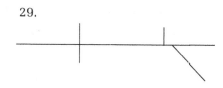

30.

LESSON 41

Capitalization: Areas, Religions, and Greetings

Dictation or Journal Entry

Vocabulary:

A *foreleg* is one of the front legs of a four-legged animal. Rex placed a *foreleg* on my knee, begging for attention.

A *fetlock* is a tuft of hair on the back part of the leg of a horse or similar animal, just above the hoof. Shetland ponies may have long *fetlocks*.

Proper capitalization becomes easier with practice. We remember to capitalize titles, family words when used as names, and the names of school subjects that come from proper nouns. Now, we shall learn more capitalization rules.

Areas of the Country We capitalize *North, South, East, West, Midwest, Northeast,* etc., when they refer to **certain areas of the country.**

The Northeast has amazing fall colors.

Many interesting reptiles live in the Southwest.

Joe draws horses and Western scenes.

Which animals come from the Far East?

However, we do not capitalize these words when they indicate a direction. See the examples below.

Sal walks west to school and north to the library.

Colorado is east of California.

That stream flows from north to south.

Religious References We capitalize **religions and their members, works regarded as sacred,** and **references to a supreme being.**

Onping was Buddhist.

Do Christians love their enemies?

Yes, Jews worship God.

Those passages are from the Koran, not the Bible.

Greeting and Closing of a Letter

We capitalize the first words in the **greeting and closing of a letter.** For example:

Dear Jim,

My thoughtful aunt,

To whom it may concern:

Yours truly,

Warmly,

Gratefully,

Example Provide capital letters as needed.

(a) Settlers moved to the west.

(b) Your home is north of mine.

(c) My friend is catholic.

(d) The man wrote, "my dear cousin," and ended his letter with, "love, tim."

Solution (a) We capitalize *West*, because it refers to a specific section of the United States.

(b) No correction is needed.

(c) We capitalize *Catholic*, for it is the name of a religion.

(d) We capitalize *My* because it is the first word of a letter's greeting. However, because "cousin" is not the name of a specific person, and because it is preceded by the word "my," we do not capitalize it. *Love* needs a capital because it is the first word of the closing. We capitalize *Tim* because it is a proper noun, or a specific person.

Practice Rewrite a–d with correct capitalization.

a. she read aloud from the king james bible.

b. when i traveled in the south, i tasted catfish and grits.

c. look at the northwest corner of the map.

d. dear mom,
    i miss you at camp.
        your son,
        jake

For e and f, replace each blank with *foreleg* or *fetlock*.

 e. A _____ is a front leg.

 f. A _____ is a tuft of hair on the back of an animal's leg.

Review Set 41 Choose the correct word to complete sentences 1–6.

 1. The (pupa, colt, sow) raced after his mother in the
 (40) meadow.

 2. Shy people tend to (flea, flee, molt) large crowds.
 (39)

 3. A (marsupial, nocturnal, sow) animal is active at night.
 (18)

 4. A fly (larva, flea, preen) is called a maggot.
 (37)

 5. Sprinklers sprayed a light (missed, fir, mist) on the ferns.
 (20)

 6. The word *walrus's* is a (possessive, plural) noun.
 (13)

 7. Add suffixes to the following words:
 (33) (a) lazy + ly   (b) tasty + er

 8. Add suffixes to the following words:
 (34) (a) spin + ing   (b) harm + less

 9. For a and b, write the word that is spelled correctly.
 (35) (a) deceit, deciet   (b) niece, neice

 10. Write each descriptive adjective from the following
 (39) sentence:

 Delicate lacewings have shiny eyes.

 11. Rewrite the following sentence, using correct capitalization.
 (41)

 john attends a baptist church in the south.

 12. Write whether the following word group is a phrase or a
 (36) clause: with silk from silk moth caterpillars

 13. In the following sentence, write the entire verb phrase,
 (12) circling each helping verb:

 Has the caterpillar been spinning a cocoon?

14. Using correct capitalization, rewrite the following song
(25) title:

"shoo, fly, don't bother me!"

15. Write the linking verb in the following sentence:
(31)
That insect looks scary.

16. Write whether the following word group is a complete
(5, 23) sentence, a sentence fragment, or a run-on sentence:

To hide among twigs and thorns.

17. Write each preposition that you find in the following
(20, 21) sentence:

At sunrise, I found a praying mantis on the petal of a rose.

18. Use a dictionary: (a) The word *nymph* is what part of
(27,30) speech? (b) Write its pronunciation. (c) Write its
etymology.

19. Rewrite the following words, circling silent letter(s):
(28, 29)
(a) fight   (b) autumn   (c) honesty

20. Rewrite and correct the run-on sentence below. There is
(24) more than one correct answer.

Gardeners welcome ladybugs they eat aphids and other
pests.

21. Write whether the following sentence is declarative,
(2) interrogative, imperative, or exclamatory:

Aphids can ruin roses, potatoes, and other crops.

22. Write the two limiting adjectives from the following
(40) sentence:

Many aphids were drinking sap from my roses.

23. For the following sentence, write the correct form of the
(18) verb:

The ladybug (present of *fly*) away.

24. For the verb *dry*, write the (a) present participle, (b) past
(19) tense, and (c) past participle.

25. Replace each blank with a descriptive adjective to add
(39) more detail to the word "fur" in the sentence below. There are many possible answers.

A dog with _____, _____ fur wags its tail.

26. Rewrite the following sentence, adding capital letters as
(26) needed:

jan asked, "how did that bee get into mr. luz's car?"

27. For a–c, write the plural of each noun.
(17, 22)
(a) handful   (b) antenna   (c) white fly

28. Diagram the simple subject and simple predicate of each
(36) clause in the following sentence:

Mary was swatting flies while her friends were napping.

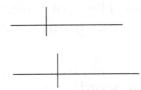

Diagram each word of sentences 29–30.

29. Kurt is writing a scary story.
(37, 40)

30. May I read that story?
(37, 40)

29.

30.

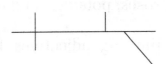

LESSON 42

Proper Adjectives

Common Adjectives An adjective can be common or proper. Common adjectives are formed from common nouns and are not capitalized.

COMMON NOUN	COMMON ADJECTIVE
beauty	beautiful
ice	iced
wind	windy
peace	peaceful

Proper Adjectives Proper adjectives are formed from proper nouns and are always capitalized. Sometimes the word does not change at all, as in the examples below.

PROPER NOUN	PROPER ADJECTIVE
Canada	Canada (geese)
Labrador	Labrador (retriever)
Idaho	Idaho (potato)
Washington	Washington (apple)

Often the form of the proper adjective does change, as in the examples below.

PROPER NOUN	PROPER ADJECTIVE
Spain	Spanish (dance)
China	Chinese (food)
America	American (flag)
Denmark	Danish (cookies)

Example 1 For sentences a–c, write each proper adjective followed by the noun it describes.

(a) How do you make Irish stew?

(b) Sid plays the French horn.

(c) Mexican food smells delicious.

Solution (a) **Irish stew** (b) **French horn** (c) **Mexican food**

Example 2 Diagram this sentence:

Nan has a Russian wolfhound.

Solution We place the proper adjective "Russian" underneath the word it describes—"wolfhound."

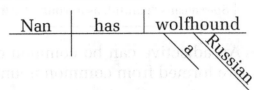

Practice For sentences a–c, write each proper adjective followed by the noun it describes.

a. Siamese cats have short hair.

b. Gardeners, beware of the Japanese beetle!

c. The Scottish terrier barked at Rex.

d. Diagram this sentence: Tim cooks Italian sausage.

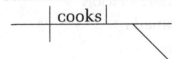

For e and f, replace each blank with *soar* or *sore*.

e. My foot is _____ where a bee stung it.

f. Gulls _____ above the cliffs.

Review Set 42 Choose the correct word to complete sentences 1–6.

1. Groomers comb the (pupa, larva, fetlocks) of a Shetland
(41)   pony before a parade.

2. Too young to be called a mare, the female horse was a
(40)   (filly, colt, buck).

3. The mouth is on the (anterior, posterior, nocturnal) part
(23)   of a fish.

4. A plant or animal lives in a (habit, habitat, foul).
(16)

5. Birds preen (there, their) feathers.
(8)

6. The word *lizard* is a(n) (abstract, concrete) noun.
(11)

7. Add suffixes to the following words:
(33)

(a) say + ed   (b) hope + ing

8. Add suffixes to the following words:
(34)

(a) win + ing   (b) snow + ed

9. For a and b, write the word that is spelled correctly.
(35)

(a) weight, wieght   (b) relieve, releive

10. Write each proper adjective from the following sentence:
(42)

For breakfast, we had French toast and Georgia peaches.

11. Rewrite the following letter, using correct capitalization.
(41)

dear tim,

      please save me some italian sausage.

                    your brother,

                    jim

12. Write whether the following word group is a phrase or a
(36) clause: if Tim ate all the Italian sausage

13. In the following sentence, write the entire verb phrase,
(12) circling each helping verb:

You might have heard a nightingale.

14. Rewrite the following sentence, using correct capitalization:
(38)

yesterday, dad wore a hawaiian shirt.

15. Write the linking verb in the following sentence:
(31)

The story sounded impossible.

16. Write whether the following word group is a complete
(5, 23) sentence, a sentence fragment, or a run-on sentence:

The skunk raised its tail the enemy ran away.

17. Write each preposition that you find in the following
(20, 21) sentence:

At dawn, we jogged through the streets.

18. Use a dictionary: (a) The word *borzoi* is what part of
(27, 30) speech? (b) Write its pronunciation. (c) Write its
etymology.

19. Rewrite the following words, circling silent letter(s):
(28, 29) (a) limb   (b) knot   (c) write

20. Rewrite and correct the following sentence fragment,
(6) making a complete sentence:

To jump like a kangaroo.

21. Write the word from this list that is *not* a linking verb:
(31) is, am, are, was, were, be, being, been, cook, feel.

22. Write the four limiting adjectives from the following
(40) sentence:

Pete chased his rabbit many times around Mom's car that
day.

23. For the following sentence, write the correct form of the
(14) verb:

I (future of *feed*) the rabbits next.

24. For the verb *step*, write the (a) present participle, (b) past
(19) tense, and (c) past participle.

25. Replace each blank with a descriptive adjective to add
(39) more detail to the word "runner" in the sentence below.
There are many possible answers.

We cheered for the _____, _____ runner.

26. Rewrite the following rhyme, adding capital letters as
(15) needed:

day is done;
gone the sun...

27. For a and b, write the plural of each noun.
(17, 22) (a) son-in-law   (b) branch

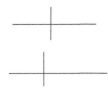

28. Diagram the simple subject and simple predicate of each
(36) clause in the following sentence:

Rex wagged his tail until he heard the sirens.

Diagram each word of sentences 29–30.

29. My thoughtful sister shares her new games.
(37, 40)

30. Do you have a new game?
(37, 40)

29.

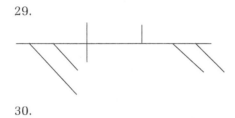

30.

No Capital Letter

Dictation or Journal Entry

Vocabulary:

A *road* is a strip of pavement or cleared, packed ground used for travel. Which *road* shall we take?

Rode is the past tense of *ride*. Nan *rode* a wild pony in yesterday's parade.

Most grammar books teach us when to capitalize words. This lesson reminds us when **not** to capitalize words.

Common Nouns

Common nouns such as animals, plants, foods, objects, medical conditions, and pastimes are not capitalized. If a proper adjective (descriptive word) appears with the noun, we capitalize only the proper adjective, not the common noun. Below are some examples:

COMMON NOUN	COMMON NOUN WITH PROPER ADJECTIVE
cow	Jersey cow
oak tree	California pepper tree
violin	Steinway piano
flu	German measles
insect	Colorado beetle
tic-tac-toe	Chinese checkers

Example 1 Add capital letters where needed.

(a) Do people eat mexican jumping beans?

(b) Mom drinks english tea, not coffee.

(c) After school, we shall play a game of checkers.

(d) Do you know how a french horn sounds?

(e) Please stay home if you have a cough or fever.

Solution (a) We capitalize *Mexican*, a proper adjective. However, *jumping beans* is not capitalized because plants and foods are common nouns.

(b) We capitalize *English*, a proper adjective. However, *tea* and *coffee* are not capitalized because foods and beverages are common nouns.

(c) We do not add capital letters. Games and pastimes such as *checkers* are common nouns.

(d) We capitalize *French*, a proper adjective. However, we do not capitalize *horn* because objects such as musical instruments are common nouns.

(e) We do not add capital letters. Most medical conditions are common nouns.

Seasons of the Year We do not capitalize **seasons of the year**: fall, winter, spring, and summer.

In winter, we wear warmer clothes than in summer.

Hyphenated Words We treat a **hyphenated word** as if it were a single word. If it is a proper noun or the first word of a sentence, we capitalize only the first word, not all the parts of the hyphenated word. See the examples below.

Twenty-one years is a long life for a cat.

Next, Attorney-at-law Dora Cruz will speak.

Example 2 Add capital letters where needed in this sentence:

Last fall, brother-in-law Joe gave me some polish sausage.

Solution We capitalize **Brother-in-law** because it is a family word used as part of a name. We capitalize **Polish** because it is a proper adjective. We do not capitalize *fall* because it is a season of the year. We do not capitalize *sausage* because it is a food, a common noun.

Practice For a and b, replace each blank with the correct vocabulary word from this lesson.

a. This _____ has very little traffic.

b. Holly _____ her bicycle to school last Monday.

For c–g, write and capitalize each word that needs a capital letter.

c. Ken has basketball practice today.

d. Grandpa plays the saxophone.

e. I toasted some russian rye bread.

f. we plant our vegetable garden in spring.

g. twenty-two children will play a game of hide-and-seek.

See "More Practice Lesson 43" in the Student Workbook.

Review Set
43

Choose the correct word to complete sentences 1–6.

1. Colorful kites (sore, soar, molt) overhead.
(42)

2. Four-legged animals have two (forelegs, pupa, fetlocks)
(41) and two back legs.

3. Too young to be called a stallion, a young male horse is
(40) called a (filly, marsupial, colt).

4. Mice will (flea, sore, flee) at the sight of a cat.
(39)

5. The tail is on the (posterior, anterior, deficient) of a fish.
(23)

6. The word *family* is a (compound, collective) noun.
(11)

7. Add suffixes to the following words:
(33)   (a) angry + ly   (b) hope + ful

8. Add suffixes to the following words:
(34)   (a) sip + ing   (b) cold + est

9. For a and b, write the word that is spelled correctly.
(35)   (a) beleif, belief   (b) weigh, wiegh

10. Write the two proper adjectives from the following
(42) sentence:

A Boston terrier lies beneath the Japanese maple tree.

11. Rewrite the following sentence, using correct
(41, 43) capitalization.

my jewish friend hannah won the eastern archery
tournament.

12. Write whether the following word group is a phrase or a
(36) clause: after a long, hard game of tennis

13. In the following sentence, write the entire verb phrase,
(12) circling each helping verb:

May I help you?

14. Rewrite the following story title, using correct
(25) capitalization: "the elves and the shoemaker"

15. Write the linking verb in the following sentence:
(31)
Aphids remained garden pests through spring.

16. Write whether the following word group is a complete
(5, 23) sentence, a sentence fragment, or a run-on sentence:

Aphids can ruin potatoes and other food crops.

17. Write each preposition that you find in the following
(20, 21) sentence:

Alongside his mother, the colt trotted through the
meadow.

18. Use a dictionary: (a) The word *aphid* is what part of
(27,30) speech? (b) Write its pronunciation. (c) Write its
etymology.

19. Rewrite the following words, circling silent letter(s):
(28, 29)
  (a) knee   (b) should   (c) ditch

20. Rewrite and correct the run-on sentence below. There is
(24) more than one correct answer.

Aphids drink rose sap this can kill roses.

21. Write whether the following sentence is declarative,
(2) interrogative, imperative, or exclamatory:

Ladybugs eat huge numbers of aphids.

22. Write the three limiting adjectives from the following
(40) sentence:

I saw some aphids and three ladybugs in Dad's garden.

23. For the following sentence, write the correct form of the
(9) verb:

Amelia (present of *rush*) out to play.

24. For the verb *jog*, write the (a) present participle, (b) past
(19) tense, and (c) past participle.

25. Replace each blank with a descriptive adjective to add
(39) more detail to the word "bicycle" in the sentence below.
There are many possible answers.

Miss Ng rode a(n) _____, _____ bicycle.

26. Rewrite the following sentence, adding capital letters as
(26) needed:

miss ng said, "the bicycle race was in france."

27. For a and b, write the plural of each noun.
(17, 22)
   (a) sheep   (b) leaf

28. Diagram the simple subject and simple predicate of each
(36) clause in the following sentence:

Miss Ng raced, and I cheered for her, but she finished last.

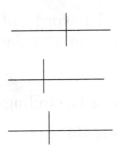

Diagram each word of sentences 29–30.

29. Those pesty aphids ruined some pretty roses.
(37, 40)

30. Did the ladybugs eat many aphids?
(37, 40)

29.

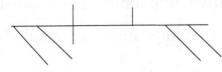

30.

Object of the Preposition •
The Prepositional Phrase

Object of the Preposition

We have learned to recognize common prepositions, connecting words that link a noun or pronoun to the rest of the sentence. In this lesson, we will identify the **object of the preposition,** which is the noun or pronoun that follows the preposition. Every preposition must have an object. Otherwise, it is not a preposition. We italicize prepositions and star their objects in the phrases below.

at *home

on her *bicycle

around the *world

within a *week

across the *street

except *him

in the *jungle

down the *drain

through a *tunnel

like a *rabbit

for your *safety

behind *her

with *joy

considering the *rain

Prepositions may have compound objects:

Rex runs *through* *puddles and *mud.

Miss Ng dreams *about* *rats and *mice.

Example 1 Circle the object (or objects) of each preposition in these sentences.

(a) *In* the morning, we walked *to* town *for* eggs and bread.

(b) I swam *under* the water and *toward* the shore.

Solution (a) *In* the (**morning**) we walked *to* (**town**) *for* (**eggs**) and (**bread**).

(b) I swam *under* the (**water**) and *toward* the (**shore**).

Prepositional Phrase   A prepositional phrase begins with a preposition and contains a noun and its modifiers. We italicize prepositional phrases below.

> Ken rode the pony *into the barn.*
>
> The filly escaped *from her stall.*
>
> *Down that road* lives Miss Ling.
>
> Rex has jam *on his snout.*

There can be more than one prepositional phrase in a sentence:

> He ate part *of my sandwich* (1) *for lunch* (2).
>
> There went a stallion *with a rider* (1) *on its back* (2).
>
> *Before dark* (1), we hiked *along the trail* (2) *by the stream* (3).

Example 2   For each sentence, write each prepositional phrase, circling the objects of the prepositions.

(a) Stories about Rex spread through town.

(b) I shall walk to the park with Rex on a leash.

(c) At the park, I shall rest on a bench in the shade.

Solution   (a) about ⓇRex   through ⓉⒽⒺtown

(b) to the ⓅⒶ park   with ⓇRex   on a ⓛⒺⒶⓈⒽ leash

(c) At the ⓅⒶ park   on a ⒷⒺⓃⒸⒽ bench   in the ⓈⒽⒶⒹⒺ shade

Practice   For sentences a–d, write each prepositional phrase, circling the object(s) of the preposition.

a. With pads on its feet, a gecko can cling to any surface.

b. Basilisks live in South America near streams and lakes.

c. They can run across the surface of water.

d. During the day, we searched for lizards.

For e and f, replace each blank with *dear* or *deer.*

e. My _____ uncle was wise and strong.

f. The _____ led its fawn into the forest.

More Practice Write each prepositional phrase, circling the object of each preposition in these sentences.

1. At noon, Rex wakes from his nap and sneaks into the kitchen.

2. He lifts his nose to the counter and sniffs around a box.

3. Inside the box is a pie for dessert.

4. In an instant, the pie is on the floor with Rex.

5. Most of the pie disappears into Rex's mouth.

6. Without doubt, Rex is in trouble.

Review Set 44 Choose the correct word to complete sentences 1–6.

1. The old car rattled on the bumpy (rode, road, sore).
(43)

2. Our legs were (soar, sore, hoarse) after the long run.
(42)

3. I combed stickers from my dog's (tale, fetlocks, fir).
(41)

4. A (filly, colt, mail) grazed near her mother.
(40)

5. One is mainly (vertical, horizontal, invertebrate) when lying in a hammock.
(24)

6. The word *puppies* is a (plural, possessive) noun.
(13)

7. Add suffixes to the following words:
(33)
   (a) beauty + ful   (b) bury + ed

8. Add suffixes to the following words:
(34)
   (a) pop + ed   (b) stir + ed

9. For a and b, write the word that is spelled correctly.
(35)
   (a) reindeer, riendeer   (b) sheild, shield

10. Write the proper adjective from the following sentence:
(42)
    An African cricket hides in a cave.

11. Rewrite the following letter, using correct capitalization.

(41, 43) dear mom,

      have you ever seen an indian cobra? i have.

          love,
          lucy

12. Write whether the following word group is a phrase or a
(36) clause: while Lucy traveled in India

13. In the following sentence, write the entire verb phrase,
(12) circling each helping verb:

Tomorrow, Rex will be napping outside.

14. Rewrite the following sentence, using correct
(38) capitalization: yes, i believe mr. sums was dad's math
teacher.

15. Write the linking verb in the following sentence:
(31)
Now Rex seems sorry.

16. Write whether the following word group is a complete
(5, 23) sentence, a sentence fragment, or a run-on sentence:

I like parrots they are colorful and smart.

17. From the following sentence, write each prepositional
(44) phrase, circling the object of each preposition:

With grace, the gull glides over the waves and lands on the
beach.

18. Use a dictionary: (a) The word *rumen* is what part of
(27, 30) speech? (b) Write its pronunciation. (c) Write its
etymology.

19. Rewrite the following words, circling silent letter(s):
(28, 29)
    (a) badger   (b) sign   (c) guest

20. Rewrite and correct the following sentence fragment,
(6) making a complete sentence:

My only pet, a hairy hamster.

21. From the following list, write the word that is *not* a linking
(31) verb: look, feel, taste, smell, sound, under.

22. Write the three limiting adjectives from the following
(40) sentence:

During the game, Miss Ng blew her whistle several times.

23. For the following sentence, write the correct form of the
(10, 19) verb:

Miss Ng (past of *try*) to be fair.

24. For the verb *stop*, write the (a) present participle, (b) past
(19) tense, and (c) past participle.

25. Replace each blank with a descriptive adjective to add
(39) more detail to the word "hamster" in the sentence below.
There are many possible answers.

Lucy has a(n) _____, _____ hamster.

26. Rewrite the following outline, adding capital letters as
(26) needed:

   i. meerkats
     a. where they live
     b. what they eat

27. For a and b, write the plural of each noun.
(17, 22)
   (a) ox   (b) penny

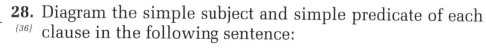

28. Diagram the simple subject and simple predicate of each
(36) clause in the following sentence:

The fun began when I opened the gate and the goats ran out.

Diagram each word of sentences 29–30.

29. Did the deer eat Mom's roses?
(37, 40)

30. My dear rabbit ate her roses.
(37, 40)

The Prepositional Phrase as an Adjective • Diagramming

Dictation or Journal Entry

Vocabulary:

Dew is air moisture that condenses in small drops upon cool surfaces during the night. In the morning, the grass was wet with *dew*.

To *do* is to perform or carry out, as an action. We must *do* our work.

Adjective Phrases We remember that a phrase is a group of words that functions as a single unit. Prepositional phrases function as a single unit, and some modify a noun or pronoun. We call these **adjective phrases.** They answer an adjective question—"Which one?" "What kind?" or "How many?"

Adjective phrases are italicized in the following sentences:

My friend *from France* speaks French. (The adjective phrase *from France* modifies the noun "friend" and tells "which one.")

Kate reads books *about birds*. (The adjective phrase *about birds* modifies the noun "books" and tells "what kind.")

The car has seatbelts *for five*. (The adjective phrase *for five* modifies the noun "seatbelts" and tells "how many.")

Example 1 Write the adjective phrase and tell which noun or pronoun it modifies.

(a) The clock in our classroom is slow.

(b) Is that a story for children?

(c) We have tickets for ten.

Solution (a) The phrase **in our classroom** modifies **clock.** It tells "which one."

(b) The phrase **for children** modifies **story.** It tells "what kind."

(c) The phrase **for ten** modifies **tickets.** It tells "how many."

Diagramming Prepositional Phrases

To diagram a prepositional phrase, we place the preposition on a slanted line attached to the word that the phrase modifies. We place the object of the preposition on a horizontal line at the bottom of the slanted preposition line:

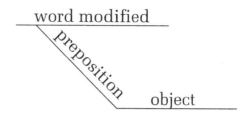

Let us diagram this sentence:

I like lemonade with ice.

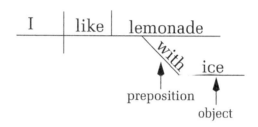

Example 2 Diagram this sentence:

The top of Mount Baldy has snow.

Solution The phrase **of Mount Baldy** modifies the subject of the sentence, **top.** We place the preposition **of** on a slanted line connected to **top.** Then, we place the object, **Mount Baldy,** on the horizontal line.

The top of Mount Baldy has snow.

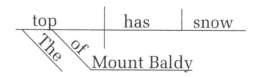

Sometimes, a prepositional phrase immediately follows another one, as in the sentence below.

Some *of the snow on the road* is melting.

In the sentence above, the first prepositional phrase, **of the snow,** modifies the subject **some.** The second prepositional phrase, **on the road,** modifies the noun **snow.**

We show this by diagramming the sentence:

Some of the snow on the road is melting.

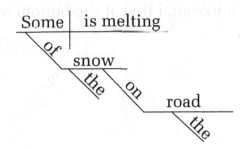

Example 3   Diagram this sentence:

I saw a bird with blue stripes on its wings.

Solution   We place each preposition on a slanted line underneath the word it modifies. Then, we place each object on a horizontal line attached to its preposition.

I saw a bird with blue stripes on its wings.

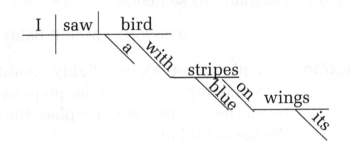

Practice   For a–c, write which noun is described by each italicized prepositional phrase.

    a. Tim drew a map *of the area.*

    b. The birds *from that nest* have flown away.

    c. Good students show respect *for their teachers.*

In sentences d and e, write the prepositional phrase. Then, write the noun it describes.

    d. Ann has a gift for Rex.

    e. Some streets in town are bumpy.

For f and g, replace each blank with *do* or *dew*.

f. I shall _____ my homework now.

g. _____ made the grass wet.

Diagram sentences h and i.

h. Kate likes stories about owls.

i. Find a recipe for soup with noodles.

Review Set 45

Choose the correct word to complete sentences 1–6.

1. (Canines, Deer, Dear) shed their antlers each year.
(44)

2. Two children (soared, road, rode) a camel at the zoo.
(43)

3. Blimps (sore, soar, paws) over football stadiums to advertise important games.
(42)

4. Limping badly, the giraffe refused to put weight on its injured (fetlock, foreleg, tale).
(41)

5. A (morning, offensive, mourning) canine looked for its lost playmate.
(25)

6. The word *joy* is a(n) (abstract, concrete) noun.
(11)

7. Add suffixes to the following words:
(33)
   (a) sleepy + ly   (b) fry + ed

8. Add suffixes to the following words:
(34)
   (a) bat + ing   (b) refer + ed

9. For a and b, write the word that is spelled correctly.
(35)
   (a) wieght, weight   (b) beleif, belief

10. Write the proper adjective from the following sentence:
(42)
   Have you heard Scottish bagpipes?

11. Rewrite the following sentence, using correct capitalization: that quaker pastor grew up in the northeast.
(41, 43)

12. Write whether the following word group is a phrase or a (36) clause:

with webbed feet and a long, flat tail

13. In the following sentence, write the entire verb phrase, (12) circling each helping verb:

We should have hidden that pie.

14. Rewrite this story title, using correct capitalization: (25)

"the wind and the sun"

15. Write the linking verb in the following sentence: (31)

Rotten potatoes smell bad.

16. Write whether the following word group is a complete (5, 23) sentence, a sentence fragment, or a run-on sentence:

Muskrats have waterproof fur.

17. From the following sentence, write each prepositional (44) phrase, circling the object of each preposition:

A platypus feeds along the bottom of the river.

18. Use a dictionary: (a) The word *hubris* is what part of (27,30) speech? (b) Write its pronunciation. (c) Write its etymology.

19. Rewrite the following words, circling silent letter(s): (28, 29)

(a) lodge   (b) rhythm   (c) wrist

20. Rewrite and correct the run-on sentence below. There is (24) more than one correct answer.

Beavers build their lodge in the river predators cannot reach them there.

21. Write whether the following sentence is declarative, (2) interrogative, imperative, or exclamatory:

Watch the beavers.

22. Write the three limiting adjectives from the following
(40) sentence:

In Miss Ng's chair lay two hamsters with their eyes
closed.

23. For the following sentence, write the correct form of the
(9) verb:

A cat (present of *hiss*).

24. For the verb *reply*, write the (a) present participle, (b) past
(19) tense, and (c) past participle.

25. Replace each blank with a descriptive adjective to add
(39) more detail to the word "stories" in the sentence below.
There are many possible answers.

Miss Kim reads _____, _____ stories.

26. Rewrite the following sentence, adding capital letters as
(26) needed: dane said, "look at the arctic fox."

27. For a and b, write the plural of each noun.
(17, 22)
    (a) Tuesday   (b) Arctic fox

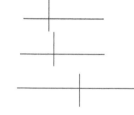

28. Diagram the simple subject and simple predicate of each
(36) clause in the following sentence:

As I watch, a cat hisses and hamsters scamper.

Diagram each word of sentences 29–30.

29. My dear friend has a collection of unusual insects.
(40, 45)

30. She continues her search for large grasshoppers.
(40, 45)

29.

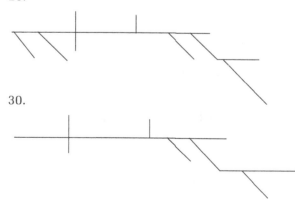

30.

LESSON 46

Indirect Objects

Dictation or Journal Entry
Vocabulary:
A *zephyr* is a west wind or a gentle wind. Treetops waved gently in the *zephyr*.

A *gale* is a very strong wind. The *gale* uprooted several trees!

Indirect Objects An action verb may have two kinds of objects: (1) A direct object receives the action directly. (2) An **indirect object** receives the action indirectly. It tells *to whom* or *for whom* the action was done.

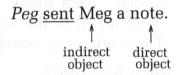

Peg <u>sent</u> Meg a note.

        ↑   ↑

    indirect direct
    object   object

In the sentences below, we have starred the direct objects and placed parentheses around the indirect objects.

Dan <u>gave</u> (them) a *gift.

<u>Did</u> *you* <u>leave</u> (her) a *message?

Please <u>toss</u> (me) the *key.

In order to have an indirect object, a sentence must have a direct object. The indirect object usually follows the verb and precedes the direct object. One test of an indirect object is that it can be expressed alternately by a prepositional phrase introduced by *to* or *for:*

Peg sent a note *to Meg.*

Dan gave a gift *to them.*

Did you leave a message *for her?*

Please toss the key *to me.*

Indirect objects can be compound:

I <u>gave</u> (Dan) and (Roy) the *address.

Example 1 Identify the indirect objects, if any, in each sentence.

(a) *Ann* <u>bought</u> Rex a new leash.

(b) *Miss Ng* <u>will give</u> her students a test.

(c) *James* <u>kicked</u> the football.

(d) We <u>found</u> the kitten a home.

Solution   (a) Ann bought a new leash *for* Rex. Therefore, **Rex** is the indirect object.

(b) Miss Ng will give a test *to* her students. Therefore, **students** is the indirect object.

(c) This sentence has **no indirect object.**

(d) We found a home *for* the kitten. Therefore, **kitten** is the indirect object.

Below is a diagram showing the simple subject, simple predicate, direct object, and indirect object of this sentence:

They <u>brought</u> (Miss Ng) *roses.

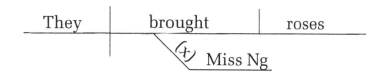

Notice that the indirect object (Miss Ng) is attached beneath the verb by a slanted line, as though it were a prepositional phrase with the preposition (x) understood, not stated.

Example 2   Diagram the simple subject, simple predicate, direct object, and indirect object of each sentence from Example 1.

Solution   (a) *Ann* <u>bought</u> Rex a new leash.

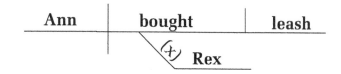

(b) *Miss Ng* <u>will give</u> her students a test.

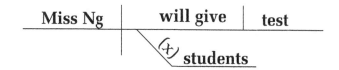

(c) *James* <u>kicked</u> the football.

James	kicked	football

(d) We <u>found</u> the kitten a home.

We	found	home

(x) kitten

Practice For a and b, replace each blank with *zephyr* or *gale*.

    a. A _____ is a strong wind.

    b. A _____ is a gentle wind.

Write the indirect object, if any, in sentences c–f.

    c. The *police* <u>could give</u> her a ticket.

    d. *Rex* <u>brings</u> Ann a bone.

    e. *Birds* <u>give</u> their babies worms.

    f. Ann <u>ran</u> around the lake.

    g. Diagram the simple subject, simple predicate, direct object, and indirect object of the sentence below.

    Miss Moore reads us stories.

Review Set 46 Choose the correct word to complete sentences 1–6.

    1. The grass sparkled with droplets of (do, dew, pupa).
    (45)

    2. Elle wrote, "(Deer, Dear, Mane) Grandma."
    (44)

    3. Workers repaired potholes in the (road, rode, habit).
    (43)

    4. His hand was (soar, sore, tale) from writing so much.
    (42)

    5. The sun rose to welcome a beautiful (mourning, morning,
    (25) prey).

6. The word *sunglasses* is a (compound, collective) noun.
(11)

7. Add suffixes to the following words:
(33, 34) (a) drip + ing   (b) tiny + est

8. Write the indirect object in the following sentence:
(46)
Mr. Cruz gives Meg trumpet lessons.

9. For a and b, write the word that is spelled correctly.
(35) (a) weigh, wiegh   (b) grief, greif

10. Write the proper adjective from the following sentence:
(42)
The African cricket has very long antennae.

11. Rewrite the following letter, using correct capitalization:
(15, 41)
dear miss ng,

     please do not give us a test this friday. i am not ready.
                           respectfully,
                            ann

12. Write whether the following word group is a phrase or a
(36) clause: if Rex jumps the fence

13. In the following sentence, write the entire verb phrase,
(12) circling each helping verb:

Could mice have eaten your grapes?

14. Rewrite the following sentence, using correct
(38) capitalization: did grandpa learn english in dr. smith's class?

15. Write the linking verb in the following sentence:
(31)
The sky remains cloudy.

16. Write whether the following word group is a complete
(5, 23) sentence, a sentence fragment, or a run-on sentence:

Head lice grip hairs with their claws.

17. From the following sentence, write the two prepositional
(44) phrases, circling the object of each preposition:

Two doves feed on the ground under the tree.

18. Use a dictionary: (a) The word *zinc* is what part of
(27,30) speech? (b) Write its pronunciation. (c) Write its
etymology.

19. Rewrite the following words, circling silent letter(s):
(28,29)
    (a) knob   (b) scent   (c) adjust

20. Rewrite and correct the following sentence fragment,
(6) making a complete sentence:

Hearing the coo of a dove.

21. From the following list, write the word that is *not* a linking
(31) verb: seem, appear, grow, between, remain, stay.

22. Write the three limiting adjectives from the following
(40) sentence:

One day, Miss Lee found three lizards under her desk.

23. For the following sentence, write the correct form of the
(14) verb:

Rex (future of *find*) his way home.

24. For the verb *magnify*, write the (a) present participle, (b)
(19) past tense, and (c) past participle.

25. Replace each blank with a descriptive adjective to add
(39) more detail to the word "shoes" in the sentence below.
There are many possible answers.

Ms. Ng wears _____, _____ shoes.

26. Rewrite the following lines of poetry, adding capital
(15) letters as needed:

cypress tall and mighty
sparrows small and flighty

27. For a–c, write the plural of each noun.
(17,22)
    (a) Friday   (b) mother-in-law   (c) beach

28. Diagram the simple subject and simple predicate of each
(36) clause in the following sentence:

Joe mops the floor, and Nam washes windows while Rex
sleeps.

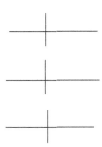

Diagram each word of sentences 29–30.

29. Grandpa combs the few hairs on the top of his head.
(40, 45)

30. Grandpa hands me the comb.
(37, 46)

29.

30.

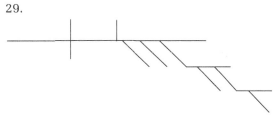

LESSON 47

The Period, Part 1

Punctuation marks help the reader to understand the meaning of what is written. **Periods** help the reader to know where a sentence begins and ends, but there are other uses for the period as well.

Declarative Sentence A **declarative sentence** (statement) needs a period at the end.

Houseflies have sticky feet.

Flies can walk upside down.

Imperative Sentence An **imperative sentence** (command) needs a period at the end.

Swat that fly.

Keep flies off your food.

Initials We place a period after each **initial** in a person's name.

Hartley F. Dailey

G. E. Wallace

M. Scott Peck

Outline In an **outline**, letters and numbers require a period after them.

I. Desert insects
A. Beetles
B. Locusts

Example Add periods where they are needed in each expression.

(a) I Soil insects
     A Cicadas
     B Mole crickets

(b) Listen to the crickets

(c) Some crickets live in caves

(d) We remember President George W Bush

Solution (a) We place a period after each number and letter in an **outline.**

    I. Soil insects
      A. Cicadas
      B. Mole crickets

(b) We place a period at the end of an **imperative sentence.**
Listen to the crickets.

(c) We place a period at the end of a **declarative sentence.**
Some crickets live in caves.

(d) We place a period after each **initial** in a person's name.
This is also a **declarative sentence.**
We remember President George W. Bush.

Practice Add periods as needed in a–d.

    a. I   Household insects
        A Bedbugs
        B Carpet beetles

    b. Susan B Anthony led women to victory

    c. Read carefully

    d. Maggots eat garbage

For e and f, replace each blank with *die* or *dye.*

    e. The _____ in my old blue jeans has faded.

    f. Fish out of water will _____.

More Practice See "More Practice Lesson 47" in the Student Workbook.

Review Set 47 Choose the correct word to complete sentences 1–6.

    1. A summer (gale, zephyr, dew) gently rustled the leaves.
    (46)

    2. We students should (do, dew, flea) our homework.
    (45)

    3. Mule (fetlocks, dear, deer) have big ears.
    (44)

    4. Coming into view was a wide (rode, road, sore).
    (43)

5. The (horizontal, vertical, nocturnal) power pole is tall.
(24)

6. The word *fly's* is a (plural, possessive) noun.
(13)

7. Add suffixes to the following words:
(33, 34) (a) fry + ing   (b) big + est

8. Write the indirect object in the following sentence:
(46)
Please send me a list of books about insects.

9. Write the word that is spelled correctly: friend, freind
(35)

10. Write the proper adjective from the following sentence:
(42)
Do hungry mice like Swiss cheese?

11. Rewrite the following sentence, using correct
(41, 43) capitalization:

deserts of the southwest get little rain.

12. Write whether the following word group is a phrase or a
(36) clause: the nest of African termites

13. In the following sentence, write the entire verb phrase,
(12) circling each helping verb:

Houseflies can carry disease.

14. Rewrite the following song title, using correct
(25) capitalization: "let there be peace on earth"

15. Write the linking verb in the following sentence:
(31)
The weather grew stormy.

16. Write whether the following word group is a complete
(5, 23) sentence, a sentence fragment, or a run-on sentence:

Lacewings, delicate insects with golden eyes.

17. From the following sentence, write each prepositional
(44) phrase, circling the object of each preposition:

Everyone in the classroom except Miss Ng saw the tarantula.

18. Use a dictionary: (a) The word *larynx* is what part of
^(27,30) speech? (b) Write its pronunciation. (c) Write its etymology.

19. Rewrite the following words, circling silent letter(s):
^(28, 29)
   (a) stalking   (b) scent

20. Rewrite the following sentence, adding periods as needed:
⁽⁴⁷⁾
   Booker T Washington was a teacher

21. Write whether the following sentence is declarative,
⁽²⁾ interrogative, imperative, or exclamatory:

   Did you find the wasps' nest?

22. Write the four limiting adjectives from the following
⁽⁴⁰⁾ sentence:

   The nurse shakes her head when she sees six fleas on Rex's back.

23. For the following sentence, write the correct form of the
⁽⁹⁾ verb:

   Rex (present of *scratch*).

24. For the verb *deny*, write the (a) present participle, (b) past
⁽¹⁹⁾ tense, and (c) past participle.

25. Replace each blank with a descriptive adjective to add
⁽³⁹⁾ more detail to the word "tale" in the sentence below.
   There are many possible answers.

   Mr. Ling tells a(n) _____, _____ tale.

26. Rewrite the following sentence, adding capital letters as
^(26, 41) needed:

   miss ng says, "that tarantula belongs in central america, not on my desk."

27. For a and b, write the plural of each noun.
^(17, 22)
   (a) ray   (b) wallaby

28. Diagram the simple subject and simple predicate of each
(36) clause in the following sentence:

Miss Ng frowns as the tarantula creeps.

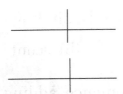

Diagram each word of sentences 29–30.

29. Rex's yelp startled the busy squirrel.
(37, 40)

30. I poured Aaron a glass of lemonade with mint.
(45, 46)

29.

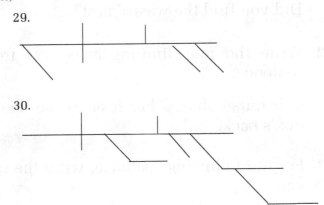

30.

Coordinating Conjunctions

Dictation or Journal Entry

Vocabulary:

A *quill* is a large, stiff feather; the hard, hollow stem of a feather; or one of the sharp spines of a porcupine or hedgehog. George Washington used a *quill* for a pen.

To *quell* is to bring to an end; to quiet. Sometimes gentle words can *quell* an argument.

Conjunctions are connecting words. They connect words, phrases, and clauses. There are three kinds of conjunctions: coordinating, correlative, and subordinating. In this lesson, we will learn to recognize coordinating conjunctions.

Coordinating Conjunctions

We use a **coordinating conjunction** to join parts of a sentence that are equal in form. Parts of sentences, such as words, phrases, and clauses, are called **elements**. A coordinating conjunction connects a word to a word, a phrase to a phrase, or a clause to a clause. When joined by a conjunction, they are called **compound elements**.

Here are the common coordinating conjunctions:

and   but   or   nor   for   yet   so

They may join a **word** to another **word**:

dog *and* cat	sooner *or* later
strong *yet* gentle	slow *but* sure

They may join a **phrase** to another **phrase**:

washing dishes *or* dusting furniture

down the street *and* around the corner

They may connect a **clause** to another **clause**:

Ann smells a skunk, *but* she cannot see it.

The porcupine rattles its quills, *for* it feels threatened.

Example Circle each coordinating conjunction that you find in these sentences.

(a) Miss Ng cleared her desk and emptied her purse and pockets, for her keys were missing.

(b) You may walk or run, but please hurry.

(c) Miss Ng is firm yet kind, so boys and girls like her.

Solution (a) Miss Ng cleared her desk (and) emptied her purse (and) pockets, (for) her keys were missing.

(b) You may walk (or) run, (but) please hurry.

(c) Miss Ng is firm (yet) kind, (so) boys (and) girls like her.

Practice a. Replace each blank to complete the list of coordinating conjunctions:
_____, but, _____, nor, _____, yet, _____

b. Replace each blank to complete the list of coordinating conjunctions:
and, _____, or, _____, for, _____, so

c. Memorize the seven coordinating conjunctions, and say them to a friend or teacher.

Write each coordinating conjunction that you find in sentences d and e.

d. I bathed and brushed Rex, but his fur is still matted and sticky.

e. Sometimes Rex will bark or howl, for sirens disturb him.

For f and g, replace each blank with *quill* or *quell*.

f. Will medicine _____ the pain?

g. I found a large _____ from the tail of a hawk.

Review Set 48 Choose the correct word to complete sentences 1–6.

1. We can (die, dye, dew) eggs by placing them in colored water.
(47)

2. A (zephyr, fetlock, gale) blew down trees and caused the windows to rattle.
(46)

3. Elle's stuffed monkey is a (dear, deer, gale) friend.
(44)

4. Morning (do, dew, flea) covers the grass with moisture.
(45)

5. We hung our clothes on the (vertical, cheep, horizontal)
(24) clothesline, which stretched between two trees.

6. The word *bravery* is a(n) (abstract, concrete) noun.
(11)

7. Add suffixes to the following words:
(33, 34) (a) say + ed   (b) win + er

8. Write the indirect object in the following sentence:
(46)

Rex took Dad the newspaper.

9. Write the word that is spelled correctly: thier, their
(35)

10. Write the two coordinating conjunctions from the
(48) following sentence:

Grandma grows apples and oranges, but she does not grow bananas.

11. Rewrite the following letter, using correct capitalization:
(41) dear jenna,

what venomous snakes live in south america?

sincerely,
mrs. hake

12. Write whether the following word group is a phrase or a
(36) clause: as Jenna said

13. In the following sentence, write the entire verb phrase,
(12) circling each helping verb:

The snake must have been molting.

14. Rewrite the following sentence, using correct capitalization:
(8, 15)
she and i flew into lima, peru, on tuesday.

15. Write the linking verb in the following sentence:
(31)

Mr. Kim sounds happy.

16. Write whether the following word group is a complete
(5, 23) sentence, a sentence fragment, or a run-on sentence:

Juan has seen egrets, pelicans, and cranes in the wetlands.

17. From the following sentence, write each prepositional phrase, circling the object of each preposition:

(44)

He lay in a bed of hay.

18. Use a dictionary: (a) The word *myth* is what part of speech? (b) Write its pronunciation. (c) Write its etymology.

(27,30)

19. Rewrite the following words, circling silent letter(s):

(28, 29)

(a) wrench   (b) scent   (c) chalk

20. Rewrite the following sentence, adding periods as needed:

(47)

Please call Dr Hyde N Seek

21. Write the word from this list that is *not* a linking verb: is, am, are, was, were, be, being, been, look, feel, waste, smell.

(31)

22. Write the proper adjective and the limiting adjective from the following sentence:

(40, 42)

Rob picked ten California oranges.

23. For the following sentence, write the correct form of the verb:

(10, 19)

Art (past of *strum*) his guitar.

24. For the verb *strum*, write the (a) present participle, (b) past tense, and (c) past participle.

(19)

25. Replace each blank with a descriptive adjective to add more detail to the word "mood" in the sentence. There are many possible answers.

(39)

Rex is in a(n) _____, _____ mood.

26. Rewrite the following outline, adding capital letters and periods as needed:

(26, 47)

i   ann's favorite activities
    a   playing games
    b   swimming
    c   reading comic books

27. For a and b, write the plural of each noun.
(17, 22)
 (a) activity (b) mouse

28. Diagram the simple subject and simple predicate of each
(36) clause in the following sentence:

When Rex yelped, I jumped, and the squirrel leaped.

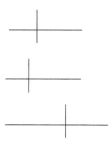

Diagram each word of sentences 29–30.

29. Does the teacher fear large, hairy spiders?
(37, 40)

30. Miss Ng gives the tarantula a sturdy box for its home.
(45, 46)

29.

30.

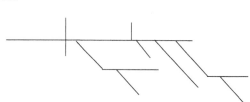

Diagramming Compound Subjects and Predicates

Dictation or Journal Entry

Vocabulary:

A *border* is a boundary line of a country or state or area. I might need a passport to cross the *border*.

A *boarder* is one who pays for a room and meals. The *boarder* thanked the cook and housekeeper.

Compound Subjects   The predicate or verb of a sentence may have more than one subject, as in the sentence below.

Rex and *Spot* <u>sniff</u>.

In this sentence, the verb "sniff" has two subjects: "Rex" and "Spot." We call this a **compound subject**.

Compound Predicates   Likewise, a subject may have more than one predicate, as in the sentence below.

Rex <u>yelps</u> and <u>howls</u>.

In this sentence, the subject "Rex" has two predicates: "yelps" and "howls." We call this a **compound predicate**.

Diagramming   To diagram a compound subject or a compound predicate, we place each part of the compound on a separate, horizontal line. We write the conjunction on a vertical dotted line that joins the horizontal lines.

COMPOUND SUBJECT DIAGRAM:

Beetles and *crickets* <u>burrow</u>.

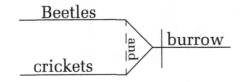

COMPOUND PREDICATE DIAGRAM:

Mosquitoes <u>swarm</u> and <u>bite</u>.

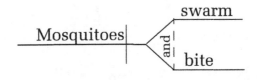

COMPOUND SUBJECT AND COMPOUND PREDICATE DIAGRAM:

Ladybugs and *lacewings* <u>come</u> and <u>go</u>.

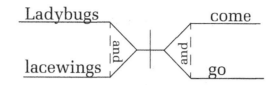

Example Diagram the simple subjects and simple predicates of each sentence.

(a) Robins and finches chirped.

(b) A bat hides and sleeps.

(c) Magpies, robins, and cardinals nest and feed here.

Solution (a) This sentence contains a compound subject.

Robins and *finches* <u>chirped</u>.

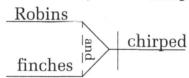

(b) This sentence has a compound predicate. The subject *bat* does two things. It <u>hides</u> and <u>sleeps</u>.

A *bat* <u>hides</u> and <u>sleeps</u>.

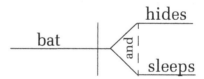

(c) This sentence has a compound subject (*Magpies, robins, cardinals*) and a compound predicate (<u>nest</u>, <u>feed</u>).

Magpies, robins, and *cardinals* <u>nest</u> and <u>feed</u> here.

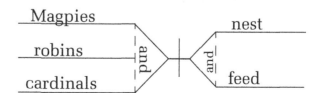

Practice For a and b, replace each blank with *border* or *boarder*.

    a. The _____ paid for her room and food.

    b. Tom lives near the eastern _____ of Tennessee.

Diagram the simple subjects and simple predicates of sentences c–e.

    c. Snakes and lizards shed their skin.

    d. A python creeps and coils.

    e. Crocodiles and alligators crawl and swim.

More Practice See "More Practice Lesson 49" in the Student Workbook.

Review Set 49 Choose the correct word to complete sentences 1–6.

    1. I found the (quell, quill, zephyr) of a porcupine.
    (48)

    2. After stinging someone, a bee (dies, dyes, sows).
    (47)

    3. A gentle (zephyr, gale, quill) moved Allie's curls.
    (46)

    4. Some people (dear, dew, do) their exercises every day.
    (45)

    5. A (male, female, mail) cat is called a tom.
    (26)

    6. The word *flock* is a (collective, compound) noun.
    (11)

    7. Add suffixes to the following words:
    (33, 34) (a) chop + ed   (b) dry + est

    8. Write the indirect object in the following sentence:
    (46) Josh offered Nate a glass of water.

    9. Write the word that is spelled correctly:
    (35) peice, piece

    10. Write the seven common coordinating conjunctions
    (48) listed in Lesson 48.

11. Rewrite the following sentence, using correct
(41, 43) capitalization:

in april, poppies bloom in the southwest.

12. Write whether the following word group is a phrase or a
(36) clause:

along the country's border

13. In the following sentence, write the entire verb phrase,
(12) circling each helping verb:

Rex might have eaten that steak.

14. Rewrite the following title, using correct capitalization:
(25) "the night of the storm"

15. Write the linking verb in the following sentence:
(31)

Mr. Moore feels hopeful.

16. Write whether the following word group is a complete
(5, 23) sentence, a sentence fragment, or a run-on sentence:

Flamingoes live in colonies they nest on mud.

17. From the following sentence, write the three
(44) prepositional phrases, circling the object of each
preposition:

With their claws, ospreys catch fish near the surface of the
water.

18. Use a dictionary: (a) The word *modest* is what part of
(27,30) speech? (b) Write its pronunciation. (c) Write its
etymology.

19. Rewrite the following words, circling silent letter(s):
(28, 29)

(a) gnat   (b) wren

20. Rewrite the following sentence, adding periods as needed:
(47)

Dan D Lyons will return

21. Write whether the following sentence is declarative, interrogative, imperative, or exclamatory:
(2)

Shall we cross the border?

22. Write each proper or limiting adjective from the following sentence:
(40, 42)

Several Canada geese landed near that pond.

23. For the following sentence, write the correct form of the verb:
(9)

Miss Ng (present of *try*) to relax.

24. For the verb *try*, write the (a) present participle, (b) past tense, and (c) past participle.
(19)

25. Replace each blank with a descriptive adjective to add more detail to the word "doghouse" in the sentence below. There are many possible answers.
(39)

Rex has a(n) _____, _____ doghouse.

26. Rewrite the following sentence, adding capital letters as needed:
(26)

the boarder moans, "there are ants in my room."

27. For a and b, write the plural of each noun.
(17, 22)

    (a) Boston terrier   (b) foot

28. Diagram the simple subject and simple predicate of each clause in the following sentence:
(36)

The wind blew, and my homework flew away before I could catch it.

Diagram each word of sentences 29–30.

29. Rob and Tom heard monkeys with shrill cries.
(45, 49)

30. Mr. Lee gave me a new book about animals of the jungle.
(45, 46)

29.

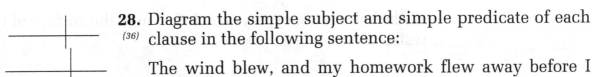

30.

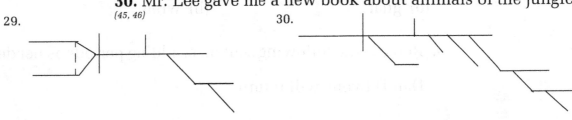

LESSON 50

The Period, Part 2: Abbreviations and Decimals

Dictation or Journal Entry
Vocabulary:
Ebb tide is falling or outgoing tide. I walk the shore at *ebb tide* so that my shoes stay dry.

Flood tide is rising or incoming tide. The *flood tide* brought seaweed and driftwood onto the sandy beach.

Abbreviations

Sometimes, we shorten words by abbreviating them. **Abbreviations** often require periods. Because there are so many abbreviations, and because some abbreviations are used for more than one word, we check our dictionaries. Below are some common abbreviations that require periods. It is important to know these abbreviations, but we do not normally use abbreviations in formal writing. **When in doubt, spell it out.**

Time of Day

a.m. (Latin *ante meridiem*, "before noon")

p.m. (Latin *post meridiem*, "after noon")

Days of the Week

Sun. (Sunday)	Thurs. (Thursday)
Mon. (Monday)	Fri. (Friday)
Tues. (Tuesday)	Sat. (Saturday)
Wed. (Wednesday)	

Months of the Year

Jan. (January)	July (no abbreviation)
Feb. (February)	Aug. (August)
Mar. (March)	Sept. (September)
Apr. (April)	Oct. (October)
May (no abbreviation)	Nov. (November)
June (no abbreviation)	Dec. (December)

Personal Titles

Mr. (Mister)	Miss (no abbreviation)

Mrs. (Mistress; a married woman)

Ms. (any woman, especially one whose marital status is unknown)

Jr. (Junior)	Sr. (Senior)
Dr. (Doctor)	Rev. (Reverend)
Prof. (Professor)	Pres. (President)

| Gen. (General) | Capt. (Captain) |
| Sen. (Senator) | Rep. (Representative) |

Proper Place Names We may abbreviate the following words when they appear in addresses as part of a proper place name (as in *Main Street*). They are not abbreviated when they are used as common nouns (as in *down the street*).

St. (Street)	Rd. (Road)
Dr. (Drive)	Blvd. (Boulevard)
Pl. (Place)	Ave. (Avenue)
Mt. (Mount, Mountain)	Bldg. (Building)

Compass Directions Compass directions may be abbreviated when they appear in addresses as part of a proper place name.

N. (North)	N.E. (Northeast)
S. (South)	N.W. (Northwest)
E. (East)	S.E. (Southeast)
W. (West)	S.W. (Southwest)

Others Here are a few other commonly used abbreviations.

Inc. (Incorporated)	etc. (Latin *et cetera*, "and so forth")
Co. (Company)	est. (estimated)
Ltd. (Limited)	cont. (continued)
govt. (government)	anon. (anonymous)
dept. (department)	misc. (miscellaneous)

Decimal Point We use a period as a **decimal point** to show dollars and cents and to show the place value of numbers. (Note: When we read a number, the "and" shows where the decimal point belongs.)

$4.10 (four dollars and ten cents)

6.2 (six and two tenths)

Example Add periods as needed in a–d.

(a) Mr Cruz lives at 270 W Oak Ave

(b) A salad costs $698 (six dollars and 98 cents).

(c) The sign reads "Grand Opening: Mon, Dec 29."

(d) I saw Dr Green at nine am yesterday.

Solution   (a) **Mr.** (Mister), **W.** (West), and **Ave.** (Avenue), are abbreviations that require periods.

(b) **$6.98** requires a period as a decimal point to show six dollars *and* ninety-eight cents.

(c) **Mon.** (Monday) and **Dec.** (December) are abbreviations that require periods.

(d) **Dr.** (doctor) and **a.m.** (*ante meridiem*, "before noon") are abbreviations that require periods.

Practice   Rewrite sentences a–f, adding periods as needed. (Note: When a sentence ends with an abbreviation that requires a period, that same period serves as the final punctuation.)

a. Mrs Chu parked on First St

b. The game will begin at 9 am

c. Ms Beck called me

d. Capt Hook lost his hand

e. Did you know Gen Patton?

f. Seemore Glass Co sells windows

For g and h, replace each blank with *ebb tide* or *flood tide*.

g. A(n) _____ is coming in.

h. A(n) _____ is going out.

More Practice   See "More Practice Lesson 50" in the Student Workbook.

Review Set 50   Choose the correct word to complete sentences 1–6.

1. We shall soon cross the state (boarder, border, quell) into
(49)   Ohio.

2. Singing a lullaby can (quill, quell, paws) a baby's cry.
(48)

3. Animals will (quill, dye, die) without food and water.
(47)

4. The weather report predicts a dangerous (zephyr, gale,
(46) boarder) along with heavy rain and hail.

5. A (male, female, mail) donkey is called a jenny.
(26)

6. The word *hawk's* is a (plural, possessive) noun.
(13)

7. Add suffixes to the following words:
(33, 34) (a) fry + ed   (b) pat + ed

8. Write the indirect object in the following sentence:
(46)
Kate tossed Nate a note.

9. Write the word that is spelled correctly:
(35)
believer, beleiver

10. Write the two coordinating conjunctions from the
(48) following sentence:

Rex does not eat corn or pickles, so I feed him spinach.

11. Rewrite the following letter, using correct capitalization:
(41, 43) dear ms. beck,

please join me for lunch on friday.

warmly,
mr. knight

12. Write whether the following word group is a phrase or a
(36) clause: if a cat scratches

13. In the following sentence, write the entire verb phrase,
(12) circling the helping verb:

Aaron might catch a fish.

14. Rewrite the following sentence, using correct
(25) capitalization:

will professor curtis allow rex in her english class?

15. Write the linking verb in the following sentence:
(31)
Do hummingbirds grow tired of humming?

16. Write whether the following word group is a complete
(5, 23) sentence, a sentence fragment, or a run-on sentence:

Other seabirds, such as terns and puffins.

17. From the following sentence, write the two prepositional
(44) phrases, circling the object of each preposition:

Some birds spend most of their time looking for food.

18. Use a dictionary: (a) The word *mullet* is what part of
(27,30) speech? (b) Write its pronunciation. (c) Write its
etymology.

19. Rewrite the following words, circling silent letter(s):
(28, 29)
(a) should   (b) castle

20. Rewrite the following sentence, adding periods as needed:
(47, 50)
Dr Bird met Mr Oman at six pm

21. Write the word from this list that is *not* a linking verb:
(31) look, feel, taste, small, sound, seem, appear, grow,
become, remain, stay.

22. Write the three proper or limiting adjectives from the
(40, 42) following sentence:

Two moths flutter around the daisies in Ana's garden.

23. For the following sentence, write the correct form of the
(10, 19) verb:

Rex (past of *beg*) for treats.

24. For the verb *beg*, write the (a) present participle, (b) past
(19) tense, and (c) past participle.

25. Replace each blank with a descriptive adjective to add
(39) more detail to the word "dog" in the sentence below.
There are many possible answers.

Rex is a(n) _____, _____ dog.

26. Rewrite the following lines of poetry, adding capital
(15) letters as needed:

old King Cole
was a merry old soul…

27. For a and b, write the plural of each noun.
(17, 22)
(a) puppy   (b) monkey

28. Diagram the simple subject and simple predicate of each
(36) clause in the following sentence:

Miss Ng lost her map, but she can use mine if she needs one.

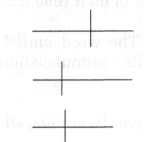

Diagram each word of sentences 29–30.

29. Can you or she read a map?
(37, 49)

30. The bakery sent us a bill for fifty dollars.
(45, 46)

29.

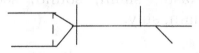

30.

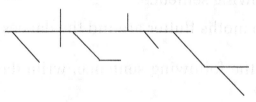

LESSON 51

The Predicate Nominative

Dictation or Journal Entry

Vocabulary:

To *close* is to shut. Remember to *close* the door.

Clothes are articles of clothing for the human body. They rinsed their muddy *clothes* in the river.

More than one name can identify people, animals, or things.

A grouse is a bird.

In the sentence above, "bird" is another name for "grouse."

Renaming the Subject
A **predicate nominative** is a noun that follows the verb and renames the subject person, animal, or thing. It explains or defines the subject. The subject and the predicate nominative are joined by a linking verb, such as *am, is, are, was, were, be, being, been, become,* or *seem.*

We remember that a linking verb does not show action, nor does it "help" the action verb. Its purpose is to connect the person, animal, or thing (the subject) to its new name (the predicate nominative).

Predicate nominatives are circled in the sentences below.

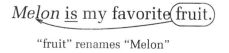

Melon is my favorite (fruit.)

"fruit" renames "Melon"

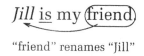

Jill is my (friend)

"friend" renames "Jill"

If we reverse the subject and the predicate nominative, as in the sentences below, the meaning of the sentence is not affected.

My favorite *fruit* is melon.

My *friend* is Jill.

Identifying the Predicate Nominative
Reversing the subject and predicate nominative in this manner helps us identify predicate nominatives. If the linking verb is not a "to be" verb, we replace it with a "to be"

verb to determine whether there is a predicate nominative that renames the subject.

The *cat* <u>became</u> a hunter.

The *cat* <u>is</u> a hunter.

"to be" linking verb

Now we reverse the subject and predicate nominative, and we see that the predicate does indeed rename the subject. The meaning is the same, so we have identified a predicate nominative.

A *hunter* <u>is</u> the cat.

Predicate nominatives are more difficult to identify in interrogative sentences. Turning the question into a statement will help.

Question: Is Miss Ng the teacher in room eight?

Statement: Miss Ng is the teacher in room eight.

In the statement above, we see that "teacher" renames "Miss Ng." Therefore, "teacher" is a predicate nominative.

Compound Predicate Nominatives

Predicate nominatives may be compound, as in the sentences below.

My best *subjects* <u>are</u> (math,) (grammar,) and (history.)

The *winners* <u>were</u> (Aaron) and (Amy.)

Diagramming

In a diagram, the predicate nominative is indicated by a line that slants back toward the subject. Here we diagram the simple subject, linking verb, and predicate nominatives of some of the sentences above.

A grouse is a bird.

Jill is my friend.

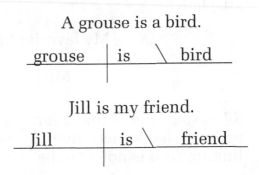

My best subjects are math, grammar, and history.

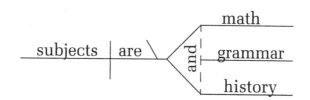

Example Diagram the simple subject, linking verb, and predicate nominatives of the following sentences. The simple subject is italicized and the linking verb is underlined to help you.

(a) An owl's *prey* <u>are</u> insects, birds, and small mammals.

(b) *Grandpa* <u>was</u> a musician.

(c) The *attic* <u>became</u> my bedroom.

Solution (a)

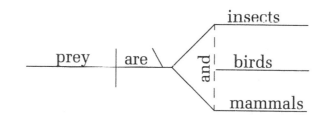

(b)

Grandpa | was \ musician

(c)

attic | became \ bedroom

Practice For a and b, replace each blank with *close* or *clothes*.

a. Please _____ the window.

b. Ana wears colorful _____.

For c–f, diagram the simple subject, linking verb, and predicate nominatives in each sentence.

c. *Dan* <u>became</u> a photographer.

d. <u>Was</u> *Miss Ling* your teacher?

e. *Nate* <u>became</u> her student.

f. *Josh* <u>is</u> an artist and a builder.

Review Set Choose the correct word to complete sentences 1–6.
51

1. At (flood, ebb, quill) tide, the lower waterline leaves a
(50) broad, sandy shore decorated with seashells.

2. The (border, boarder, zephyr) attends classes at a nearby
(49) university.

3. Stroking the cat's fur might (quill, gale, quell) its fear of
(48) people.

4. Children can use (dye, die, dew) to color their eggs.
(47)

5. The (offensive, defensive, fowl) cat pestered the little
(13) mouse.

6. The word *metamorphosis* is a(n) (abstract, concrete)
(11) noun.

7. Add suffixes to the following words:
(33, 34)(a) lazy + est   (b) big + er

8. Write the indirect object in the following sentence:
(46)
Aaron gave Lucy the key.

9. Write the word that is spelled correctly:
(35)
weigh, wiegh

10. Write the seven common coordinating conjunctions
(48) listed in Lesson 48.

11. Rewrite the following sentence, using correct
(8, 41) capitalization:

miss ng said, "bolivia is in south america."

12. Write whether the following word group is a phrase or a
(36) clause:

a large wasp with a powerful sting

13. In the following sentence, write the entire verb phrase,
(12) circling each helping verb:

I have been mending clothes all day.

14. Rewrite the following song title, using correct
(25) capitalization:

"listen to the mockingbird"

15. Write the predicate nominative in the following sentence:
(51)

Quan remains captain of our team.

16. Write whether the following word group is a complete
(5, 23) sentence, a sentence fragment, or a run-on sentence:

Most reptile eggs have soft, leathery shells.

17. From the following sentence, write each prepositional
(44) phrase, circling the object of each preposition:

After the storm, Rex ran out the door and into the yard.

18. Use a dictionary: (a) The word *junco* is what part of
(27,30) speech? (b) Write its pronunciation. (c) Write its
etymology.

19. Rewrite the following words, circling silent letter(s):
(28, 29)
   (a) know   (b) sight

20. Rewrite the following sentence, adding periods as needed:
(47, 50)
   Dr Ow will give flu shots on Oct 1

21. Write the linking verb from the following sentence:
(31)

The milk smelled sour.

22. Write each proper or limiting adjective from the
(40, 42) following sentence:

An Indian python lay at Lucy's feet.

23. For the following sentence, write the correct form of the
(9) verb:

Quan (present of *wish*) for good weather.

24. For the verb *carry*, write the (a) present participle, (b)
(19) past tense, and (c) past participle.

25. Replace each blank with a descriptive adjective to add
(39) more detail to the word "purse" in the sentence below.
There are many possible answers.

Miss Flores carries a(n) _____, _____ purse.

26. Rewrite the following sentence, adding capital letters as
(26) needed:

dr. ow says, "roll up your sleeve."

27. For a and b, write the plural of each noun.
(17, 22)
(a) glassful   (b) child

28. Diagram the simple subject and simple predicate of each
(36) clause in the following sentence:

If Lucy likes snakes, she can draw one when she has time.

Diagram each word of sentences 29–30.

29. Miss Ng is Quan's teacher and a friend of Dr. Ow.
(49, 51)

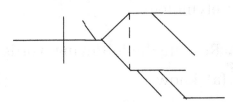

30. A big, mature tarantula gave Miss Ng a fright.
(37, 46)

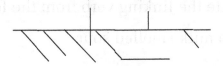

LESSON 52

Noun Case, Part 1: Nominative and Possessive

Dictation or Journal Entry

Vocabulary:

A *cirrus* is a high, white, thin, wispy cloud made of ice crystals. The *cirrus* looked like a large white feather high in the sky.

A *cumulus* is a dense cloud shaped like rounded mounds billowing upward from a flat base. After the rain, a huge *cumulus* formed over the valley.

We can group nouns into three **cases:** *nominative, possessive,* and *objective.* The case of the noun explains how the noun is used in the sentence. In this lesson, we will learn to identify nouns that are in the nominative and possessive cases.

Nominative Case

SUBJECT OF A SENTENCE   (NOMINATIVE CASE) ⎹_____

A noun is in the **nominative case** when it is the subject of a sentence. In the sentence below, the noun *frog* is in the nominative case because it is the subject of the sentence.

A *frog* sits on a rock.

PREDICATE NOMINATIVE   (NOMINATIVE CASE) ⎹ linking verb \ (NOMINATIVE CASE)

A noun is also in the **nominative case** when it is used as a predicate nominative. A predicate nominative follows a linking verb and renames the subject. In the sentence below, *amphibians* renames the subject, *frogs. Amphibians* is in the nominative case because it is a predicate nominative.

Frogs are *amphibians.*

Possessive Case

We are familiar with nouns that show possession or ownership. These nouns are in the **possessive case**. In the sentence below, the possessive noun *Mary's* is in the possessive case.

Dilly is *Mary's* bullfrog.

Example

Tell whether the italicized noun in each sentence is in the nominative case or the possessive case. If it is in the nominative case, tell whether it is the subject of the sentence or a predicate nominative.

(a) The *toad* ate a cricket.

(b) Dilly is my *pet.*

(c) *Dilly's* habitat is lovely.

Solution   (a) The word *toad* is in the **nominative case.** It is the **subject of the sentence.**

(b) The word *pet* is in the **nominative case.** It is a **predicate nominative**; it follows the linking verb *is* and renames the subject.

(c) *Dilly's* is in the **possessive case.** It shows possession; it tells "whose habitat."

Practice   For sentences a–e, tell whether the italicized noun is in the nominative case or the possessive case. If it is in the nominative case, tell whether it is the subject of the sentence or a predicate nominative.

a. Two big green *frogs* croak loudly.

b. Dilly was a *tadpole.*

c. The *tadpole's* legs are developing.

d. Do *frogs* have hair?

e. The pond is a lovely *habitat.*

For f and g, replace each blank with *cirrus* or *cumulus.*

f. The dense _____ was shaped like a cauliflower.

g. A _____ is thin and wispy.

Review Set   Choose the correct word to complete sentences 1–6.
52   **1.** On a cold winter day, we (clothes, close, boarder) the
     (51) windows.

2. A beach dweller might stack sandbags to prepare for the
(50) (flood, ebb, quell) tide.

3. He made a rock (boarder, border, quill) around the
(49) garden.

4. Before the invention of ballpoint pens, writers dipped
(48) (quells, gales, quills) into ink.

5. The (offensive, defensive, nocturnal) cat swiped the
(13) attacking dog with its claws.

6. The word *group* is a (compound, collective) noun.
(11)

7. Add suffixes to the following words:
(33, 34)
(a) happy + est   (b) sit + ing

8. Write the indirect object in the following sentence:
(46)
Lucy hands Aaron a pen.

9. Write the word that is spelled correctly: relief, releif
(35)

10. Write each coordinating conjunction from the following
(48) sentence:

Meg tossed Rex a bone and a toy, yet he kept howling.

11. Rewrite the following letter, using correct capitalization:
(15, 41)
dear miss ng,

please forgive me. i forgot to close the cage.

regretfully,
mr. hake

12. Write whether the following word group is a phrase or a
(36) clause: as hamsters play

13. In the following sentence, write the entire verb phrase,
(12) circling each helping verb:

Some might have escaped.

14. Using correct capitalization, rewrite the following sentence:
(38)
does uncle john know officer cruz?

15. Write the predicate nominative in the following sentence:
(51)
The gift was a book.

16. Write whether the following word group is a complete
(5, 23) sentence, a sentence fragment, or a run-on sentence:

A picture book about horses.

17. From the following sentence, write each prepositional
(44) phrase, circling the object of each preposition:

A bat with big ears sleeps under the bridge.

18. Use a dictionary: (a) The word *irate* is what part of
(27,30) speech? (b) Write its pronunciation. (c) Write its
etymology.

19. Rewrite the following words, circling silent letter(s):
(28, 29)
(a) whom   (b) hymn   (c) match

20. Rewrite the following sentence, adding periods as needed:
(47, 50)
Ms Moll left for Peru on Aug 5

21. Write whether the following sentence is declarative,
(2) interrogative, imperative, or exclamatory:

When will she return?

22. Write the four adjectives from the following sentence:
(40, 42)
The young bats cling together in a dark cave.

23. For the following sentence, write the correct form of the
(10, 19) verb:

Rex (past of *rip*) the newspaper.

24. For the verb *rip*, write the (a) present participle, (b) past
(19) tense, and (c) past participle.

25. Write whether the circled word in the sentence below is
(52) in the nominative case or the possessive case:

An ape is a (mammal).

26. Rewrite the following outline, adding periods and capital
(26, 47) letters as needed:

 i types of ants
  a winged queen
  b winged male
  c soldier
  d worker

27. For a and b, write the plural of each noun.
(17, 22)

(a) thief   (b) math teacher

28. Diagram the simple subject and simple predicate of each
(36) clause in the following sentence: After I milk the cows, I
shall feed the chickens.

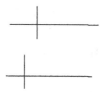

Diagram each word of sentences 29–30.

29. Ana is a cheerful worker and a good friend.
(49, 51)

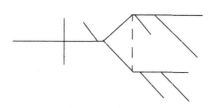

30. Rex brought me a wet, muddy ball.
(46)

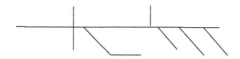

Noun Case, Part 2: Objective

Dictation or Journal Entry

Vocabulary:
A *bough* is a branch of a tree, especially a main one. The *bough* bent low because of its heavy fruit.

To *bow* is to bend the head or upper body forward in respect or greeting. The actors will *bow* to the audience after the play.

We have learned to identify nouns that are in the nominative and possessive cases. In this lesson, we will see examples of nouns that are in the objective case.

Objective Case A noun is in the **objective case** when it is used as a *direct object*, an *indirect object*, or the *object of a preposition*. Let us review these "objects."

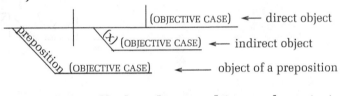

Direct Object A noun or pronoun is called a **direct object** when it is the direct receiver of the action of the verb. Direct objects are circled in the sentences below.

Rob made (pancakes).
(Rob made *what*?)

I fried (eggs).
(I fried *what*?)

Indirect Object An **indirect object** is the noun or pronoun that tells "to whom" or "for whom" the action was done. In the following examples, the indirect objects are circled.

Did you bring (Meg) flowers?
(Did you bring flowers for *Meg*?)

I tossed (Rex) the ball.
(I tossed the ball to *Rex*.)

Object of a Preposition A noun or pronoun that follows a preposition is called the **object of a preposition.** Objects of the prepositions are circled in the examples below.

on the (beach)   through the (tunnel)

around the (world)   besides (her)

near (them)   during (class)

Example 1 For sentences a–c, tell whether each circled noun is a direct object, an indirect object, or the object of a preposition.

(a) Ed sent (Peg) pictures.

(b) I washed the (car).

(c) Earth revolves around the (sun).

Solution (a) *Peg* is an **indirect object,** telling "to whom" the pictures were sent.

(b) *Car* is a **direct object.** It is the receiver of the action verb *washed.*

(c) *Sun* is the **object of the preposition** *around.*

Example 2 Tell whether the circled noun is in the nominative, possessive, or objective case.

(a) Nan grew (pumpkins).

(b) My yard is smaller than (Nan's).

(c) Nan is an excellent (gardener).

(d) She wakes at (dawn).

Solution (a) *Pumpkins* is a direct object. Therefore, it is in the **objective case.**

(b) *Nan's* is a possessive noun. Therefore, it is in the **possessive case.**

(c) *Gardener* is a predicate nominative. Therefore, it is in the **nominative case.**

(d) *Dawn* is the object of a preposition. Therefore, it is in the **objective case.**

Practice For sentences a–f, write whether the circled noun is a direct object (D.O.), an indirect object (I.O.), or the object of a preposition (O.P.).

a. Rex dug under the (gate.)

b. Bob threw (Sam) a rope.

c. Sam caught the (rope).

d. The cow jumped over the (moon).

e. Joe plays the (oboe).

f. He gave the (voter) a ballot.

For g–i, write whether the circled noun is in the nominative, possessive, or objective case.

g. Did (Rex) find his bone?

h. Rats ate my (seeds).

i. Bunny nibbled (Rex's) ear.

For j and k, replace each blank with *bough* or *bow*.

j. People might _____ before a king or queen.

k. The fir _____ broke, for it was heavy with snow.

Review Set 53

Choose the correct word to complete sentences 1–6.

1. Wispy (cumulus, cirrus, zephyr) clouds streaked the blue
(52) sky.

2. She packed all her (close, clothes, boarders) into one
(51) suitcase.

3. During (ebb, flood, quell) tide, the tide is going out.
(50)

4. A fence might mark the (boarder, border, roots) of one's
(49) property.

5. Spoiled milk has a (foul, fowl, defensive) odor.
(14)

6. The word *anteaters* is a (plural, possessive) noun.
(13)

7. Add suffixes to the following words:
(33, 34) (a) fry + s   (b) pop + ing

8. Write the indirect object in the following sentence:
(46)
Nan tossed Rex a treat.

9. Write the word that is spelled correctly: belief, beleif
(35)

10. Write the seven common coordinating conjunctions
(48) listed in Lesson 48.

11. Rewrite the following sentence, using correct
(15, 41) capitalization:

corn grows tall in the midwest.

12. Write whether the following word group is a phrase or a
(36) clause: under the mallard's wing

13. In the following sentence, write the entire verb phrase,
(12) circling each helping verb:

By next Monday, the eggs will have hatched.

14. Rewrite the following story title, using correct
(25) capitalization: "the fox and the grapes"

15. Write the predicate nominative in the following sentence:
(51)
Is the Euphrates a river?

16. Write whether the following word group is a complete
(5, 23) sentence, a sentence fragment, or a run-on sentence:

Puffins find food at sea, they dive underwater.

17. From the following sentence, write the two prepositional
(44) phrases, circling the object of each preposition:

Seabirds can glide over the waves for long distances.

18. Use a dictionary: (a) The word *mange* is what part of
(27,30) speech? (b) Write its pronunciation. (c) Write its
etymology.

19. Rewrite the following words, circling silent letter(s):
(28, 29)
(a) guest   (b) knock

20. Rewrite the following sentence, adding periods as needed:
(47, 50)
I shall see Dr Ow at one pm today

21. Write the word from this list that is *not a* linking verb:
(31)
is, am, are, wax, were, be, being, been

22. Write the four adjectives from the following sentence:

(39, 40)

Three fuzzy ducklings slept in the warm nest.

23. For the following sentence, write the correct form of the verb:

(14)

We (future of *wax*) the car tomorrow.

24. For the verb *flap*, write the (a) present participle, (b) past tense, and (c) past participle.

(19)

25. Write whether the circled word in the sentence below is in the nominative, possessive, or objective case:

(52, 53)

The gull flapped its (wings).

26. Rewrite the following sentence, adding capital letters as needed:

(26)

mrs. tern said, "next, i shall teach you to fly."

27. For a–c, write the plural of each noun.

(17, 22)

(a) colony   (b) bird of prey   (c) Monday

28. Diagram the simple subject and simple predicate of each clause in the following sentence:

(36)

If weather permits, we shall explore the dunes until school starts.

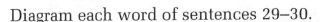

Diagram each word of sentences 29–30.

29. Bob's older brother is a musician and an artist.

(49, 51)

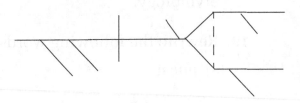

30. Bob and I gave Bill an idea.

(46, 49)

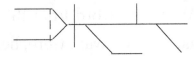

The Predicate Adjective

Dictation or Journal Entry

Vocabulary:

Then means "at that time." Men wore powdered wigs *then*. *Then* also means "immediately or soon afterward." Lightning flashed, and *then* we heard thunder. In addition, *then* means "in that case, or therefore." If she wants a good grade, *then* she will work hard.

Than introduces the second part of a comparison. He is taller *than* I. She would rather play games *than* study. I have less *than* two dollars.

We have learned that a predicate nominative follows a linking verb and *renames* the subject.

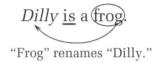

"Frog" renames "Dilly."

Describes the Subject A **predicate adjective** follows a linking verb and *describes* or gives more detail about the subject.

"Old" describes "Dilly."

In the sentence above, the word "old" is a predicate adjective. It describes "Dilly"— old Dilly.

Here is another example:

Wally was gentle

In the sentence above, the word "gentle" is a predicate adjective. It describes "Wally"— gentle Wally.

The linking verb that connects the subject to the predicate adjective may be a "to be" verb (*is, am, are, was, were, be, been, being*), but other linking verbs such as *become, seem, feel, appear, look, taste,* and *smell* also can link the predicate adjective to the subject.

Wally looks strong.

The *berry* tastes sweet.

Dilly seems tired.

The *milk* smells sour.

Identifying Predicate Adjectives

To help us identify the predicate adjective, we can replace a possible linking verb with a "to be" verb.

$$\underset{\text{Wally lo}\cancel{\text{oks}}\text{ strong.}}{\underset{\text{is}}{\Big|}} \longleftarrow \text{"to be" verb}$$

In the sentence above, we see that "strong" describes the subject "Wally"— strong Wally. Therefore, "strong" is a predicate adjective.

$$\underset{\text{The }berry\text{ ta}\cancel{\text{stes}}\text{ sweet.}}{\underset{\text{is}}{\Big|}} \longleftarrow \text{"to be" verb}$$

In the sentence above, we see that "sweet" describes the subject "berry"— sweet berry. "Sweet" is a predicate adjective.

Compound Predicate Adjectives

A predicate adjective may be compound, as in the sentence below. Predicate adjectives are circled.

Her *shoes* are (stylish) and (comfortable).

Diagramming

We diagram a predicate adjective in the same way we diagram a predicate nominative. Here is a diagram of the simple subject, linking verb, and predicate adjectives of the sentence above:

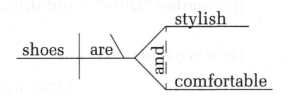

stylish and comfortable shoes

Example

Diagram the simple subject, linking verb, and predicate adjectives in sentences a–d.

(a) Kittens <u>are</u> playful.

(b) Dilly <u>appears</u> shy.

(c) Miss Ng <u>looks</u> angry.

(d) Wally <u>seems</u> strong but gentle.

Solution

(a)   <u>Kittens | are \ playful</u>

(b)

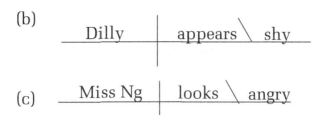

(c)

(d)

Practice For sentences a–d, diagram the simple subjects, linking verbs, and predicate adjectives.

    a. Gulls <u>appear</u> graceful.

    b. Peacocks and parrots <u>are</u> colorful.

    c. The nest <u>looks</u> warm and dry.

    d. <u>Is</u> the owl wise?

For e and f, replace each blank with *then* or *than*.

    e. Dilly is older _____ I am.

    f. First we think, and _____ we speak.

Review Set 54 Choose the correct word(s) to complete sentences 1–8.

    1. Fir (bows, boughs, quells) sway in the wind.
    (53)

    2. Huge, fluffy (zephyr, cirrus, cumulus) clouds looked like
    (52) marshmallows in the sky.

    3. I shall (close, clothes, bow) my eyes and go to sleep.
    (51)

    4. During (ebb, flood, bough) tide, seawater rises to the top
    (50) of the wall.

    5. Because fish are (invertebrates, nocturnal, vertebrates),
    (15) the backbone must be removed before eating.

    6. The word *anteaters* is a(n) (abstract, concrete) noun.
    (11)

7. Rex (tryed, tried) not to bark.
(33, 34)

8. The (neighbor, nieghbor) has a cat.
(35)

9. Write the indirect object in the following sentence:
(46)

Nan taught Jo some bird calls.

10. Write each coordinating conjunction in the following
(48) sentence:

Gannets and kittiwakes nest high on cliffs, but cormorants nest lower.

11. Rewrite the following letter, using correct capitalization:
(8, 41) dear officer cruz,

    people drive too fast on main street.

                with concern,
                miss moore

12. Write whether the following word group is a phrase or a
(36) clause: when Dilly saw me

13. In the following sentence, write the entire verb phrase,
(12) circling each helping verb:

You must have seen pheasants.

14. Using correct capitalization, rewrite the following sentence:
(38)

is dilly older than uncle john?

15. Write the predicate adjective in the following sentence:
(54)

The bird sounds lonely.

16. Write whether the following word group is a complete
(5, 23) sentence, a sentence fragment, or a run-on sentence:

Seabirds with waterproof feathers, webbed feet, and sharp bills.

17. From the following sentence, write the three prepositional
(44) phrases, circling the object of each preposition:

From sunrise until sunset, gulls swooped over our boat.

18. Use a dictionary: (a) The word *pathos* is what part of
(27, 30) speech? (b) Write its pronunciation. (c) Write its etymology.

Grammar and Writing 4   **256**   **Student Edition**
                                                                                                        Lesson 54

19. Rewrite the following words, circling silent letter(s):
(28, 29)
    (a) wrist   (b) calf

20. Rewrite the following outline, adding periods as needed:
(47, 50)
    I Shorebirds
     A Stilts
     B Sandpipers

21. Write whether the following sentence is declarative,
(2) interrogative, imperative, or exclamatory:

Where do gulls live?

22. Write the three adjectives from the following sentence:
(39, 40)
With long legs, the stilt can feed in deep water.

23. For the following sentence, write the correct form of the
(9) verb:

A gull (present of *cry*) overhead.

24. For the verb *cry*, write the (a) present participle, (b) past
(19) tense, and (c) past participle.

25. Write whether the circled word in the sentence below is
(52, 53) in the nominative, possessive, or objective case:

The (moon) waxes and wanes.

26. Rewrite the following lines of poetry, adding capital
(15) letters as needed:

life is not dull
when you fly like a gull.

27. For a and b, write the plural of each noun.
(17, 22)
    (a) story   (b) lunchbox

28. Diagram the simple subject and simple predicate of each
(36) clause in the following sentence:

When Miss Ng sees Mr. Hake, she will tease him.

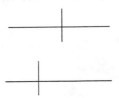

Diagram each word of sentences 29–30.

29. Our teacher has been feeling happy and hopeful.
(49, 54)

30. Nan and Jo gave us a report on shorebirds.
(46, 49)

29.

30.

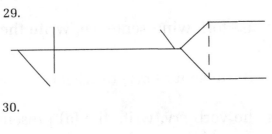

LESSON 55

Comparison Adjectives

Dictation or Journal Entry
Vocabulary:
Idle means "not busy; inactive." The *idle* student was daydreaming.

An *idol* is an object of worship. The athlete became an *idol* for many young people.

Adjectives are often used to compare nouns or pronouns. These **comparative adjectives** have three forms that show greater or lesser degrees of quality, quantity, or manner: **positive**, **comparative**, and **superlative**. Below are examples of the positive, comparative, and superlative forms of some adjectives.

POSITIVE	COMPARATIVE	SUPERLATIVE
tall	taller	tallest
low	lower	lowest
hard	harder	hardest
easy	easier	easiest
lazy	lazier	laziest

Positive Form The positive form describes a noun or pronoun without comparing it to any other. (Do not confuse *positive* with *good*. Here, *positive* simply means "possessing the quality." The quality itself may be good, bad, or neutral.)

Dilly is *old*.

Berries are *sweet*.

Miss Ng is *pretty*.

Comparative Form The comparative form compares **two** persons, places, or things.

Dilly is *older* than Rex.

Are berries *sweeter* than lemons?

Miss Ng is *prettier* than a princess.

Superlative Form The superlative form compares **three or more** persons, places, or things.

Of my four pets, Dilly is the *oldest*.

Are berries the *sweetest* of all the fruits?

Miss Ng is the *prettiest* of the three teachers.

Example 1 Choose the correct adjective for each sentence.

(a) My dog is (thin, thinner, thinnest) than yours.

(b) Of the three, Nan is the (busy, busier, busiest).

(c) Dan is the (fast, faster, fastest) of the two skaters.

(d) Of all the actors, Bob was the (silly, sillier, silliest).

Solution (a) My dog is **thinner** than yours. We use the comparative form because we are comparing two dogs.

(b) Of the three, Nan is the **busiest.** We use the superlative form because we are comparing three or more people.

(c) Dan is the **faster** of the two skaters. We use the comparative form because we are comparing only two.

(d) Of all the actors, Bob was the **silliest.** We use the superlative form because we are comparing three or more actors.

Forming Comparison Adjectives How we create the comparative and superlative forms of an adjective depends on how the adjective appears in its positive form. There are three main categories to remember.

One-Syllable Adjectives We create the comparative form of most one-syllable adjectives by adding *er* to the end of the word. The superlative form is created by adding *est.*

POSITIVE	COMPARATIVE	SUPERLATIVE
big	bigger	biggest
wide	wider	widest
new	newer	newest

Two-Syllable Adjectives Most adjectives with two or more syllables do not have comparative or superlative forms. Instead, we use the word "more" (or "less") before the adjective to form the comparative, and the word "most" (or "least") to form the superlative.

POSITIVE	COMPARATIVE	SUPERLATIVE
mature	more mature	most mature
fearful	less fearful	least fearful
serious	more serious	most serious

Two-Syllable Adjectives That End in y	When a two-syllable adjective ends in *y*, we create the comparative and superlative forms by changing the *y* to *i* and adding *er* or *est*.	

POSITIVE	COMPARATIVE	SUPERLATIVE
fuzzy	fuzzier	fuzziest
happy	happier	happiest
cloudy	cloudier	cloudiest

Exceptions There are exceptions to these guidelines. Below are a few examples of two-syllable adjectives whose comparative and superlative forms are created by adding *er* or *est*.

POSITIVE	COMPARATIVE	SUPERLATIVE
little (size, not amount)	littler	littlest
quiet	quieter	quietest
stable	stabler	stablest
yellow	yellower	yellowest
clever	cleverer	cleverest
simple	simpler	simplest

We check the dictionary if we are unsure how to create the comparative or superlative form of a two-syllable adjective.

Spelling Reminders Remember that when adding *er* or *est* to the positive form of an adjective, we often must alter the word's original spelling. We apply the same rules we use when adding *ed* to form a past-tense verb.

When an adjective ends with **two or more consonants**, *er* or *est* is simply added to the positive form of the adjective.

brown	browner	brownest
young	younger	youngest
bright	brighter	brightest

When an adjective ends with a **single consonant following one vowel**, we double the final consonant before adding *er* or *est*.

sad	sadder	saddest
red	redder	reddest

When an adjective ends with a **single consonant following two vowels**, we do not double the final consonant.

loud	louder	loudest
green	greener	greenest

When a one-syllable adjective ends in **w, x, or y preceded by a vowel**, we do not double the final consonant.

new	newer	newest
gray	grayer	grayest

When a two-syllable adjective ends in **y**, we change the *y* to *i* before adding *er* or *est*.

crazy	crazier	craziest
wavy	wavier	waviest

When an adjective ends with a **silent e**, we drop the *e* and add *er* or *est*.

tame	tamer	tamest
blue	bluer	bluest

Example 2 Complete the comparison chart by adding the comparative and superlative forms of each adjective.

POSITIVE	COMPARATIVE	SUPERLATIVE
(a) strong	_____	_____
(b) full	_____	_____
(c) tasty	_____	_____
(d) beautiful	_____	_____
(e) red	_____	_____
(f) brave	_____	_____

Solution

POSITIVE	COMPARATIVE	SUPERLATIVE
(a) strong	stronger	strongest
(b) full	fuller	fullest
(c) tasty	tastier	tastiest
(d) beautiful	more beautiful (or less beautiful)	most beautiful (or least beautiful)
(e) red	redder	reddest
(f) brave	braver	bravest

Practice Choose the correct adjective for each sentence, and write whether it is comparative or superlative.

    a. Your bag is (heavier, heaviest) than mine.

    b. Jill is the (younger, youngest) of the three sisters.

    c. Miss Ng is the (more, most) helpful of all the teachers.

    d. Was Rex (more, most) active today or yesterday?

    e. Isn't this the (long, longer, longest) of the four routes?

    f. Josh has short hair, but Nate's is (shorter, shortest).

For g and h, write the comparative and superlative of each adjective.

    g. muddy   **h.** defensive

For i and j, replace each blank with *idle* or *idol*.

    i. A person might worship an _____.

    j. Dan was not busy; he was _____.

Review Set 55 Choose the correct word(s) to complete sentences 1–9.

    1. If you read the directions carefully, (than, then, their) you
    ⁽⁵⁴⁾ will make fewer mistakes.

    2. In some countries, people (quill, bough, bow) to one
    ⁽⁵³⁾ another to show respect.

    3. (Gale, Cumulus, Cirrus) clouds look like giant feathers
    ⁽⁵²⁾ across the azure sky.

    4. Nate asked for dry (close, clothes, roots) after falling into
    ⁽⁵¹⁾ the pool.

    5. Jellyfish and other (vertebrates, fowl, invertebrates) were
    ⁽¹⁵⁾ grouped together at the aquarium.

    6. The word *family* is a (compound, collective) noun.
    ⁽¹¹⁾

    7. Nan is (fameous, famous) for her (funy, funny) stories.
    ^(33, 34)

8. Have the winners (received, recieved) (there, their)
_(8, 35)_ rewards?

9. Chief was the (tall, taller, tallest) of the two horses.
_(55)_

10. Write the seven common coordinating conjunctions
_(48)_ listed in Lesson 48.

11. Rewrite the following sentence, using correct
_(41, 43)_ capitalization:

sal attends a catholic school in the northeast.

12. Write whether the following word group is a phrase or a
_(36)_ clause: with Tim and his two pythons

13. Write the indirect object in the following sentence:
_(46)_
Elle handed Sal a pencil with an eraser.

14. Rewrite the following book title, using correct
_(25)_ capitalization:

how to care for frogs

15. Write the predicate adjective in the following sentence:
_(54)_
That milk smells sour.

16. Write whether the following word group is a complete
_(5, 23)_ sentence, a sentence fragment, or a run-on sentence:

The puffin dove underwater.

17. From the following sentence, write the three prepositional
_(44)_ phrases, circling the object of each preposition:

Millions of birds nest in colonies along the shore.

18. Use a dictionary: (a) The word _gannet_ is what part of
_(27,30)_ speech? (b) Write its pronunciation. (c) Write its
etymology.

19. Rewrite the following words, circling silent letter(s):
_(28, 29)_
(a) would   (b) guide

20. Rewrite the following sentence, adding periods as needed:
(47, 50)

Mr R W Potts lives at 24 E Oak Dr

21. Write the word from this list that is *not* a linking verb:
(31)

look, feel, paste, smell, sound, seem, appear

22. Write the four adjectives from the following sentence:
(40, 42)

With a sharp bill, the seabird can catch slippery prey.

23. For the following sentence, write the correct form of the
(10) verb:

Its feathers (past of *dry*) quickly.

24. For the verb *dry*, write the (a) present participle, (b) past
(19) tense, and (c) past participle.

25. Write whether the circled word in the sentence below is
(52, 53) in the nominative, possessive, or objective case:

Kittiwakes are small (gulls).

26. Rewrite the following sentence, adding capital letters as
(26) needed:

miss ng said, "listen to the hawk."

27. For a and b, write the plural of each noun.
(17, 22)

(a) shoe box   (b) branch

28. Diagram the simple subject and simple predicate of each
(36) clause in the following sentence:

Hummingbirds sip nectar as condors soar over the Andes.

Diagram each word of sentences 29–30.

29. An eagle's wings are huge and powerful.
(37, 49)

30. Hawks and owls give Dilly tremors.
(37, 49)

29.

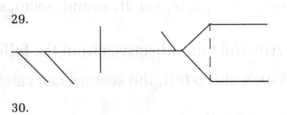

30.

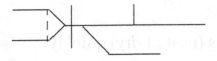

Irregular Comparison Adjectives

Dictation or Journal Entry

Vocabulary:

Optic means "of or relating to vision or the eye." The *optic* nerve carries information from the eye to the brain.

Auditory means "of or relating to the sense of hearing." The *auditory* exam showed that her hearing was perfect.

Some adjectives have irregular comparative and superlative forms. We must learn these if we haven't already.

POSITIVE	COMPARATIVE	SUPERLATIVE
little (amount, not size)	less	least
good, well	better	best
bad, ill	worse	worst
far	farther	farthest
many, much, some	more	most

Little or Few? We use *little*, *less*, and *least* with things that cannot be counted. We use *few*, *fewer*, and *fewest* with things that can be counted.

> CANNOT BE COUNTED:
> I drink *less* milk than water.

> CAN BE COUNTED:
> I eat *fewer* bananas than she does.

Much or Many? We use *much* with things that cannot be counted, and we use *many* for things that can be counted.

> CANNOT BE COUNTED:
> We do not have *much* time.

> CAN BE COUNTED:
> We have *many* things to do.

Example 1 Choose the correct adjective for each sentence.

(a) (Little, less, least) rain falls in the desert than in the forest.

(b) That tornado was the (baddest, worst) one ever.

(c) Are there (less, fewer) eagles in Arizona than in Alaska?

(d) Today, there is (less, fewer) fog over the ocean.

(e) (Many, Much) of the geese have flown away.

Solution   (a) **Less** rain falls in the desert than in the forest. (The sentence is comparing rainfall in two places, so we use the comparative form of "little.")

(b) That tornado was the **worst** one ever. ("Baddest" is not a word.)

(c) Are there **fewer** eagles in Arizona than in Alaska? ("Eagles" can be counted.)

(d) Today, there is **less** fog over the ocean. ("Fog" cannot be counted.)

(e) **Many** of the geese have flown away. ("Geese" can be counted.)

Avoid Double Comparisons   We do not use double comparisons. In other words, we do not use *more* with *er*, or *most* with *est*.

NO: The goose was *more fatter* than the gander.
YES: The goose was *fatter* than the gander.

NO: He was the *most biggest* bird on the lake.
YES: He was the *biggest* bird on the lake.

Absolute Adjectives   Some adjectives do not normally permit comparison. Adjectives that represent an ultimate condition (*square, round, maximum, equal, fatal, unique, dead*, etc.) cannot be increased by degree. (For example, a square cannot be "squarer" than another square; it is either square or it is not.) When necessary, careful writers can modify these adjectives by using words like *almost, near,* and *nearly* instead of *more/less* and *most/least*.

NO: That tree looks *deader* now.
YES: That tree looks *nearly dead* now.

Example 2   Choose the correct adjective for each sentence.
(a) Are hogs (stinkier, more stinkier) than cattle?

(b) The giraffe is the (tallest, most tallest) of all.

Solution   (a) Are hogs **stinkier** than cattle? ("More stinkier" is a double comparison. We do not use *more* with *er*.)

(b) The giraffe is the **tallest** of all. ("Most tallest" is a double comparison. We do not use *most* with *est*.)

Practice For a–f, choose the correct adjective for each sentence.

    a. (Much, Many) seabirds nest on cliffs.

    b. Seabirds find (many, much) food in the ocean.

    c. Of the two trails, this one has the (better, best) view.

    d. This rainforest has (more, most) parrots than toucans.

    e. Nan spends (few, little) time watching television.

    f. The cobra looks (more scary, more scarier) than the garter snake.

For g and h, replace each blank with *optic* or *auditory*.

    g. An _____ exam checks hearing.

    h. An _____ exam checks vision.

More Practice Choose the correct adjective for each sentence.

    1. (Little, Less) snow falls at sea level than on the mountain.

    2. Her music sounds (gooder, better) than his.

    3. That storm was the (worse, worst) in history.

    4. Of all the birds, that one has the (more, most) eggs.

    5. Our new car is (safer, more safer) than our old one.

    6. Rex has (more, most) energy than I have.

    7. Who is the (more idle, most idle) of the three?

    8. Is Tim the (younger, youngest) of the two?

Review Set 56 Choose the correct word(s) to complete sentences 1–10.

    1. The room was silent, for the noisy printer was (idol, idle,
    ₍₅₅₎ dew).

    2. Abraham Lincoln is more famous (than, then, there) I.
    ₍₅₄₎

3. Several tree (bows, boughs, paws) fell during the storm.
(53)

4. Puffy (cirrus, cumulus, zephyr) clouds have well-defined edges.
(52)

5. The zoo improved the Asian elephants' (nocturnal, habit, habitat).
(16)

6. The word *cats* is a (plural, possessive) noun.
(13)

7. The (begining, beginning) of the tale was (sader, sadder) than the ending.
(33, 34)

8. My (neice, niece) collects insects.
(35)

9. Chief is the (tall, taller, tallest) of the three horses.
(55)

10. Fido's fur is (redder, more redder) than Rex's.
(55)

11. Rewrite the following letter, using correct capitalization:
(15, 41)

dear mr. sting,

    i cannot find my classroom key.

        regretfully,
        miss ng

12. Write whether the following word group is a phrase or a clause: when you finish
(36)

13. Write each coordinating conjunction in the following sentence:
(48)

Tim and Tom were small but mighty.

14. Rewrite the following sentence, using correct capitalization:
(38)

does mr. h. r. wu speak english?

15. Write the predicate nominative in the following sentence:
(51)

Friday's lunch will be fish.

16. Write whether the following word group is a complete sentence, a sentence fragment, or a run-on sentence:
(5, 23)

Frigatebirds steal food from other birds vultures do too.

17.
(44) From the following sentence, write each prepositional phrase, circling the object of each preposition:

Are nests on cliffs safe from predators?

18.
(27,30) Use a dictionary: (a) The word *tern* is what part of speech? (b) Write its pronunciation. (c) Write its etymology.

19.
(28, 29) Rewrite the following words, circling each silent letter(s):

(a) whole   (b) sketch

20.
(47, 50) Rewrite the following sentence, adding periods as needed:

Mr Sting wrote, "There will be no school on Fri , Apr 22"

21.
(2) Write whether the following sentence is declarative, interrogative, exclamatory, or imperative:

What long legs the stilt has!

22.
(39, 40) Write the three adjectives from the following sentence:

That tall bird prefers shallow water.

23.
(9) For the following sentence, write the correct form of the verb:

The tumbler (present of *polish*) rocks.

24.
(19) For the verb *sip*, write the (a) present participle, (b) past tense, and (c) past participle.

25.
(52, 53) Write whether the circled word in the sentence below is in the nominative, possessive, or objective case:

Rex wags his (tail)

26.
(26, 47) Rewrite the following outline, adding periods and capital letters as needed:

   i seabirds
      a gulls
      b gannets
      c terns

27.
(17, 22) For a and b, write the plural of each noun.

(a) cat box   (b) handful

28. Diagram the simple subject and simple predicate of each
(36) clause in the following sentence:

Students are waiting, for Miss Ng is searching for the key.

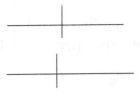

Diagram each word of sentences 29–30.

29. Miss Ng's students seem patient and kind.
(49, 54)

30. Will the principal bring Miss Ng a key for her classroom?
(45, 46)

29.

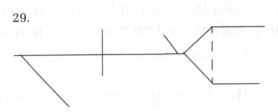

30.

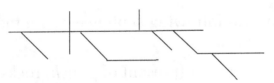

The Comma, Part 1: Dates, Addresses, and Series

Dictation or Journal Entry

Vocabulary:

The Latin root *lumen* means "light." To *illuminate* is to light up. The sun *illuminates* the sky.

Luminous is an adjective meaning bright, shining, or full of light. Fireflies are *luminous* in the darkness.

Commas are the most frequently used form of punctuation. We use commas to separate elements within sentences. Using commas correctly helps us clarify the meaning of a phrase or a sentence.

Parts of a Date We use commas to separate the **parts of a date.** When we write a complete date, we always place a comma between the day and the year.

February 22, 1732

If a complete date appears in the middle of a sentence, we place a comma after the year.

On February 22, 1732, George Washington was born.

If the day of the week appears as part of the date, we place a comma after the day.

People remember Tuesday, September 11, 2001.

Note: When just the month and the year appear in a sentence, no comma is required.

What makes July 1776 important?

Example 1 Insert commas wherever they are needed in the parts of the date in this sentence:

Ed was born on Wednesday March 23 2011 at noon.

Solution We place a comma after day of the week (Wednesday). We also place a comma after the date (March 23). Last, because the date appears in the middle of a sentence, we place a comma after the year.

Ed was born on Wednesday, March 23, 2011, at noon.

Parts of an Address We use commas to separate the **parts of an address** and the names of geographical places or political divisions.

The parts of a street address are separated by commas according to the following pattern:

house number and street, city, state and zip code

106 Race Street, Denver, Colorado 80206

243 Fox Avenue, Trenton, NJ 07719

Note: We use the state abbreviation when addressing a letter or package.

We also use commas to separate the names of geographical places or political divisions.

Sutter County, California   Sucre, Bolivia

London, England, UK   Banff, Alberta, Canada

If the city and state or country appear in the middle of the sentence, a comma is required after the state or country.

They visited Paris, France, last summer.

Example 2   Insert commas wherever they are needed in these sentences.
(a) We saw the Betsy Ross House at 239 Arch Street Philadelphia Pennsylvania.

(b) The race began in Salem Oregon at six a.m.

Solution   (a) We separate the parts of the address with commas. One comma goes after the house number and street, and another goes between the city and the state.

We saw the Betsy Ross House at 239 Arch Street, Philadelphia, Pennsylvania.

(b) We place a comma between the city and the state. We place another comma after the state because it is in the middle of a sentence.

The race began in Salem, Oregon, at six a.m.

Words in a Series We use commas to separate **three or more words or phrases in a series**.

> My cats' names are Dash, Fluffy, and Pepper.
>
> They like balls of yarn, warm food, and long naps.

Example 3 Insert commas as needed in this sentence:

> Exercise sleep and good nutrition improve our health.

Solution We separate the items in the series with commas.

> Exercise, sleep, and good nutrition improve our health.

Practice For a and b, replace each blank with *illuminate* or *luminous*.

a. In the sun, the butterfly's wings appeared _____.

b. The full moon will _____ our path at night.

Rewrite sentences c–e, inserting commas where necessary to separate parts of a date.

c. Aaron turned a year old on Wednesday April 6 2011.

d. August 2010 was hot.

e. Chinese New Year fell on Thursday February 3 2011.

Rewrite sentences f and g, inserting commas to separate parts of an address.

f. Mr. Flores moved to 121 First Lane Boise Idaho.

g. Boise Idaho was his son's birthplace.

Rewrite sentences h and i, inserting commas to separate words in a series.

h. Rex knows nothing about math grammar or history.

i. Dash chased two mice a blue jay and a squirrel.

More Practice See "More Practice Lesson 57" in the Student Workbook.

Review Set
57 Choose the correct word(s) to complete sentences 1–10.

1. The eye has a blind spot where the (optic, auditory,
(56) vertical) nerve leaves the retina.

2. Wisdom literature warns against making money one's
(55) (mane, idle, idol).

3. Diligent students will complete their homework; (than,
(54) then, there) they will play games.

4. Drama players (border, bough, bow) after a performance.
(53)

5. The nurse (knew, new, whose) how to care for the sick.
(17)

6. The word *tale* is a(n) (abstract, concrete) noun.
(11)

7. Those (flys, flies) are the (bigest, biggest) I've ever seen.
(33, 34)

8. Did you (beleive, believe) the tall tale?
(35)

9. Ed is now the (tall, taller, tallest) of the two boys.
(55)

10. She ate (fewer, less) peanuts than I.
(56)

11. Rewrite the following letter, using correct capitalization:
(15, 41)
    dear nan,
        shall we play tag after school?
                        your friend,
                        ann

12. Write whether the following word group is a phrase or a
(36) clause:
    on the butterfly's luminous wings

13. Write the indirect object in the following sentence:
(46) I gave Ann a hint.

14. Rewrite the following song title, using correct capitalization:
(25) "give a little whistle"

15. Write the predicate adjective in the following sentence:
(54) The sunrise was magnificent.

16. Write whether the following word group is a complete
^(5, 23) sentence, a sentence fragment, or a run-on sentence:

Rainforests remain a rich habitat for many animals.

17. From the following sentence, write each prepositional
⁽⁴⁴⁾ phrase, circling the object of each preposition:

A variety of insects live in the trees.

18. Use a dictionary: (a) The word *mantis* is what part of
^(27,30) speech? (b) Write its pronunciation. (c) Write its
etymology.

19. Rewrite the following words, circling silent letter(s):
^(28, 29)
(a) light   (b) gnat

20. Rewrite the following sentence, adding periods as needed:
^(47, 50)
Go to Dr Yu's office on S First Street

21. Write the word from this list that is *not* a linking verb:
⁽³¹⁾
grow, become, remove, stay

22. Write the three adjectives from the following sentence:
^(39, 40)
Some insects have sharp, pointed jaws.

23. Rewrite the following sentence, adding commas as
⁽⁵⁷⁾ needed:

Abraham Lincoln was born on February 12 1809 in
Kentucky.

24. For the verb *chop*, write the (a) present participle, (b) past
⁽¹⁹⁾ tense, and (c) past participle.

25. Write whether the circled word in the sentence below is
^(52, 53) in the nominative, possessive, or objective case:

Dash chases Rex's tail.

26. Rewrite the following sentence, adding capital letters as
⁽²⁶⁾ needed:

nora asked, "may i help you?"

27. For a and b, write the plural of each noun.
(17, 22)

    (a) baby   (b) dog dish

28. Diagram the simple subject and simple predicate of each
(36) clause in the following sentence:

    Mr. Sting brings a key, and Miss Ng thanks him.

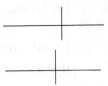

Diagram each word of sentences 29–30.

29. Dash's green eyes look large and luminous.
(49, 54)

30. Did Ann and Nan offer Miss Ng a bowl of cherries?
(45, 46)

29.

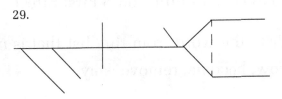

30.

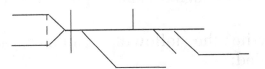

LESSON 58

Appositives

Appositives A word or group of words that immediately follows a noun to identify or give more information about the noun is called an **appositive.** In the sentences below, the appositives are italicized.

> Tim lives near Sacramento, *the capital of California.*

> Samuel de Champlain, *an explorer from France,* established Quebec in Canada.

> Ed, *my oldest cousin,* plays the violin.

> Henry Hudson, *an Englishman,* searched for the Northwest Passage.

Example 1 Identify the appositives from each sentence.
(a) We flew over Lake Superior, the largest of the Great Lakes.

(b) Julius Caesar, a Roman leader, invaded Egypt long ago.

Solution (a) The appositive ***the largest of the Great Lakes*** gives more information about the noun "Lake Superior."

(b) The appositive ***a Roman leader*** identifies the noun "Julius Caesar."

Improving Our Writing Using appositives skillfully can improve our writing. With an appositive, we can combine two choppy sentences to make one good one.

> TWO CHOPPY SENTENCES:
> Julius Caesar loved Cleopatra. Cleopatra was queen of Eqypt.

> ONE GOOD SENTENCE:
> Julius Caesar loved Cleopatra, queen of Egypt.

Example 2 Combine each pair of choppy sentences to make one longer sentence by using an appositive.

  (a) Julius Caesar was a proud conqueror. Julius Caesar died in the year 44 B.C.

  (b) Roman senators killed Julius Caesar on the Ides of March. The Ides of March was the Romans' name for March 15.

Solution (a) **Julius Caesar, a proud conqueror, died in the year 44** B.C.

  (b) **Roman senators killed Julius Caesar on the Ides of March, the Romans' name for March 15.**

Diagramming an Appositive We diagram an appositive by placing it in parentheses beside the noun it identifies or describes. If the appositive contains adjectives, we place them on slanted lines directly beneath the appositive.

Brutus, Caesar's friend, was an assassin.

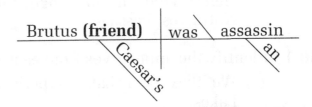

The Roman in the picture is Julius Caesar, a proud dictator.

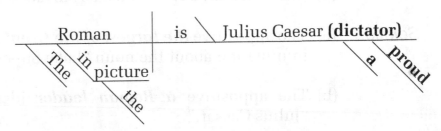

Practice For a and b, replace each blank with *illusion* or *illusory*.

  a. The movie's monster was not real; it was only an

  _____.

  b. The _____ character deceived many people.

For c and d, write the appositive from each sentence.

  c. The whale, a mammal, breathes with lungs.

  d. Ed broke a leg bone, the tibia.

e. Diagram the sentence below.

Elle, a musician, plays the flute.

For f and g, combine each pair of sentences into one sentence by using an appositive.

f. Louis played the trumpet. The trumpet is a brass instrument.

g. Louis Armstrong played the trumpet. Louis Armstrong was a famous jazz musician.

More Practice   See "Funny Fill-in #3" in the Student Workbook.

Review Set 58   Choose the correct word to complete sentences 1–10.

1. Candles (pause, paws, illuminate) a dark room.
(57)

2. Some people are (optic, auditory, main) learners. They learn by listening.
(56)

3. Max is usually busy; he is rarely (idol, idle, mane).
(55)

4. Elle likes drawing more (fur, than, then) Josh and Nate do.
(54)

5. Bats and owls are (marsupial, nocturnal, foul) birds.
(18)

6. The word *seashore* is a (compound, collective) noun.
(11, 13)

7. Nan (trys, tries) to brush Rex's (mated, matted) fur.
(33, 34)

8. I (received, recieved) a phone call.
(35)

9. Of the two rulers, Julius Caesar was the (proud, prouder, proudest).
(55)

10. Ed has (less, fewer) freckles than Ted.
(56)

11. Rewrite the following letter, using correct capitalization:
(15, 41)

dear mr. tellem,

what happened to queen cleopatra?

regards,

nan c. davis

12. Write whether the following word group is a phrase or a
(36) clause: for we received it

13. Write the seven coordinating conjunctions listed in
(48) Lesson 48.

14. Rewrite the following sentence, using correct
(38) capitalization:

did you call dr. stein, father?

15. Write the predicate nominative in the following sentence:
(51)
Dr. Stein has been a rabbi for ten years.

16. Write whether the following word group is a complete
(5, 23) sentence, a sentence fragment, or a run-on sentence:

Marc Antony, one of Julius Caesar's best friends.

17. From the following sentence, write each prepositional
(44) phrase, circling the object of each preposition:

You can visit the ruins of the Forum in Rome.

18. Use a dictionary: (a) The word *placid* is what part of
(27,30) speech? (b) Write its pronunciation. (c) Write its
etymology.

19. Write the appositive in the following sentence:
(58)
Octavian became Augustus Caesar, Rome's first emperor.

20. Rewrite the following sentence, adding periods as needed:
(47, 50)
Get off the bus at First Ave and Elm St

21. Write whether the following sentence is declarative,
(2) interrogative, imperative, or exclamatory:

Our calendar comes from the Romans.

22. Write the four adjectives from the following sentence:
(40, 42)
I wiped Polly's sticky fingers with a damp rag.

23. Rewrite the following sentence, adding commas as
(57) needed:

Mercury Mars and Pluto were Roman gods.

24. For the verb *reply*, write the (a) present participle, (b) past
(19) tense, and (c) past participle.

25. Write whether the circled word in the sentence below is
(52, 53) in the nominative, possessive, or objective case:

Polly likes toast with (honey).

26. Rewrite the following lines of poetry, adding capital
(15) letters as needed:

hey diddle diddle,
the cat and the fiddle...

27. For a and b, write the plural of each noun.
(17, 22)
(a) lady   (b) earful

28. Diagram the simple subject and simple predicate of each
(36) clause in the following sentence:

Romans ate jellyfish, but I prefer tuna.

Diagram each word of sentences 29–30.

29. Mr. Sting, the principal, appears grouchy and grim.
(54, 58)

30. Nan gave Rex two cupfuls of dry dog food.
(45, 46)

29.

30.

The Comma, Part 2: Direct Address and Academic Degrees

Dictation or Journal Entry

Vocabulary:

Mire is an area of wet, soft ground; mud. Our tires were stuck in the *mire*.

A *mirage* is an optical illusion, something that seems real but is not. The sheet of water far ahead on the road was only a *mirage*.

In this lesson, we will discuss more uses for commas.

Nouns of Direct Address

A **noun of direct address** names the person who is being spoken to (the person who is receiving the information in the sentence). The noun can be the person's name or a "name" you are using for him or her. Nouns of direct address can appear anywhere in a sentence. We offset them with commas.

Rex, come.

Where, Nan, did you find the keys?

Do not play with fire, Ed!

There may be more than one noun of direct address in a sentence. Also, like any noun, a noun of direct address can be modified by adjectives. We offset the entire noun phrase with commas, as in the sentences below.

Here are your tickets, Josh and Nate.

Speak up, my dear friend, so that we can hear you.

Example 1 Insert commas to offset the noun of direct address in the sentence below.

Fred are you cold?

Solution We insert a comma after "Fred" because he is being spoken to. Fred is a noun of direct address.

Fred, are you cold?

Example 2 Insert commas to offset the noun of direct address in the sentence below.

Fly away little ladybug to your home.

Solution We offset the entire noun phrase "little ladybug" because the ladybug is being spoken to, and "little" modifies "ladybug."

Fly away, little ladybug, to your home.

Academic Degrees When an **academic degree** or similar title follows a person's name, it is usually abbreviated. Here are some abbreviations you are likely to see:

M.D. (Doctor of Medicine)

D.D.S. (Doctor of Dental Surgery)

D.V.M. (Doctor of Veterinary Medicine)

Ph.D. (Doctor of Philosophy)

Ed.D. (Doctor of Education)

D.D. (Doctor of Divinity)

R.N. (Registered Nurse)

L.P.N. (Licensed Practical Nurse)

M.B.A. (Master of Business Administration)

We use commas to offset academic degrees or other titles that follow a person's name.

Yin Yu, C.P.A., enjoys math.

Dan's professional name is Daniel Cruz, Ph.D.

Example 3 Insert commas to offset the academic degree in this sentence.

Kim Kane D.V.M. examined Rex.

Solution Since "D.V.M." is an academic degree, it is offset with commas.

Kim Kane, D.V.M., examined Rex.

Practice Rewrite sentences a and b, using commas to offset nouns of direct address.

a. Amir have you seen Dilly?

b. Please know my dear cousin that I miss you.

Rewrite sentences c and d, using commas to offset academic degrees or other titles.

c. Katie Canz R.N. cares for heart patients.

d. Does Yang Kim D.D.S. pull teeth?

For e and f, replace each blank with *mire* or *mirage*.

    e. A _____ is an optical illusion.

    f. _____ is mud.

More Practice   See "More Practice Lesson 59" in the Student Workbook.

Review Set 59   Choose the correct word to complete sentences 1–10.

1. Making a rabbit appear in a hat is a magician's (illusory,
(58) illusion, tail).

2. Some (auditory, idol, luminous) objects glow in the
(57) dark.

3. The (auditory, optic, illusory) nerve sends visual pictures
(56) to the brain.

4. Athletes become the (idles, idols, borders) of some
(55) people.

5. (Marsupials, Spiders, Insects) often make webs.
(19)

6. The word *Henrys* is a (plural, possessive) noun.
(13)

7. Will the (winer, winner) of the contest become (fameous,
(33, 34) famous)?

8. Did you (recieve, receive) my message?
(35)

9. Spot is the (friendlier, friendliest) of the three pups.
(55)

10. Dash has caught (less, fewer) rats than Pepper.
(56)

11. Rewrite the following sentence, using correct capitalization:
(41, 43)
     on a hot day in the southwest, ed plays soccer.

12. Write whether the following word group is a phrase or a
(36) clause:
     during the hottest part of the day

13. Write the indirect object in the following sentence:
(46)
     Ed told Lucy a lie.

14. Rewrite the following poem title, using correct
(25) capitalization:

"for want of a nail"

15. Write the predicate adjective in the following sentence:
(54)

Ed feels miserable.

16. Write whether the following word group is a complete
(5, 23) sentence, a sentence fragment, or a run-on sentence:

July is named after Julius Caesar August is named after
Augustus Caesar.

17. From the following sentence, write each prepositional
(44) phrase, circling the object of each preposition:

May comes from Maia, the Roman goddess of spring.

18. Rewrite the following words, circling silent letter(s).
(28, 29)

(a) wrist   (b) stalk

19. Use an appositive to combine the following two
(58) sentences into one sentence.

March comes from Mars.

Mars is the Roman god of war.

20. Rewrite the following sentence, adding periods as needed:
(47, 50)

Meet me on Mon at ten am

21. Write the word from this list that is *not* a linking verb:
(31)

is, am, are, buzz, were, be, being, been, look, feel, taste

22. Write each adjective from the following sentence:
(39, 40)

Marc Antony married the famous Cleopatra.

23. Rewrite the following sentence, adding commas as
(57, 59) needed:

Nan please bring apples grapes and crackers.

24. For the verb *smile*, write the (a) present participle, (b)
(19) past tense, and (c) past participle.

25. Write whether the circled word in the sentence below is
(52, 53) in the nominative, possessive, or objective case:

Ed eats fried(rice) with eggs.

26. Rewrite the following sentence, adding capital letters as
(26) needed:

mr. kim said, "no, rex, you may not come to school."

27. For a and b, write the plural of each noun.
(17, 22)

(a) topic sentence   (b) olive tree

28. Diagram the simple subject and simple predicate of each
(36) clause in the following sentence:

Mr. Kim says that Rex must go.

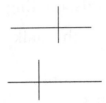

Diagram each word of sentences 29–30.

29. Miss Ng, Nan's teacher, is a writer and an illustrator.
(51, 58)

30. Miss Ng drew Nan a picture of Rex.
(45, 46)

29.

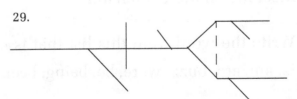

30.

LESSON 60

The Comma, Part 3: Appositives

Dictation or Journal Entry

Vocabulary:

Essential means "necessary." Your help is *essential* to our success.

The prefix *non* means "not." Therefore, *nonessential* means "not necessary." Candy is a *nonessential* part of our diet.

In this lesson, we will discuss another use for commas.

Appositives

An **appositive** is a word or group of words that immediately follows a noun to identify or give more information about the noun. In the sentence below, "a wicked emperor" is an appositive. Notice how commas offset it from the rest of the sentence.

> Nero, a wicked emperor, killed many people.

In the sentence below, "Nero" is also an appositive. But it is not offset by a comma. Why?

> The emperor Nero saw Rome burning.

Essential and Nonessential Appositives

Whether or not an appositive is offset with commas depends on how essential it is to the meaning of the sentence.

Let's look at the first sentence above. If we remove the appositive, the sentence still makes sense:

> Nero killed many people.

The name "Nero" has already identified the person the sentence is about. The appositive "a wicked emperor" is informative but **nonessential** to the meaning of the sentence. **Nonessential appositives are offset with commas.**

Now let's remove the appositive from the second sentence:

> The emperor saw Rome burning.

The emperor? Which emperor? The appositive "Nero" is **essential** to the meaning of the sentence. **Essential appositives are not offset by commas.**

Example Insert commas to offset the nonessential appositive in the sentence below.

Pliny a Roman author wrote about a huge volcano.

Solution We see that "a Roman author" is a nonessential appositive, so we offset it with commas:

Pliny, a Roman author, wrote about a huge volcano.

Practice Rewrite sentences a–c, using commas to offset nonessential appositives.

a. Cupid a little boy with wings was a Roman god.

b. Mount Vesuvius a volcano erupted near the town of Pompeii.

c. Dr. Adam the head physician has the flu.

For d and e, replace each blank with *essential* or *nonessential*.

d. Comic books are fun, but they are _____ for my education.

e. Food, water, and shelter are _____ for people.

More Practice See "More Practice Lesson 60" in the Student Workbook.

Review Set 60 Choose the correct word to complete sentences 1–10.

1. The adventurous cousins sank deep in the swampy
(59) (bough, mirage, mire).

2. The (illusory, illusion, luminous) label did not give the
(58) true contents of the package.

3. Fireflies (illuminate, luminous, illusory) the summer
(57) night.

4. A dalmation with hearing loss might not react to
(56) (auditory, optic, heard) stimuli.

5. When sailors were (sufficient, deficient, mourning) in
(21) vitamin C, they suffered from scurvy.

6. The word *education* is a(n) (abstract, concrete) noun.
(11)

7. Rex (trys, tries) to find the (bigest, biggest) bone.
(33, 34)

8. My (friend, freind) has lost (wieght, weight).
(35)

9. Of the two classes, this one is the (quieter, quietest).
(55)

10. There are not (much, many) rats in the house.
(56)

11. Rewrite the following letter, using correct capitalization:
(41, 43)

dear cousin kate,

please meet me at paco's cafeteria on tuesday.
love,
lulu

12. Write whether the following word group is a phrase or a
(36) clause: as you know

13. Write each coordinating conjunction that you find in the
(48) following sentence:

I must do my homework now or later, so I might as well do it now.

14. Rewrite the following sentence, using correct
(38) capitalization:

why, dr. green, must i learn latin?

15. Write the predicate nominative in the following sentence:
(51)

Kerry has been a drummer for many years.

16. Write whether the following word group is a complete
(5, 23) sentence, a sentence fragment, or a run-on sentence:

We can visit the ancient city of Pompeii.

17. From the following sentence, write each prepositional
(44) phrase, circling the object of each preposition:

Rex ran out the gate and down the street.

18. Use a dictionary: (a) The word *plebs* is what part of
(27,30) speech? (b) Write its pronunciation. (c) Write its etymology.

19. Rewrite the following sentence, using commas to offset
(60) the nonessential appositive:

My mother Mrs. Cozak makes good soup.

20. Rewrite the following sentence, adding periods as needed:
(47, 50)
Have Mr and Mrs Hahn climbed Mt Everest?

21. Write whether the following sentence is declarative,
(2) interrogative, imperative, or exclamatory:

Please listen carefully.

22. Write each adjective from the following sentence:
(39, 40)
The poor Romans did hard work.

23. Rewrite the following sentence, adding commas as
(57, 59) needed:

I spoke with Maribel Galindo Ph.D. on June 2 2012.

24. For the verb *hurry*, write the (a) present participle, (b)
(19) past tense, and (c) past participle.

25. Write whether the circled word in the sentence below is
(52, 53) in the nominative, possessive, or objective case:

Rex is a friendly (dog)

26. Rewrite the following outline, adding periods and capital
(26, 47) letters as needed:

i leg bones
    a tibia
    b fibula
    c femur

27. For a and b, write the plural of each noun.
(17, 22)
    (a) journal entry   (b) arm muscle

28. Diagram the simple subject and simple predicate of each
(36) clause in the following sentence:

Fish are cold-blooded, but birds are warm-blooded.

Diagram each word of sentences 29–30.

29. Nero, a Roman emperor, was cruel and murderous.
(54, 58)

30. My sister sang me a song about a weasel.
(45, 46)

29.

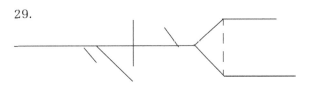

30.

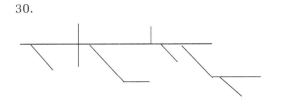

LESSON 61

The Progressive Verb Forms

> **Dictation or Journal Entry**
> **Vocabulary:**
> *Sent* is the past tense and past participle of *send*. Yesterday, she *sent* her package. I had *sent* mine the day before.
>
> A *cent* is a penny; a U.S. coin equal to one hundredth of a dollar. I would not pay one *cent* for that boring movie.

We have learned three main verb tenses:

    1. present   walk(s)

    2. past   walked

    3. future   will/shall walk

All three of these main verb tenses also have a **progressive form.** A progressive verb phrase shows action in "progress," or continuing action.

    Present progressive   = action still in progress
                               at the time of speaking

    Past progressive   = action in progress through
                               a specific time in the past

    Future progressive   = action that will be in
                               progress in the future

Progressive verb forms are expressed with some form of the verb *to be* and the present participle ("ing" added to the main verb).

Present Progressive The present progressive form consists of the appropriate present tense of *to be* (am/is/are) plus the present participle (verb + *ing*).

PRESENT PROGRESSIVE = <u>IS</u> OR <u>AM</u> OR <u>ARE</u> + <u>PRESENT PARTICIPLE</u>

Ed <u>is walking</u> to the park.

Rex and Ted <u>are going</u> with him.

I <u>am baking</u> a pie.

Past Progressive The past progressive form consists of a past form of *to be* (was/were) plus the present participle.

> PAST PROGRESSIVE = <u>WAS</u> OR <u>WERE</u> + <u>PRESENT PARTICIPLE</u>
>
> The mouse <u>was nibbling</u> at the cheese.
>
> Squirrels <u>were dropping</u> acorns.

Future Progressive We form the future progressive by adding the present participle to the future of the *to be* verb (shall be/will be).

> FUTURE PROGRESSIVE = <u>SHALL BE</u> OR <u>WILL BE</u> + <u>PRESENT PARTICIPLE</u>
>
> My family <u>will be going</u> to the desert on Friday.
>
> I <u>shall be celebrating</u> my ninth birthday this year.

Example 1 For sentences a–c, tell whether the progressive verb form is present, past, or future tense.

(a) The women <u>were chatting</u> on the phone.

(b) Soon, you <u>will be diagramming</u> long sentences.

(c) Molly <u>is dreaming</u> about vacation.

Solution (a) We notice that "were" is the past tense form of *to be*, so we know that "were chatting" is the **past progressive**.

(b) "Will be" is the future form of *to be*, so the verb phrase is **future progressive**.

(c) "Is" is a present form of *to be*, so the verb phrase is **present progressive**.

Example 2 Complete each sentence, using the progressive form of the italicized verb.

(a) Elle (past progressive of *listen*) carefully.

(b) Soon, the infant (future progressive of *walk*).

(c) The farmer (present progressive of *pray*) for rain.

Solution (a) Elle **was listening** carefully.

(b) Soon, the infant **will be walking**.

(c) The farmer **is praying** for rain.

Practice For sentences a–c, write whether the verb is present progressive, past progressive, or future progressive.

a. Nan <u>is telling</u> Pam a story.

b. This weekend, I <u>will be sailing</u>.

c. The cat <u>was licking</u> her kitten.

Complete sentences d–f using the progressive form of the italicized verb.

d. Rex (present progressive of *bark*).

e. Nan (past progressive of *brush*) Rex.

f. This Saturday, Dad (future progressive of *work*).

For g and h, replace each blank with *sent* or *cent*.

g. A _____ is a coin.

h. I _____ thank-you notes for the gifts.

Review Set 61 Choose the correct word to complete sentences 1–10.

1. Unnecessary words are (essential, nonessential, illusory).
(60)

2. The (mirage, mire, illuminate) looked like water to the
(59) thirsty traveler.

3. Police could not find the (illusion, illuminous, illusory)
(58) thief.

4. The night sky sparkled with (luminous, illuminate,
(57) illusion) stars.

5. The story of Pecos Bill is a tall (tail, tale, mane) of the Old
(6) West.

6. The word *team* is a (compound, collective) noun.
(11)

7. Speak (gentlely, gently), please.
(33, 34)

8. The Puritans would not give up (thier, their) strong
(35) (beleifs, beliefs).

9. Of the three boys, Bala is the (quieter, quietest).
(55)

10. Rex has (less, fewer) fleas than Spot.
(56)

11. Rewrite the following sentence, using correct
(41, 43) capitalization:

do oak trees grow in the south?

12. Write whether the following word group is a phrase or a
(36) clause:

after the fall of Rome

13. Write the indirect object in the following sentence:
(46)

Did God give Moses ten commandments?

14. Rewrite the following title, using correct capitalization:
(25)

the wind in the willows

15. Write the predicate adjectives in the following sentence:
(54)

The story is clever and funny.

16. Complete the following sentence, using the correct verb
(61) tense.

Mole (past progressive of *working*) hard all morning.

17. From the following sentence, write each prepositional
(44) phrase, circling the object of each preposition:

Mole sat on the bank of the river.

18. Rewrite the following words, circling silent letter(s):
(28, 29)(a) scent   (b) though

19. Use an appositive to combine the following two
(58) sentences into one sentence.

Water Rat is Mole's neighbor.

Water Rat enjoys rowing on the river.

20. Rewrite the following sentence, adding periods as needed:
(47, 50)Mr C A Bird rises at six am

21. Write the word from this list that is *not* a linking verb:
⁽³¹⁾

is, am, car, was, were, be, being, been

22. Write each adjective from the following sentence:
^(39, 40)

A gentle current sent golden leaves downstream.

23. Rewrite the following sentence, adding commas as
^(57, 59) needed:

Nan you may interview Ivan Rivas D.D. on Friday January 6.

24. For the verb *tag*, write the (a) present participle, (b) past
⁽¹⁹⁾ tense, and (c) past participle.

25. Write whether the circled word in the sentence below is
^(52, 53) in the nominative, possessive, or objective case:

Rex digs ⟨holes⟩.

26. Rewrite the following sentence, adding capital letters as
⁽²⁶⁾ needed:

miss ng asked, "have you seen my pen?"

27. For a and b, write the plural of each noun.
^(17, 22)

(a) wrench   (b) dishful

28. Diagram the simple subject and simple predicate of each
⁽³⁶⁾ clause in the following sentence:

As Mole rows the boat, he falls into the river.

Diagram each word of sentences 29–30.

29. Mole, a silly fool, looks sorry and wet.
^(54, 58)

30. Rat offers Mole his friendship.
^(37, 46)

29.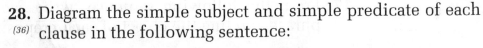

30.
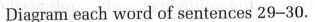

Pronouns and Antecedents

Dictation or Journal Entry

Vocabulary:

Claws are sharp nails, usually curved, on the feet of birds or other animals. The cat scratched my arm with its *claws*.

A *clause* is a word group containing a subject and a predicate. We learned the difference between a phrase and a *clause*.

Pronouns A **pronoun** is a word that takes the place of a noun or a noun phrase. Rather than using the same noun over and over again, we use pronouns.

Without pronouns, our language would be quite tiresome:

> Annabelle Elizabeth was using Annabelle Elizabeth's uncle's tools to put a new tire on Annabelle Elizabeth's old bicycle. Annabelle Elizabeth thought that Annabelle Elizabeth could do the job by Annabelle Elizabeth's self, so Annabelle Elizabeth did not ask Annabelle Elizabeth's uncle for help. Soon, Annabelle Elizabeth's bicycle was in many pieces, and Annabelle Elizabeth was ready to lose Annabelle Elizabeth's temper.

Pronouns (italicized) simplify the passage:

> Annabelle Elizabeth was using *her* uncle's tools to put a new tire on *her* old bicycle. *She* thought that *she* could do the job by *her*self, so *she* did not ask *her* uncle for help. Soon, *her* bicycle was in many pieces, and *she* was ready to lose *her* temper.

Pronouns are the words (such as *he, she, it, we, they*) that we use to refer to people, places, and things that have already been mentioned. Pronouns are italicized in the examples below.

> Nan read the note, and then *she* passed *it* to Ed.

In the sentence above, the pronoun *she* replaces "Nan," and the pronoun *it* replaces "note."

Antecedents The noun or noun phrase to which the pronoun refers is called the **antecedent.** The prefix *ante* means "before," and the root *ced* means "go." The antecedent usually "goes before" the pronoun. In the example above, "Nan" and "note" are antecedents for the pronouns *she* and *it*.

Notice the antecedents for the pronouns *him* and *it* in this sentence:

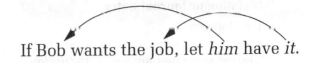

If Bob wants the job, let *him* have *it*.

The antecedent of the pronoun *him* is "Bob," and the antecedent of the pronoun *it* is "job."

Often, we find an antecedent in an earlier sentence:

> Yesterday, Ed (antecedent) made tacos (antecedent).
> *He* served *them* for dinner.

Sometimes, the antecedent comes after the pronoun:

> Although *she* likes tacos,
> Nan (antecedent) was not hungry.

An antecedent might be another pronoun:

> *They* (antecedent) washed *their* dishes.

A pronoun can also have more than one antecedent:

> After Nan (antecedent) and Ed (antecedent) washed the dishes, *they* cleaned the kitchen.

Likewise, a noun can serve as the antecedent for more than one pronoun.

> Julius Caesar (antecedent) was surprised when *he* saw *his* old friend Brutus.

Example 1 Write the antecedent for each italicized pronoun in a–d. (Example: *his*/Dan)

(a) Dan scratches *his* head as *he* thinks.

(b) Although *she* was tired, Nan kept working.

(c) Pam fed the horse. *She* also brushed *it*.

(d) It took them three hours to do *their* homework.

Solution (a) *his*/**Dan**, *he*/**Dan**

(b) *she*/**Nan**

(c) *She*/**Pam**, *it*/**horse**

(d) *their*/them

Each pronoun needs a clear antecedent. The meaning of the sentence below is unclear because the antecedent is unclear:

The teacher thinks *she* talks too much.
Who talks too much?
What is the antecedent of *she*?

The following sentences are unclear because they each contain a pronoun that has more than one possible antecedent:

Luz and Leah planted *her* garden.
Whose garden?
Luz's? Leah's?

Ed left Dan with *his* bicycle.
Which is the antecedent of *his*?
Is it Ed, or is it Dan?

Rose picked up Daisy when *she* was finished.
Does *she* refer to Rose or to Daisy?

To make our meaning clear, we can use nouns instead of pronouns, we can rearrange a few words, or we can rewrite the whole sentence:

Luz and Leah planted Luz's garden.

Ed left his bicycle with Dan.

When Rose was finished, she picked up Daisy.

Example 2 Write the clearer sentence of each pair.
(a) She hurried home.

Nan hurried home.

(b) Luz played tag with Leah and lost her shoe.

Luz lost her shoe while playing tag with Leah.

Solution (a) We choose the second sentence because it clearly tells *who* hurried home.

Nan hurried home.

(b) We choose the second sentence because it clearly tells *whose* shoe was lost.

Luz lost her shoe while playing tag with Leah.

Practice For a–d, write the antecedent for each italicized pronoun.
a. Rose left class early, but *she* returned the next day.

b. Ted helps as much as *he* can.

c. Nan and Ed wore muddy boots to my house, but *they* left *them* outside.

d. Although the car is old, *it* still runs fine.

For e and f, write the clearer sentence of each pair.

e. While Rose and Daisy were waiting, she read a story.

While Rose and Daisy were waiting, Rose read a story.

f. It crackled and popped.

The fire crackled and popped.

For g and h, replace each blank with *clause* or *claws*.

g. We know the difference between a phrase and a
_____.

h. Cats have sharp _____.

Review Set 62

Choose the correct word(s) to complete sentences 1–10.

1. The clerk (cent, sent, road) a letter to the judge.
(61)

2. A nutritious diet is (nonessential, essential, illuminous)
(60) to good health.

3. A magician's tricks are merely (auditory, luminous,
(58) illusions).

4. I was stuck, for my tires sank deeper in the (mirage, mire,
(59) optic).

5. We need (sufficient, deficient, illusory) sunlight for
(21) healthy bones.

6. The word *bear's* is a (plural, possessive) noun.
(13)

7. Rex acts (happyest, happiest) when Nan is (smiling,
(33, 34) smileing).

8. Leah was (relieved, releived) when her (nieghbor,
(35) neighbor) caught the snake.

9. Dilly is the (smarter, smartest) of the two frogs.
(55)

10. Dilly is the (smartest, most smartest) frog of all.
(55)

11. Rewrite the following letter, using correct capitalization:
(38, 41)

dear mrs. trapper,

thank you for catching that snake on monday.

gratefully,
leah

12. Write the antecedent of the circled pronoun in the
(62) following sentence:

Miss Ng had a new key, but she lost(it)somewhere.

13. Write the coordinating conjunction that you find in the
(48) following sentence:

Jill and her sister live in a tent.

14. Rewrite the following sentence, using correct
(38) capitalization:

may i feed this stray cat, mother?

15. Write the predicate nominative in the following sentence:
(51)

Is Pat a nurse?

16. Complete the following sentence, using the correct verb
(61) tense:

Mole (present progressive of *working*) hard.

17. From the following sentence, write each prepositional
(44) phrase, circling the object of each preposition:

During the day, Dilly hides under a rock.

18. Use a dictionary: (a) The word *blithe* is what part of
(27, 30) speech? (b) Write its pronunciation. (c) Write its
etymology.

19. Rewrite the sentence below, using commas to offset the
(60) nonessential appositive.

Jill's only sister Lucy collects stamps.

20. Rewrite the following sentence, adding periods as needed:
(47, 50) Mr Wong moved to N Oak Dr in Dallas

21. Write whether the following sentence is declarative,
(2) interrogative, imperative, or exclamatory:

Stay on the trail.

22. Write each adjective from the following sentence:
(39, 40)
The Romans ate many unusual foods.

23. Rewrite the following sentence, adding commas as
(57, 59) needed:

Mother have you ever been in Rome Italy?

24. For the verb *dance*, write the (a) present participle, (b)
(19) past tense, and (c) past participle.

25. Write whether the circled word in the sentence below is
(52, 53) in the nominative, possessive, or objective case:

(Rex's) tail whips back and forth.

26. Rewrite the following lines of poetry, adding capital
(15) letters as needed:

for want of a nail, the shoe was lost,
for want of a shoe, the horse was lost, ...

27. For a and b, write the plural of each noun.
(17, 22) (a) goddess   (b) Roman god

28. Diagram the simple subject and simple predicate of each
(36) clause in the following sentence:

The Romans ate jellyfish, but I prefer pasta.

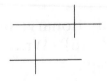

Diagram each word of sentences 29–30.

29. The remains of the Colosseum appear old but magnificent.
(45, 54)

30. The Colosseum, a Roman amphitheater, held many
(37, 58) spectators.

29.

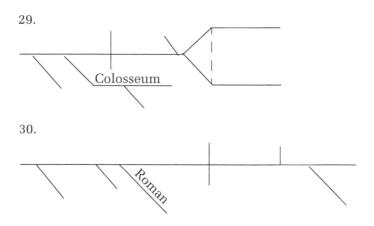

30.

LESSON 63

The Comma, Part 4: Greetings and Closings and Last Name First

> **Dictation or Journal Entry**
>
> **Vocabulary:**
> A *proboscis* is an elephant's trunk; a long, flexible snout; or the long tubular mouth part of such insects as mosquitoes and butterflies. A butterfly drinks through its *proboscis.*
>
> A *mandible* is the lower jaw bone in a vertebrate; part of an insect's mouth. Bugs use their *mandibles* for biting and chewing.

In this lesson, we will learn more uses for commas.

Greeting We use a comma after the **greeting** of a friendly letter.

Dear Roy,

My faithful friend,

Closing We use a comma after the **closing** of a letter.

Sincerely yours,

Gratefully,

Example 1 Place commas where they are needed in the letter below.

Dear Ed

Thank you for the circus tickets.

Love

Nan

Solution We place commas after the greeting and closing of the letter.

Dear Ed,

Thank you for the circus tickets.

Love,

Nan

Last Name First When we alphabetize a list of names, we usually alphabetize by the person's last name. We place the last name first and the first name (followed by middle names, if any) last. They are separated by a comma, as shown:

Baba, Ali

Díaz, Maria

McCoy, Lee R.

Sayat, Edna

Vanhook, Paul

Other than in lists, we do not often write names this way. When we do, we are usually referring to or "quoting from" a list. Quotation marks are a good way of indicating this:

The last name on the class list was "Zwissler, Bruce."

"Watts, Isaac" completed the list of famous American poets.

I am listed as "Wang, Lisa T." in the phone book.

Example 2 Insert a comma where it is needed in the sentence below.

"Abas Sam" was the first name on the class list.

Solution We use a comma in inverted names.

"Abas, Sam" was the first name on the class list.

Practice Rewrite a and b, inserting commas as needed.

a. Dear Pete

Thank you for the guest list. I see that the first name is "Abrams Don."

Gratefully
Gina

b. The index lists "Carroll Lewis" as the author of "The Crocodile."

For c and d, replace each blank with *proboscis* or *mandible*.

c. A _____ is used for biting and chewing.

d. A _____ is a long, flexible snout.

Review Set 63 Choose the correct word(s) to complete sentences 1–10.

1. The bear's sharp (clause, claws, tale) dug deep into the
(62) tree's bark.

2. A penny is one (cent, sent, clause).
(61)

3. We need (nonessential, essential, illuminous) vitamins.
(60)

4. A (cent, mire, mirage) seems real but is not.
(59)

5. Carrots are a (route, root, claws) vegetable.
(22)

6. The word *joy* is a(n) (abstract, concrete) noun.
(11)

7. Almost (dayly, daily), Mr. Lee tells (funy, funny) jokes.
(33, 34)

8. Did you (recieve, receive) a call from the fire (chief, cheif)?
(35)

9. Of the twins, Bing has the (darker, darkest) eyes.
(55)

10. Bing's eyes are the (darkest, most darkest) in the whole family.
(56)

11. Rewrite the following letter, adding commas and capital letters as needed:
(41, 63)

dear mrs. haji

thank you for saving rex from the coyote last tuesday.

gratefully

nan

12. Write whether the following word group is a phrase or a clause:
(36)

for a glass of cold water with ice

13. Write the indirect object in the following sentence:
(46)

Nan sends Mrs. Haji a card.

14. Rewrite the following title, using correct capitalization:
(25)

"ali baba and the forty thieves"

15. Write the predicate adjectives in the following sentence:
(54)

Cassim was rich but jealous.

16. Complete the following sentence, using the correct verb tense.
(61)

The thieves (past progressive of *search*) for Ali Baba.

17. From the following sentence, write each prepositional phrase, circling the object of each preposition:
(44)

I have been looking for Dilly since Monday.

18. Use a dictionary: (a) The word *proboscis* is what part of
(27, 30) speech? (b) Write its pronunciation. (c) Write its
etymology.

19. Use an appositive to combine the following two
(58) sentences into one sentence.

Willy is my youngest cousin.

Willy pulls Rex's tail.

20. Rewrite the following sentence, adding periods as needed:
(47, 50) The catnip will cost $250 (two dollars and fifty cents)

21. Write the linking verb from the following sentence:
(31) Cassim is a thief.

22. Write each adjective from the following sentence:
(40, 42) Julia wore a long blue toga.

23. Rewrite the following sentence, adding commas as
(57, 59) needed:

Nan we have class on Wednesday Thursday and Friday.

24. For the verb *wag*, write the (a) present participle, (b) past
(19) tense, and (c) past participle.

25. Write whether the circled word in the sentence below is
(52, 53) in the nominative, possessive, or objective case:

Rex's ⟨tail⟩ wagged back and forth.

26. Rewrite the following sentence, adding capital letters as
(26) needed:

alex asked, "who spilled the honey?"

27. For a and b, write the plural of each noun.
(17, 22)
(a) sea slug   (b) thief

28. Diagram the simple subject and simple predicate of each
(36) clause in the following sentence:

Roy made fewer errors on today's test than he did on the
last test, for he has been studying.

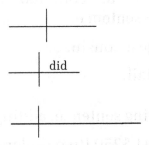

Diagram each word of sentences 29–30.

29. Was Friday's dictation long and difficult?
(40, 54)

30. Aladdin, the son of a tailor, shows his mother some
(46, 58) precious jewels.

29.

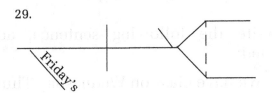

30.

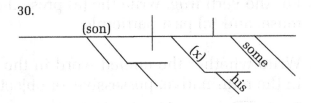

Personal Pronouns

> **Dictation or Journal Entry**
> **Vocabulary:**
> The Latin root *ped-* or *pedi-* means "foot" or "feet."
> A *biped* is a two-footed animal. Some dinosaurs were *bipeds*.
>
> *Pinnipeds* are fin-footed animals, which means they have flippers. Seals and walruses are *pinnipeds*.

There are five main categories of pronouns: personal, relative, indefinite, interrogative, and demonstrative. We will begin with personal pronouns.

Just like nouns, **personal pronouns** refer to people and things (and also places, if you think of a place as an "it"). In the following sentences, the personal pronouns are italicized.

She will help *us*.

Do *you* have *my* pen?

They say *we* must not eat *it*.

It makes a good bear habitat.

There are three forms of personal pronouns: person, number, and case.

Person   *First person* is the speaker: *I, me, mine, we, us, ours.*

I try hard.

We shall succeed.

That error was *mine*.

Second person is the person being spoken to: *you, yours.*

Will *you* come also?

All of *you* are invited.

That seat is *yours*.

Third person is the person being spoken about: *he, she, it, him, her, his, hers.*

He and *she* left.

They left also.

That hat is *his*.

Send *it* to *her*.

Example 1 For each sentence below, write the pronoun and tell whether it is first person, second person, or third person.

(a) We studied pinnipeds.

(b) Dan pitched him the ball.

(c) Did you read the article?

Solution (a) *We* is **first person.** It indicates the speaker.

(b) *Him* is **third person,** the person being spoken about.

(c) *You* is **second person,** the person being spoken to.

Number Some personal pronouns are singular:

> *I, me, mine, you, yours, he, him, his, she, her, hers, it*

Others are plural:

> *we, us, ours, you, yours, they, them, theirs*

Notice that *you* and *yours* appear in both lists. These words can be either singular or plural. In fact, we cannot always tell which the writer means.

Example 2 For a–d, write each personal pronoun and tell whether it is singular or plural.

(a) *They* ran.

(b) That is *mine*.

(c) Meg has *hers*.

(d) *You* are kind.

Solution (a) *They* is **plural.**

(b) *Mine* is **singular.**

(c) *Hers* is **singular.**

(d) *You* might be **singular** or **plural.** We cannot tell.

Case Like nouns, pronouns appear in **cases.** We remember that case shows how a noun or pronoun is used in a sentence.

Some pronouns are used as *subjects*:

> *He* eats snails. *She* wants one too. *I* do not. Do *they* save the shells?

Others are used as *objects*:

> Nan eats *them* also. (direct object)

Ed gave *her* the last one. (indirect object)

Roy is waiting for *us*. (object of a preposition)

Some pronouns show *possession*:

Is this *yours?*

Roy lost *his.*

I hid *mine.*

Theirs are rotten.

Example 3 Tell whether each circled pronoun shows possession or whether it is used as a subject or an object. If it is an object, tell what kind (direct object, indirect object, object of a preposition).

(a) Nan sent (him) a postcard.

(b) (She) pressed the gas pedal.

(c) Ed believes (her.)

(d) This is (yours).

Solution (a) The pronoun *him* is an **indirect object.**

(b) The pronoun *She* is the **subject** of the sentence.

(c) The pronoun *her* is a **direct object.**

(d) The pronoun *yours* shows **possession.**

Practice For a and b, replace the blank with *biped* or *pinniped*.

a. A _____ has flippers.

b. A _____ has two feet.

For sentences c–e, write the personal pronoun and tell whether it is first, second, or third person.

c. Dan agrees with me.

d. He agrees with Dan.

e. Do you agree with Dan?

For f and g, write the personal pronoun and tell whether it is singular or plural.

    f. Please help us.   **g.** Look at me.

For h–k, tell whether the circled personal pronoun is used as a subject, direct object, indirect object, object of a preposition, or whether it shows possession.

    h. (I) woke at dawn.

    i. Rex greets (her) with a woof.

    j. Miss Ng hands (us) our tests.

    k. This bus is (ours).

More Practice

For sentences 1–5, write each personal pronoun and write whether it is first, second, or third person. Also write whether it is singular or plural. (Example: 1. we, first person plural; you, second person singular)

    1. May we help you?

    2. Are they bipeds?

    3. Please pour him some milk.

    4. They removed their hats.

    5. Have you seen my keys?

For sentences 6–10, write each personal pronoun and label it "subject," "object," or "possessive."

    6. The snake beside her hissed.

    7. We took our frogs to the stream and freed them.

    8. I gave them my name.

    9. They understand me.

    10. She came with us.

Review Set 64

Choose the correct word(s) to complete sentences 1–10.

    1. The elephant's (pinniped, mandible, proboscis) reached
    ⁽⁶³⁾ for a peanut on the ground.

2. Cats use their (clause, claws, proboscis) for climbing.
(62)

3. I (cent, sent) my brother a package.
(61)

4. We do not need (essential, nonessential, illuminous) things.
(60)

5. The map showed two (mandibles, roots, routes) to the beach.
(22)

6. The word *landlord* is a (compound, collective) noun.
(11, 13)

7. We (moped, mopped) the deck and (dryed, dried) it with rags.
(33, 34)

8. My (freind, friend) Pat plays center (feild, field).
(35)

9. They don't have (much, many) points yet.
(56)

10. The pronoun *I* is (first, second, third) person (singular, plural).
(64)

11. Rewrite the following letter, adding commas and capital letters as needed:
(57, 63)

dear nan

please keep rex out of my fish pond flower bed and chicken coop.

sincerely
mrs. haji

12. Write the antecedent of the circled pronoun in the following sentence:
(62)

Miss Ling bought cereal, but (she) forgot the milk.

13. Write each coordinating conjunction that you find in the following sentence:
(48)

I shall plant lettuce or spinach here.

14. Rewrite the following sentence, using correct capitalization:
(38)

my uncle, dr. ivan cruz, studied latin.

15. Write the predicate nominative in the following sentence:
(51)

The first day of spring is tomorrow.

16. Write whether the following word group is a complete
(5, 23) sentence, a run-on sentence, or a sentence fragment:

Fierce warriors from the North.

17. From the following sentence, write each prepositional
(44) phrase, circling the object of each preposition:

Rex stays in the kitchen beside Nan.

18. Rewrite the word *ridge*, circling the silent letter.
(28, 29)

19. Rewrite the sentence below, using commas to offset the
(60) nonessential appositive.

A Viking discovered Greenland a land of ice and snow.

20. Rewrite the following sentence, adding periods as needed:
(47, 50)
Dr Luz said this: Go west to Main St and turn left

21. Write whether the following sentence is declarative,
(2) interrogative, imperative, or exclamatory:

Eric the Red sailed past Iceland.

22. Write whether the following word group is a phrase or a
(36) clause:

when Vikings ruled the seas

23. Rewrite the following sentence, adding commas as
(57, 59) needed:

Bob shall we fly to Denver Colorado?

24. For the verb *apply*, write the (a) present participle, (b)
(19) past tense, and (c) past participle.

25. Write whether the circled pronoun in the sentence below
(64) is used as a subject or an object:

Rex barks at me.

26. Rewrite the following outline, adding periods and capital
(26, 47) letters as needed:

    i new teachers

      a mrs curtis

      b mr yu

27. For a and b, write the plural of each noun.
(17, 22)

    (a) Viking ship   (b) wolf

28. Diagram the simple subject and simple predicate of each
(36) clause in the following sentence:

Meg made fewer errors on today's test than she did before
because she has been working hard.

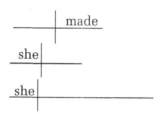

Diagram each word of sentences 29–30.

29. Did Nero become a kind ruler or a cruel tyrant?
(49, 51)

30. Mr. Yu, a new teacher, showed us a statue of Leif Ericson.
(46, 58)

29.

30.

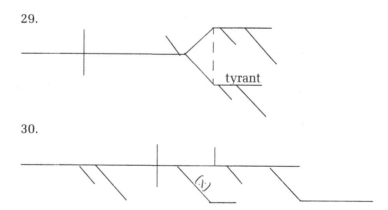

Irregular Verbs, Part 2

We form the past tense of regular verbs by adding *d* or *ed* to the present tense of the verb. We form the past tense of irregular verbs in different ways. There are no rules for forming the past tense and past participles of these verbs. Fortunately, we recognize the principal parts of most irregular verbs just by hearing them. We must memorize the irregular verb parts that we do not know already.

Irregular verbs cause people trouble because it is easy to confuse the past tense and past participle.

He has gone (NOT *went*) to school.

Class began (NOT *begun*) on time.

We can group many irregular verbs because they follow similar patterns. Here we list four groups of irregular verbs:

	Verb	Past Tense	Past Participle
1.	blow	blew	(has) blown
	know	knew	(has) known
	throw	threw	(has) thrown
	grow	grew	(has) grown
2.	bear	bore	(has) born
	tear	tore	(has) torn
	wear	wore	(has) worn
	swear	swore	(has) sworn
3.	begin	began	(has) begun
	ring	rang	(has) rung
	shrink	shrank	(has) shrunk

sing	sang	(has) sung
drink	drank	(has) drunk

4. choose	chose	(has) chosen
freeze	froze	(has) frozen
speak	spoke	(has) spoken
break	broke	(has) broken
steal	stole	(has) stolen

Remember, there are many more irregular verbs. Some of them follow the patterns above, but others do not. Always consult the dictionary if you are unsure.

Example Write the correct verb form for sentences a–d.

(a) The lake has (froze, frozen) solid already.

(b) Amelia (threw, thrown) a snowball at Andrew.

(c) My sweater (shrank, shrunk) in the dryer.

(d) Ed has (grew, grown) an inch taller this month.

Solution (a) The lake has **frozen** solid already.

(b) Amelia **threw** a snowball at Andrew.

(c) My sweater **shrank** in the dryer.

(d) Ed has **grown** an inch taller this month.

Practice For a and b, replace each blank with *weak* or *week*.

a. She wants to spend a _____ at the beach.

b. He needs help, for he feels _____.

For c–j, write the correct verb form for each sentence.

c. Roy (blew, blown) out all the candles.

d. Amy has (wore, worn) out her socks.

e. Abe (sang, sung) an old hymn.

f. Have you (spoke, spoken) to Meg?

g. Miss Ng (tore, torn) the paper airplane.

h. Pat has (knew, known) Sam since preschool.

i. A crow (stole, stolen) a nut from a squirrel.

j. Have you (rang, rung) the bell yet?

For k–v, write the past tense and past participle of each verb.

k. grow   **l.** bear   **m.** ring   **n.** sink

o. sing   **p.** drink   **q.** choose   **r.** break

s. wear   **t.** know   **u.** blow   **v.** begin

Review Set 65   Choose the correct word(s) to complete sentences 1–10.

1. Birds are (pinnipeds, week, bipeds).
(64)

2. A tapir's elongated nose is called a (proboscis, clause, mandible).
(63)

3. Dogs use (proboscis, claws, clause) to dig holes.
(62)

4. The nurse (mire, cent, sent) the ill child home.
(61)

5. Listen to the (wail, whale, morning) of the lost cat.
(27)

6. The word *fillies* is a (plural, possessive) noun.
(13)

7. In the (begining, beginning), I was (worryed, worried).
(33, 34)

8. You have (achieved, acheived) much.
(35)

9. Kate is the (better, best) of the two swimmers.
(56)

10. The pronoun *we* is (first, second, third) person (singular, plural).
(64)

11. Rewrite the following letter, adding commas and capital
(41, 63) letters as needed:

dear uncle max

her number is in the directory under "luna eva."

your niece
kate

12. Write the antecedent of the circled pronoun in the
(62) following sentence:

Caligula was an arrogant Roman emperor, and people
cheered when (he) died.

13. Write the indirect object in the following sentence:
(46)
Ed bought Rex a new collar.

14. Rewrite the following title, using correct capitalization:
(25)
"androcles and the lion"

15. Write the predicate adjective in the following sentence:
(54)
The lion looks fierce.

16. Complete the following sentence, using the correct verb
(61) tense.

A lion (present progressive of *lick*) Androcles's face!

17. From the following sentence, write each prepositional
(44) phrase, circling the object of each preposition:

He stepped into the arena with the lion.

18. Write the third person singular pronoun from this
(64) sentence:

Did you see him in the arena?

19. Use an appositive to combine the following two
(58) sentences into one sentence.

Tulip likes to trot through puddles.

Tulip is a white mare.

20. Rewrite the following sentence, adding four periods as
(47, 50) needed:

By one am, Ms Perfect had torn up her essay twice

21. Write the word from this list that is *not* a linking verb:
(31)

look, feel, paste, smell, sound, seem, appear, grow

22. Write whether the following word group is a phrase or a
(36) clause:

for the third time in a week

23. Rewrite the following sentence, adding commas as
(57, 59) needed:

I saw you Ed on Monday June 2 2011.

24. For the irregular verb *blow*, write the (a) present
(19, 65) participle, (b) past tense, and (c) past participle.

25. Write whether the circled pronoun in the sentence below
(64) is used as a subject or an object:

She is Rex's best friend.

26. Rewrite the following lines of poetry, adding capital
(15) letters as needed:

the emperor Nero
was not a hero.

27. For a and b, write the plural of each noun.
(17, 22)
(a) rosebush   (b) bagful

28. Diagram the simple subject and simple predicate of each
(36) clause in the following sentence:

Roy lost his wallet, but Ed found it before a thief did.

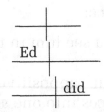

Diagram each word of sentences 29–30.

29. Ed remains an honest young man and Roy's good friend.
(49, 51)

30. Ed, an honest young man, handed Roy the wallet.
(46, 58)

29.

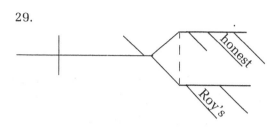

30.

Nominative Pronoun Case

Dictation or Journal Entry

Vocabulary:

An *arc* is a curved line, or part of a circle. The rainbow formed a giant *arc* in the sky.

An *ark* is a large boat. Did Noah build an *ark?*

Nominative Case We remember that nouns can be grouped into three cases: nominative, objective, and possessive. We also remember that the same is true of pronouns. This lesson shows the **nominative case.** A pronoun used as a subject or predicate nominative is in the nominative case.

He wears glasses. (subject)

The boy with glasses is *he.* (predicate nominative)

I mow the lawn. (subject)

The mower is *I.* (predicate nominative)

She sweeps. (subject)

The sweeper is *she.* (predicate nominative)

We are the gardeners. (subject)

The gardeners are *we.* (predicate nominative)

Example 1 Complete this chart by replacing each blank with the correct nominative case pronoun.

NUMBER	PERSON		NOMINATIVE CASE (subject or predicate nominative)
Singular	First		_____
	Second		_____
	Third	(masc.)	_____
		(fem.)	_____
		(neuter)	_____
Plural	First		_____
	Second		_____
	Third		_____

We complete the chart as follows:

Number	Person		Nominative Case (subject or predicate nominative)
Singular	First		I
	Second		you
	Third	(masc.)	he
		(fem.)	she
		(neuter)	it
Plural	First		we
	Second		you
	Third		they

Subjects   These sentences use nominative case personal pronouns as subjects:

I sang two songs.

She joined me.

When we use the pronoun *I* as part of a compound subject, it is polite to refer to ourselves last:

Pam and *I* sang duets.

Ed and *I* are cousins.

Example 2   Which sentence is more polite?

Both *we* and *they* like the rain.

Both *they* and *we* like the rain.

Solution   It is more polite to refer to ourselves (*we*) last.

Both *they* and *we* like the rain.

Example 3   Write a sentence using a nominative case personal pronoun as a subject.

Solution   Your answer will be unique. Here are some correct examples:

***We* shall learn a new song.**

***She* drew an arc.**

Noah and *they* built an ark.

Predicate Nominatives These sentences use nominative case personal pronouns as predicate nominatives.

The winner was *he* with the glasses.

The person in charge is *she*.

Predicate nominatives can also be compound:

The singers are Ed and *he*.

The drummers will be *she* and *I*.

Example 4 Write a sentence using a nominative case pronoun as a predicate nominative.

Solution Your answer will be unique. Here are some correct examples:

It was *I* who broke the window.

The best drummer is *she*.

The helpers will be *they* and *I*.

Practice **a.** Study the nominative case pronoun chart from Example 1. Then try to reproduce it from memory. You may abbreviate (1st, 2nd, 3rd, sing., pl., etc.).

b. Unscramble these words to make a sentence with a personal pronoun as a subject:

listeners good they are

c. Unscramble these words to make a sentence with a personal pronoun as a predicate nominative:

listener best he was the

For d and e, replace each blank with *arc* or *ark*.

d. The _____ floated upon the water.

e. He drew an _____, a curved line.

f. Write the sentence that is more polite:

I and he wore blue.

He and I wore blue.

g. Write each nominative case pronoun from this list: me, him, I, she, them, they, he, her, we, us.

Choose the nominative case pronoun for sentences h–k.

h. The man in the photo is (he, him).

i. The highest jumpers were Nan and (her, she).

j. The woman in the red hat was (her, she).

k. It is (I, me).

Review Set 66 Choose the correct word(s) to complete sentences 1–10.

1. The poor fox appeared (illusory, week, weak), for it was
(65) starving.

2. A (pinniped, biped, mirage) walks on two feet.
(64)

3. People chew using their (proboscis, mandibles, mirages).
(63)

4. "If I memorize my dictation" is a (clause, claws, mirage).
(62)

5. Baleen (pinnipeds, bipeds, whales) strain seawater
(27) through their comb-like mouths.

6. The word *weakness* is a(n) (abstract, concrete) noun.
(11)

7. I think Noah (prefered, preferred) (sunnyer, sunnier)
(33, 34) weather.

8. Before the flight, we must (wiegh, weigh) each (piece,
(35) peice) of luggage.

9. We have (less, fewer) apples than oranges.
(56)

10. The pronoun *you* is (first, second, third) person.
(64)

11. Rewrite the following letter, adding commas and capital
(41, 63) letters as needed:

dear aunt grace

please come to father's birthday party on friday
june 7.

your niece
amelia

12. Write the antecedent of the circled pronoun in the
(62) following sentence:

Noah built an ark, and (it) saved his family.

13. Write each coordinating conjunction that you find in the
(48) following sentence:

Ron and Eve sang hymns and carols, but they did not sing
folk songs.

14. Rewrite the following sentence, using correct
(38) capitalization:

eve learned all about music from her father, dr. tseng.

15. Write the predicate nominative in the following sentence:
(51)

George Gershwin was a composer.

16. Write whether the following sentence is a complete
(5, 23) sentence, a run-on sentence, or a sentence fragment:

By a twentieth-century American composer.

17. From the following sentence, write each prepositional
(44) phrase, circling the object of each preposition:

With the rainbow in the background, this picture reminds
me of the story about the ark.

18. Rewrite the word *guilt*, circling the silent letter.
(28, 29)

19. Rewrite the sentence below, using commas to offset the
(60) nonessential appositive.

My littlest sister Hope found a bird's nest.

20. Rewrite the following sentence, adding periods as needed:
(47, 50)

Dr Seuss wrote humorous verse

21. Write the nominative case pronoun to complete the
(66) following sentence:

The woman in the red hat is (she, her).

22. Write whether the following word group is a phrase or a
(36) clause:

if you swallow the seeds

23. Rewrite the following sentence, adding commas as
(59) needed:

Lilly I would like you to meet Kim Yu R.N.

24. For the irregular verb *bear*, write the (a) present
(19, 65) participle, (b) past tense, and (c) past participle.

25. Write whether the circled pronoun in the sentence below
(64) is used as a subject or an object:

Rex trusts(her).

26. Rewrite the following sentence, adding capital letters as
(26) needed:

ed said, "this wallet belongs to roy."

27. For a and b, write the plural of each noun.
(17, 22)

    (a) cupful   (b) cup of tea

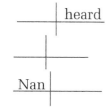

28. Diagram the simple subject and simple predicate of each
(36) clause in the following sentence:

When they heard about the contest, Ed baked an apple
pie, and Nan made a peanut butter pie.

Diagram each word of sentences 29–30.

29. Will the winner of the contest be Ed or she?
(45, 51)

30. Nan, an excellent cook, showed me her lovely pie.
(46, 58)

29.

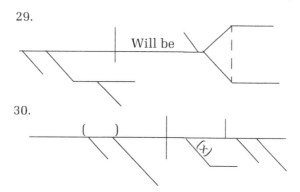

30.

LESSON 67

The Comma, Part 5: Introductory and Interrupting Elements and Afterthoughts

> **Dictation or Journal Entry**
>
> **Vocabulary:**
> The *abdomen* is the belly, the large body part of a creature that contains the stomach and other organs. The cow's *abdomen* was swollen, for she was about to give birth.
>
> The *thorax* is the chest, the part of a creature's body between the head and the abdomen. In people and other vertebrates, the *thorax* contains the heart, lungs, and ribs.

Comma = Pause   When we speak, we often pause between words. If we wrote down exactly what we were saying, many of those pauses would be indicated by commas. Pauses usually occur when we insert words or phrases that interrupt the natural flow of the sentence. Notice how commas are used to offset the italicized words, phrases, and clauses in the sentences below.

No, I have not gone to the moon.

There, *I think,* people cannot find food.

Earth is our habitat, *after all.*

These sentences show natural pauses that occur with introductory elements, interrupting elements, and afterthoughts. Let us look at more examples.

Introductory Elements   An **introductory element** begins a sentence. It sometimes expresses the writer's attitude about what is being said. An introductory element can also be a request or command.

Yes, it rained last night.

On the other hand, today is sunny.

Besides, today is a holiday.

In addition, my cousins are coming.

Example 1   Rewrite these sentences, using commas to offset introductory phrases.

(a) Without a doubt ice covers the roads.

(b) In my opinion we should stay home.

Solution (a) "Without a doubt" is an introductory element. We offset it with a comma.

Without a doubt, ice covers the roads.

(b) The phrase "In my opinion" is an introductory element. We offset it with a comma.

In my opinion, we should stay home.

Interrupting Elements An **interrupting element** appears in the middle of a sentence, interrupting the flow from subject to verb to object. An interrupting element can be removed without changing the meaning of the sentence.

Swamps, *it would seem,* breed mosquitoes.

Walk home, *if you can,* before dark.

Kerry, *not Joe,* was playing the drums.

Example 2 Rewrite these sentences, using commas to offset interrupting phrases.

(a) How in the world you ask did I run so fast?

(b) She wanted soup not salad for lunch.

Solution (a) We look for a word or phrase that interrupts the flow of the sentence and can be removed without changing its meaning. (It's not unusual to find that you must read the sentence two or three times in order to decide.) In this sentence, the phrase "you ask" is an interrupting element, so we offset it with commas.

How in the world, **you ask,** did I run so fast?

(b) The phrase "not salad" is an interrupting element. We offset it with commas.

She wanted soup, **not salad,** for lunch.

Afterthoughts **Afterthoughts** are similar to introductory and interrupting elements except that they are added to the ends of sentences.

The door is unlocked, *by the way.*

I am fine, *thank you.*

She raises chickens, *if I remember correctly.*

Some afterthoughts turn the sentence into a question:

It's not snowing, *is it?*

Hand me the hammer, *would you?*

We all have to help, *don't we?*

Example 3 Rewrite these sentences, using commas to offset afterthoughts.

(a) You are right of course.

(b) You told the truth didn't you?

Solution (a) The phrase "of course" is an afterthought, so we offset it with a comma.

You are right, **of course**.

(b) The questioning phrase "didn't you" is an afterthought. We offset it with a comma.

You told the truth, **didn't you?**

Practice Rewrite sentences a and b, inserting commas to offset introductory elements.

a. Yes I understand.

b. However I do not agree.

Rewrite sentences c and d, inserting commas to offset interrupting elements.

c. Her mother I believe came from Scotland.

d. The lion it is said rules the jungle.

For e and f, replace each blank with *abdomen* or *thorax*.

e. A creature's heart is part of its _____.

f. A creature's stomach is part of its _____.

More Practice See "More Practice Lesson 67" in the Student Workbook.

Review Set 67 Choose the correct word(s) to complete sentences 1–10.

1. With a compass, one can draw circles and (clauses, arks, arcs).
(66)

2. In one (biped, week, weak), Anna completed her monthly social studies assignment.
(65)

3. Kangaroos are (pinnipeds, bipeds, luminous).
(64)

4. He could not chew because his (mandible, thorax, proboscis) was broken.

5. Ms. Flight's colorful parakeets (molt, preen, cheap) themselves daily.

6. The word *Rex's* is a (plural, possessive) noun.

7. Ed (frys, fries) the (flatest, flattest) pancakes!

8. Miss Flores gave a (breif, brief) speech.

9. Of all the storms, that was the (worse, worst).

10. The pronoun *she* is (first, second, third) person (singular, plural).

11. Rewrite the following letter, adding commas and capital letters as needed:

dear amelia

yes i shall come to your father's party on friday june 7.

love
aunt grace

12. Write the antecedent of the circled pronoun in the following sentence:

Miss Ng asked Ed if he had seen her keys.

13. Write the indirect object in the following sentence:

The ranger gave us information about geysers.

14. Rewrite the following title, using correct capitalization:

a christmas carol

15. Write the predicate adjective in the following sentence:

Brer Rabbit is clever.

16. Complete the following sentence, using the correct verb tense:

The lion (past progressive of *roar*).

17.
(44)
From the following sentence, write each prepositional phrase, circling the object of each preposition:

Mole sat in the stern of the boat.

18.
(28, 29)
Rewrite the word *two*, circling the silent letter.

19.
(58)
Use an appositive to combine the following two sentences into one sentence.

Shanghai is a big city in China.

Tom flew to Shanghai.

20.
(47, 50)
Rewrite the following sentence, adding periods as needed:

Dr Kim will arrive on Aug 10

21.
(66)
Write the nominative case pronoun to complete the following sentence:

It is (me, I) who should wash dishes.

22.
(36)
Write whether the following word group is a phrase or a clause:

with a belt around his abdomen

23.
(57, 59)
Rewrite the following sentence, adding commas as needed:

If you have time Ed please call your sister your brother and me.

24.
(19, 65)
For the irregular verb *begin*, write the (a) present participle, (b) past tense, and (c) past participle.

25.
(64)
Write whether the circled pronoun in the sentence below is used as a subject or an object:

Does (he) like Rex?

26.
(26, 47)
Rewrite the following outline, adding periods and capital letters as needed:

i famous composers
  a bach
  b beethoven

27. For a and b, write the plural of each noun.
(17, 22)

    (a) bag of flour   (b) penny

28. Diagram the simple subject and simple predicate of each
(36) clause in the following sentence:

    I winked at him, for I thought that I knew him.

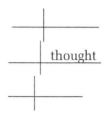

Diagram each word of sentences 29–30.

29. Will the winner of the race be you or I?
(45, 51)

30. Todd, a generous friend, has loaned me his best shoes.
(46, 58)

29.

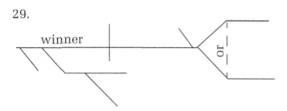

30.

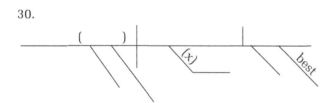

The Comma, Part 6: Clarity

Dictation or Journal Entry
Vocabulary:
To *meet* is to come upon or across; or to make the acquaintance of. Please *meet* me at the library.

Meat is a part of a plant or animal used for food. The *meat* of a coconut tastes sweet.

Clarity To *clarify* is to "make clear." When something is clear, it has *clarity*. We use commas to separate words, phrases, or clauses in order to **clarify meaning**, or to "make clear" the meaning of our sentences. Without commas, the meaning of the sentences below is unclear.

UNCLEAR: To Ben Franklin was always a hero.
CLEAR: To Ben, Franklin was always a hero.

UNCLEAR: Shortly after the rooster crowed.
CLEAR: Shortly after, the rooster crowed.

Example Rewrite each sentence, using commas to clarify meaning.
(a) During the week it snowed.

(b) To Lilly the cook was a friend.

Solution (a) Without a comma, this sentence is incomplete. During the week it snowed... *what?* They wore boots? We played inside? To avoid confusion, we insert a comma to clarify our intended meaning:

During the week, it snowed.

(b) Is Lilly a cook? If we read the sentence carefully, we see that she is not. A comma makes this much clearer.

To Lilly, the cook was a friend.

Practice Rewrite sentences a–c, using commas to clarify meaning.
a. To Lucy Clark meant trouble.

b. While passing the runner waved.

c. After John Henry sang.

For d and e, replace each blank with *meet* or *meat*.
d. Carnivores eat _____.

e. Please _____ me after school.

Review Set 68 Choose the correct word(s) to complete sentences 1–10.

1. Most of the digestion of food occurs in the (proboscis,
(67) thorax, abdomen).

2. Flatboats, also called (arks, arcs, bipeds), floated on the
(66) Mississippi River.

3. Muscles will become (weak, week, illusory) if they are
(65) not used.

4. (Bipeds, Pinnipeds, Mandibles) use flippers to swim
(64) through the water.

5. A snake (preens, molts, claws) its old skin.
(28)

6. The sentence below is (declarative, interrogative,
(2) imperative, exclamatory).

Was Eric the Red a Viking?

7. Lee is (shoping, shopping) for a (beautyful, beautiful)
(33, 34) ring.

8. Did you (recieve, receive) the package?
(35)

9. Of the two storms, the first one was (worse, worst).
(56)

10. The pronoun *they* is (first, second, third) person
(64) (singular, plural).

11. Rewrite the following letter, adding commas and capital
(63, 67) letters as needed:

dear aunt grace

if possible bring paper plates cups and napkins
to father's party.

many thanks
amelia

12. Write the antecedent of the circled pronoun in the
(62) following sentence:

Miss Ng asked Ed if (he) had seen her keys.

Grammar and Writing 4   **337**   **Student Edition Lesson 68**

13. Write each coordinating conjunction that you find in the
(48) following sentence:

Did Eric and Leif come from Norway or Denmark?

14. Rewrite the following sentence, using correct
(38) capitalization:

i'll ask mother how to say the danish words.

15. Write the predicate adjective in the following sentence:
(54)
The Vikings seemed fierce.

16. Write whether the following is a complete sentence, a
(5, 23) run-on sentence, or a sentence fragment:

Do you know what a *fjord* is?

17. Rewrite the sentence below, using a comma to clarify the
(68) meaning:

To rescue that dog Rex would do anything.

18. Use a dictionary: (a) The word *fjord* is what part of
(27, 30) speech? (b) Write its pronunciation. (c) Write its
etymology.

19. Rewrite the sentence below, using commas to offset the
(60) nonessential appositive.

Miss Ng a middle school teacher needs help.

20. Rewrite the following sentence, adding periods as needed:
(47, 50)
At one pm, Mrs Svelt arrived from Sweden

21. Write the nominative case pronoun to complete the
(66) following sentence:

The drummers were Sam and (her, she).

22. Write whether the following word group is a phrase or a
(36) clause:

if they eat meat

Grammar and Writing 4   **338**   **Student Edition
Lesson 68**

23. Rewrite the following sentence, adding commas as
(57, 59) needed:

If you can Mr. Moore please come Monday June 8.

24. For the irregular verb *choose*, write the (a) present
(19, 65) participle, (b) past tense, and (c) past participle.

25. Write whether the circled pronoun in the sentence below
(64) is used as a subject or an object:

Rex has a dish with his name on(it.)

26. Rewrite the following lines of poetry, adding capital
(26, 47) letters as needed:

one man went to mow,
went to mow the meadow.
one man and his dog
went to mow the meadow.

27. For a and b, write the plural of each noun.
(17, 22)
    (a) leash   (b) family

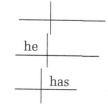

28. Diagram the simple subject and simple predicate of each
(36) clause in the following sentence:

Rex barks at Nan, for he thinks that she has treats.

Diagram each word of sentences 29–30.
29. Has Rex been faithful and obedient?
(49, 54)

30. My funny friend Kay ordered us burgers without meat.
(46, 58)

29.

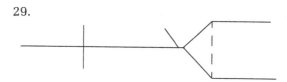

30.

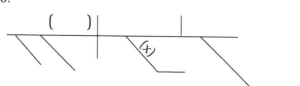

Objective Pronoun Case

Dictation or Journal Entry
Vocabulary:
Feet is the plural of "foot." New boots made blisters on my *feet.*

A *feat* is an amazing act of strength or skill. Climbing that mountain was a *feat.*

We have learned that pronouns used as subjects and predicate nominatives are in the **nominative case**, and that pronouns that show possession are in the **possessive case**. In this lesson, we will focus on the **objective case**.

Pronouns are in the **objective case** when they are used as direct objects, indirect objects, or objects of a preposition.

A bee stung *him.* (direct object)

I gave *him* ice. (indirect object)

I shall sit with *him.* (object of a preposition)

Please take *them.* (direct object)

Did you give *them* water? (indirect object)

You can sit by *them.* (object of a preposition)

Miss Ng likes *us.* (direct object)

Please fix *us* lunch. (indirect object)

This map belongs to *us.* (object of a preposition)

Example 1 Complete this chart by replacing each blank with the correct objective case pronoun.

NUMBER	PERSON		OBJECTIVE CASE (direct object, indirect object, or object of a preposition)
Singular	First		_____
	Second		_____
	Third	(masc.)	_____
		(fem.)	_____
		(neuter)	_____
Plural	First		_____
	Second		_____
	Third		_____

Solution We complete the chart as follows:

NUMBER	PERSON		OBJECTIVE CASE (direct object, indirect object, or object of a preposition)
Singular	First		me
	Second		you
	Third	(masc.)	him
		(fem.)	her
		(neuter)	it
Plural	First		us
	Second		you
	Third		them

Direct Objects The following sentences use personal pronouns as direct objects. We remember to use objective case pronouns.

The cow likes *her.* (not *she*)

Miss Ng taught Jeff and *me.* (not *I*)

Jeff called *them.* (not *they*)

Example 2 Write a sentence using a personal pronoun as a direct object.

Solution Your answer will be unique. Here are some correct examples:

Sam ignores *him.*

Jeff will meet Al and *her.*

The dog chewed *it.*

Indirect Objects These sentences use personal pronouns as indirect objects. Note that the pronouns are in the objective case.

Quan gave *her* a pen. (not *she*)

Nan loaned Ed and *me* a rake. (not *I*)

Al bakes *us* biscuits. (not *we*)

Example 3 Write a sentence using an objective case personal pronoun as an indirect object.

Solution Your answer will be unique. Here are some correct examples:

Nan told *him* a secret.

Jay gave *them* a clue.

Mike read Ed and *her* the story.

Objects of a Preposition The sentences below use personal pronouns as objects of a preposition. The pronouns are in the objective case.

Mike read a story to *them.* (not *they*)

Kim waited for *me.* (not *I*)

Gulls flew over *us.* (not *we*)

Example 4 Write a sentence using a personal pronoun as an object of a preposition.

Solution Your answer will be unique. Here are some correct examples:

A gull lands near *them.*

The gull takes bread from *us.*

Rex hides behind *me.*

Compound Objects Objective case pronouns can be compound. We politely mention ourselves last.

Dad hugged *him* and *me.* (compound direct object)

Ed gave *her* and *me* a gift. (compound indirect object)

Gulls flew around *them* and *us.*
(compound object of a preposition)

Example 5 Choose the sentence that is both correct and polite.

Joy sang for me and him.

Joy sang for he and I.

Joy sang for him and me.

Joy sang for him and I.

Solution The objective case pronouns are *him* and *me.* Also, we politely mention ourselves last.

Joy sang for him and me.

Practice   **a.** Study the objective case pronoun chart from Example 1. Then try to reproduce it from memory.

b. Unscramble these words to make a sentence with a personal pronoun as a direct object:

bobcat   the   frightened   him

c. Unscramble these words to make a sentence with a personal pronoun as an indirect object:

made   Jeff   soup   me

d. Unscramble these words to make a sentence with a personal pronoun as an object of a preposition:

came   Joy   us   with

For e and f, replace each blank with *feet* or *fcat.*

e. Digging the tunnel was a _____.

f. I washed my dirty _____.

g. Write the sentence that is more polite.

Do not forget me or her.
Do not forget her or me.

h. Write each objective case pronoun from this list:

me	him	I	she	them
they	he	her	we	us

Choose the objective case pronoun for sentences i–k.

i. Geese chased Ed and (he, him).

j. I'll give Nan and (him, he) the key.

k. A boa wrapped itself around Roy and (me, I).

Review Set 69   Choose the correct word to complete sentences 1–10.

1. The student council (bares, meats, meets) once a month.
(68)

2. In mammals, the (proboscis, thorax, abdomen) consists of
(67) the sternum, vertebrae, and ribs.

3. The rainbow formed a beautiful (arc, ark, mandible) in
(66) the sky.

4. Once a (week, weak, clause), the boy bathes his dog.
(65)

5. Whale (bulls, cows, bears) nurse their babies for more
(29) than a year.

6. The word *Vikings* is a (plural, possessive) noun.
(13)

7. The pronoun *them* is in the (nominative, objective,
(66, 69) possessive) case.

8. They caught the (thief, theif).
(35)

9. We have had (less, fewer) tornados this year.
(56)

10. The pronoun *it* is (first, second, third) person (singular,
(64) plural).

11. Rewrite the following letter, adding commas and capital
(63, 67) letters as needed:

dear aaron

   as i remember your uncle is listed as " zamora
herbert."

warmly
aunt alba

12. Write the antecedent of the circled pronoun in the
(62) following sentence:

Nan, if the telephone rings, please answer (it.)

13. Write the indirect object in the following sentence:
(46)

The noise gave her a headache.

14. Rewrite the following title, using correct capitalization:
(25)

"beauty and the beast"

15. Write the predicate nominative in the following sentence:
(51)

The Vikings were sailors.

16. Complete the following sentence, using the correct verb
(61) tense:

Vikings (past progressive of *attack*) their neighbors.

17. Rewrite the sentence below, using a comma to clarify the
(68) meaning:

To Nan Vikings seemed cruel.

18. Rewrite the word *knees*, circling the silent letter.
(28, 29)

19. Use an appositive to combine the following two
(58) sentences into one sentence.

Leif Ericson sailed from Greenland.

Leif Ericson was the son of Eric.

20. Rewrite the following sentence, adding periods as needed:
(47, 50)
Mr E F Hum lived on S Oak Ave

21. Write whether the circled pronoun in the sentence below
(64) is used as a subject or an object.

Does (she) like dogs?

22. Write whether the following word group is a phrase or a
(36) clause:

with muddy feet and messy hair

23. Rewrite the following sentence, adding commas as
(57, 67) needed:

On June 2 2011 I turned ninety my dear.

24. For the irregular verb *know*, write the (a) present
(19, 65) participle, (b) past tense, and (c) past participle.

25. Write the objective case pronoun to complete the
(69) following sentence:

Rex zooms past Nan and (I, me).

26. Rewrite the following sentence, adding capital letters as
(26) needed:

eric asked, "was i named after uncle eric?"

27. For a and b, write the plural of each noun.
(17, 22)
 (a) dollar bill   (b) butterfly

28. Diagram the simple subject and simple predicate of each
(36) clause in the following sentence:

Rex jumps and barks, for he is excited.

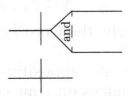

Diagram each word of sentences 29–30.

29. Will Rex become calm and obedient?
(49, 54)

30. My dear friend Ben brought Fay and me glasses of cold
(46, 58) water.

29.

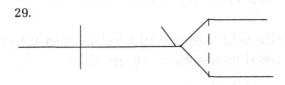

30.

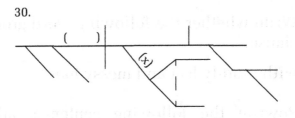

LESSON 70

Personal Pronoun Case Forms

Dictation or Journal Entry

Vocabulary:

A *hare* is a mammal related to and larger than the rabbit. We read a story about a tortoise and a *hare*.

Hair is the fine, threadlike growth on the skin of mammals. He combed his shiny *hair*.

Case Forms The following chart helps us to sort out the three personal pronoun **case forms:** (1) If a pronoun is a subject or predicate nominative, it is *nominative case*. (2) A pronoun used as a direct object, indirect object, or object of a preposition is *objective case*. (3) If a pronoun shows possession, it is *possessive case*.

NUMBER	PERSON	CASE		
		NOMINATIVE	OBJECTIVE	POSSESSIVE
Singular	First	I	me	mine
	Second	you	you	yours
	Third (masc.)	he	him	his
	(fem.)	she	her	hers
	(neuter)	it	it	its
Plural	First	we	us	ours
	Second	you	you	yours
	Third	they	them	theirs

Example 1 Tell whether each italicized pronoun is nominative, objective, or possessive case.

(a) Joy, Ann, and *she* swam.

(b) The dog saved *her*.

(c) *Yours* is here.

Solution (a) **nominative case**

(b) **objective case**

(c) **possessive case**

The pronoun case form depends on how the pronoun is used in the sentence. We refer to the chart to decide which pronoun is correct for this sentence:

(We, Us) students try hard.

The pronoun *we* identifies "students," which is the subject of the sentence. We use the nominative case pronoun *we* (NOT *us*) as a subject. Therefore, we write:

We students try hard.

Example 2 Tell how the pronoun is used in each sentence (subject, direct object, indirect object, object of a preposition, or possession).

(a) Miss Ng teaches *him*.

(b) That brush is *hers*.

(c) *We* planted seeds.

(d) Ed gave *her* a shovel.

(e) Joy and Ann swam with *them*.

Solution (a) *Him* is a **direct object.**

(b) *Hers* shows **possession.**

(c) *We* is the **subject.**

(d) *Her* is an **indirect object.**

(e) *Them* is an **object of a preposition.**

Example 3 Determine how the pronoun is used in each sentence. Then refer to the chart above to help you choose the correct pronoun. Rewrite each sentence correctly.

(a) Voters elected Beth and (I, me).

(b) Ed and (she, her) cheered.

(c) The mail was sent to Ed and (she, her).

Solution (a) The pronoun is a **direct object,** so we choose the objective case pronoun *me.*

Voters elected Beth and *me.*

(b) The pronoun is part of the **subject** of the sentence, so we choose the nominative case pronoun *she.*

Ed and *she* cheered.

(c) The pronoun is an **object of the preposition** *to,* so we choose the objective case pronoun *her.*

The mail was sent to Ed and *her.*

Practice For a–c, tell whether the pronoun is nominative, objective, or possessive case.

a. Joy noticed *her.*

b. *He* fed the hare.

c. That herd is *his.*

For d–h, tell how the pronoun is used in each sentence (subject, direct object, indirect object, object of a preposition, or possession).

d. A bough broke beneath *me.*

e. *I* bow my head.

f. A flea bit *him.*

g. Ed tosses *her* a note.

h. That note is *hers.*

For i and j, choose the correct pronoun.

i. The Smiths and (they, them) heard a wail.

j. Mom rode with Ed and (I, me).

For k and l, replace each blank with *hare* or *hair.*

k. I forgot to comb my _____.

l. A _____ runs fast.

**Review Set
70**

Choose the correct word(s) to complete sentences 1–10.

1. I try to land with both (feat, feet, meat) on the ground.
(69)

2. Some people do not eat red (meet, meat, feat).
(68)

3. A pregnant cow has a large (proboscis, abdomen, thorax).
(67)

4. A large (mandible, ark, arc) floated down the river.
(66)

5. A (bull, cow) does not give birth.
(29)

6. The word *hare* is a(n) (abstract, concrete) noun.
(11)

7. The pronoun *we* is (nominative, objective, possessive)
(66, 69) case.

8. The horse (troted, trotted) (steadyly, steadily) along the
(33, 34) road.

9. Nan has the (prettiest, most prettiest) hair today!
(55, 56)

10. The pronoun *I* is (first, second, third) person (singular,
(64) plural).

11. Rewrite the following letter, adding commas and capital
(41, 63) letters as needed:

dear aunt alba

　　i found uncle herbert's name address and phone
number.

> thankfully
> aaron

12. Write the antecedent of the circled pronoun in the
(62) following sentence:

Ken cheered until (he) was hoarse.

13. Write each coordinating conjunction that you find in the
(48) following sentence:

Jen or Ken will cook today, but Phil will cook tomorrow.

14. Rewrite the following sentence, using correct
(8, 38) capitalization:

yes, mother, you will see dr. heal on monday.

15. From the following sentence, write each prepositional
(44) phrase, circling the object of each preposition.

The hare hopped across the field and through the woods.

16. Write whether the following is a complete sentence, a
(5, 23) run-on sentence, or a sentence fragment:

Packing their clothes for the trip.

17. Rewrite the sentence below, using a comma to clarify the
(68) meaning:

Soon after Ed heard noises.

18. Use a dictionary: (a) The word *gene* is what part of
(27, 30) speech? (b) Write its pronunciation. (c) Write its
etymology.

19. Rewrite the sentence below, using commas to offset the
(60) nonessential appositive.

London the capital of Great Britain is on the Thames
River.

20. Rewrite the following sentence, adding periods as needed:
(47, 50)
Col Hahn guards a bank in St Louis

21. Write the nominative case pronoun to complete the
(66) sentence below.

The woman in the fake fur coat is (her, she).

22. Write whether the following word group is a phrase or a
(36) clause:

if Aaron cuts his hair

23. Rewrite the following sentence, adding commas as
(57, 59) needed:

Professor Garza Ph.D. studies spiders insects and
vertebrates.

24. For the irregular verb *tear*, write the (a) present
(19, 65) participle, (b) past tense, and (c) past participle.

25. Which sentence is more polite? Write *A* or *B*.
(69)   A. Rex missed me and him.

      B. Rex missed him and me.

26. Rewrite the following outline, adding periods and capital
(26, 47) letters as needed:

    i brass instruments
     a trumpets
     b bugles

27. For a and b, write the plural of each noun.
(17, 22)
     (a) child   (b) sister-in-law

28. Diagram the simple subject and simple predicate of each
(36) clause in the following sentence:

Rex snorts and scratches, for he has fleas.

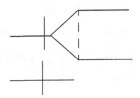

Diagram each word of sentences 29–30.

29. Will the tortoise and the hare become friends?
(49, 51)

30. The tortoise, a slow traveler, gives the hare and me
(46, 58) advice.

29.

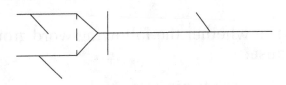

30.

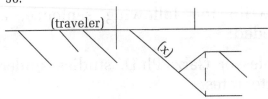

LESSON
71

Diagramming Pronouns

Dictation or Journal Entry
Vocabulary:
An *ant* is an insect. *Ants* live in colonies.

An *aunt* is the sister of one's father or mother. My *aunt* raises poodles.

As you may have already noticed, we diagram pronouns in the same way that we diagram nouns.

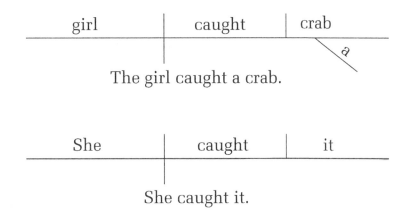

The girl caught a crab.

She caught it.

Diagramming a sentence helps us determine which pronoun to use because it clearly shows *how* the pronoun is used in the sentence. We diagram the sentence below to help us choose the correct pronoun:

Nan talks to my brother and (I, me).

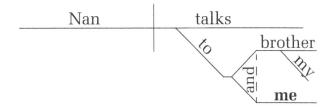

We see from the diagram that the pronoun is an object of the preposition *to*, so we choose the objective case pronoun *me*.

Nan talks to my brother and *me*.

Note: For some reason, we are more likely to use the wrong pronoun when it is part of a compound subject or object, as in the sentence above. If we remove the other half of the subject or object, the correct pronoun is usually obvious:

Nan talks to ~~my brother and~~ (I, me).

Our ears tell us that "talks to me" is correct. "Talks to I" does not sound right; it is incorrect.

Example Diagram the following sentence in order to choose the correct pronoun. Then, rewrite the sentence correctly.

Peter and (he, him) will play tag.

Solution We diagram the sentence this way:

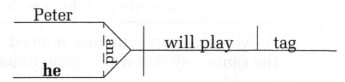

We see from our diagram that the pronoun is part of the subject of the sentence, so we choose the nominative case pronoun *he*.

Peter and *he* will play tag.

Practice For a and b, replace each blank with *ant* or *aunt*.

a. My _____ and uncle live in Arkansas.

b. An _____ crawled into the sugar bowl.

Diagram sentences c–e, choosing the correct pronoun.

c. Don and (him, he) play checkers.

d. Ling wrote Deb and (me, I) a letter.

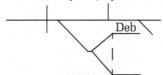

e. Aunt Ruth called Meg and (she, her).

Review Set Choose the correct word(s) to complete sentences 1–10.
71
　1. Rabbits and (claws, hares, hairs) are similar.
　(70)

　2. Swimming the English Channel is an amazing (feat, feet,
　(69) week).

　3. The friends often (meat, feat, meet) at the park.
　(68)

4. The (ark, proboscis, thorax) is between an insect's head
⁽⁶⁷⁾ and its abdomen.

5. A (buck, doe, ark) is a male deer or goat.
⁽³⁰⁾

6. The word *herd* is a (compound, collective) noun.
⁽¹¹⁾

7. The pronoun *us* is (nominative, objective, possessive)
^(66, 69) case.

8. Did they find (thier, their) (freind, friend)?
⁽³⁵⁾

9. There are not (much, many) plums on that tree.
⁽⁵⁶⁾

10. The pronoun *we* is (first, second, third) person (singular,
⁽⁶⁴⁾ plural).

11. Rewrite the following letter, adding commas and capital
^(57, 63) letters as needed:

dear amelia

    the date has been changed to saturday june 3.

                love
              aunt grace

12. Write the antecedent of the circled pronoun in the
⁽⁶²⁾ following sentence:

Hakeem followed the car until(it)turned onto Main Street.

13. Write the direct object in the following sentence:
⁽³⁷⁾

Englishmen captured Pocahontas.

14. Rewrite the following title, using correct capitalization:
⁽²⁵⁾

"the hunting of the great bear"

15. Write the predicate nominative in the following sentence:
⁽⁵¹⁾

That graceful tree with thin branches and long, narrow
leaves is a willow.

16. Complete the following sentence, using the correct verb
⁽⁶¹⁾ tense:

In 1608, colonists (past progressive of *build*) forts in
Jamestown.

17. Rewrite the sentence below, using a comma to clarify the meaning:

(68)

As you know everyone needs a friend.

18. Rewrite the word *lulk*, circling the silent letter.

(29)

19. Use an appositive to combine the following two sentences into one sentence.

(58)

John Smith was a strong leader.

John Smith took charge of the colony.

20. Rewrite the following sentence, adding periods as needed:

(47, 50)

Mr James Ham, Jr, works for Victors, Inc, in Boston

21. Write whether the circled pronoun in the sentence below is used as a subject or an object.

(64)

Will ⟨they⟩ tell the truth?

22. Write whether the following word group is a phrase or a clause:

(36)

without a care in the world

23. Rewrite the following sentence, adding commas as needed:

(57, 59)

Lalita my new address is 456 First Avenue Nashville Tennessee.

24. For the irregular verb *sing*, write the (a) present participle, (b) past tense, and (c) past participle.

(19, 65)

25. Write the objective case pronoun to complete the sentence below.

(69)

Rex brought Nan and (she, her) a bone.

26. Rewrite the following sentence, adding capital letters as needed:

(26)

nan said, "thank you, rex."

27. For a and b, write the plural of each noun.

(17, 22)

(a) branch   (b) daisy

28. Diagram the simple subject and simple predicate of each
(36) clause in the following sentence:

Rex yips and jumps when Nan and Ed arrive.

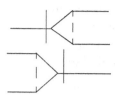

Diagram each word of sentences 29–30.

29. Will Nan and Ed remain friends?
(49, 51)

30. Ed, a friendly boy, shows Nan the impolite side of his
(46, 58) personality.

29.

30.

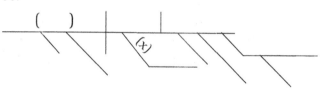

Possessive Pronouns and Possessive Adjectives

Dictation or Journal Entry

Vocabulary:

A *drought* is a long period of dry weather without normal rainfall. Plants and trees died during the *drought*.

A *famine* is an extreme and widespread food shortage. People starved during the *famine*.

Possessive Pronouns
We have learned that a pronoun takes the place of a noun. The possessive pronouns *mine, yours, his, hers, ours,* and *theirs* replace nouns to tell "whose."

That's *mine,* not *yours.*

His is green, and *hers* is yellow.

Theirs are ready, so why aren't *ours?*

Notice that in each of the sentences above, the possessive pronoun **replaces a noun** and stands alone.

Possessive Adjectives
There is another group of words that is very similar to possessive pronouns except that they **come before a noun** rather than replace it. These words are the possessive adjectives *my, your, his, her, its, our,* and *their.*

Please keep *your* feet off *my* table.

Her cat is standing on *our* table and arching *its* back.

In each of the sentences above, the possessive adjective comes before a noun to tell "whose."

Many people consider possessive adjectives to be pronouns. Others see them as adjectives because they always come before nouns to modify them. What is important is using them correctly.

POSSESSIVE ADJECTIVE (IN FRONT OF A NOUN)	POSSESSIVE PRONOUN (STANDING ALONE)
my	mine
your	yours
his	his
her	hers
its	its *(very seldom used)*
our	ours
their	theirs

Errors to Avoid Possessive pronouns do not have apostrophes. The words *yours, hers, its,* and *ours* are already possessive.

> INCORRECT: I saw Dad's car but not **her's**.
> CORRECT: I saw Dad's car but not **hers**.

> INCORRECT: The choice is **your's**.
> CORRECT: The choice is **yours**.

Also, we must not confuse contractions and possessive adjectives.

POSSESSIVE ADJECTIVE	CONTRACTION	
your	you're	(you are)
their	they're	(they are)
its	it's	(it is)

Example Choose the correct word to complete each sentence.

(a) Is (your, you're) dog lonely?

(b) (Its, It's) ears are droopy.

(c) Is the poodle also (their's, theirs)?

(d) This dog is meaner than (yours, your's).

Solution (a) Is **your** dog lonely?

(b) **Its** ears are droopy.

(c) Is the poodle also **theirs**?

(d) This dog is meaner than **yours**.

Practice Choose the correct word to complete sentences a–e.

a. The horse is limping; (its, it's) leg is sore.

b. Rob and Tom took (their, they're) shoes off.

c. Mr. Yu has his key, but Miss Lee forgot (her's, hers).

d. Give us (your, you're) advice.

e. The gray car is (ours, our's).

For f and g, replace each blank with *drought* or *famine*.

    f. There was little to eat during the _____.

    g. We try to save water, especially during a _____.

More Practice   Choose the correct word(s) to complete each sentence.

    1. How do swans find (there, they're, their) way home?

    2. (They're, There, Their) able to do it somehow.

    3. That swan has injured (its, it's) foot.

    4. Is a swan's eyesight better than (ours, our's)?

    5. Are all these cygnets (her's, hers)?

    6. Is that nest (their's, theirs)?

    7. That swan wants (your, you're) lunch!

    8. (It's, Its) flapping (its, it's) wings.

Review Set 72   Choose the correct word to complete sentences 1–10.

    1. (Aunts, Ants, Hares) are social insects that live in
    (71) colonies.

    2. (Hare, Hair, Feat) color can be brown, black, gray, red,
    (70) or blond.

    3. (Feet, Feat, Meet) bear the weight of the human body.
    (69)

    4. Ham, chicken, and roast beef are different kinds of (feat,
    (68) meet, meat).

    5. A (doe, buck, boar) is a female.
    (30)

    6. The sentence below is (declarative, interrogative,
    (2) imperative, exclamatory).

       Can an ostrich fly?

    7. The pronoun *our* is (nominative, objective, possessive)
    (66, 69) case.

    8. (Your, You're) shoes are muddy.
    (72)

9. That was the (better, best) of the two recipes.
(56)

10. The pronoun (*I, you, he, she, it, they*) is second person.
(64)

11. Rewrite the following letter, adding commas and capital
(57, 63) letters as needed:

dear aunt grace

    i shall blow up balloons bake a cake and wrap
presents for the party.

                    love
                  amelia

12. Write the antecedent of the circled pronoun in the
(62) following sentence:

Ed wants me to wait for (him)

13. Write the indirect object in the following sentence:
(46)

Jo tossed the swan a bread crumb.

14. Rewrite the following sentence, using correct
(38) capitalization:

her classes include math, history, and english.

15. Add suffixes:
(33, 34) (a) flap + ing   (b) glory + ous

16. Write whether the following is a complete sentence, a
(5, 23) run-on sentence, or a sentence fragment:

Sal writes songs he also plays the drums.

17. Rewrite the sentence below, using a comma to clarify the
(68) meaning:

Because of John Smith was late.

18. Use a dictionary: (a) The word *cygnet* is what part of
(27, 30) speech? (b) Write its pronunciation. (c) Write its
etymology.

19. Rewrite the sentence below, using commas to offset the
(60) nonessential appositive.

Roger Williams a Puritan minister believed in religious
freedom.

20. Rewrite the following sentence, adding periods as needed:
(47, 50)

Mr Chan wrote, "Homework is due on Fri, Feb 3"

21. Write the nominative case pronoun to complete the
(66) sentence below.

It was (me, I) who dropped the ball.

22. Write whether the following word group is a phrase or a
(36) clause:

if you have time

23. Rewrite the following sentence, adding commas as
(57, 59) needed:

No Lalita I have not lived in Atlanta Georgia.

24. For the irregular verb *freeze*, write the (a) present
(19, 65) participle, (b) past tense, and (c) past participle.

25. Which sentence is more polite? Write *A* or *B*.
(69)   A. Rex growled at her and me.

B. Rex growled at me and her.

26. From this list, write the word that is *not* a possessive
(72) adjective: my, your, its, it's.

27. For a and b, write the plural of each noun.
(17, 22)
(a) match   (b) dictionary

28. Diagram the simple subject and simple predicate of each
(36) clause in the following sentence:

Amy smiles and waves as Nan and Ed jog by.

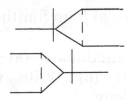

Diagram each word of sentences 29–30.

29. Does Teo's fear of sharks seem reasonable?
(45, 54)

30. Olivia, Teo's lovely wife, told me a funny story about her
(46, 58) husband.

29.

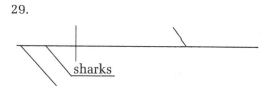

30.

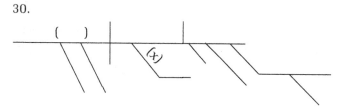

LESSON 73

Dependent and Independent Clauses • Subordinating Conjunctions

> **Dictation or Journal Entry**
>
> **Vocabulary:**
> The *bow* (rhymes with *cow*) of a boat or ship is the forward end. From the *bow* of the ship, I could see whales swimming ahead of us.
>
> The *stern* of a boat or ship is its rear part. From the *stern* of the ship, I could see where we had been.

Independent Clauses

There are two types of clauses. One type is the **independent clause**, also called the main clause. An independent clause expresses a complete thought.

> The sun rises.
>
> Bill plays the bugle.

Dependent Clauses

The other type of clause is the **dependent clause**. It cannot stand by itself and is sometimes called the subordinate clause. It depends upon additional information to complete a thought.

> If Jo feeds the birds …
>
> When I found a dollar …

Even though the dependent clauses above each contain a subject and a predicate, they do not complete a thought. However, if we remove the introductory words "if" and "when," they become independent clauses and can stand alone:

> Jo feeds the birds.
>
> I found a dollar.

Example 1

For a–d, tell whether the clauses are dependent or independent.

(a) as soon as they awake

(b) the horse trots home

(c) although it snowed

(d) they find peace

Solution (a) This is a **dependent** clause. It depends on another clause to complete a thought.

(b) This is an **independent** clause. It can stand alone and does not require another clause to complete a thought.

(c) This is a **dependent** clause. It needs another clause to complete the thought.

(d) This is an **independent** clause and can stand by itself.

Subordinating Conjunctions

A **subordinating conjunction** introduces a dependent clause. We can turn an independent clause into a dependent clause by adding a subordinating conjunction. In the dependent clauses below, *though* and *because* are subordinating conjunctions.

INDEPENDENT CLAUSE	DEPENDENT CLAUSE
I like rain.	*Though* I like rain,…
It looks old.	*Because* it looks old,…

Below are some common subordinating conjunctions. There are many more.

after	*because*	*so that*	*when*
although	*before*	*than*	*whenever*
as	*even though*	*that*	*where*
as if	*if*	*though*	*wherever*
as soon as	*in order that*	*unless*	*while*
as though	*since*	*until*	

Many of these words also function as prepositions. Sometimes phrases begin with prepositions such as *after*, *before*, *since*, or *until*. In this case, these words are not subordinating conjunctions but prepositions. Remember that a clause has both a subject and a verb. Notice how the word *before* is used in the two sentences below.

SUBORDINATING CONJUNCTION:
Amy came *before* lunch was served. (introducing the **clause** "before lunch was served")

PREPOSITION:
Amy came *before* lunch. (part of the **phrase** "before lunch")

Example 2 Identify the subordinating conjunctions in the following sentences.

    (a) Polly felt sorry because she had lied.

    (b) If we go, we'll need a map.

Solution (a) *Because* is the subordinating conjunction. It introduces the dependent clause "because she had lied."

    (b) *If* is the subordinating conjunction. It introduces the dependent clause "If we go."

Practice For a–d, write whether the clause is dependent or independent.

    a. since Gus left

    b. the bough broke

    c. he quells their anger

    d. wherever they soar

For e–g, write each subordinating conjunction.

    e. Unless we finish our work, we will not play.

    f. I walked to town, even though it was stormy.

    g. When Ana came, we cheered.

For h and i, replace each blank with *bow* or *stern*.

    h. A ship's _____ is in the rear.

    i. A ship's _____ is in the front.

More Practice See "More Practice Lesson 73" in the Student Workbook.

Review Set 73 Choose the correct word(s) to complete sentences 1–10.

    1. A (drought, famine, clause) is a long period of dry
    (72) weather.

    2. An (aunt, ant, illusion) is an insect that lives on every
    (71) continent but Antarctica.

3. A snowshoe (feat, hair, hare) has very large hind feet.
(70)

4. Heather considers Kylie's project an amazing (feat, feet, meet).
(69)

5. Adult male (sows, boars, does) develop tusks.
(31)

6. The word *donkey's* is a (plural, possessive) noun.
(13)

7. The pronoun *he* is (nominative, objective, possessive) case.
(66, 69)

8. Is this bag (your's, yours)?
(72)

9. That was the (better, best) of the four essays.
(56)

10. The pronoun *she* is (first, second, third) person (singular, plural).
(04)

11. Rewrite the following letter, adding commas and capital letters as needed:
(57, 63)

dear carl

     please come to my art show on saturday may 3 2012 at noon.

                        your cousin
                        joe

12. Write the antecedent of the circled pronoun in the following sentence:
(62)

I think Miss Ng left (her) key in the lock.

13. From the following sentence, write each prepositional phrase, circling the object of each preposition.
(44)

Look in the drawer for a pair of scissors.

14. Write the subordinating conjunction in this sentence:
(73)

I shall hum while you sing.

15. Add suffixes:
(33, 34)

    (a) clap + ing   (b) sandy + er

16. Complete the following sentence, using the correct verb
(61) tense.

They (future progressive of *sing*), but I shall be humming.

17. Rewrite the sentence below, using a comma to clarify the
(68) meaning:

The day after we found paw prints.

18. Rewrite the word *light*, circling the silent letters.
(28, 29)

19. Use an appositive to combine the following two
(58) sentences into one sentence.

Lulu was the smallest girl.

Lulu won the sack race at the picnic.

20. Rewrite the following sentence, adding periods as needed:
(47, 50)
Capt Picket lives on N Lemon Ave

21. Write whether the circled pronoun in the sentence below
(64) is used as a subject or an object.

Lulu spilled punch on Nan and (me).

22. Write whether the clause below is dependent or
(73) independent:

if the stairs creak

23. Rewrite the following sentence, adding commas as
(57, 59) needed:

Mother this is Ms. Nit R.N.

24. For the irregular verb *blow*, write the (a) present
(19, 65) participle, (b) past tense, and (c) past participle.

25. Write the objective case pronoun to complete the
(69) sentence below.

Lulu gave Nan and (me, I) napkins.

26. Rewrite the following sentence, adding capital letters as
(26) needed:

lulu said, "please forgive me."

27. For a and b, write the plural of each noun.
(17, 22)
    (a) Tuesday   (b) life

28. Diagram the simple subject and simple predicate of each
(36) clause in the following sentence:

Lulu likes red, and Nan likes blue, but I prefer yellow.

Diagram each word of sentences 29–30.

29. Did Lulu's story about the goat sound believable?
(45, 54)

30. My canine friend Rex gave Dan and me his bark of
(46, 58) approval.

29.

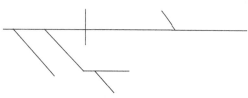

30.

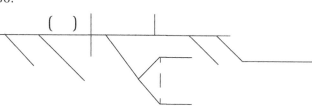

LESSON 74

The Comma, Part 7: Descriptive Adjectives and Dependent Clauses

Dictation or Journal Entry

Vocabulary:

Girth is the distance around something; the circumference. The *girth* of the redwood tree was more than twenty feet!

Breadth is the measure of a surface from side to side; the width. Because of the *breadth* of the river, we dare not cross it without a boat.

We remember that commas are used to indicate the natural pauses of speech. Let's look at more places where we use commas.

Descriptive Adjectives We use a comma to separate two or more **descriptive adjectives.**

> Ed has a *neat, orderly* desk.

> It was a *long, cold* winter.

There are some exceptions. For example, if one adjective is a color, we do not use a comma to separate it from another adjective.

> A *rude red* rooster crows too early.

One way to decide whether a comma is needed is to insert the word "and" between the adjectives.

> IF YOU COULD SAY: It was a *hot and humid* day.
> YOU DO NEED A COMMA: It was a *hot, humid* day.

> YOU WOULDN'T SAY: I saw an *old and blue* truck.
> SO YOU DO NOT NEED A COMMA: I saw an *old blue* truck.

Example 1 Insert commas where they are needed in the sentences below.

(a) They smell a strong foul odor.

(b) It has long shiny black fur.

Solution (a) We place a comma between the two adjectives "strong" and "foul."

They smell a **strong, foul** odor.

(b) We separate the adjectives "long" and "shiny" with a comma, but we do not place a comma before the color adjective "black."

It has **long, shiny black** fur.

Dependent Clauses We remember that a **dependent clause** cannot stand alone. However, an independent clause, or main clause, makes sense without the dependent clause. We use a comma after a dependent clause when it comes before the main clause.

When I entered the barn, I saw hundreds of bats.
(DEPENDENT CLAUSE)   (INDEPENDENT/MAIN CLAUSE)

However, we do **not** use a comma when the dependent clause follows the main clause and is essential to the meaning of the main clause.

I saw hundreds of bats *when I entered the barn*.
(INDEPENDENT/MAIN CLAUSE)   (DEPENDENT CLAUSE)

Example 2 Insert commas as needed in the sentences below.

(a) Although he fell twice he finished the race.

(b) I must scrub until the sink sparkles.

Solution (a) We place a comma after the dependent clause "Although he fell twice" because it comes before the main clause.

Although he fell twice, he finished the race.

(b) We do not place a comma in this sentence because the dependent clause "until the sink sparkles" follows the main clause.

Practice Rewrite sentences a and b, inserting commas to separate descriptive adjectives.

a. We ran from the huge angry bear.

b. I took my thickest warmest coat to Alaska, but all I really needed was my thin blue jacket.

Rewrite sentences c–e, inserting a comma after each dependent clause.

c. When you go to the market buy some apples.

d. If they look wormy get bananas instead.

e. As soon as you come home we'll make lunch.

For f and g, replace each blank with *girth* or *breadth*.

f. The _____ of something is its width.

g. _____ is the distance around something.

Review Set 74 Choose the correct word(s) to complete sentences 1–10.

1. Standing on the (girth, stern, bow) of the ship, we can see where we are going.
(73)

2. One hundred days without rain created a (drought, illusion, stern) in Texas.
(72)

3. Queen (ants, aunts, mandibles) have wings.
(71)

4. (Hairs, Hares, Aunts) box one another with their paws.
(70)

5. The tusks of a male (sow, deer, boar) were used as tools or weapons.
(31)

6. The word *illusion* is a(n) (abstract, concrete) noun.
(11)

7. The pronoun *him* is (nominative, objective, possessive) case.
(66, 69)

8. Is this bag (her's, hers)?
(72)

9. The attic has (less, fewer) mice than rats.
(56)

10. The pronoun *it* is (first, second, third) person (singular, plural).
(64)

11. Rewrite the following letter, adding commas and capital letters as needed:
(57, 63)

dear joe

　　on saturday may 3 i shall be in dover delaware.

　　　　　　　　regretfully
　　　　　　　　carl

12. Write the antecedent of the circled pronoun in the following sentence:
(62)

Miss Ng lost her key, but I found (it.)

13. Write each coordinating conjunction in the following sentence:
(48)

Ali and Pat imitate horses, but they like to pretend.

14. Write the subordinating conjunction in this sentence:
₍₇₃₎

After you sort the socks, put them away.

15. Add suffixes:
_(33, 34) (a) sip + ing   (b) penny + less

16. Write whether the following is a complete sentence, a
_(5, 23) sentence fragment, or a run-on sentence.

Philadelphia means "city of brotherly love."

17. Rewrite the sentence below, using a comma to clarify the
₍₆₈₎ meaning:

To paint Nan needs a brush.

18. Use a dictionary: (a) The word *cello* is what part of
_(27, 30) speech? (b) Write its pronunciation. (c) Write its
etymology.

19. Rewrite the sentence below, using commas to offset the
₍₆₀₎ nonessential appositive.

William Penn a wealthy gentleman came to North
America from England.

20. Rewrite the following sentence, adding periods as needed:
_(47, 50)
Henry Hudson sailed for the Dutch East India Co in the
1600s

21. Write the nominative case pronoun to complete the
₍₆₆₎ sentence below.

The cellists were Dan and (her, she).

22. Write whether the clause below is dependent or
₍₇₃₎ independent:

she spun wool

23. Rewrite the following sentence, adding commas as
₍₇₄₎ needed:

If English people owed money they might have been sent
to a dark filthy prison.

24. For the irregular verb *tear*, write the (a) present
(19, 65) participle, (b) past tense, and (c) past participle.

25. Write the objective case pronoun to complete the
(69) sentence below.

Meg rode with Beth and (she, her).

26. Rewrite the following outline, adding periods and capital
(26, 47) letters as needed:

i southern colonies
  a virginia
  b georgia
  c carolina

27. For a and b, write the plural of each noun.
(17, 22)
(a) northern colony   (b) king of England

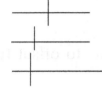

28. Diagram the simple subject and simple predicate of each
(36) clause in the following sentence:

If you catch a rat before I return, I shall reward you.

Diagram each word of sentences 29–30.
29. Did the bear in the basement seem hungry?
(45, 54)

30. My neighbor Rob sent Gus and me a scary picture of the
(46, 58) bear in their basement.

29.

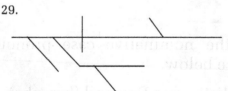

30.

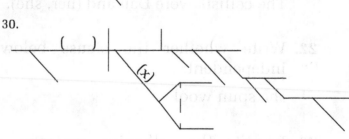

LESSON
75

Compound Sentences •
Coordinating Conjunctions

Dictation or Journal Entry
Vocabulary:
Elytra are the hard, protective forewings of beetles and other insects. The ladybug's *elytra* were red with black spots.

Antennae are sense organs, or feelers, on the heads of centipedes, millipedes, insects, crustaceans, and some other creatures. Can ants "talk" to each other by touching *antennae*?

Compound Sentences Two or more simple sentences (independent clauses) joined by a connecting word such as *and*, *or*, or *but* form a **compound sentence**. Only sentences closely related in thought should be joined to form a compound sentence. Below, we connect two simple sentences to form a compound sentence.

TWO SIMPLE SENTENCES:
My uncle is a chef.
He works in Denver.

ONE COMPOUND SENTENCE:
My uncle is a chef, and he works in Denver.

Here we diagram the simple subjects and simple predicates of the compound sentence above:

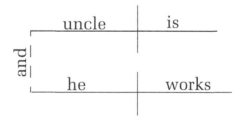

Notice that the compound sentence is made up of two independent clauses that can each stand alone and make sense.

Any number of independent clauses can be joined to form a compound sentence. For example, here we join four independent clauses (simple sentences) to form one compound sentence:

Bill counts whales, and Fred counts dolphins, but I just ride along, and Zoe drives the boat.

Grammar and Writing 4 **375** Student Edition
Lesson 75

Coordinating Conjunctions

A **coordinating conjunction** can join two simple sentences to form a compound sentence. We have learned that the following are coordinating conjunctions:

> and   but   or   nor   for   yet   so

Notice how coordinating conjunctions are used in the compound sentences below.

> *AND* INDICATES ADDITIONAL INFORMATION:
> My uncle works in Denver, *and* he likes his job.

> *BUT* SHOWS CONTRAST:
> My uncle works in Denver, *but* he lives in Boulder.

> *OR* SHOWS A CHOICE:
> I can fly to Illinois, *or* I can take the train.

Conjunctions may also connect the parts of a compound subject or predicate. Do not confuse a compound subject or a compound predicate with a compound sentence. A compound sentence has both a subject and a predicate on each side of the conjunction. A compound sentence follows this pattern:

> *SUBJECT* <u>PREDICATE</u>, (CONJUNCTION) *SUBJECT* <u>PREDICATE</u>

> *You* <u>may walk,</u>   (or)   *you* <u>may ride</u>.
> *He* <u>has been resting</u>,   (but)   *she* <u>has been working</u>.
> *Aaron* <u>plays</u> guitar,   (and)   *Melody* <u>sings</u> a solo.

Example 1 Tell whether each sentence is simple or compound. If it is compound, write the coordinating conjunction that joins the two independent clauses.

(a) *Kate* <u>felt</u> weak, yet *she* <u>finished</u> the race.

(b) The *race* <u>was</u> long, but *Kate* <u>was</u> determined.

(c) *Kate* <u>ran</u> and <u>jogged</u> the whole distance.

Solution (a) We find a subject and a predicate on each side of the conjunction: *Kate* <u>felt</u>, (conjunction) *she* <u>finished</u>. Therefore, the sentence is **compound**. The coordinating conjunction joining the two independent clauses is **yet**.

(b) This sentence is **compound**. It consists of two independent clauses joined by the coordinating conjunction **but**.

(c) This is a **simple** sentence. It is a single, independent clause with one subject (*Kate*) and a compound predicate (<u>ran</u> and <u>jogged</u>).

Diagramming To diagram the simple subjects and simple predicates of a compound sentence, we follow these steps:

1. Diagram each simple sentence, one below the other.

2. Join the two sentences with a dotted line on the left side.

3. Write the coordinating conjunction on the dotted line.

Below, we diagram the simple subjects and simple predicates of this compound sentence:

Rex sees a thief, so he is growling.

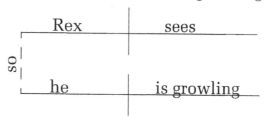

Example 2 Diagram the simple subjects and simple predicates of this compound sentence:

Rex barks at Grandma, and she frowns.

Solution We diagram the simple subject and simple predicate of each simple sentence and place one below the other. Then we join them with a dotted line on which we write the coordinating conjunction "and."

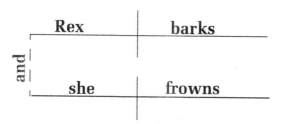

Practice For a–c, write whether each sentence is simple or compound. If it is compound, write the coordinating conjunctions that join the two or more independent clauses.

   a. *Colonists* in Maryland <u>traded</u> with friendly Indians.

b. *Sir George Calvert* <u>died</u>, but his *son* <u>carried</u> on.

c. *Nate* <u>grew</u> potatoes, and *Josh* <u>grew</u> tomatoes, so *they* <u>had</u> enough food.

d. Diagram the simple subjects and simple predicates of this compound sentence:

You will need boots, for the trail is rocky.

For e and f, replace each blank with *elytra* or *antennae*.

e. _____ protect a beetle's wings.

f. Insects "feel" with their _____.

Review Set 75

Choose the correct word to complete sentences 1–10.

1. The clerk measures the (bow, stern, girth) of a poster tube
(74) to determine its mailing cost.

2. From the (stern, bow, girth) of the ship, we can see where
(73) we have been.

3. People are hungry during a (feat, feet, famine).
(72)

4. One of Elle's (ants, aunts, illusions) has red hair.
(71)

5. (Sows, Boars, Deer) bear piglets.
(31)

6. The word *bunch* is a (compound, collective) noun.
(11)

7. The pronoun *his* is (nominative, objective, possessive)
(66, 69) case.

8. Are these tools (yours, your's)?
(72)

9. Of the two swimmers, Ted is (faster, fastest).
(56)

10. The pronoun *them* is (first, second, third) person
(64) (singular, plural).

11. Rewrite the following letter, adding commas and capital
(57, 63) letters as needed:

dear mr. yu

my address is 212 oak street austin texas.

sincerely

mr. cruz

12. Write whether the sentence below is simple or
(75) compound.

They lost their tools, but Kim found them.

13. Write the predicate nominative in the following sentence:
(51)
Pigs are mammals.

14. Write the subordinating conjunction in this sentence:
(73)
The floor creaks as Mom sneaks.

15. Write the word that is spelled correctly:
(35)
(a) view, veiw   (b) sliegh, sleigh

16. Complete the following sentence, using the correct verb
(61) tense.

They (past progressive of *sing*), and Jo was playing the
piano.

17. Rewrite the sentence below, using a comma to clarify the
(68) meaning:

To coach Meg needs a whistle.

18. Rewrite the word *drought*, circling the silent letters.
(28, 29)

19. Use an appositive to combine the following two
(58) sentences into one sentence.

Roger Williams was a Puritan.

Roger Williams believed in religious freedom.

20. Rewrite the following sentence, adding periods as needed:
(47, 50)
Dr Nick will be 45 min late

21. Write whether the circled pronoun in the sentence below
(64) is used as a subject or an object.

The doctor will call (him) next week.

22. Write whether the word group below is a phrase or a
(36) clause:

with shiny brown elytra

23. Rewrite the following sentence, adding commas as needed:
(74)

When we opened the box we found an old faded flag.

24. For the irregular verb *ring*, write the (a) present
(19, 65) participle, (b) past tense, and (c) past participle.

25. Which sentence is more polite? Write *A* or *B*.
(69) A. Gus sang with me and Zoe.

B. Gus sang with Zoe and me.

26. Rewrite the following sentence, adding capital letters as
(26) needed:

zoe said, "the goat ate my homework!"

27. For a and b, write the plural of each noun.
(17, 22)
(a) dish (b) city

28. Diagram the simple subject and simple predicate of each
(75) clause in the following compound sentence:

You spoke clearly, so we understood you.

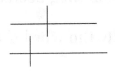

Diagram each word of sentences 29–30.

29. Did the deer in the woods look young?
(45, 54)

30. Dan, the photographer, showed Ana and me his photo of
(46, 58) the deer.

29.

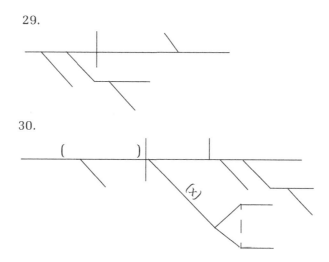

30.

LESSON 76

The Comma, Part 8: Compound Sentences and Direct Quotations

Compound Sentences

We remember that independent clauses joined by a coordinating conjunction (*and, but, or, for,* etc.) form a compound sentence. We place a comma between the first independent clause and the coordinating conjunction in a compound sentence.

> The tortoise raced hard, but the hare was ahead.

> Nan made salad, and we ate it for dinner.

The following coordinating conjunctions signal the need for a comma in a compound sentence.

> and   but   or   nor   for   yet   so

Example 1 Identify the coordinating conjunction in each compound sentence.

(a) She has not slept, nor has she eaten.

(b) She should rest now, or she will be too tired.

(c) Ivy was late, so she missed the bus.

Solution (a) **nor**   (b) **or**   (c) **so**

Example 2 Insert a comma before the coordinating conjunction to separate the two independent clauses in the sentences below.

(a) They did not play soccer for it was hailing.

(b) Jin threw the ball and Pablo caught it.

Solution We place a comma between the first independent clause and the coordinating conjunction.

(a) **They did not play soccer, for it was hailing.**

(b) **Jin threw the ball, and Pablo caught it.**

Direct Quotations

We use a comma or commas to offset the exact words of a speaker, a **direct quotation**, from the rest of the sentence.

Nan asked, "Is a bat a bird?"

"I think," said Zoe, "that a bat is a mammal."

"You are right," said Miss Ling.

Notice that the comma stays next to the word it follows. If a comma follows a direct quote, the comma goes inside the quotation marks.

YES: "Let's fly kites," said Gus.

NO: "Let's fly kites", said Gus.

Example 3

Rewrite sentences a and b, inserting commas as needed to offset direct quotations from the rest of the sentence.

(a) Nan yelled "Did you see that hawk? It was huge!"

(b) "Its nest is in that tree" said Carlos.

Solution

(a) We place a comma just before Nan's words.

Nan yelled, "Did you see that hawk? It was huge!"

(b) We place a comma after Carlos's words. The comma goes inside the quotation marks.

"Its nest is in that tree," said Carlos.

Practice

a. List the seven coordinating conjunctions.

For b–d, write the coordinating conjunction in each sentence.

b. Gus is a botanist, for he studies plants.

c. Bats are mammals, yet they fly!

d. Mom's eyes are blue, but mine are brown.

Rewrite these compound sentences, inserting commas before the coordinating conjunctions.

e. The man felt weak and his shoulders sagged.

f. He wanted water but there wasn't any.

Rewrite sentences g and h, inserting commas to offset direct quotations.

g. Gus said "Good night."

h. "And God bless you" he added.

For i and j, replace each blank with *botany* or *entomology*.

i. _____ is the study of insects.

j. _____ is the study of plants.

More Practice See "More Practice Lesson 76" in the Student Workbook.

Review Set 76 Choose the correct word to complete sentences 1–10.

1. The (elytra, stern, antennae) of beetles hide the wings
(75) that they use for flying.

2. Let us measure the (bow, girth, breadth), or width, of the
(74) flag.

3. A ship's (bow, stern, girth) cuts through the water.
(73)

4. During a drought, crop failure can create a (mire, idol,
(72) famine).

5. A large (heard, herd, preen) of bison blocked the
(32) highway.

6. The sentence below is (declarative, interrogative,
(2) imperative, exclamatory).

What ever happened to Henry Hudson?

7. The pronoun *she* is (nominative, objective, possessive)
(66, 69) case.

8. Those oars are (our's, ours).
(72)

9. I made (much, many) errors.
(56)

10. The pronoun *us* is (first, second, third) person (singular,
(64) plural).

11. Rewrite the following poem title, adding capital letters as needed:

"the owl and the pussycat"

12. Write the antecedent of the circled pronoun in the following sentence:

Gus opened the cage but failed to close (it).

13. Write the direct object in the following sentence:

Bees guard the queen of their hive.

14. Write the subordinating conjunction in this sentence:

Although he had sailed for Asia, John Cabot landed in Canada.

15. Add suffixes:

(a) crazy + er   (b) spin + ing

16. Write whether the following is a complete sentence, a sentence fragment, or a run-on sentence.

The colonists worked hard many died.

17. Rewrite the sentence below, using a comma to clarify the meaning:

To John Smith was a hero.

18. From the following sentence, write each prepositional phrase, circling the object of each preposition.

Charles I was bad news for the Puritans of Massachusetts.

19. Rewrite the following sentence, using commas to offset the nonessential appositive.

John Winthrop a wealthy lawyer encouraged the Puritans.

20. Rewrite the following sentence, adding periods as needed:

Gov Winthrop did not trust Mrs Hutchinson

21. Write the nominative case pronoun to complete the
(66) sentence below.

The heroes were Rex and (him, he).

22. Write whether the clause below is dependent or
(73) independent.

before the cock crows

23. Rewrite the following sentence, adding commas and
(26, 76) capital letters as needed:

gus said "the lizard was there but now it isn't."

24. For the irregular verb *choose*, write the (a) present
(19, 65) participle, (b) past tense, and (c) past participle.

25. Write the objective case pronoun to complete the
(69) sentence below.

Ted went with Zoe and (I, me).

26. Write the seven common coordinating conjunctions
(76) listed in this lesson.

27. For a and b, write the plural of each noun.
(17, 22)
(a) class   (b) pen name

28. Diagram the simple subject and simple predicate of each
(75) clause in the following compound sentence:

Ed has chosen work, but I have chosen play.

Diagram each word of sentences 29–30.

29. Will ten pounds of potatoes be sufficient?
(45, 54)

30. My friend Joe will bring you and me a large sack of
(46, 58) potatoes.

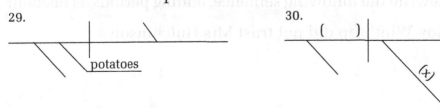

Relative Pronouns

Dictation or Journal Entry

Vocabulary:
The Latin prefix *in-* means "in" or "into." The Latin prefix *ex-* means "out of" or "from."

To *inhale* is to draw into the lungs; to breathe in. I try not to *inhale* dust and smoke.

To *exhale* is to expel from the lungs; to breathe out. Why can you see your breath when you *exhale* in cold weather?

Relative Pronouns

Relative pronouns play the part of subject or object in clauses:

> Sal and Kay, *who* train horses, live on a ranch. (subject)

> The trainers, *whom* I admire, have much patience. (object)

Relative pronouns often refer to nouns that have preceded them, making the sentence more compact.

> WORDY:
> Gus cares for pandas, and the pandas came from China.

> COMPACT:
> Gus cares for pandas, *which* came from China.

Simple

The following are simple relative pronouns:

> *who, whom, whose, what, which, that*

WHO REFERS TO PEOPLE (AND SOMETIMES ANIMALS):

> The girl *who* lives next door is nine.

> I have a cat *who* likes water.

WHICH REFERS TO ANIMALS OR THINGS:

> The calf, *which* had already eaten, still nibbled grass.

> He stared at his hair, *which* had not been cut in months.

THAT REFERS TO PEOPLE, ANIMALS, OR THINGS:

> She is the kind of person *that* everyone likes.

> The mule *that* escaped belongs to Jeb.

> The howl *that* you heard last night was a wolf.

Example 1   Choose the correct relative pronoun for each sentence.

(a) The woman (who, which) lives next door has a llama.

(b) That bridge, (who, which) has been wobbly for years, might fall.

(c) There is the child (which, that) I told you about.

Solution   (a) We choose **who** because it refers to "woman," a person. We do not use *which* for people.

(b) We choose **which** because it refers to "bridge," a thing. We do not use *who* for things.

(c) We choose **that** because it refers to "child," a person. We do not use *which* for people.

Errors to Avoid   The relative pronoun *who* can cause problems, because *who* changes form depending on the part it plays in the clause:

SUBJECT	OBJECT	POSSESSIVE
who	*whom*	*whose*

In the sentences below, we diagram the dependent clause to show how the pronoun is used.

SUBJECT:
Miss Ng, *who* was my teacher, will call today.

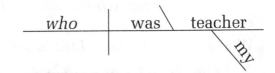

OBJECT:
Miss Ng, *whom* you met, will call today.

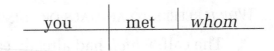

POSSESSIVE:
Miss Ng, *whose* help I appreciate, will call today.

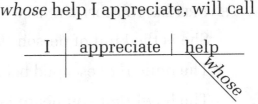

Example 2 Diagram the dependent clause to help you determine whether the pronoun is a subject or an object in the clause. Then, choose the correct pronoun form.

(a) That friend, (who, whom) I miss, has moved to Mexico.

(b) Kate, (who, whom) lives nearby, raises finches.

(c) Stan, (who, whom) writes music, has two guitars.

(d) Only Ben, (who, whom) I recognized, wore a tie.

Solution (a) That friend, ***whom*** I miss, has moved to Mexico. (object)

(b) Kate, ***who*** lives nearby, raises finches. (subject)

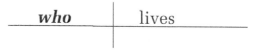

(c) Stan, ***who*** writes music, has two guitars. (subject)

who	writes	music

(d) Only Ben, ***whom*** I recognized, wore a tie. (object)

I	recognized	***whom***

Compound The following are compound relative pronouns:

whoever, whomever, whosoever
whatever, whatsoever, whichever

He may choose *whichever* color he wants.

Whatever you do, be there on time.

Notice that we carefully choose *whoever* or *whomever* depending on the part the compound relative pronoun plays in the clause.

You may invite *whomever* you want. (object)

Whoever is hungry may come for snacks. (subject)

Practice Choose the correct relative pronoun for sentences a–d.

    a. Children (who, which) have pets should care for them.

    b. The student (who, whom) took the key must return it.

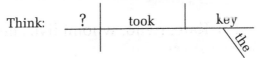

    c. The man (that, which) owns the store went home.

    d. Ted, (who, whom) I saw at school, asked me to babysit his puppy.

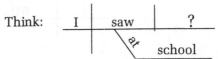

    e. Diagram the dependent clause in the sentence below to show how the pronoun is used.

    Kim, *who* is my best friend, helps me with math.

For f and g, replace each blank with *inhale* or *exhale*.

    f. When we _____, we fill our lungs.

    g. We _____ to blow out candles.

More Practice Choose the correct relative pronoun for each sentence.

    1. We thank all (who, whom) help.

        Think: ? | help

    2. Nan, (who, whom) washes windows, works as a volunteer.

        Think: ? | washes | windows

3. The volunteers, (who, whom) I shall thank, gave me new hope.

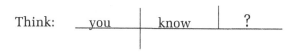

Think: I | shall thank | ?

4. Some of the volunteers, (who, whom) you know, stayed until dark.

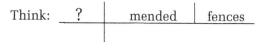

Think: you | know | ?

5. Ed, (who, whom) you met yesterday, mopped floors.

Think: you | met | ?

6. Those (who, whom) mended fences finished at sunset.

Think: ? | mended | fences

Review Set 77

Choose the correct word(s) to complete sentences 1–11.

1. In a(n) (entomology, metamorphosis, botany) class, we
(76) study plants.

2. On insects, (breadth, girth, antennae) are located on the
(75) forehead, between the eyes.

3. We measured the (stern, bow, girth) of the giant sequoia
(74) tree.

4. The (bow, stern, girth) is the back of a ship.
(73)

5. Damien (herd, heard, rode) the sirens.
(32)

6. The word *baby's* is a (plural, possessive) noun.
(13)

7. The pronoun *they* is (nominative, objective, possessive)
(66, 69) case.

8. (You're, Your) seat is in front.
(72)

9. Sid has made (less, fewer) errors than I.
(56)

10. The pronoun *our* is (first, second, third) person (singular,
(64) plural).

11. Penny, (who, whom) I admire, collects coins.
(77)

Think:	I	admire	?

12. Write whether the sentence below is simple or compound.
(75)

Annabelle may call, write, or email her aunt.

13. Write the predicate adjective in the following sentence:
(54)

His hair is curly.

14. Write the subordinating conjunction in this sentence:
(73)

Rex is scratching because he has fleas.

15. For a and b, write the word that is spelled correctly.
(35)

(a) ieght, eight   (b) piece, peice

16. Complete the following sentence, using the correct verb tense.
(61)

Nan (present progressive of *curl*) her hair.

17. Rewrite the sentence below, using a comma to clarify the meaning:
(68)

Without Abe Scott feels lonely.

18. Rewrite the word *bought*, circling the silent letters.
(28, 29)

19. Using an appositive, combine the following two sentences into one sentence.
(58)

The cerebrum is the largest part of the brain.

The cerebrum controls the body's movements.

20. Rewrite the following sentence, adding periods as needed:
(47, 50)

Mrs Cox's baby, Ian P Cox, Jr, weighed 9 pounds at birth

21. Write whether the circled pronoun in the sentence below is used as a subject or an object.
(64)

Abe and (he) will rake leaves.

22. Write whether the word group below is a phrase or a
(36) clause.

the largest part of the brain

23. Rewrite the following sentence, adding commas and
(15, 74) capital letters as needed:

as i took a step i nearly crushed a big ugly cockroach.

24. For the irregular verb *grow*, write the (a) present
(19, 65) participle, (b) past tense, and (c) past participle.

25. Which sentence is more polite? Write *A* or *B*.
(69)   A. The big bug startled her and me.

  B. The big bug startled me and her.

26. Rewrite the following compound sentence, adding a
(76) comma before the coordinating conjunction.

Joe is playing games for he has finished his work.

27. Rewrite the following letter, adding commas and capital
(41, 63) letters as needed.

dear ana
    please call write or email me soon.

                love
                aunt belle

28. Diagram the simple subject and simple predicate of each
(75) clause in the following compound sentence:

Joe is playing games, for he has finished his work.

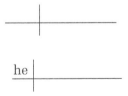

Diagram each word of sentences 29–30.

29. Is Ana's aunt lonely or ill?
(49, 54)

30. Ana, an excellent reader, could read her aunt an article
(46, 58) from a magazine.

29.

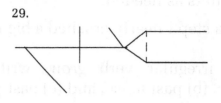

30.

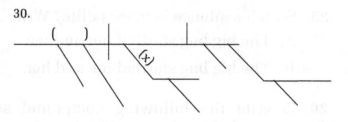

Pronoun Usage

Dictation or Journal Entry

Vocabulary:

The Latin root *centum* means "hundred."

A *centimeter* is a unit of measure equal to one hundredth of a meter. One hundred *centimeters* equal one meter.

A *centipede* (Latin *centum* + *pes,* foot) is a wormlike invertebrate with many pairs of legs. Does a *centipede* really have a hundred feet?

In this lesson, we shall discuss situations in which pronoun usage can be troublesome.

Written vs. Spoken Language

Traditionally, pronouns that follow a form of "to be" must be in the nominative case, as in the examples below:

It is *I.*

Was it *they* who called?

I thought it was *she.*

When we write, we should follow this rule. When we are speaking, however, we tend to be less formal. Our ear tells us that in casual conversation, "It is I" sounds stiff. Instead, we are more likely to say:

It is *me.*

Was it *them* who called?

I thought it was *her.*

This relaxed pronoun usage is acceptable in casual conversation, but it would be unacceptable in formal speech or any form of writing.

Now, we will discuss two more areas that often cause trouble in pronoun usage.

Appositions

We remember than an appositive renames a person or thing. An **apposition** is a pronoun used to rename a noun for emphasis.

Only one student, *you,* may read ahead.

Miss Ng named the winners of the essay contest, *you* and *him.*

The apposition must be in the same case form as the noun it renames. Consider the examples below.

> SUBJECT:
> *We* (NOT *us*) students took the test.
>
> OBJECT:
> Teachers like *us* (NOT *we*) young people.
>
> SUBJECT:
> Both girls, Grace and *she* (NOT *her*), ran laps.

Example 1 Choose the correct apposition for this sentence:

> Miss Ng sent two boys, Gus and (him, he).

Solution The apposition "Gus and him" renames "boys," which is a direct object, so we use the objective case pronoun:

> Miss Ng sent two boys, Gus and **him.**

Comparisons In comparison sentences, words are sometimes omitted. This usually occurs following the words *than* or *as*.

> She writes better than *I*. ("do" is omitted)
>
> I can climb as high as *he*. ("can" is omitted)

Notice that the pronouns in the sentences above are in the nominative case because they are used as the subjects of clauses whose verbs are understood (not stated).

The pronoun used in a comparison is important because it can change the meaning of the sentence:

> Ed loves Rex as much as *she*. ("does" is omitted)
> [MEANING: Ed loves Rex as much as she does.]
>
> Ed loves Rex as much as *her*. ("he loves" is omitted)
> [MEANING: Ed loves Rex as much as he loves her.]

Example 2 Choose the correct pronoun for the following sentences.
(a) We draw better than (they, them).

(b) Ed is as tall as (she, her).

Solution (a) We draw better than **they**. ("do" is omitted)

(b) Ed is as tall as **she**. ("is" is omitted)

Practice   Choose the correct pronoun for sentences a–e.

   a. (We, Us) girls can try harder.

Think: <u>   ?   </u> | <u>can try</u>

   b. It is okay with (we, us) boys if you build a fort.

Think:

   c. A thud startled (we, us) boys.

Think: <u>thud</u> | <u>startled</u> | ?

   d. He is a better cook than (I, me). ["am" omitted]

   e. Sid travels as far as (we, us). ["do" omitted]

For f and g, replace each blank with *centimeter* or *centipede*.

   f. A _____ might have a hundred feet.

   g. A _____ is one hundredth of a meter.

More   Choose the correct pronoun for each sentence.
Practice

   1. Ron has more freckles than (she, her). ["does" omitted]

   2. (We, Us) students enjoy math.

Think: <u>   ?   </u> | <u>enjoy</u>

   3. Miss Ng gave (we, us) students the answer.

Think: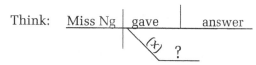

   4. Gus and (her, she) will redo the problem.

Think: <u>   ?   </u> | <u>will redo</u>

   5. We met two new girls, Ava and (her, she).

Think: <u>We</u> | <u>met</u> | ?

   6. Ed hiked farther than (he, him). ["did" omitted]

7. Nan sleeps later than (she, her). ["does" omitted]

8. I sing higher than (they, them). ["do" omitted]

9. (We, Us) girls laughed and laughed.

Think: ___?___ | laughed

10. The water cooled (we, us) workers.

Think: ___water___ | cooled | ?

Review Set 78

Choose the correct word(s) to complete sentences 1–12.

1. To (exhale, inhale, preen) smoke is harmful to one's
(77) lungs.

2. Those who want to study bugs should enroll in a(n)
(76) (entomology, botany, pollination) class.

3. Some beetles have shiny green (antennae, pollen, elytra)
(75) covering their bodies.

4. The (girth, stern, breadth) of the river was too narrow for
(74) large ships to pass one another.

5. A coupon made the item (cheep, cheap, feat).
(33)

6. The word *centipede* is a(n) (abstract, concrete) noun.
(11)

7. The pronoun *I* is (nominative, objective, possessive) case.
(66, 69)

8. This key is (her's, hers).
(72)

9. Of the two brothers, Aaron has the (curlier, curliest) hair.
(56)

10. The pronoun *their* is (first, second, third) person
(64) (singular, plural).

11. Penny, (who, whom) collects coins, owes me a dime.
(77)

Think: ___?___ | collects | coins

12. (We, Us) students like Fridays best.
(78)

Think: ___?___ | like

13. Write the seven common coordinating conjunctions
(48, 75) listed in lessons 48 and 75.

14. Write the subordinating conjunction in this sentence:
(73)

Everyone knows that slavery is wrong.

15. Write the antecedent for the pronoun circled in the
(62) sentence below.

Some people wish that (they) could fly.

16. Write whether the following is a complete sentence, a
(5, 23) sentence fragment, or a run-on sentence.

The Great Wall in ancient China.

17. Rewrite the sentence below, using a comma to clarify the
(68) meaning:

After the rain puddles were deep.

18. Use a dictionary: (a) The word *debt* is what part of
(27, 30) speech? (b) Write its pronunciation. (c) Write its
etymology.

19. Rewrite the sentence below, using commas to offset the
(60) nonessential appositive.

James Oglethorpe an Englishman wanted to give debtors
a second chance.

20. Rewrite the following sentence, adding periods as needed:
(47, 50)
Al's Tire Co is on N First St in Laketown

21. Write the nominative case pronoun to complete the
(66) sentence below.

My nurses were Addy and (him, he).

22. Write whether the clause below is dependent or
(73) independent.

Oglethorpe founded the colony of Georgia

23. Rewrite the following sentence, adding commas and
(74) capital letters as needed:

when oglethorpe returned to england he faced a fair
morciful jury.

24. For the irregular verb *swear*, write the (a) present
(19, 65) participle, (b) past tense, and (c) past participle.

25. Write the objective case pronoun to complete the
(69) sentence below.

Hand the coin to Penny or (she, her).

26. Rewrite the following compound sentence, adding a
(76) comma before the coordinating conjunction.

I played chess but I did not win.

27. Rewrite the following title, adding capital letters as needed:
(25)
"the people could fly"

28. Diagram the simple subject and simple predicate of each
(75) clause in the following compound sentence:

The oak has frozen, and boughs have broken.

Diagram each word of sentences 29–30.

29. Whom shall I ask?
(77)

30. Did Buzz, the barber, give Alex a short haircut?
(46, 58)

29.

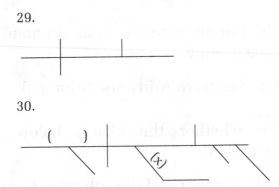

30.

Interrogative Pronouns

Dictation or Journal Entry

Vocabulary:

Audible means "loud enough to be heard." Did God speak in an *audible* voice?

The Latin prefix *in-* means "not" or "without."

Inaudible means "cannot be heard." The whisper was almost *inaudible*.

When a relative pronoun introduces a question, it is called an **interrogative pronoun**. *Who, whom, whose, what, which, whoever, whomever, whichever,* and *whatever* are interrogative pronouns.

> *Who* is there?

> *What* do you want?

> *Which* shall I choose?

> *Whom* are you calling?

> *Whoever* would do that?

A sentence does not have to end with a question mark to contain an interrogative pronoun. Sometimes, an interrogative pronoun introduces a question that is contained inside a declarative sentence:

> Nan asked *who* was there.

> Ed wondered *what* they wanted.

> I do not know *which* is best.

Example 1 Write each interrogative pronoun that you find in each sentence.

(a) We wonder what will happen next.

(b) Who ate the egg roll?

(c) I cannot guess which he will choose.

(d) Whose old shoe is this?

Solution (a) **what**   (b) **Who**   (c) **which**   (d) **Whose**

Who or Whom To decide whether we should use *who* or *whom*, we must determine what part the interrogative pronoun plays in the sentence. If it functions as a subject or a predicate nominative, we use *who*.

Who sang the solo? (subject)

$$\underline{\quad Who \quad \big| \quad sang \quad }$$

The soloist was *who*? (predicate nominative)

$$\underline{\quad soloist \quad \big| \quad was \; \backslash \, who \quad }$$

If the interrogative pronoun is an object (direct object, indirect object, or object of a preposition), we use *whom*.

Whom did Ed call? (direct object)

$$\underline{\quad Ed \quad \big| \quad did\ call \; \big| \; Whom \quad }$$

Nan gave *whom* a gift? (indirect object)

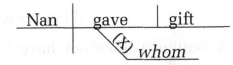

To check whether we have used *who* or *whom* correctly, we can turn the questions above into statements, substituting *he* or *she* for *who* and *him* or *her* for *whom*:

RIGHT: Ed <u>did call</u> *him*.
WRONG: Ed <u>did call</u> *he*.

RIGHT: Nan <u>gave</u> *her* a gift.
WRONG: Nan <u>gave</u> *she* a gift.

Errors to Avoid   Do not confuse *whose* and *who's*. *Whose* is a possessive or interrogative pronoun. *Who's* is a contraction for "who is." **Possessive pronouns do not have apostrophes.**

Who's that? (Who is that?)

Whose bag is that?

Example 2   Choose the correct interrogative pronoun for each sentence.

(a) (Who, Whom) caught the crab?

(b) (Who, Whom) did you expect?

(c) To (who, whom) are you speaking?

(d) This one is mine, but (who's, whose) is that?

Solution (a) The pronoun is used as the subject, so we choose *Who.*

Who caught the crab?

(b) The pronoun is used as an object, so we choose *Whom.*

Whom did you expect?

you | did expect | *Whom*

To check whether we have used *who* or *whom* correctly, we change the question into a statement, substituting *he* or *she* for *who* and *him* or *her* for *whom.*

RIGHT: You <u>did expect</u> *him.*
WRONG: You <u>did expect</u> *he.*

(c) The pronoun is used as an object of a preposition, so we choose *whom.*

To **whom** are you speaking?

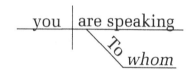

(d) *Who's* is a contraction for "who is." We choose the interrogative pronoun *whose.*

This one is mine, but **whose** is that?

Practice For a–c, write the interrogative pronoun from each sentence.

a. I cannot imagine what he wanted.

b. Which shall we choose?

c. Whose sack lunch is that ?

For d–f, choose the correct interrogative pronoun for each sentence.

d. (Who, Whom) will you ask for help?

e. (Who's, Whose) little black dog is that?

f. (Who, Whom) wants more soup?

For g and h, replace each blank with *audible* or *inaudible*.

g. The sound was _____; I could not hear it.

h. The sound was _____; I could hear it clearly.

More Practice Choose the correct word to complete each sentence.

1. (Who's, Whose) whispering?

2. (Who's, Whose) voice do I hear?

3. (Who, Whom) made the soup?
   Think: <u> ? </u>|<u> made </u>

4. To (who, whom) does this bag belong?
   Think: <u>To</u> ?

5. (Who, Whom) are you calling?
   Think: <u> you </u>|<u> are calling </u>|<u> ? </u>

6. (Who's, Whose) the woman in the green hat?

7. (Who's, Whose) book is this?

8. With (who, whom) would you like to speak?
   Think: <u>With</u> ?

9. (Who, Whom) will play?
   Think: <u> ? </u>|<u> will play </u>

10. (Who, Whom) did you invite?
    Think: <u> you </u>|<u> did invite </u>|<u> ? </u>

Review Set 79 Choose the correct word(s) to complete sentences 1–13.

1. An inch equals 2.54 (girths, breadths, centimeters).
   (78)

2. People inhale oxygen and (sent, cent, exhale) carbon
   (77) dioxide.

3. Plant biology is also called (metamorphosis, botany,
   (76) entomology).

4. Crabs have two pairs of (antennae, elytra, feat) for
   (75) sensing.

5. We heard the chicks (cheep, cheap, feat).
(33)

6. The word *windmill* is a (compound, collective) noun.
(11, 13)

7. The pronoun *me* is (nominative, objective, possessive)
(66, 69) case.

8. (They're, Their) noses are cold.
(72)

9. Of the three cousins, Aaron has the (curlier, curliest) hair.
(55)

10. The pronoun *you* is (first, second, third) person.
(64)

11. Zoe, (who, whom) the bee stung, will be more careful
(77) next time.

Think: bee | stung | ?

12. Gus invited (we, us) fourth graders.
(78)

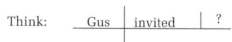

Think: Gus | invited | ?

13. (Who, Whom) are you missing?
(79)

Think: you | are missing | ?

14. Write the subordinating conjunction in this sentence:
(73)

We swam until the sun went down.

15. Write whether the sentence below is simple or
(75) compound.

Dutch colonists built windmills in New Netherland, but
their government failed.

16. Write the interrogative pronoun in the following
(79) sentence:

Who named New York City?

17. Rewrite the sentence below, using a comma to clarify the
(68) meaning:

This Charles could do.

18. Rewrite the word *reign*, circling the silent letter.
(28)

19. Use an appositive to combine the following two
(58) sentences into one sentence.

Carolina was an English colony.

Carolina split into two colonies.

20. Rewrite the following sentence, adding periods as needed:
(47, 50) Mr Brink grew corn, rice, etc, in Georgia

21. Write whether the circled pronoun in the sentence below
(64) is used as a subject or an object.

Bees stung Zoe and (me)!

22. From the following sentence, write each prepositional
(44) phrase, circling the object of each preposition.

All the hikers except Ed stepped over the snake.

23. Rewrite the following sentence, adding commas and
(74) capital letters as needed:

when dad was ten he marched with a small lively band.

24. For the irregular verb *sing*, write the (a) present
(19, 65) participle, (b) past tense, and (c) past participle.

25. Which sentence is more polite? Write *A* or *B*.
(69)   A. Please hand the tools to me or him.

   B. Please hand the tools to him or me.

26. Rewrite the following sentence, adding commas and
(26, 76) capital letters as needed.

   beth said "i was born on november 16 1975 so how old
   am i?"

27. Rewrite the following letter, adding commas and capital
(57, 63) letters as needed.

   dear aunt belle
        if you want i could bring mom dad and rex.
                                          love
                                          ana

28. Diagram the simple subject and simple predicate of each
(75) clause in the following sentence:

Colonists had planted seeds, and the seeds were sprouting.

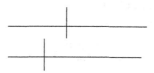

Diagram each word of sentences 29–30.

29. The new student is who?
(77)

30. Our teacher, Mr. Flores, loaned whom the key to his car?
(46, 58)

29.

30.

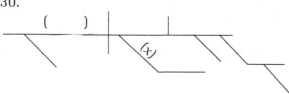

LESSON 80

Quotation Marks, Part 1

Dictation or Journal Entry

Vocabulary:

The Latin root *vad-* means "to go" or "to walk."

To *evade* is to escape something by trickery. One might *evade* answering the question by changing the subject.

To *invade* is to enter forcefully. Ants will *invade* a house if food crumbs are on the floor.

Direct Quotation

A **direct quotation** gives a speaker's exact words. To indicate a direct quotation, we enclose the speaker's words in quotation marks.

> Miss Ng told me, "Don't give up."

> "You can do it," she said.

Notice that in each of the examples above, the punctuation mark following the direct quotation appears **inside** the quotation marks.

Example 1

Place quotation marks where they are needed in the sentence below.

> Try again, said Miss Ng.

Solution

We place quotation marks before and after Miss Ng's words (including the comma that follows them).

> **"Try again," said Miss Ng.**

Direct Quotation with Explanatory Note

Sometimes, a direct quotation is interrupted by an **explanatory note,** such as *he said, she replied, the teacher explained,* etc. We enclose in quotation marks only the speaker's exact words, not the explanatory note. Notice that both parts of the direct quotations below are enclosed in quotation marks.

> "I can't do this," moaned Ed, "because it's too hard."

> "If you keep trying," she said, "you'll succeed."

Example 2

Place quotation marks where they are needed in the sentence below.

> Did you know, asked Miss Ng, that I have failed many times?

Solution We place quotation marks around both parts of Miss Ng's direct quotation, but we do not enclose the explanatory note (asked Miss Ng) in quotation marks.

"Did you know," asked Miss Ng, "that I have failed many times?"

Indirect Quotations An **indirect quotation** gives the main idea of what someone said, but it does not give the speaker's exact words. We do not use quotation marks with indirect quotations.

Miss Ng told me that I should never give up.

She explained that there is always hope for those who keep trying.

Example 3 Add quotation marks as needed in the sentence below.

Miss Ng said that she, too, has failed.

Solution **No quotation marks** are necessary, because this is not a direct quotation. It is an **indirect quotation.**

Practice For a–d, correctly rewrite each sentence that needs quotation marks. If the sentence does not need quotation marks, write "none."

  a. My classmate Ed complains that grammar is too hard.

  b. He tells me that he wants to quit.

  c. Read carefully, said Mr. Kim.

  d. Take your time, said the teacher, and you will do better.

For e and f, replace each blank with *invade* or *evade.*

  e. If you do not want to do something, you might try to _____ it.

  f. Please do not allow that bear to _____ our tent!

More Practice See "More Practice Lesson 80" in the Student Workbook.

Review Set 80 Choose the correct word(s) to complete sentences 1–13.

  1. Was the dog's whimpering (week, mist, audible) to the
  (79) neighbors?

2. Despite their name, (centipedes, hoarses, horses) do not
(78) always have one hundred feet.

3. We (inhale, exhale, stern) to smell roses.
(77)

4. (Entomology, Botany, Metamorphosis) is a branch of
(76) zoology focused on insects.

5. Water is relatively (creak, cheep, cheap) when one
(33) considers its value.

6. The sentence below is (declarative, interrogative,
(2) imperative, exclamatory).

The cello is a stringed instrument.

7. The pronoun *my* is (nominative, objective, possessive)
(66, 69) case.

8. (Who's, Whose) nose is cold?
(79)

9. I have (less, fewer) blisters than (him, he). ["has" omitted]
(56, 78)

10. The pronoun *I* is (first, second, third) person (singular,
(64) plural).

11. Nan, (who, whom) loves her cat, worries about coyotes.
(77)

Think:	?	loves

12. (We, Us) cellists need practice.
(78)

Think:	?	need	practice

13. (Who, Whom) will play the cello?
(79)

Think:	?	will play	cello

14. Write the subordinating conjunction in this sentence:
(73)

Whenever her cat goes out, Nan worries.

15. Write the antecedent to the circled pronoun in the
(62) sentence below.

If her cat goes out, Nan worries about(him).

16. Write the predicate adjective in the following sentence:
(54)

Ed felt hopeless.

17. Rewrite the sentence below, using a comma to clarify the
(68) meaning:

For that Jeff paid a fortune.

18. Use a dictionary: (a) The word *canteen* is what part of
(27, 30) speech? (b) Write its pronunciation. (c) Write its
etymology.

19. Rewrite the sentence below, using commas to offset the
(60) nonessential appositive.

The tuba a brass instrument adds low notes to music.

20. Rewrite the following sentence, adding periods as needed:
(47, 50)

Come to the lake on Sat, Aug 10

21. Write the nominative case pronoun to complete the
(66) sentence below.

Our two bass players are Zoe and (he, him).

22. Write whether the clause below is dependent or
(73) independent.

because it hurts

23. Rewrite the following sentence, adding commas, capital
(76, 80) letters, and quotation marks as needed:

i have broken two pencils said ed but i shall keep
working.

24. For the irregular verb *break*, write the (a) present
(19, 65) participle, (b) past tense, and (c) past participle.

25. Write the objective case pronoun to complete the
(69) sentence below.

Send postcards to Lulu and (he, him).

26. Rewrite the following outline, adding periods and capital
(26, 47) letters as needed.

> i woodwind instruments
>   a flute
>   b oboe

27. Rewrite the following letter, adding commas and capital
(41, 63) letters as needed.

> dear ana
>   bring your family and i shall make lunch.
>   many thanks
>   aunt belle

28. Diagram the simple subject and simple predicate of each
(75) clause in the following compound sentence:

Ed broke two pencils, so he needs a new one.

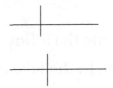

Diagram each word of sentences 29–30.

29. Whom will voters elect?
(77)

30. Will Roy, the skillful violinist, play Zoe and me a piece
(46, 58) by Tchaikovsky?

29.

30.

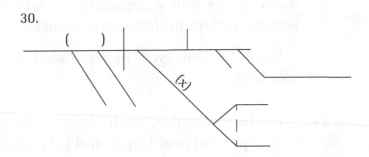

LESSON 81

Quotation Marks, Part 2

Dictation or Journal Entry

Vocabulary:

The Latin prefixes *ab-, a-,* and *abs-* mean "away."

An *aversion* is a strong dislike. Many people have an *aversion* to sharks.

Absent means "not present; away." Megaladon are now *absent* from the world's oceans.

Speaker Changes A set of quotation marks can contain the words of only one speaker. When the speaker changes, we use a new set of quotation marks. Also, when writing dialogue (conversation), we start a new paragraph every time the speaker changes.

Notice how quotation marks are used as the speaker changes in this dialogue:

"How old are you?" asked Sid.

"I am ten," replied Ben. "How old are you?"

"I'll be ten next month," answered Sid. "Would you like to play tag?"

"Yes," said Ben, "and I'll be *it*."

Example 1 Rewrite the following dialogue, inserting quotation marks as needed.

Where were you? he asked me in a sharp tone.

I was at Lulu's house, I said. Were you looking for me?

Yes, I was worried about you! he exclaimed.

Solution We know that a new paragraph means that the speaker has changed. We place quotation marks around the actual words of each speaker.

"Where were you?" he asked me in a sharp tone.

"I was at Lulu's house," I said. "Were you looking for me?"

"Yes, I was worried about you!" he exclaimed.

Titles The titles of short literary works are enclosed in quotation marks. This includes short stories, parts of books (chapters, lessons, sections, etc.), essays and sermons, one-act plays, newspaper and magazine articles, and short poems. We also enclose in quotation marks the titles of songs.

> Lewis Carroll's poem "Father William" makes me smile.
>
> Next, I shall read the story "The River Bank."
>
> Ed titled his essay "Life Is Not Fair."
>
> Please whistle something besides "Yankee Doodle."

We do not use quotation marks for larger works such as books, plays, movies, television programs, or operas. Instead, these titles are underlined or italicized (for example: Charlotte's Web, *Mr. Popper's Penguins*). We shall discuss this more in another lesson.

Example 2 Rewrite the sentences below, inserting quotation marks where they are needed.

(a) Does Nan sing Happy Birthday often?

(b) Kim wrote an article called John Muir's Adventures.

(c) Ed skipped the first chapter, Basic Concepts.

Solution (a) We place quotation marks around "Happy Birthday" because it is a song title.

Does Nan sing "Happy Birthday" often?

(b) We enclose "John Muir's Adventures" in quotation marks because it is the name of an article.

Kim wrote an article called "John Muir's Adventures."

(c) We enclose "Basic Concepts" in quotation marks because it is the title of a chapter in a book.

Ed skipped the first chapter, "Basic Concepts."

Practice For a and b, replace each blank with *aversion* or *absent*.

a. Some people have an _____ to hard work.

b. Julia was _____ from school, for she was ill.

Rewrite sentences c–e, inserting quotation marks as needed.

c. Have you ever read the poem Can't by Edgar Guest?

d. Let's sing Jingle Bells.

e. The short story The Devoted Friend is about loyalty.

f. Rewrite this dialogue, inserting quotation marks where they are needed.

> Sit here, Ed, and tell me about yourself. How are you doing? asked Nan.
>
> I am doing well in grammar, Ed said.

More Practice See "More Practice Lesson 81" in the Student Workbook.

Review Set 81 Choose the correct word(s) to complete sentences 1–13.

1. People sometimes stretch the truth to (inhale, invade, evade) trouble.
_(80)_

2. The student's question was (audible, inaudible, horse), so the teacher asked for it to be louder.
_(79)_

3. A (centipede, centimeter, elytra) is a unit of length in the metric system.
_(78)_

4. To blow out a candle, we (inhale, exhale, prey).
_(77)_

5. Known as the fertilizing part of flowering plants, (fir, pollen, stamen) can cause allergic reactions.
_(34)_

6. The word *friend's* is a (plural, possessive) noun.
_(13)_

7. The pronoun *their* is (nominative, objective, possessive) case.
_(66, 69)_

8. This seat is (your's, yours).
_(72)_

9. Of all the dogs, Fido has the (least, fewer, fewest) fleas.
_(56)_

10. The pronoun *we* is (first, second, third) person (singular, plural).
_(64)_

11. Nan, (who, whom) you know, has an aversion to coyotes.
_(77)_

> Think: ___you_ | know | ?

12. They have more time than (us, we). ["have" omitted]
(78)

13. For (who, whom) shall we sing?
(79)

Think:　　　　For
　　　　　　　　　　　　　　　　　?

14. Write the subordinating conjunction in this sentence:
(73)
As soon as she finds her cat, Nan will relax.

15. Write whether the sentence below is simple or
(75) compound.

William Penn joined the Society of Friends.

16. Write the interrogative pronoun in the following
(79) sentence:

Whom will you visit?

17. Rewrite the sentence below, using a comma to clarify the
(68) meaning:

That Jake can take home.

18. Write the plural form of the singular noun *family*.
(16)

19. Use an appositive to combine the following two
(58) sentences into one sentence.

Jan Vermeer was a Dutch artist.

Jan Vermeer painted *The Milkmaid*.

20. Rewrite the following sentence, adding periods as needed:
(47, 50)

Dr Peña works at 26 S Second Ave in Arcadia

21. Write whether the circled pronoun in the sentence below
(64) is used as a subject or an object.

Abe and (she) are friends.

22. Rewrite the sentence below, adding commas and capital
(26, 67) letters as needed.

ed replied "no i have not seen nan's cat."

23. Rewrite the following sentence, adding commas, capital
(74, 80) letters, and quotation marks as needed:

if i see a young furry cat said ed i'll tell nan.

24. For the irregular verb *drink*, write the (a) present
(19, 65) participle, (b) past tense, and (c) past participle.

25. Rewrite the sentence below, adding capital letters and
(25, 81) quotation marks as needed.

let us hum the song row, row, row your boat.

26. Rewrite the compound sentence below, adding a comma
(76) before the coordinating conjunction.

Rex chews my shoes yet I forgive him.

27. Rewrite the following letter, adding commas and capital
(57, 63) letters as needed.

dear officer truant
    some healthy lazy students were absent on monday
tuesday and wednesday.
                           respectfully
                           mrs. barton R.N.

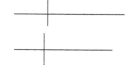

28. Diagram the simple subject and simple predicate of each
(75) clause in the following compound sentence:

We must hide our shoes, or Rex will chew them.

Diagram each word of sentences 29–30.

29. The healthy, lazy students are who?
(77)

30. Mrs. Barton, a nurse, gave the officer and me a report on
(46, 58) the health of each student.

29.

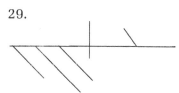

30.

LESSON 82

Demonstrative Pronouns

Pointing Pronouns

This, that, these, and *those* are **demonstrative pronouns.** Some people call them "pointing pronouns" because they seem to point out the person or thing being referred to, distinguishing it from others.

This is a ladybug.

That is a scorpion.

These are ants.

Those are termites.

A demonstrative pronoun must agree in number with its antecedent (the noun that it points out).

SINGULAR: *This* is a horse.

PLURAL: *These* are horses.

SINGULAR: *That* is a vertebrate.

PLURAL: *Those* are vertebrates.

This, These

We use *this* and *these* to point out persons or things that are nearby in space, time, or awareness.

This is a hamster.

These are my tools.

This has been a happy day.

That, Those

We use *that* and *those* to point out persons or things that are farther away.

That is a stray cat.

That was a good idea.

Those were fun games.

Errors to Avoid

We never add "here" or "there" to a demonstrative pronoun.

NO: This *here* is my plan.
YES: This is my plan.

NO: That *there* is the kindest woman.
YES: That is the kindest woman.

We do not use "them" in place of "these" or "those."

NO: *Them* are the ripe ones.
YES: *These* are the ripe ones.

NO: *Them* taste sweet.
YES: *Those* taste sweet.

Adjective or Pronoun? The demonstrative pronouns *this, that, these,* and *those* also function as demonstrative adjectives.

It is easy to tell the difference. If they stand alone, they are demonstrative pronouns. If they come before a noun, they are demonstrative adjectives.

These are too big. (pronoun)

These boots are too big. (adjective)

She wrote *this*. (pronoun)

She wrote *this* story. (adjective)

Example Choose the correct demonstrative pronoun for each sentence, and write the noun that it points to.

(a) (This here, This) is a picture of Rex.

(b) Is (that, those) the reason you came?

(c) (This, These) are the boots I like best.

(d) (Them, Those) are the socks I wore yesterday.

Solution (a) **This, picture**   (b) **that, reason**

(c) **These, boots**   (d) **Those, socks**

Practice For a and b, replace each blank with *brontosaurus* or *brontophobia.*

a. A _____ was a four-legged dinosaur that ate plants.

b. One who fears thunder suffers from _____.

For c–g, choose the correct demonstrative pronoun, and write the noun it points to.

    c. (This, These) is a friend of mine.

    d. (That, Those) are the colors of autumn.

    e. (This, These) is my youngest cousin.

    f. (These, That) are my ideas for fun.

    g. (This, This here) is the book I was looking for.

Review Set 82 Choose the correct word(s) to complete sentences 1–13.

    1. Some people have a(n) (mourning, stamen, aversion) to
(81) large dogs.

    2. Bedbugs can (evade, meat, invade) your house.
(80)

    3. Her voice was (inaudible, audible, week) only to those
(79) sitting near her.

    4. A(n) (centimeter, elytra, centipede) has a pair of legs on
(78) each body segment.

    5. The pollen produced by the (larva, pupa, stamen) is
(34) carried by wind, water, or animals to the flower.

    6. The word *aversion* is a(n) (abstract, concrete) noun.
(11)

    7. The pronoun *its* is (nominative, objective, possessive)
(66, 69) case.

    8. (Who's, Whose) key is this?
(79)

    9. Carl is the (better, best) of the two drummers.
(56)

    10. The pronoun *he* is (first, second, third) person (singular,
(64) plural).

    11. (Who, Whom) were they expecting?
(77, 79)

        Think: they | were expecting | ?

    12. (We, Us) pianists shall play a duet.
(78)

13. (That, Those) were heavy boots.
(82)

14. Write the subordinating conjunction in this sentence:
(73)
Since I came, the parrot has not spoken.

15. Add suffixes:
(33, 34)
(a) win + ing   (b) angry + er

16. Write whether the following is a complete sentence, a
(5, 23) run-on sentence, or a sentence fragment.

William Penn started a colony it was Pennsylvania.

17. Rewrite the sentence below, using a comma to clarify the
(68) meaning:

To Julius Caesar seems proud.

18. Use a dictionary: (a) The word *forage* is what part of
(27, 30) speech? (b) Write its pronunciation. (c) Write its
etymology.

19. Rewrite the following sentence, using commas to offset
(60) the nonessential appositive.

Rembrandt van Rijn a Dutch artist painted *Belshazzar's Feast*.

20. Rewrite the following sentence, adding periods as needed:
(47, 50)
You may see Dr Vásquez on Mon, Jan 7

21. Write the nominative case pronoun to complete the
(64) sentence below.

Ed and (he, him) spoke briefly.

22. From the following sentence, write each prepositional
(44) phrase, circling the object of each preposition.

A brontosaurus plods through the valley, alongside a river.

23. Rewrite the following sentence, adding commas, capital
(74, 80) letters, and quotation marks as needed:

ed said although i was born in boise idaho i now live in
iowa.

24. For the irregular verb *steal*, write the (a) present
(19, 65) participle, (b) past tense, and (c) past participle.

25. Rewrite the sentence below, adding capital letters and
(25, 80) quotation marks as needed.

let us read this short story titled uncle wiggily and the big
dog.

26. Rewrite the compound sentence below, adding a comma
(76) before the coordinating conjunction.

Rex ate my pencil so I could not do my math.

27. Rewrite the following letter, adding commas and capital
(63, 67) letters as needed.

dear mrs. barton R.N.
  the students i believe were fishing without licenses.
                              respectfully
                              officer truant

28. Diagram the simple subject and simple predicate of each
(75) clause in the following compound sentence:

King Belshazzar was feasting, and a hand wrote a
message on the wall.

Diagram each word of sentences 29–30.

29. The great Dutch artist painted whom?
(77)

30. A hand wrote Belshazzar a message about the end of his
(46) reign.

29.

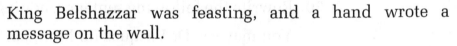

30.

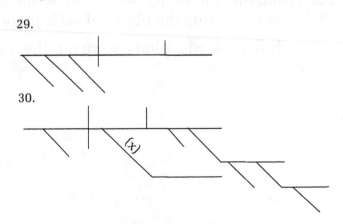

Indefinite Pronouns

A pronoun that does not have a known antecedent is called an **indefinite pronoun.** It refers only generally to a person or thing.

Anybody can come.

Several will walk.

Something is missing.

Singular Some indefinite pronouns refer to only one person or thing. They are singular and take singular verbs:

another	*anybody*	*anyone*
anything	*neither*	*either*
everybody	*everyone*	*everything*
each	*nobody*	*no one*
nothing	*other*	*one*
somebody	*someone*	*something*
much		

Everybody <u>needs</u> a friend.

Each of the friends <u>takes</u> a turn.

Neither of us <u>is</u> perfect.

Nothing <u>is</u> impossible.

Plural The following indefinite pronouns refer to more than one person or thing. They take plural verbs:

several	*both*	*few*
ones	*many*	*others*

Both <u>are</u> fine.

Few <u>were</u> quiet.

Many <u>are</u> excited.

Others <u>seem</u> nervous.

Singular or Plural The following indefinite pronouns can be singular or plural depending on their use in the sentence.

all	any	more
none	some	most

They are plural when they refer to things that can be counted.

Most docents <u>are</u> helpful.

They are singular when they refer to something that cannot be counted.

Most of the snow <u>is</u> gone.

Example 1 Write each indefinite pronoun and tell whether it is singular or plural in the sentence.

(a) *Much* has been written about sharks.

(b) *Each* writes his or her own report.

(c) *Many* of the sharks are dangerous.

(d) *All* of the snow has melted.

(e) *All* are invited to the picnic.

(f) *None* of the horses were docile.

Solution (a) ***Much*, singular** (b) ***Each*, singular**

(c) ***Many*, plural** (d) ***All*, singular**

(e) ***All*, plural** (f) ***None*, plural**

Example 2 Choose the correct verb form (singular or plural) to match the indefinite pronoun in each sentence.

(a) *All* of you (is, are) welcome.

(b) *Many* (need, needs) new shoes.

(c) *Few* (has, have) enough patience.

(d) (Is, Are) *anything* more fun than grammar?

Solution   (a) *All* of you **are** welcome.

(b) *Many* **need** new shoes.

(c) *Few* **have** enough patience.

(d) **Is** *anything* more fun than grammar?

Adjective or Pronoun? Just like demonstrative pronouns, when indefinite pronouns are placed before nouns, they function as indefinite adjectives.

Some are too sour. (pronoun)

Some plums are too sour. (adjective)

She gave one to *each*. (pronoun)

She gave one to *each* person. (adjective)

Agreement with Antecedents If an indefinite pronoun is the antecedent for a personal pronoun, the personal pronoun must agree in number, person, and gender.

SINGULAR: *Everything* has *its* purpose.

(antecedent)   (personal pronoun)

PLURAL: *Both* have *their* purpose.

(antecedent)   (personal pronoun)

Example 3 Choose the correct personal pronoun to match the antecedent.

(a) *Something* left (their, its) footprints in the sand.

(b) *Neither* of the girls forgot (their, her) money.

(c) *Some* have paid (their, his or her) money already.

Solution (a) The antecedent *something* is singular, so we choose the singular personal pronoun *its*.

Something left **its** footprints in the sand.

(b) The antecedent *neither* is singular, so we choose the singular personal pronoun **her.**

        Neither of the girls forgot **her** money.

(c) The antecedent *some* refers to people, who can be counted. We choose the plural personal pronoun ***their.***

        Some have paid **their** money already.

Practice For sentences a and b, write the indefinite pronoun and tell whether it is singular or plural.

    a. All of us are learning.

    b. Nobody plays better than she.

For sentences c–e, choose the correct verb form to match the indefinite pronoun.

    c. *None* of the orders (is, are) ready.

    d. *Some* of the players (is, are) practicing.

    e. *Each* of us (is, are) working hard.

For f–h, choose the correct personal pronoun and verb form to match the indefinite pronoun antecedent.

    f. *Something* (have, has) left (its, their) fur here.

    g. *Many* musicians (polishes, polish) (his, her, their) instruments daily.

    h. *None* of his art (sell, sells) for what (it, they) (is, are) worth.

For i and j, replace each blank with *docent* or *docile.*

    i. One can teach a _____ animal.

    j. One can learn much from a good _____.

More Practice Tell whether each indefinite pronoun is singular, plural, or either. (S = singular; P= plural; E = either)

    1. both   **2.** most   **3.** anybody   **4.** neither

    5. either   **6.** ones   **7.** everyone   **8.** few

9. everything   **10.** some   **11.** many   **12.** each

13. something   **14.** nothing   **15.** none   **16.** more

17. several   **18.** another   **19.** others   **20.** all

Review Set 83

Choose the correct word(s) to complete sentences 1–14.

1. Some students express interest in gigantic dinosaurs like
(82) the (brontophobia, brontosaurus, centipede).

2. (*Audible, Inaudible, Absent*) means "not present."
(81)

3. The thief cannot (invade, evade, inhale) capture for long.
(80)

4. A(n) (audible, inaudible, week) sound cannot be heard.
(79)

5. Very little water flowed in the (creak, creek, rode).
(35)

6. The word *choir* is a (compound, collective) noun.
(11)

7. The pronoun *they* is (nominative, objective, possessive)
(66, 69) case.

8. Is this car (their's, theirs)?
(72)

9. Abe caught (less, fewer, fewest) fish than I.
(56)

10. The pronoun *him* is (first, second, third) person (singular,
(64) plural).

11. The docent (who, whom) told the story was friendly.
(77, 79)

Think:	?	told	story

12. The docent showed (we, us) tourists a famous painting.
(78)

13. Everybody (is, are) here.
(83)

14. Nothing left (its, their) mark.
(83)

15. Write the subordinating conjunction in this sentence:
(73)

Wherever they go, they spread joy.

16. Write the predicate nominative in the sentence below.
(51)

Rembrandt was a great artist.

17. Rewrite the sentence below, using a comma to clarify the
(68) meaning:

To eat Nan needs a fork.

18. Write the plural form of the singular noun *boundary*.
(17, 22)

19. Use an appositive to combine the following two
(58) sentences to make one sentence.

Louis Armstrong was a jazz musician.

Louis Armstrong played the trumpet.

20. Write the antecedent to the circled pronoun in the
(62, 83) sentence below.

Both had (their) violins.

21. Write whether the circled pronoun in the sentence below
(66) is used as a subject or an object.

Will Officer Truant and (she) find the students?

22. Write whether the clause below is dependent or
(73) independent.

Some forgot their passwords.

23. Rewrite the following sentence, adding periods, commas,
(76, 80) capital letters, and quotation marks as needed:

mrs barton RN said sleep well eat well and drink plenty
of water

24. For the irregular verb *throw*, write the (a) present
(19, 65) participle, (b) past tense, and (c) past participle.

25. Write the objective case pronoun to complete the
(69) sentence below.

Ivy gave the officer and (her, she) a poor excuse.

26. Rewrite the outline below, adding periods and capital
(26, 47) letters as needed.

    i american artists
      a mary cassatt
      b edward hicks

27. Rewrite the following letter, adding periods, commas, and
(57, 67) capital letters as needed.

    dear officer truant
        if possible return the runaways to their school on e
    pine street topeka kansas
                      sincerely
                     mrs barton RN

28. Diagram the simple subject and simple predicate of each
(75) clause in the following compound sentence:

Ivy's boat capsized, for a wave hit it, and Ivy screamed.

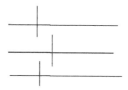

Diagram each word of sentences 29–30.

29. Whom should Officer Truant arrest?
(77)

30. Pooch, a docile poodle, brings his master the newspaper.
(46, 58)

29.

30.

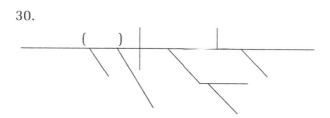

LESSON 84

Italics or Underline

The word *italics* refers to a slightly slanted style of type that is used to indicate the titles of larger literary works or to bring special emphasis to a word or phrase in a sentence. The book title below is in italics.

Making Thirteen Colonies

When we handwrite material, or when the italic style of type is not available, we **underline** the word or words that would require italics in print.

<u>Making Thirteen Colonies</u>

Here are some of the main categories of words and phrases that should be italicized or underlined.

Longer Literary Works, Movies, CDs, etc.
We italicize or underline titles of books, magazines, newspapers, pamphlets, plays, book-length poems, television programs, movies, films, record albums, tapes, and CDs.

Grandma watched TV shows like *Sheriff John*.

Have you read <u>The First Americans</u> by Joy Hakim?

Paintings, Sculptures, and Artwork
We italicize or underline the titles of paintings, sculptures, and other works of art.

Edvard Munch painted *The Scream* with bold colors and wavy lines.

The American artist Faith Ringgold made <u>Tar Beach</u>, a quilt that tells a story.

Ships, Planes, and Trains   We italicize or underline the names of ships, planes, and trains. (Words such as "The" and "U.S.S." are not treated as part of the vehicle's name.)

> Pilgrims sailed on the *Mayflower*.
>
> We travel by train on the <u>Coastal Express</u>.

Example 1   For sentences a–c, underline all the words that should be italicized or underlined.

(a) Great Grandpa flew a plane called the Bobcat.

(b) Leaves of Grass is a long poem by Walt Whitman.

(c) Pinkie is a famous painting by Thomas Lawrence.

Solution   (a) We underline **<u>Bobcat</u>** because it is the name of a plane. ("The" is not considered part of the name.)

(b) **<u>Leaves of Grass</u>** is a book-length poem.

(c) **<u>Pinkie</u>** is a painting.

Words as Words   We italicize or underline a word when the sentence calls attention to the word **as a word**.

> What does the word *pompous* mean?
>
> He used *really* too often in his essay.
>
> *Fish* can be a verb, but *tuna* cannot.

This is also true for numerals and lowercase letters.

> Make each lowercase *b* the same height as the numeral *4*.

Foreign Words and Phrases   We italicize or underline foreign words that are not used as part of everyday English language.

> The Dutch say *goedemorgen* (good morning) in the morning.
>
> We cannot change a <u>fait accompli</u> (an accomplished fact).

Genus and Species Names   We italicize or underline the scientific names for a genus, species, or subspecies.

> Horses, donkeys, and zebras are members of the genus *Equus*.
>
> *Castor canadensis* and *Castor fiber* are two species of beavers.

Example 2 For sentences a and b, underline each word that should be italicized or underlined.

(a) The simple predicate in this sentence is were swimming.

(b) Beau monde means "fashionable world" in French.

Solution (a) The sentence calls attention to the words **were swimming**.

(b) **Beau monde** is a foreign phrase.

Practice For a and b, replace each blank with *dinosaur* or *dinothere*.

a. The _____ had curved tusks.

b. _____ means "terrible lizard."

Write and underline the words that should be italicized in sentences c–g.

c. Appleseeds has been a popular magazine for children.

d. His speech had too many extra words, like well.

e. The scientific name for the cedar tree is Cedrus.

f. Spanish speakers use bonita for pretty.

g. My great grandparents sailed on the Queen Mary.

More Practice See "More Practice Lesson 84" in the Student Workbook.

Review Set 84 Choose the correct word(s) to complete sentences 1–14.

1. The local museum provided a(n) (ant, pinniped, docent)
(83) to guide the tour.

2. A violent storm might cause (drought, brontophobia, zephyr)
(82) in some children.

3. Some people have a(n) (aversion, illusion, pollination) to
(81) hard work.

4. Fleas can (evade, invade, absent) the furry coat of an
(80) animal.

5. The old wooden bridge might (invade, evade, creak)
_(35)_ when we cross it.

6. The sentence below is (declarative, interrogative,
_(2)_ imperative, exclamatory).

The Arctic Ocean surrounds the North Pole.

7. The pronoun _them_ is (nominative, objective, possessive)
_(66, 69)_ case.

8. (You're, Your) poem gave me goosebumps.
_(72)_

9. Of the two photos, this one is the (better, best).
_(56)_

10. The pronoun _they_ is (first, second, third) person
_(64)_ (singular, plural).

11. The students, (who, whom) you know, caught two fish.
_(77, 79)_

Think: __you__ | know | ?

12. Rex is docile, but Lady is more docile than (he, him).
_(78)_ ["is" omitted]

13. (Is, Are) everyone ready?
_(83)_

14. (Has, Have) everyone finished (their, his or her) essay?
_(83)_

15. Write the subordinating conjunction in this sentence:
_(73)_
The team plays soccer, even though it is raining.

16. Write the interrogative pronoun in the sentence below.
_(79)_
What have they done?

17. Write and underline the words that should be italicized
_(84)_ in the sentence below.

French speakers greet people with bonjour.

18. Rewrite the word _calm_, circling the silent letter.
_(28, 29)_

19. Rewrite the following sentence, using commas to offset the nonessential appositive.
(60)

Louisa May Alcott a popular American author wrote novels for children.

20. Write the antecedent to the circled pronoun in the
(62, 83) sentence below.

Neither had (her) umbrella.

21. Write the nominative case pronoun to complete the
(66) sentence below.

The most docile are Rex and (her, she).

22. Write whether the word group below is a phrase or a
(36) clause.

with long green socks and black shoes

23. Rewrite the following sentence, adding periods, commas,
(74, 80) capital letters, and quotation marks as needed:

officer truant replied yes as soon as i can i shall return the students to class

24. For the irregular verb *wear*, write the (a) present
(19, 65) participle, (b) past tense, and (c) past participle.

25. Which sentence is more polite? Write *A* or *B*.
(69)
A. You may ride with me or Edwin.

B. You may ride with Edwin or me.

26. Rewrite the sentence below, adding capital letters,
(67, 81) periods, commas, and quotation marks as needed.

yes i have read the fable titled the fox and the grapes

27. Rewrite the following letter, adding periods, commas, and
(57, 67) capital letters as needed.

dear mrs barton RN

on friday may 4 i shall lecture on school attendance
sincerely
officer truant

28. Diagram the simple subject and simple predicate of each
(75) clause in the following compound sentence:

Along comes the fox, for he wants some grapes, but can
he reach them?

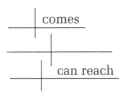

Diagram each word of sentences 29–30.

29. Are the grapes on the vine sour?
(45, 54)

30. Edwin gave Sam and me a ride to the library.
(46)

29.

30.

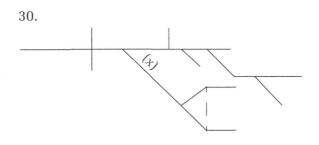

LESSON 85

Irregular Verbs, Part 3

Dictation or Journal Entry
Vocabulary:
The Latin *jocu* or *joct-* means "joke" or "humorous."

A *jester* is someone who likes to make people laugh. My uncle, the *jester* of the family, makes me giggle.

Jocular means "humorous." The *jocular* entertainer made funny faces at the crowd.

We have already learned that there are no rules for forming the past tense and past participle of irregular verbs. In this lesson, we will look at some additional irregular verbs.

Remember that we must memorize the principal parts of irregular verbs. To test yourself, cover the past tense and past participle forms; then try to write or say the past tense and past participle for each verb. Make a new list of the ones you miss, and work to memorize them.

VERB	PAST TENSE	PAST PARTICIPLE
beat	beat	(has) beaten
bite	bit	(has) bitten
bring	brought	(has) brought
build	built	(has) built
burst	burst	(has) burst
buy	bought	(has) bought
catch	caught	(has) caught
come	came	(has) come
cost	cost	(has) cost
dive	dived or dove	(has) dived
draw	drew	(has) drawn
drive	drove	(has) driven
eat	ate	(has) eaten
fall	fell	(has) fallen

feel	felt	(has) felt
fight	fought	(has) fought
find	found	(has) found
flee	fled	(has) fled
fly	flew	(has) flown
forget	forgot	(has) forgotten
forgive	forgave	(has) forgiven

Example 1 Write the past tense and past participle forms of each verb.
(a) beat   (b) bite   (c) build   (d) burst

Solution (a) beat, **beat, (has) beaten**

(b) bite, **bit, (has) bitten**

(c) build, **built, (has) built**

(d) burst, **burst, (has) burst**

Example 2 Write the correct verb form for each sentence.
(a) Some of us (feeled, felt) sad on the last day of school.

(b) Others (fleed, fled) without looking back.

(c) The last day had (come, came).

(d) It had (catched, caught) me by surprise.

Solution (a) Some of us **felt** sad on the last day of school.

(b) Others **fled** without looking back.

(c) The last day had **come**.

(d) It had **caught** me by surprise.

Errors to Avoid People sometimes treat a regular verb as if it were irregular. For example, the past tense of *drag* is *dragged*, not "drug." The past tense of *drown* is simply *drowned*, not "drownded." Avoid these errors by memorizing the irregular verbs and consulting a dictionary when in doubt. If the dictionary does not list the verb's principal parts, the verb is regular.

Practice For a–h, write the past tense and past participle form of each verb.

    a. catch   **b.** come   **c.** cost   **d.** dive

    e. drag   **f.** draw   **g.** drown   **h.** drive

For i–p, write the correct verb form for each sentence.

    i. After I had (ate, eaten) the stew, she told me what was in it.

    j. Where did you say she (find, found) the key?

    k. He (drived, drove) a red truck.

    l. The shoes must have (cost, costed) her fifty dollars.

    m. They (forgave, forgived) each other afterward.

    n. The lizard has (catched, caught) some crickets.

    o. Bats (flied, flew) everywhere.

    p. Rain (fell, falled) as we hiked the trail.

For q and r, replace each blank with *jester* or *jocular*.

    q. A _____ person is humorous.

    r. A _____ tries to be funny.

More Practice See "More Practice Lesson 85" in the Student Workbook.

Review Set 85 Choose the correct word(s) to complete sentences 1–14.

    1. The brontosaurus and stegosaurus are species of
    (84) (centipedes, pinnipeds, dinosaurs).

    2. The (docent, docile, defensive) sea lion performed many
    (83) tricks.

    3. The gigantic (brontosaurus, centipede, pinniped) had a
    (82) very long neck.

    4. Seven students were (audible, inaudible, absent) from
    (81) class because of the flu.

5. The (mandible, creek, creak) has more water when it
(35) rains.

6. The word *jesters* is a (plural, possessive) noun.
(13)

7. The pronoun *their* is (nominative, objective, possessive)
(66, 69) case.

8. My backpack is orange; (her's, hers) is blue.
(72)

9. Of the three photos, this one is the (better, best).
(56)

10. The pronoun *them* is (first, second, third) person
(64) (singular, plural).

11. Do you know anyone (who, whom) tells funny jokes?
(77, 79)
Think: ? | tells | jokes

12. Miss Ng gave (we, us) students a hint.
(78)

13. Many have (come, came) to sketch the old mansion.
(85)

14. Some (has, have) sketched (their, his or her) friends
(83) instead.

15. Write the subordinating conjunction in this sentence:
(73)
Until you succeed, you must keep trying.

16. Write the interrogative pronoun in the sentence below.
(79)
Whose long green socks are those?

17. Write and underline the words that should be italicized
(84) in the sentence below.

Let's read Ralph Ellison's novel Invisible Man.

18. Write the plural form of the singular noun *butterfly*.
(17, 22)

19. Use an appositive to combine the following two
(58) sentences into one sentence.

Robert Frost is an American poet.

Robert Frost wrote a poem called "The Road Not Taken."

20. Write whether the sentence below is simple or compound.
(75)

The Grinch is mean, so he steals everyone's presents.

21. Write whether the circled pronoun in the sentence below
(64) is used as a subject or an object.

Nan and (she) have forgiven each other.

22. From the following sentence, write each prepositional
(44) phrase, circling the object of each preposition.

Gulliver traveled to Brobdingnag, a land of giants.

23. Rewrite the following sentence, adding periods, commas,
(76, 80) capital letters, and quotation marks as needed:

oscar said yes my goose laid an egg but it was not golden

24. For the irregular verb *forgive*, write the (a) present
(19, 85) participle, (b) past tense, and (c) past participle.

25. Write the objective case pronoun to complete the
(69) sentence below.

Nan may ride with Ed or (me, I).

26. Rewrite the sentence below, adding capital letters,
(67, 81) periods, commas, and quotation marks as needed.

yes i know the song london bridge is falling down

27. Rewrite the following letter, adding periods, commas, and
(57, 63) capital letters as needed.

dear miss ng
　　　get plenty of rest exercise and fresh air
　　　　　　　　　　　　　　　sincerely
　　　　　　　　　　　　　　　mrs barton RN

28. Diagram the simple subject and simple predicate of each
(75) clause in the following compound sentence:

Into the lake dives Ivy, for she needs exercise, and the water is cool.

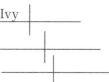

Diagram each word of sentences 29–30.

29. Can the Grinch steal the spirit of Christmas?
(45)

30. The people teach the Grinch a lesson about happiness.
(46)

29.

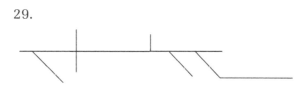

30.

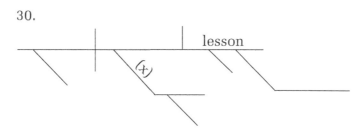

LESSON 86

Irregular Verbs, Part 4

Dictation or Journal Entry
Vocabulary:
The Latin *laps-* means "to slip" or "to fall."

To *collapse* means "to crumble or to fall suddenly." A bridge might *collapse* under the weight of many trucks.

Elapse means "to slip or to pass by." Many years have *elapsed* since dinosaurs roamed the earth.

In this lesson, we will look at more irregular verbs, whose principal parts we must memorize. To test yourself, cover the past tense and past participle forms; then try to write or say the past tense and past participle for each verb. Make a new list of the ones you miss, and work to memorize them.

VERB	PAST TENSE	PAST PARTICIPLE
get	got	(has) gotten
give	gave	(has) given
go	went	(has) gone
hang (execute)	hanged	(has) hanged
hang (suspend)	hung	(has) hung
hide	hid	(has) hidden or hid
hold	held	(has) held
keep	kept	(has) kept
lay (place)	laid	(has) laid
lead	led	(has) led
lend	lent	(has) lent
lie (recline)	lay	(has) lain
lie (deceive)	lied	(has) lied
lose	lost	(has) lost
make	made	(has) made
mistake	mistook	(has) mistaken

put	put	(has) put
ride	rode	(has) ridden
rise	rose	(has) risen
run	ran	(has) run
see	saw	(has) seen
sell	sold	(has) sold

Example 1 Write the past tense and past participle forms of each verb.
(a) see   (b) ride   (c) go   (d) give   (e) make

Solution (a) see, **saw, (has) seen**

(b) ride, **rode, (has) ridden**

(c) go, **went, (has) gone**

(d) give, **gave, (has) given**

(e) make, **made, (has) made**

Example 2 Write the correct verb form for each sentence.
(a) The moon (rised, rose) at seven p.m.

(b) Oh dear, I've (losed, lost) another tooth!

(c) Yesterday, I (run, ran) a mile.

Solution (a) The moon **rose** at seven p.m.

(b) Oh dear, I've **lost** another tooth!

(c) Yesterday, I **ran** a mile.

Practice For a–h, write the past tense and past participle form of each verb.

a. hide	**b.** hold	**c.** lay	**d.** lead
e. lend	**f.** mistake	**g.** put	**h.** sell

For i–l, write the correct verb form for each sentence.
i. Ed (hided, hid) the gift in a sack.

j. Grandpa (held, holded) a garter snake.

k. She had (laid, lain) her key on the desk.

l. That goat has (leaded, led) the others away.

For m and n, replace each blank with *collapse* or *elapse.*

m. Do not let many days _____ before you water the garden again.

n. The desk was wobbly and ready to _____.

More Practice   See "More Practice Lesson 86" in the Student Workbook.

Review Set 86   Choose the correct word(s) to complete sentences 1–14.

1. Circus clowns are sometimes called (inaudible, stern, jesters).
(85)

2. A stegosaurus is a (mandible, dinothere, dinosaur).
(84)

3. The (docent, pinniped, illusion) shared many facts about the exhibit.
(83)

4. (Brontophobia, Elytra, Entomology) may cause animals to panic in a thunderstorm.
(82)

5. A door needing oil will (creak, creek, preen) when opened.
(35)

6. The word *faith* is a(n) (abstract, concrete) noun.
(11)

7. The pronoun *we* is (nominative, objective, possessive) case.
(66, 69)

8. (Who's, Whose) green socks are these?
(79)

9. Edwin has (less, fewer) sheep than goats.
(56)

10. The pronoun *we* is (first, second, third) person (singular, plural).
(64)

11. (Who, Whom) were they calling?
(77, 79)

Think: | they | were calling | ? |

12. Nate is almost as jocular as (me, I). ["am" omitted]
(78)

13. Some have (went, gone) fishing.
(86)

14. Someone (have, has) laid (their, his or her) old shoe on my desk.
(83)

15. Write the two subordinating conjunctions in the sentence below.
(73)

Edwin acts as if he doesn't care that his goat ate my jacket.

16. Write the predicate adjective in the sentence below.
(54)

Does he seem jocular?

17. Write and underline the words that should be italicized in the sentence below.
(84)

We shall name our boat Dolphin Dreams.

18. Use a dictionary: (a) The word *hedge* is what part of speech? (b) Write its pronunciation. (c) Write its etymology.
(27, 30)

19. Rewrite the following sentence, using commas to offset the nonessential appositive.
(60)

The Grinch a nasty creature learns an important lesson.

20. Add suffixes:
(33, 34)

(a) messy + er   (b) thin + est

21. Write the nominative case pronoun to complete the sentence below.
(64)

The leaders were Ivy and (they, them).

22. Write whether the following is a phrase or a clause.
(36)

as cold as an ice cube

23. Rewrite the following sentence, adding periods, commas, capital letters, and quotation marks as needed:
(74, 80)

nan said although his goat ate my jacket i shall forgive edwin

24. For the irregular verb *drive*, write the (a) present
(19, 85) participle, (b) past tense, and (c) past participle.

25. Write the objective case pronoun to complete the
(69) sentence below.

Dad drove Ed and (me, I) to the library.

26. Rewrite the sentence below, adding capital letters,
(67, 81) periods, commas, and quotation marks as needed.

if you can recite the nursery rhyme hey diddle diddle

27. Rewrite the following letter, adding periods, commas, and
(57, 67) capital letters as needed.

my dear miss ng
          you may see dr payne on monday may 7
                              warm regards
                              mrs barton RN

28. Diagram the simple subject and simple predicate of each
(75) clause in the following compound sentence:

Ivy has swum for hours, so she is tired, but she must do
her chores before bedtime.

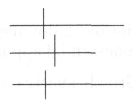

Diagram each word of sentences 29–30.

29. Is every joke funny?
(54)

30. Did Edwin lend you a new jacket with a hood?
(45, 46)

29.

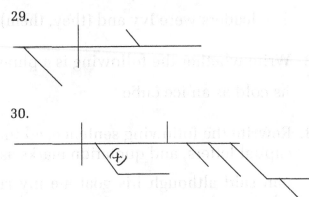

30.

Irregular Verbs, Part 5

Dictation or Journal Entry

Vocabulary:

The Latin *que-* means "to ask" or "to seek."

To *inquire* means "to ask." A detective may *inquire* about a criminal's past police record.

A *quest* is a search to find something. Good students are on a *quest* for knowledge.

In this lesson, we will look at one last group of irregular verbs, whose principal parts we must memorize. To test yourself, cover the past tense and past participle forms; then, try to write or say the past tense and past participle for each verb. Make a new list of the ones you miss, and memorize them.

VERB	PAST TENSE	PAST PARTICIPLE
sct	set	(has) set
shake	shook	(has) shaken
shine (light)	shone	(has) shone
shine (polish)	shined	(has) shined
shut	shut	(has) shut
sit	sat	(has) sat
slay	slew	(has) slain
sleep	slept	(has) slept
spring	sprang or sprung	(has) sprung
stand	stood	(has) stood
strive	strove	(has) striven
swim	swam	(has) swum
swing	swung	(has) swung
take	took	(has) taken

teach	taught	(has) taught
tell	told	(has) told
think	thought	(has) thought
wake	woke	(has) woken
weave	wove	(has) woven
wring	wrung	(has) wrung
write	wrote	(has) written

Example 1 Write the past tense and past participle forms of each verb.
(a) write   (b) think   (c) swim   (d) sleep   (e) stand

Solution (a) write, **wrote, (has) written**

(b) think, **thought, (has) thought**

(c) swim, **swam, (has) swum**

(d) sleep, **slept, (has) slept**

(e) stand, **stood, (has) stood**

Example 2 Write the correct verb form for each sentence.
(a) The wet dog had (shook, shaken) water all over the place!

(b) Pat has (wove, woven) two rugs on the loom.

(c) He (swang, swung) the bat and hit a home run.

Solution (a) The wet dog had **shaken** water all over the place!

(b) Pat has **woven** two rugs on the loom.

(c) He **swung** the bat and hit a home run.

Practice For a–h, write the past tense and past participle form of each verb.

a. take   **b.** set   **c.** teach   **d.** tell

e. wake   **f.** spring   **g.** strive   **h.** shut

For i–p, write the correct verb form for each sentence.

i. Have you ever (wrote, written) a poem?

j. Ben (sleeped, slept) well after exercising.

k. Have you (thought, thinked) about your future?

l. Has Miss Lee ever (teached, taught) art?

m. She (telled, told) me the truth.

n. Have you (woken, woke) at midnight before?

o. Ed (sitted, sat) at his desk.

p. The door (shutted, shut) with a bang.

For q and r, replace each blank with *inquire* or *quest*.

q. Detectives are on a _____ for the truth.

r. We shall _____ at the train station about the price of tickets.

More Practice See "More Practice Lesson 87" in the Student Workbook.

Review Set 87 Choose the correct word(s) to complete sentences 1–14.

1. Starving people might (elapse, collapse, invade) from
(86) hunger.

2. A (docent, dinothere, jester) is supposed to make people
(85) laugh.

3. A (centipede, hare, dinosaur) is an extinct reptile.
(84)

4. A(n) (mature, immature, docile) dog nips, yaps, jumps,
(36) and disobeys.

5. (*Docent, Docile, Audible*) means "teachable."
(83)

6. The word *grassland* is a (compound, collective) noun.
(11)

7. The pronoun *us* is (nominative, objective, possessive)
(66, 69) case.

8. This box is (their's, theirs).
(72)

9. Abe is the (better, best) of the two divers.
(56)

10. The pronoun *I* is (first, second, third) person (singular,
(64) plural).

11. Vera, (who, whom) I just called, will be late.
(77, 79)

Think:	I	called	?

12. I think (we, us) students should have a party.
(78)

13. I (lied, lay) down and (sleeped, slept) for an hour.
(86, 87)

14. Each (have, has) (their, his or her) own nickname.
(83)

15. Write the two subordinating conjunctions in the sentence
(73) below.

You may dry the car after I wash it, if you don't mind.

16. Write whether the following is a complete sentence, a
(5, 23) sentence fragment, or a run-on sentence.

The Eiffel Tower stands in Paris, France.

17. Write the sentence below, adding a comma to clarify the
(68) meaning.

After that time passed quickly.

18. Write the plural form of the singular noun *handful*.
(17, 22)

19. Use an appositive to combine the following two
(58) sentences into one sentence.

Robin Hood is a legendary English outlaw.

Robin Hood stole from the rich to give to the poor.

20. Write the antecedent to the pronoun circled below.
(62)

Robinson Crusoe survived even though (he) was
shipwrecked.

21.
(64)
Write whether the circled pronoun in the sentence below is used as a subject or an object.

Ed smiled at Nan and (her).

22.
(44)
From the following sentence, write each prepositional phrase, circling the object of each preposition.

Across the field, under the gate, and through the garden hopped the rabbit.

23.
(76, 80)
Rewrite the following sentence, adding periods, commas, capital letters, and quotation marks as needed:

ed said i wrote to ms mott but she has not written back

24.
(19, 85)
For the irregular verb *bring*, write the (a) present participle, (b) past tense, and (c) past participle.

25.
(60)
Which sentence is more polite? Write *A* or *B*.

A. Dad drove me and her to the library.

B. Dad drove her and me to the library.

26.
(67, 81)
Rewrite the sentence below, adding capital letters, periods, commas, and quotation marks as needed.

that song i believe is called down in the valley

27.
(41, 47)
Rewrite the following letter, adding periods, commas, and capital letters as needed.

dear aunt jen
    you have taught me much thank you for your help
                love
                lucas

28.
(75)
Diagram the simple subject and simple predicate of each clause in the following compound sentence:

Into the garden sneaks Peter, for he is hungry, and the lettuce looks tasty.

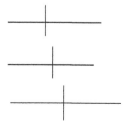

Diagram each word of sentences 29–30.

29. Is Peter's quest for food a mistake?
(45, 51)

30. Miss Ng, our wonderful teacher, told Nan and me a story
(46, 58) about Ali Baba.

29.

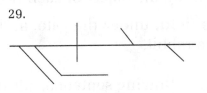

30.

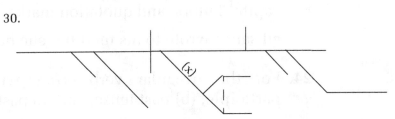

The Exclamation Mark • The Question Mark

Dictation or Journal Entry

Vocabulary:

The Latin *sag-* means "wise" or "shrewd."

A *sage* is a person of great wisdom. People admire the elderly *sage* for his experience and good judgment.

Sagacious means "shrewd; having or showing keen perception and sound judgment." *Sagacious* people think before they speak.

Almost every sentence ends with one of three punctuation marks. The period, the exclamation mark, and the question mark are called final punctuation marks.

Exclamation Mark   We use an **exclamation mark** after an exclamatory sentence (a sentence showing strong emotion).

It was a great white shark!

We can also use an exclamation mark after a word or phrase showing strong emotion. We call this an **interjection**.

Hooray!   Well done!   Oh no!

Careful writers try to limit their use of exclamation marks. Think of it as shouting. Sometimes shouting is appropriate, but someone who shouts all the time is soon ignored. Use exclamation marks sparingly.

Question Mark   We place a **question mark** at the end of an interrogative sentence (one that asks a question).

What is the cat's name?

Remember that a sentence can contain a questioning phrase without being an interrogative sentence.

I wonder what the cat's name is.

With Quotation Marks   When using exclamation marks and question marks with quotation marks, we must decide whether to place the final punctuation mark *inside* or *outside* the quotation marks. We do this by determining if the final punctuation mark punctuates the whole sentence or just the part in quotation marks.

In the sentence below, only the words in quotation marks ask a question. The question mark punctuates only the direct quotation, so it goes *inside* the quotation marks.

Someone asked, "Where have you been?"

In the next sentence, the question mark punctuates the whole sentence, so it goes *outside* the quotation marks:

Have they sung "America"?

Example Rewrite sentences a–d, inserting exclamation or question marks as needed.

(a) Was Robin Hood a real person

(b) What a surprise

(c) She exclaimed, "There he is"

(d) Can you sing "The Star Spangled Banner"

Solution (a) **Was Robin Hood a real person?** (interrogative sentence)

(b) **What a surprise!** (exclamatory sentence)

(c) The exclamation mark goes inside the quotation marks because it punctuates only the direct quotation.

She exclaimed, "There he is!"

(d) The question mark goes outside the quotation marks because it punctuates the entire sentence.

Can you sing "The Star Spangled Banner"?

Practice Rewrite sentences a–d, placing exclamation marks or question marks where they are needed.

a. Wow That detective is sagacious

b. Does she speak English

c. Who invented the telephone

d. I know It was Alexander Graham Bell

For e and f, replace each blank with *sage* or *sagacious*.

e. The _____ guide led many travelers safely through dangerous territory.

f. Because of her deep wisdom, the woman was called a _____.

Review Set 88

Choose the correct word(s) to complete sentences 1–14.

1. To (quest, collapse, inquire) means "to ask."
(87)

2. Much time has (elapsed, collapsed, inquired) since I borrowed that book.
(86)

3. Jake was happy, and we enjoyed his (weak, illusory, jocular) behavior.
(85)

4. Displayed in the case were huge bones from a (brontosaurus, hare, docent).
(82)

5. Beginning riders usually prefer a (cheep, mourning, mature) horse.
(36)

6. The sentence below is (declarative, interrogative, imperative, exclamatory).
(2)

Remove your hat, please.

7. The pronoun *me* is (nominative, objective, possessive) case.
(66, 69)

8. (Who, Whom) called you?
(79)

9. Abe is the (better, best) of the two divers.
(56)

10. The pronoun *it* is (first, second, third) person (singular, plural).
(64)

11. Vera, (who, whom) you have met, will be here soon.
(77, 79)

Think: ___you___ | have met | ?

12. Can you walk as fast as (her, she)? ["can" omitted]
(78)

13. Ed has (took, taken) many photos and (hanged, hung) them in his room.
(86, 87)

14. Both (have, has) (their, his or her) passes.
(83)

15. Write the two subordinating conjunctions in the sentence
(73) below.

While you wash the car, I shall dump the trash so that we
can surprise Dad.

16. Write the predicate adjective in the sentence below.
(54)

Ali Baba appears sagacious.

17. Write and underline the word that should be italicized
(84) in the sentence below.

Ivy tried to use the word jocular in a sentence.

18. Rewrite the word *bough*, circling the silent letters.
(28, 29)

19. Rewrite the sentence below, using commas to offset the
(60) nonessential appositive.

Superman a comic book hero protects people from evil.

20. Write whether the sentence below is simple or
(75) compound.

Baby Tarzan is abandoned in the jungle, but he becomes a
hero.

21. Write the nominative case pronoun to complete the
(64) sentence below.

Ed and (she, her) make salads.

22. Write whether the following is a phrase or a clause.
(36)

through drought and famine

23. Rewrite the following sentence, adding capital letters and
(80, 88) punctuation marks as needed:

nan asked have you heard from ms mott

24. For the irregular verb *buy*, write the (a) present participle,
(19, 85) (b) past tense, and (c) past participle.

25. Write the objective case pronoun to complete the
(69) sentence below.

Please come with Ed and (I, me).

26. Rewrite the sentence below, adding capital letters and
(81, 88) punctuation marks as needed.

what a funny story you should title it the forgetful sage

27. Rewrite the following letter, adding capital letters and
(41, 63) punctuation marks as needed.

dear amy
     have you found my missing purse it is red white and
blue

                    love
                    grandma

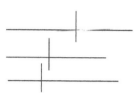

28. Diagram the simple subject and simple predicate of each
(75) clause in the following compound sentence:

Pinocchio tells lies, so his nose grows longer, yet he
proves his worthiness.

Diagram each word of sentences 29–30.

29. Has Ali Baba been sagacious?
(54)

30. Pinocchio, a wooden puppet with a long nose, shows
(46, 58) Geppetto and them his bravery.

29.

30.

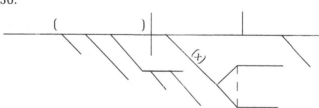

LESSON 89

Subject-Verb Agreement, Part 1

Just as a pronoun must agree with its antecedent, a verb must agree with the subject of the sentence in **person** and **number**.

Person Verbs and personal pronouns are the only parts of speech that change their form to show person (point of view).

When we learned about the irregular verbs *be, have,* and *do* in Lesson 18, we used a chart similar to the one below. Here we show two regular verbs (*work* and *wish*) and one irregular verb (*be*) in the first, second, and third person. (Most regular verbs form the third person singular by adding *-s* or *-es.* The irregular verbs must be memorized.)

	SINGULAR	PLURAL
1ST PERSON	**I** work, wish, am	**we** work, wish, are
2ND PERSON	**you** work, wish, are	**you** work, wish, are
3RD PERSON	**he** works, wishes, is	**they** work, wish, are

If the subject of a sentence is in the **first person** (*I, we*), the verb must also be in the first person:

> *I* work hard.   *We* wish them well.
>
> *I* am docile.   *We* are thankful.

If the subject of a sentence is in the **second person** (*you*), the verb must also be in the second person:

> *You* work hard.

If the subject of a sentence is in the **third person** (*he, she, it,* or any noun), the verb must also be in the third person:

> *He* walks home.   *They* walk home.
>
> *Nan* wishes her well.   *People* wish her well.
>
> The *jester* is funny.   The *jesters* are funny.

Number If the subject of a sentence is **singular**, the verb must also be singular:

I <u>work</u> hard.

She <u>wishes</u> me well.

If the subject of a sentence is **plural**, the verb must also be plural:

We <u>work</u> hard.

They <u>wish</u> us well.

Notice that the pronoun *you* always takes a plural verb, even when it is singular.

You <u>are</u> amazing, Ruth.

You <u>are</u> both outstanding.

Compound Subjects It is sometimes difficult to determine if the subject of a sentence is singular or plural.

Compound subjects joined by *and* are considered plural and require a plural verb.

Ed and *Ivy* <u>admire</u> your talent.

The *boys* and their *uncle* <u>fix</u> old cars.

Compound subjects joined by *or*, *nor*, *either/or*, or *neither/nor* can be singular or plural, depending on the subjects themselves:

If both subjects are singular, we use a singular verb.

Neither *Nan* nor *Ivy* <u>is</u> ready.

Either *Van* or *Don* <u>teaches</u> golf.

If both subjects are plural, we use a plural verb.

Neither the *pears* nor the *apples* <u>look</u> ripe.

My *sisters* or *brothers* <u>use</u> my nickname.

If one subject is singular and the other is plural, the verb should agree with the part of the subject it is closest to.

Neither the *dog* nor the *cats* <u>are eating</u> today.

Either the *violins* or the *cello* <u>sounds</u> out of tune.

Example Choose the correct verb form for each sentence.
(a) My sisters-in-law (is, are) nurses.

(b) Either Carl or Kate (has, have) the key.

(c) Neither the boys nor the girls (wants, want) homework.

(d) Ed or his sisters (sweep, sweeps) every day.

Solution (a) The subject "sisters-in-law" is plural, so we use the plural verb form: My sisters-in-law **are** nurses.

(b) When compound singular subjects are joined by *either/or*, we use the singular verb form: Either Carl or Kate **has** the key.

(c) Compound plural subjects joined by *neither/nor* require the plural verb form: Neither the boys nor the girls **want** homework.

(d) When compound subjects are joined by *or*, the verb agrees with the part of the subject it is closest to: Ed or his sisters **sweep** every day.

Practice For a–f, choose the correct verb form for each sentence.
a. Miss Cruz (was, were) sorry after the conflict.

b. The Cruzes (was, were) quick to forgive.

c. Abe and he (raise, raises) goats.

d. The rabbit or the pig (make, makes) a good pet.

e. Rabbits or pigs (make, makes) good pets.

f. Neither the cows nor the horse (has, have) been fed.

For g and h, replace each blank with *reticent* or *tacit.*
g. Her frown showed _____ disagreement.

h. One who is _____ is slow to speak.

More Practice Choose the correct verb form for each sentence.
1. Neither the guitar nor the drums (sound, sounds) right.

2. Either the dog or the wolves (is, are) howling.

3. Trout and salmon (swim, swims) in this stream.

4. The phoebe and the finch (is, are) small birds.

5. Either a duck or a goose (has, have) eaten my lunch!

6. A mole and a gopher (was, were) digging for food.

7. Either the jay or the squirrels (has, have) eaten the last nut.

8. Neither the cats nor the dog (see, sees) the chipmunk.

Review Set 89

Choose the correct word(s) to complete sentences 1–15.

1. A respected (fetlock, sage, pupa) offers good advice.
(88)

2. Knights were known for their (quests, hares, clauses) to save damsels.
(87)

3. People sometimes (elapse, collapse, invade) in extreme heat.
(86)

4. (Sages, Jesters, Pinnipeds) made the king and queen laugh.
(85)

5. The (optic, mire, mature) tree grew large, juicy peaches.
(36)

6. The word *finch's* is a (plural, possessive) noun.
(13)

7. The pronoun *mine* is (nominative, objective, possessive) case.
(66, 69)

8. (There, Their) dog is docile; (yours, your's) is not.
(72)

9. Ed has broken (less, fewer) pencils than Abe.
(56)

10. The pronoun *its* is (first, second, third) person (singular, plural).
(64)

11. Kim, (who, whom) lives in Boston, jogs up the hill every day.
(77, 79)

Think: _____?_____ | lives

12. You may call (we, us) workers if you need help.
(78)

13. The hero has (keeped, kept) his promise; he has (slew, slain) the beast.
(86, 87)

14. Neither (have, has) (their, his or her) money.
(83)

15. Neither Rex nor Fido (like, likes) coyotes.
(89)

16. Write the predicate nominative in the sentence below.
(51)

Will you become a botanist someday?

17. Write and underline the words that should be italicized in the sentence below.
(84)

The artist is Monet, and the painting is called The Japanese Footbridge.

18. Write the plural form of the singular noun *canine tooth*.
(17, 22)

19. Use an appositive to combine the following two sentences into one sentence.
(60)

Scott Joplin was an American pianist.

Scott Joplin composed ragtime pieces.

20. Add suffixes:
(33, 34)

(a) funny + er (b) worry + some

21. Write whether the circled pronoun in the sentence below is used as a subject or an object.
(64)

Although Rex likes treats, he shares (them).

22. Write whether the clause below is dependent or independent.
(73)

yellow and blue make green

23. Rewrite the following, adding capital letters and punctuation marks as needed:
(80, 88)

ava shouted help since you are taller than i can you reach that shelf

24. For the irregular verb *draw*, write the (a) present participle, (b) past tense, and (c) past participle.
(19, 85)

Grammar and Writing 4   **462**   Student Edition
Lesson 89

25. Write the objective case pronoun to complete the
(69) sentence below.

Please give Rex and (he, him) fresh water.

26. Rewrite the sentence below, adding capital letters and
(67, 81) punctuation marks as needed.

that song i think is called little liza jane

27. Rewrite the following letter, adding capital letters and
(63, 88) punctuation marks as needed.

dear ruby

why is your cat so mean have you taught him to scratch

with concern
opal

28. Write the two subordinating conjunctions in the sentence
(73) below:

Although it is stormy, we must hike until the sun sets.

Diagram each word of sentences 29–30.

29. Has Opal become a victim of Ruby's mean cat?
(45, 51)

30. Superman, a hero, shows Lois and them his great strength.
(46, 58)

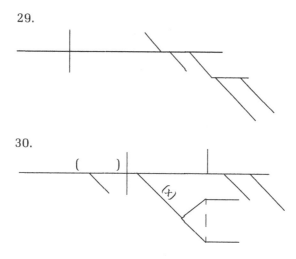

29.

30.

LESSON 90

Subject-Verb Agreement, Part 2

Problems with subject-verb agreement occur when it is difficult to identify the subject of the sentence. Until we do that, we cannot determine whether it is singular or plural.

Words Between the Subject and Verb

Words that come between the subject and the verb must not distract us. Be aware of prepositional phrases, appositives, and other words that might be mistaken for the subject of the sentence. Diagramming the simple subject and simple predicate helps us to determine which verb form to use.

That game for kids (was, were) fun!

| game | was (not *were*) |

Every one of you (knows, know) your multiplication tables.

| one | knows (not *know*) |

Alex, who lives with his cousins, (is, are) here.

| Alex | is (not *are*) |

Example 1 Diagram the simple subject and simple predicate in order to show the correct verb form for each sentence.

(a) A bowl of grapes (was, were) on the table.

(b) The arrival of my friends (make, makes) me happy.

(c) The anole, like many lizards, (eats, eat) crickets.

(d) The noise of the power saws (disturb, disturbs) us.

Solution   (a) A bowl of grapes **was** on the table.

$$\underline{\quad \text{bowl} \mid \text{was} \quad}$$

(b) The arrival of my friends **makes** me happy.

$$\underline{\quad \text{arrival} \mid \text{makes} \quad}$$

(c) The anole, like many lizards, **eats** crickets.

$$\underline{\quad \text{anole} \mid \text{eats} \quad}$$

(d) The noise of the power saws **disturbs** us.

$$\underline{\quad \text{noise} \mid \text{disturbs} \quad}$$

Reversed Subject-Verb Order   If the subject follows the verb, we can better identify the subject by diagramming:

Across the street (is, are) my uncle's house.

$$\underline{\quad \text{house} \mid \text{is} \quad}$$

There on the porch (was, were) the muddy old boots.

$$\underline{\quad \text{boots} \mid \text{were} \quad}$$

Here (comes, come) the Belgian horses.

$$\underline{\quad \text{horses} \mid \text{come} \quad}$$

There (is, are) many ants on that peach.

$$\underline{\quad \text{ants} \mid \text{are} \quad}$$

There (was, were) some tall, high-stepping horses in the parade.

$$\underline{\quad \text{horses} \mid \text{were} \quad}$$

Example 2 Diagram the simple subject and simple predicate in order to show the correct verb form for each sentence.

(a) There (is, are) tall, skinny cypress trees in the park.

(b) Beside the kittens (sit, sits) the fluffy gray mother cat.

(c) There (was, were) different kinds of soil in the area.

(d) First in the races (was, were) our team!

Solution (a) There **are** tall, skinny cypress trees in the park.

trees	are

(b) Beside the kittens **sits** the fluffy gray mother cat.

cat	sits

(c) There **were** different kinds of soil in the area.

kinds	were

(d) First in the races **was** our team!

team	was

Practice Diagram the simple subject and simple predicate in order to determine the correct verb form for sentences a–e.

a. In the album (was, were) pictures of my father.

b. Along the winding road (was, were) two small towns.

c. Here (is, are) the more sensible types of clothing.

d. There (goes, go) the herder of the goats.

e. Up the hill (come, comes) trucks full of fruit.

For f and g, replace each blank with *ichthyology* or *ichthyosaur*.

f. A book on _____ tells about fish.

g. The _____ was a huge sea creature that looked like a fish.

More Practice Choose the correct verb form for each sentence.

1. A basket of berries (sit, sits) beside me.

2. That bag of potatoes (weigh, weighs) ten pounds.

3. A busload of children (is, are) coming.

4. There (go, goes) the runners!

5. There (is, are) many kinds of fruit.

6. The sound of many voices (break, breaks) the silence.

7. The aroma of biscuits in the oven (make, makes) me hungry.

8. That fish with sharp spines (look, looks) dangerous.

Review Set 90 Choose the correct word(s) to complete sentences 1–15.

1. A(n) (jocular, reticent, idol) person is slow to speak.
(89)

2. The (sagacious, docile, inaudible) leader spoke wisely.
(88)

3. The customer (elapsed, inquired, invaded) about the prices of several items.
(87)

4. Sixty minutes had (collapsed, invaded, elapsed) since I began working on my report.
(86)

5. A (larva, fetlock, flea) is usually wormlike.
(37)

6. A basket of berries (sell, sells) for two dollars.
(90)

7. The word *ichthyology* is a(n) (abstract, concrete) noun.
(11)

8. (Who's, Whose) books are those?
(79)

9. Of all the writers, Ed has broken the (least, less, fewer, fewest) pencils.
(56)

10. The pronoun *our* is (first, second, third) person (singular, plural).
(64)

11. Abe and Ed, (who, whom) you mentioned, went fishing.
(77, 79)

Think: | you | mentioned | ? |

12. The parrots are big, but the hornbill is bigger than (them,
(78) they). ["are" omitted]

13. The sun has (rose, risen), and Rex has (woke, woken).
(86, 87)

14. Everything (has, have) (their, its) place.
(83)

15. Neither Nan nor her friends (like, likes) bedbugs.
(89)

16. Write whether the following is a complete sentence, a
(5, 23) sentence fragment, or a run-on sentence:

Pretending to gallop at full speed.

17. Rewrite the sentence below, using a comma to clarify the
(68) meaning.

With this Carl can fix the tire.

18. Use a dictionary: (a) The word *linnet* is what part of
(27, 30) speech? (b) Write its pronunciation. (c) Write its
etymology.

19. Rewrite the following sentence, using commas to offset
(58, 60) the nonessential appositive.

The Great Wall of China an ancient stone wall runs along
China's northern border.

20. Write the antecedent to the circled pronoun in the
(62) sentence below.

Woody sings folk songs, and we enjoy (them).

21. Write the nominative case pronoun to complete the
(64) sentence below.

Nan's tallest friends are Kim and (her, she).

22. From the following sentence, write each prepositional
(44) phrase, circling the object of each preposition.

At dawn, linnets woke me with beautiful songs.

23. Rewrite the following, adding capital letters and
(80, 88) punctuation marks as needed:

nan cries watch out glass has broken and it might cut you

24. For the irregular verb *beat*, write the (a) present
(19, 85) participle, (b) past tense, and (c) past participle.

25. Write the objective case pronoun to complete the
(69) sentence below.

Let's walk Rex and (she, her) to the park.

26. Rewrite the sentence below, adding capital letters and
(67, 81) punctuation marks as needed.

as i remember the fairy tale was called sleeping beauty

27. Rewrite the following letter, adding capital letters and
(41, 63) punctuation marks as needed.

dear opal
  i have had my cat for only two weeks three days and
one hour he is just a kitten
       your friend
       ruby

28. Write the subordinating conjunction in the sentence
(73) below:

Because food is scarce, the fish eats whatever it finds.

Diagram each word of sentences 29–30.

29. Ruby's cat is small but mighty.
(49, 54)

30. Ruby will give her cat tips on friendliness.
(45, 46)

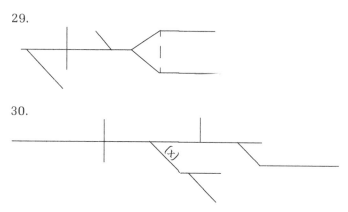

29.

30.

Subject-Verb Agreement, Part 3

> **Dictation or Journal Entry**
>
> **Vocabulary:**
> The Latin *avi-* means "bird."
>
> An *aviary* is a place for keeping birds. Mrs. Flight kept her parakeets in the *aviary*.
>
> To *aviate* is to operate an aircraft. A student pilot learns to *aviate*.

Indefinite Pronouns

We remember that some indefinite pronouns are singular, some are plural, and some can be either. If an indefinite pronoun is the subject of a sentence, the verb must agree with it in number. (See Lesson 83 for the complete list of indefinite pronouns.)

SINGULAR	*Everybody* <u>is</u> welcome.
PLURAL	*Few* <u>are</u> poisonous.
SINGULAR	*Some* of the pie <u>was</u> gone.
PLURAL	*Some* of the children <u>were</u> asleep.

Prepositional Phrases

Sometimes people are confused when a prepositional phrase comes between the subject and predicate. Diagramming the simple subject and simple predicate helps us to see which verb is correct.

Neither of her sons (lives, live) nearby.

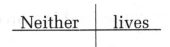

Each of you (has, have) talents.

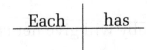

Many in the group (was, were) singing.

Many	were

Several in the room (look, looks) sad.

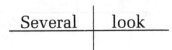

Example 1 Choose the correct verb form for each sentence.

(a) Somebody (were, was) here.

(b) Few (have, has) such courage.

(c) Nobody on these teams (know, knows) my name.

Solution   (a) The indefinite pronoun *somebody* is singular. It takes a singular verb: Somebody **was** here.

(b) The indefinite pronoun *few* takes a plural verb: Few **have** such courage.

(c) The indefinite pronoun *nobody* takes a singular verb: Nobody on these teams **knows** my name.

Contractions   Contractions can cause us to use the wrong verb. We expand them, if necessary, to be sure the subject and verb agree.

The *ship* isn't (<u>is</u> not) at the dock.

The *ships* aren't (<u>are</u> not) at the dock.

The *girl* wasn't (<u>was</u> not) reticent.

The *girls* weren't (<u>were</u> not) reticent.

He doesn't (<u>does</u> not) hunt deer.

They don't (<u>do</u> not) hunt deer.

Errors to Avoid   The contraction *there's* ("there is" or "there has") can only be used with singular subjects.

There's (There <u>is</u>) only one *boot* here.

There's (There <u>has</u>) been a *mistake*.

NO: There's two *ships* at the dock.

YES: There <u>are</u> two *ships* at the dock.

Also, we do not use the contraction *ain't*. It is informal.

He isn't (NOT *ain't*) here.

I haven't (NOT *ain't*) seen him.

Example 2   Choose the correct contraction for each sentence.

(a) (There's, There are) Kurt's sisters.

(b) Lucas (don't, doesn't) need any help.

(c) My boots (hasn't, haven't) any laces.

(d) That answer (ain't, isn't) correct.

Solution　(a) The subject *sisters* is a plural noun, so we use a plural verb: There **are** Kurt's sisters.

(b) *Lucas* is a singular subject: Lucas **doesn't** need any help.

(c) *Boots* is a plural subject, so we use a plural verb: My boots **haven't** any laces.

(d) *Ain't* is informal, so we choose *isn't*: That answer **isn't** correct.

Practice　For a–e, choose the correct verb form or contraction for each sentence.

　　a. Nan exclaimed, "You (ain't, aren't) going to believe this!"

　　b. Someone with gifts (is, are) at the door.

　　c. The goats and their owner (wasn't, weren't) there.

　　d. (There's, There are) only two seats left.

　　e. Each of the socks (have, has) a hole.

For f and g, replace each blank with *aviary* or *aviate*.

　　f. A pilot learns to _____ in bad weather.

　　g. You might see birds in an _____.

More Practice　Choose the correct verb form for each sentence.

　　1. Everybody (is, are) surprised.

　　2. Either (is, are) fine with me.

　　3. Each (need, needs) water.

　　4. Neither (want, wants) more food.

　　5. One of his friends (is, are) helping him.

　　6. Anybody in the upper grades (know, knows) Mr. Ling.

　　7. Nobody in all the classes (has, have) run faster than he.

　　8. Anyone with pets (know, knows) how Nan feels.

　　9. (There's, There are) two peacocks!

　　10. (There's, There are) another peacock!

11. Dad (ain't, isn't) home yet.

12. Ed (don't, doesn't) have lunch money.

13. Nan and Ava (don't, doesn't) have any either.

14. We (ain't, aren't) finished with math.

15. They (isn't, aren't) finished either.

Review Set 91

Choose the correct word(s) to complete sentences 1–16.

1. (Brontophobia, Entomology, Ichthyology) is the study of
(90) fish.

2. Her frown was a(n) (optic, tacit, docile) "no."
(89)

3. A (brontosaurus, pupa, sage) has great wisdom.
(88)

4. The explorer's (feet, quest, claws) was to discover new
(87) lands.

5. A larva becomes a (preen, pupa, stamen) before it
(37) becomes a butterfly.

6. There (was, were) six on our team.
(90)

7. The word *team* is a (compound, collective) noun.
(11)

8. Is this (you're, your) jacket?
(72)

9. Rex is the (friendlier, friendliest) of the two dogs.
(56)

10. The pronoun *your* is (first, second, third) person.
(64)

11. (Who, Whom) is it?
(77, 79)

> Think: it | is \ ?

12. Carl is bringing (we, us) workers a snack.
(78)

13. Yesterday, Luis (swam, swum) fast and (lead, led) the
(86, 87) team to victory.

14. Many on the team (has, have) (their, his or her) shoes off.
(83, 91)

15. My aunt or my uncle (know, knows) my nickname.
(89)

16. (There's, There are) ants in the kitchen.
(91)

17. Write and underline the word that should be italicized
(84) in the sentence below.

Only one train, the Beeline, will take you to Buzztown.

18. Rewrite the word *eight*, circling the silent letters.
(28, 29)

19. Use an appositive to combine the following two
(60) sentences into one sentence.

Harriet Tubman was an escaped slave.

Harriet Tubman helped many other slaves to gain their
freedom.

20. Write whether the sentence below is simple or
(75) compound.

During the Civil War, Harriet Tubman was a nurse, scout,
and spy for the Union army.

21. Write whether the circled pronoun in the sentence below
(64) is used as a subject or an object.

Would the slaves and (she) survive?

22. Write whether the clause below is dependent or
(73) independent.

as they soared through the air

23. Rewrite the following, adding capital letters and
(80, 88) punctuation marks as needed:

amy yells stop look both ways before you cross

24. For the irregular verb *fall*, write the (a) present participle,
(19, 85) (b) past tense, and (c) past participle.

25. Which sentence is more polite? Write *A* or *B*.
(69)
A. Amy gave them and me a warning.

B. Amy gave me and them a warning.

26. Rewrite the outline below, adding capital letters and
(26, 47) punctuation marks as needed.

    i hebrew scriptures
      a genesis
      b exodus
      c leviticus

27. Rewrite the following letter, adding capital letters and
(41, 57) punctuation marks as needed.

    dear ruby
        please come to my party on tuesday june 2 but do not
    bring your cat
                           your friend
                           opal

28. Write the subordinating conjunction in the sentence
(73) below:

    I shall come if my cat can come.

Diagram each word of sentences 29–30.

29. Will Opal's party be fancy and fun?
(49, 54)

30. Is our friend Carl bringing us a package of crackers and
(46, 58) cheese?

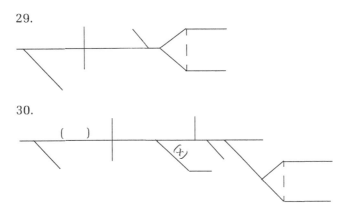

29.

30.

LESSON 92

Subject-Verb Agreement, Part 4

Dictation or Journal Entry

Vocabulary:

The prefix *pre-* means "before" in place, time, order, or position.

To *prearrange* is to arrange beforehand. Did Miss Ng *prearrange* a field trip for the class?

A *precaution* is something that one does beforehand to avoid danger or harm. We take *precaution* against injury by wearing seat belts in the car.

In this lesson, we shall look at nouns that can cause difficulty with subject-verb agreement.

Collective Nouns
We remember that a collective noun refers to a group or unit (a collection of people, places, animals, or things). Most of the time, these nouns take singular verbs.

If the group or unit is "acting" as one, we use a singular verb.

The *class* elects a president.

The *team* is winning.

A *bunch* of grapes sits in the bowl.

However, if members of the group are "acting" individually, we use a plural verb.

The *majority* finish the race.

What *fraction* of the runners quit?

A *group* of people wait in line.

Special Nouns
Some nouns refer to a single "thing" but are still considered plural. When used as the subject of a sentence, nouns such as *pants*, *slacks*, *trousers*, *scissors*, *pliers*, *shears*, and *eyeglasses* require plural verbs.

These *scissors* are sharp.

His *slacks* were too baggy.

However, watch for sentences like the one below. The word *pair* is the subject. *Pair* is singular and takes a singular verb.

This *pair* of scissors is sharp.

Other nouns, especially ones that end in -*s*, appear to be plural but are considered singular. Nouns such as *measles*, *mumps*, *news*, and *lens* require singular verbs.

The *news* is good!

Mumps is less common now.

Some nouns have the same form whether they are singular or plural. *Corps, series, means, species,* and *gross,* as well as many animal names (*sheep, trout, bison, salmon,* etc.), are some examples. Use the meaning of the sentence to decide which verb form to use.

SINGULAR: This *series* of novels is exciting.

PLURAL: Two new *series* are coming.

SINGULAR: That *sheep* looks lost.

PLURAL: Several *sheep* have wandered away.

Finally, nouns that end in -*ics*, such as *athletics, economics, ethics, mathematics,* and *politics,* can also be either singular or plural, depending on their meaning in the sentence. If we are referring to a body of knowledge, the noun is singular. If we are referring to a series of actions, the noun is plural:

Body of knowledge: *Mathematics* is fun.

Series of actions: His *mathematics* are accurate.

Example Choose the correct verb form for each sentence.

(a) Economics (is, are) an interesting subject.

(b) The committee (decide, decides) what to do next.

(c) Some species (is, are) endangered.

(d) Measles (was, were) miserable.

Solution (a) "Economics" is singular, for it is a body of knowledge. Economics **is** an interesting subject.

(b) "Committee" is a collective noun, and its members are acting as one. The committee **decides** what to do next.

(c) The adjective "some" tells us that "species" is plural. Some species **are** endangered.

(d) "Measles" is singular. Measles **was** miserable.

Practice Choose the correct verb form for sentences a–d.

    a. An army of ants (cover, covers) the jelly jar.

    b. A popular dog species (is, are) the beagle.

    c. The theater staff (has, have) chosen new shows.

    d. The morning news (was, were) on at nine o'clock.

For e and f, replace each blank with *prearrange* or *precaution*.

    e. Bikers take _____ by wearing helmets.

    f. Mike will _____ for someone to pick him up from soccer practice.

Review Set 92 Choose the correct word to complete sentences 1–16.

    1. The (boarder, aviary, lumen) features exotic birds.
    (91)

    2. In prehistoric times, there were huge, dolphin-like marine reptiles called (brontosauruses, dinotheres, ichthyosaurs).
    (90)

    3. (*Audible, Jocular, Reticent*) means "reserved or silent."
    (89)

    4. (Sagacious, Inaudible, Jocular) counselors provide us wisdom.
    (88)

    5. A tadpole changes into a frog by a process called (pollination, metamorphosis, nocturnal).
    (38)

    6. Here (comes, come) my buddies.
    (90)

    7. The sentence below is (declarative, interrogative, imperative, exclamatory).
    (2)

    There's a pack of coyotes!

    8. To (who, whom) were they speaking?
    (79)

    9. Some toddlers don't use (much, many) words.
    (56)

10. The pronoun *your* is (nominative, objective, possessive)
_(66, 69) case.

11. The winner of the contest was (who, whom)?
_(77, 79)

Think: <u>winner</u> | was \\ ?

12. Ed is more cautious than (me, I). ["am" omitted]
₍₇₈₎

13. I have (sat, sitted) in the car and have (rode, ridden) too
_(86, 87) long.

14. No one in the group (has, have) (their, his or her) helmet.
_(83, 91)

15. The boys and their mother (hike, hikes) together.
₍₈₉₎

16. The whole batch of biscuits (has, have) burned!
₍₉₂₎

17. Write and underline the words that should be italicized
₍₈₄₎ in the sentence below.

Falco peregrinus is a species of falcon, a hawk-like bird of prey.

18. Write the plural form of the singular noun *batch*.
_(17, 22)

19. Rewrite the sentence below, using commas to offset the
₍₅₈₎ nonessential appositive.

The flamingo a tropical bird wades in shallow water.

20. Add suffixes.
_(33, 34)
(a) true + ly   (b) penny + less

21. Write the nominative case pronoun to complete the
₍₆₄₎ sentence below.

Mr. Cox and (her, she) play the bugle.

22. Write whether the following is a phrase or a clause.
₍₃₆₎

at the end of the day

23. Rewrite the following, adding capital letters and
_(80, 88) punctuation marks as needed:

may i please have some carrots asked tom

24. For the irregular verb *find*, write the (a) present
(19, 85) participle, (b) past tense, and (c) past participle.

25. Write the objective case pronoun to complete the
(69) sentence below.

Nan gave Tom and (I, me) some carrots.

26. Rewrite the sentence below, adding capital letters and
(26, 47) punctuation marks as needed.

nan said yes ed you may have some carrots

27. Rewrite the following letter, adding capital letters and
(41, 63) punctuation marks as needed.

dear opal
my cat will be kind gentle and friendly
your friend
ruby

28. Write the two subordinating conjunctions in the sentence
(73) below:

After the sun went down, I turned on the lights until Mr.
Cox played taps.

Diagram each word of sentences 29–30.

29. My faithful friends are Mrs. Cox and he.
(49, 51)

30. Mr. Cox, an excellent musician, played Mrs. Cox and us a
(46, 58) jazzy version of taps.

29.

30.

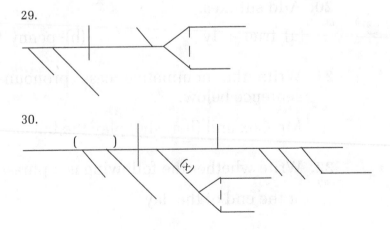

Negatives • Double Negatives

Dictation or Journal Entry

Vocabulary:

The Latin *cedere* means "to yield" or "to go."

To *cede* means "to give up a possession or to surrender." A war-torn country might *cede* territory to its enemy.

To *precede* means "to go or to come before." A drought might *precede* a brush fire.

Negatives Negatives are modifiers, usually adverbs, that mean "no" or "not." We will learn more about adverbs later. In this lesson, we will learn to recognize negatives and to use them correctly. Negatives are italicized in the sentences below.

She *never* saw him.

He had *nowhere* to go.

They had *scarcely* enough food.

We could *not* hear you.

Here is a list of common negatives:

no	*not*	*never*
hardly	*scarcely*	*barely*
nowhere	*none*	*no one*
nothing	*nobody*	

Because the word *not* is a negative, the contraction *n't* is also a negative:

Ed does*n't* like spinach.

Dessert is*n't* essential.

We have*n't* much time.

Example 1 Write each negative that you find in these sentences.

(a) I could barely hear him.

(b) No one believed that he had nothing to hide.

(c) They did not invite anybody, so nobody came.

(d) Hardly anyone knew the secret.

Solution (a) **barely**   (b) **No one, nothing**

(c) **not, nobody**   (d) **Hardly**

Double We use only one negative to express a negative idea. In the
Negatives English language, two negatives in the same clause "cancel
each other out," and the idea becomes positive again.
Therefore, it is incorrect to use two negatives with one verb.
We call this a **double negative,** and we avoid it.

NO: Rob *never* wants *no* help.
YES: Rob *never* wants help.
YES: Rob wants *no* help.

NO: Meg has*n't no* pen.
YES: Meg has*n't* a pen.
YES: Meg has *no* pen.

NO: *Scarcely none* are left.
YES: *Scarcely any* are left.
YES: Almost *none* are left.

Example 2 Choose the correct word to complete each sentence.
(a) We (could, couldn't) hardly see the trail.

(b) Ed doesn't want (no, any) spinach.

(c) Your sister isn't (nothing, anything) like mine.

(d) Hardly (nobody, anybody) could see the trail.

Solution (a) "Couldn't" and "hardly" are both negatives, so we choose
"could." We **could** hardly see the trail.

(b) "Doesn't" and "no" are both negatives. (To *not* want *no*
spinach is to want some spinach!) Ed doesn't want **any**
spinach.

(c) "Isn't" and "nothing" are both negatives. Your sister isn't
anything like mine.

(d) "Hardly" and "nobody" are both negatives. Hardly
anybody could see the trail.

Correcting Double Negatives To correct a double negative, we can replace one of the negatives with a positive word. Look at the positive forms of the negatives below:

NEGATIVE		POSITIVE
hardly	→	almost
no	→	any, a
nobody	→	anybody
nowhere	→	anywhere
never	→	ever
neither	→	either
none	→	any
no one	→	anyone
nothing	→	anything

                               anything
Rex didn't take ~~nothing~~.

               a
He is not ~~no~~ thief.

                           either
I don't want spinach, ~~neither~~.

Example 3 Rewrite this sentence, correcting the double negative:

Neither of them saw nobody.

Solution We replace the second negative, *nobody*, with a positive form—*anybody*:

Neither of them saw *anybody*.

Remember that a sentence can contain more than one negative, as long as the negatives are not in the same clause. The sentence below is not an example of a double negative because each negative is in a different clause.

I *didn't* go to the store, so I have *no* eggs.

Practice Choose the correct word to complete sentences a–e.

a. They (had, hadn't) scarcely any water.

b. I (could, couldn't) see no paw prints.

c. We had never done (anything, nothing) more fun!

d. That hasn't (ever, never) happened to us before.

e. He's not (ever, never) going to find it.

For f and g, replace each blank with *cede* or *precede*.

f. One predator might _____ its prey to a stronger predator.

g. Dark clouds might _____ a storm.

More Practice Choose the correct word to complete these sentences.

1. I haven't seen (no, any) bears, and I don't want to see (none, any) today.

2. Ava didn't see (no, any) bears, either.

3. Rob doesn't want (nobody, anybody) to disturb him.

4. Mr. Cox doesn't, (neither, either).

5. They haven't heard (no one, anyone).

6. Ava hasn't gone (nowhere, anywhere).

7. Ed didn't eat (none, any) of the spinach.

8. Yin hasn't (never, ever) met Mr. Flores.

9. They have hardly (no, any) water left.

10. Ed didn't eat (nothing, anything).

Review Set 93 Choose the correct word(s) to complete sentences 1–16.

1. We shall (quest, prearrange, elapse) transportation and
(92) lodging for our trip.

2. A helicopter is a challenge to (inquire, aviate, aviary).
(91)

3. Interested in fish, my aunt Martha studies (ichthyology,
(90) brontophobia, entomology).

4. His smile revealed his (tacit, reticent, week) approval.
(89)

5. A butterfly's (fetlock, foreleg, larva) is a caterpillar.
(37)

6. There (go, goes) the pinnipeds!
(90)

7. The word *pinniped's* is a (plural, possessive) noun.
(13)

8. I (can, can't) hardly see the stars.
(93)

9. Kim built the (taller, tallest) of the two towers.
(56)

10. The pronoun *me* is (first, second, third) person (singular, plural).
(64)

11. (Who, Whom) stole (her's, hers)?
(72, 79)

Think:

12. Please listen to (we, us) teachers.
(78)

Think:

13. I have (maked, made) the beds and (shook, shaken) the rugs.
(86, 87)

14. One of the boys (haven't, hasn't) any of (their, his) books today.
(83, 91)

15. The boys or their father (plant, plants) the corn.
(89)

16. (There's, There are) ants!
(92)

17. Rewrite the sentence below, adding a comma to clarify the meaning.
(68)

For washing machines are helpful.

18. Write the plural form of the singular noun *emperor of Japan*.
(17, 22)

19. Use an appositive to combine the two sentences below into one sentence.
(60)

London is the capital of Great Britain.

London is on the Thames River.

20. Write whether the following sentence is simple or compound.
(75)

He is from Denmark, and she is from Spain.

21. Write whether the circled pronoun in the sentence below is used as a subject or an object.
(64)

I heard that Kim and (she) ran fast.

22. From the following sentence, write each prepositional phrase, circling the object of each preposition.
(44)

At the end of the day, Mr. Cox played taps.

23. Rewrite the following, adding capital letters and punctuation marks as needed:
(80, 88)

this corn is sweet exclaims meg

24. For the irregular verb *build*, write the (a) present participle, (b) past tense, and (c) past participle.
(19, 85)

25. Write the objective case pronoun to complete the sentence below.
(69)

I shall vote for Pat and (she, her).

26. Rewrite the sentence below, adding capital letters and punctuation marks as needed.
(26, 47)

meg said please pass the corn dad

27. Rewrite the following letter, adding capital letters and punctuation marks as needed.
(41, 63)

dear ruby
    there is a cat hotel at 27 main street frankfort kentucky
                                    your friend
                                    opal

28. Write the subordinating conjunction in the sentence below:
(73)

If Kitty goes to the party, she must hide in Ruby's purse.

Diagram each word of sentences 29–30.

29. Ruby's cat might feel unwanted.
(54)

30. Does the hotel in Frankfort offer cats fancy cakes and
(46) strawberries?

29.

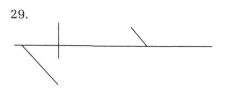

30.

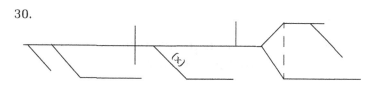

LESSON 94

The Hyphen: Compound Nouns and Numbers

> **Dictation or Journal Entry**
>
> **Vocabulary:**
>
> *Mater* means "mother" in Latin.
>
> A *matriarch* is the female head of a family. The *matriarchs* of each family gathered to plan the celebration.
>
> *Maternal* means "motherly." The doe's *maternal* instincts caused her to take good care of her fawn.

The **hyphen** is a punctuation mark used to connect elements of compound words and to express numbers.

Compound Nouns

We have learned that some compound nouns are hyphenated. There are no absolute rules for spelling a compound noun as one word, as two words, or as a hyphenated word. However, certain categories of compound nouns are often hyphenated.

- Compound nouns that end in prepositional phrases:

  right-of-way   son-in-law   bump-on-a-log

  artist-at-large   man-about-town   attorney-at-law

- Compound nouns containing the prefix *ex-* or *self-* or the suffix *-elect*:

  ex-president   self-control   mayor-elect

- Compound nouns that are units of measurement:

  man-hour   light-year

- Compound nouns that end with the prepositions *in, on,* or *between*:

  drive-in   stand-in   trade-in

  add-on   goings-on   go-between

Nouns Without Nouns?

The English language is so flexible that we can create nouns from almost any part of speech. Look at the last category (compound nouns that end with prepositions) and notice that some of them do not contain an actual noun. Following are more examples of compound nouns formed from other parts of speech. We join the elements (words) with hyphens.

go-getter	show-off	has-been
get-together	look-alike	have-nots
sit-up	know-how	talking-to

The dictionary lists many of these words. But no dictionary can show every single combination of words that might make up a compound noun. If you need a unique combination, use any similar words you can find in the dictionary to decide how to punctuate your compound noun.

Example 1 Write the words that should be hyphenated in sentences a–c. Be prepared to use the dictionary.

(a) We need self discipline to succeed.

(b) His essay was runner up in the contest.

(c) She is prideful; she is a know it all.

Solution These compound words need hyphens:

(a) **Self-discipline** contains the prefix *self-* and so should be hyphenated.

(b) The dictionary tells us that **runner-up** is hyphenated.

(c) **Know-it-all** is being used as a noun but does not actually contain a noun. It should be hyphenated. (The dictionary lists *know-it-all* as an informal noun or adjective.)

Numbers Hyphens are often used to join elements in the expression of numbers and inclusive sets or sequences.

Numbers as Words We use a hyphen in compound numbers from twenty-one to ninety-nine:

thirty-five	one hundred fifty-two pages
twenty-first day	two twenty-fifths ($\frac{2}{25}$)

A Range of Numbers A hyphen is used to indicate a range of numbers or an inclusive set or sequence.

pages 11-22	the years 1980-1990
60-70 percent	the week of May 10-17

Because the hyphen takes the place of words in pairs such as *from/through*, *from/to*, or *between/and*, we do not use one of the words and a hyphen.

INCORRECT: between 1986-1991

CORRECT: between 1986 and 1991

Example 2   Write the numbers that should be hyphenated in sentences a–c.

(a) Miss Ng is forty six.

(b) She was born on the twenty third of June.

(c) The story appears on pages 60 64.

Solution   (a) **Forty-six** is hyphenated because it is a number between 21 and 99.

(b) **Twenty-third** is hyphenated because it is a number between 21 and 99.

(c) The numerals **60-64** are hyphenated because they represent a sequence.

Practice   For a and b, replace each blank with *matriarch* or *maternal*.

a. Niki gives her baby doll _____ care.

b. Aunt Liz was the _____ of her family.

For c–f, write each expression that should be hyphenated. Use the dictionary, if necessary.

c. Does she have the know how to bathe a dog?

d. He read the write up in the newspaper.

e. We have twenty five minutes to play outside.

f. He will be camping July 12 19.

More Practice   For 1–8, use words to write each number.

1. 45	**2.** 56	**3.** 42	**4.** 99
5. 31st	**6.** 22nd	**7.** 45th	**8.** 63rd

Write each expression that should be hyphenated in sentences 9–12. Use a dictionary, if necessary.

9. Practice helps our self confidence.

10. Planting those trees took about 11 man hours!

11. My brother in law is a go getter.

12. I must not play games all day; I must use self restraint.

Review Set 94

Choose the correct word(s) to complete sentences 1–16.

1. The toddler refused to (precede, cede, prearrange) the toy
(93) to a playmate.

2. Before crossing the street, we take (precaution, aversion,
(92) breadth) by looking both ways.

3. A(n) (dinothere, mandible, aviary) should be cleaned
(91) regularly to keep birds healthy.

4. The fish-like (dinotheres, brontosauruses, ichthyosaurs)
(90) were as long as thirteen feet.

5. Peach trees depend on (metamorphosis, pollination,
(38) precaution) to bear fruit.

6. A can of peas (sit, sits) on the shelf.
(90)

7. The word *weakness* is a(n) (concrete, abstract) noun.
(11)

8. We don't have (no, any) flour.
(93)

9. Kim built the (taller, tallest) of the four towers.
(56)

10. The pronoun *me* is (nominative, objective, possessive)
(66, 69) case.

11. (Your's, Yours) is here, but (their's, theirs) is missing.
(72)

12. Mr. Luna can identify more butterflies than (me, I).
(78) ["can" omitted]

13. She has (wove, woven) baskets and (selled, sold) them.
(86, 87)

14. Three in the class (haven't, hasn't) written (their, his or
(91) her) essays.

15. Either the hens or the rooster (wake, wakes) first.
(89)

16. Mumps (was, were) common when Grandpa was young.
(92)

17. Write and underline the word that should be italicized
(84) in the sentence below.

The word dance can be either a noun or a verb.

18. Use a dictionary: (a) The word *exceed* is what part of
(27, 30) speech? (b) Write its pronunciation. (c) Write its
etymology.

19. Rewrite the sentence below, adding hyphens as needed.
(94)

Thirty four girls came to the get together.

20. Write the antecedent of the circled pronoun in the
(62) sentence below.

The cygnet flapped (its) wings.

21. Write the nominative case pronoun to complete the
(64, 66) sentence below.

Ed and (them, they) are in my class.

22. Write whether the following is a phrase or a clause.
(36)

with long antennae

23. Rewrite the following, adding capital letters and
(80, 88) punctuation marks as needed:

if the baby cries will you rock him asked tom

24. For the irregular verb *catch*, write the (a) present
(19, 85) participle, (b) past tense, and (c) past participle.

25. Which sentence is more polite? Write *A* or *B*.
(69)
A. Will you vote for her and me?

B. Will you vote for me and her?

26. Rewrite the sentence below, adding capital letters and punctuation marks as needed.
_(15, 81)

i shall title my story a long dry summer

27. Rewrite the following letter, adding capital letters and punctuation marks as needed.
_(41, 63)

dear opal
      does the hotel have cat food catnip and cat toys
              love
              ruby

28. Write the subordinating conjunction in the sentence below:
₍₇₃₎

After Clara Barton organized relief during the Civil War, she founded the American Red Cross.

Diagram each word of sentences 29–30.

29. Clara Barton, a nurse, was brave and kind.
_(49, 54)

30. Clara Barton fed the weary soldier a bowl of soup and a piece of bread.
_(46, 58)

29.

30.

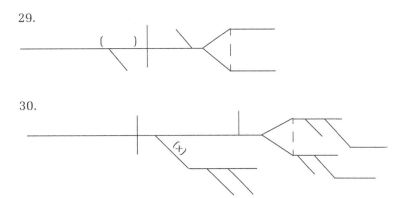

LESSON 95

Adverbs That Tell "How"

Adverbs are descriptive words that modify or add information to verbs, adjectives, and other adverbs. They answer the questions "how," "when," "where," and "how much" (or "to what extent"). The italicized adverbs below modify the verb *talks*:

> HOW: Nan talks *quietly*.
>
> WHEN: Nan talks *now*.
>
> WHERE: Nan talks *there*.
>
> HOW MUCH: Nan talks *more*.

"How"   An adverb that tells "how" usually modifies a verb or verb phrase and often ends in the suffix *-ly*. For example, let's think about how Al drives:

> Al drives *slowly*.

Al might also drive *carefully, smoothly, cautiously, fast, recklessly,* or *happily*. These adverbs all answer the question "how."

Example 1   Write the adverbs that tell "how" from this sentence:

> Miss Ng spoke loudly and firmly.

Solution   The adverbs **loudly** and **firmly** tell "how" Miss Ng spoke.

Suffix -ly Below are the adjective and adverb forms of some nouns. Notice that the adverb is formed by adding -ly to the adjective.

Noun	Adjective	Adverb
joy	joyful	joyfully
nature	natural	naturally
help	helpful	helpfully
danger	dangerous	dangerously
storm	stormy	stormily

Of course, not every word that ends in -ly is an adverb. *Lovely*, *friendly*, *orderly*, and *lonely* are all adjectives.

Adjective or Adverb? Some words, such as *hard*, *fast*, *right*, *early*, and *long*, have the same form whether they are used as adjectives or adverbs. However, we can always tell how the word is being used because an adjective modifies a noun or pronoun, and an adverb modifies a verb, adjective, or other adverb.

ADJECTIVE: The test was *hard*. (modifies the noun "test")
ADVERB: Meg worked *hard*. (modifies the verb "worked")

ADJECTIVE: It was a *fast* pace. (modifies the noun "pace")
ADVERB: Ed ran *fast*. (modifies the verb "ran")

ADJECTIVE: I ate an *early* dinner. (modifies the noun "dinner")
ADVERB: I ate dinner *early*. (modifies the verb "ate")

We must learn to see the difference between an adverb and a predicate adjective. Look at the following sentence:

The dog looks friendly.

It might seem that *friendly* tells "how" the dog looks. However, we remember that we can identify a predicate adjective by replacing a possible linking verb (*looks*) with a "to be" verb:

The dog *was* friendly. (friendly dog)

The word *friendly* describes the dog, not the act of looking. It is an adjective. Compare this to a sentence containing an action verb:

A tiger moves silently.

If we replace an action verb with a "to be" verb, the sentence no longer makes sense:

A tiger *is* silently. (silently tiger?)

Silently does not describe the tiger. It describes the act of moving. It is an adverb.

Example 2 Tell whether the italicized word in each sentence is an adjective or adverb. Also, tell which word it modifies.

(a) Kim works *hard*.

(b) I admire *hard* work.

(c) Two wild parrots grew *friendly*.

Solution (a) The word *hard* is an **adverb. It modifies the verb "works."** *Hard* tells "how" Kim works.

(b) The word *hard* is an **adjective. It modifies the noun "work."** *Hard* tells "what kind" of work.

(c) The word *friendly* is an **adjective. It modifies the noun "parrots."** *Friendly* tells "what kind" of parrots.

Practice For sentences a–c, write each adverb that tells "how," and write the word or phrase it modifies.

a. An eagle flies swiftly.

b. The old tire burst suddenly.

c. Sal fixed the tire quickly and easily.

For d–g, write whether the italicized word is an adjective or an adverb, and write the word or phrase it modifies.

d. Her speech seemed *long*.

e. Did she speak *long*?

f. Ed made a *left* turn.

g. Ed turned *left*.

For h and i, replace each blank with *fraternity* or *fraternal*.

h. Mr. Green has made friends in his _____.

i. Boy Scouts of America is a _____ organization.

Choose the correct word(s) to complete sentences 1–16.

1. (Ichthyosaurs, Matriarchs, Jesters) discussed family concerns.
(94)

2. Lightning (preens, aviates, precedes) thunder.
(93)

3. Working parents (prearrange, aviate, elapse) childcare for
(92) their children.

4. Unlike earthworms, butterfly larvae undergo (pollination,
(38) metamorphosis, morning).

5. Is a large airplane harder to (aviate, precede, cede)?
(91)

6. Josh, one of the twins, (is, are) playing tag.
(90)

7. The word *basketball* is a (compound, collective) noun.
(11)

8. He doesn't need (no, any) help.
(93)

9. Ruth counted (less, fewer) ducks than geese.
(56)

10. The pronoun *we* is (first, second, third) person (singular,
(64) plural).

11. (Who, Whom) shall I choose?
(79)

Think:	I	shall choose	?

12. Please give (us, we) painters more time.
(78)

13. Dan (mistook, mistaken) me for someone else; he
(86, 87) (thinked, thought) I was a sixth grader.

14. Some in the group (haven't, hasn't) written (their, his or
(83, 91) her) essays.

15. Either the rooster or the hens (wake, wakes) first.
(89)

16. Measles (was, were) common when Grandpa was young.
(92)

17. Write and underline the words that should be italicized in the sentence below.
(84)

I saw Venus de Milo, a Greek statue, in Paris.

18. Write the plural form of the singular noun *bookshelf*.
(17, 22)

19. Rewrite the sentence below, adding hyphens as needed.
(94)

I do thirty five sit ups each morning.

20. Write whether the sentence below is simple or compound.
(75)

Josh is playing tag, but Nate is napping.

21. Write the objective case pronoun to complete the sentence below.
(69)

I shall call Luke and (he, him).

22. Write whether the clause below is dependent or independent.
(73)

they are fraternal twins

23. Rewrite the following, adding capital letters and punctuation marks as needed:
(80, 88)

ed said i went to paris but i didn't go to the eiffel tower

24. For the irregular verb *eat*, write the (a) present participle, (b) past tense, and (c) past participle.
(19, 85)

25. From the sentence below, write each adverb and the word or phrase it modifies.
(95)

Most of the speakers spoke clearly.

26. Rewrite the sentence below, adding capital letters and punctuation marks as needed.
(81)

the funniest chapter was titled uncle's new hairdo

27. Rewrite the following sentence, adding capital letters and punctuation marks as needed.
(57, 67)

the colors of mexico's flag as i recall are green white and red

28. Write the two subordinating conjunctions in the sentence
(73) below:

It looks as though the weeds have grown taller since it
rained.

Diagram each word of sentences 29–30.

29. Nan's report on fraternal twins was short but interesting.
(45, 54)

30. Lucy, an identical twin, showed us a picture of her twin
(46, 58) sister.

29.

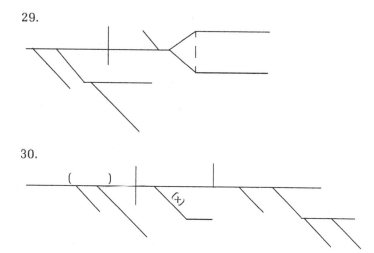

30.

Using the Adverb *Well*

Dictation or Journal Entry

Vocabulary:

In Greek, *megas* means "large."

A *megalodon* was a species of shark that reached ninety feet in length. The *megalodon* is now extinct.

The *megamouth*, a rare deepwater shark, swims with its mouth wide open.

Good   The words *good* and *well* are difficult parts of speech. *Good* is a descriptive adjective or a predicate adjective. It modifies a noun or pronoun, as in these sentences:

Ed is a *good* cook.
(descriptive adjective modifying "cook")

He makes *good* chili.
(descriptive adjective modifying "chili")

The chili tastes *good*.
(predicate adjective describing "chili")

Well   The word *well* is usually an adverb. It modifies an action verb and explains "how" someone does something.

Zack sings *well*.

Rita plays basketball *well*.

How *well* do you read?

We do not use the word *good* as an adverb.

NO: Amelia draws *good*.
YES: Amelia draws *well*.

NO: This pen works *good*.
YES: This pen works *well*.

Example 1   Replace each blank with *well* or *good*.

(a) Melody slept _____.

(b) Did you have a _____ weekend?

(c) Elle paints _____.

(d) She is a _____ painter.

Solution   (a) Melody slept **well.** *Well* is an adverb that modifies the verb *slept*. It tells "how" Melody slept.

(b) Did you have a **good** weekend? *Good* is an adjective that modifies the noun *weekend*.

(c) Elle paints **well.** *Well* is an adverb that modifies the verb *paints*. It tells "how" Elle paints.

(d) She is a **good** painter. *Good* is an adjective that modifies the noun *painter*.

Feeling Well? The word *well* is used as an adjective when referring to the state of one's health. You feel *good* about passing a test, for example, but when you wish to state that you are in good health, it is preferable to say that you are *well*.

He feels *well* today.

Is he *well*, or is he sick?

Example 2 Choose either *well* or *good* to complete each sentence.
(a) I don't think she feels (good, well).

(b) Ed felt (well, good) about finishing his work.

Solution (a) I don't think she feels **well.** We use *well* when referring to one's health.

(b) Ed felt **good** about finishing his work. We do not use *well* because we are not referring to the state of Ed's health.

Practice Choose the correct descriptive word for sentences a–e.
a. The boys worked (good, well) together.

b. Ava wrote a (good, well) story.

c. Nan can draw (good, well).

d. Molly is a (good, well) pianist.

e. She plays (good, well).

For f and g, replace each blank with *megalodon* or *megamouth.*
f. The _____ swims with its mouth open.

g. The _____ shark grew very long.

Choose the correct descriptive word for each sentence.

1. Grapes grow (good, well) in California.

2. How (good, well) do you swim?

3. Sal swims (good, well).

4. He is a (good, well) swimmer.

5. This soup tastes (good, well).

6. Ben feels (good, well) about his grades.

7. Nan and Ed paint (well, good).

8. They've painted some (good, well) pictures.

9. May sings (good, well).

10. Dan is a (good, well) singer, too.

**Review Set
96**

Choose the correct word(s) to complete sentences 1–16.

1. Twins who are not identical are called (maternal,
(95) fraternal, nocturnal) twins.

2. (Maternal, Fraternal, Nocturnal) instincts cause mothers
(94) to care for their babies.

3. Great Britain (preceded, ceded, inquired) the American
(93) colonies after the American Revolution.

4. Take great (quest, aversion, precaution) when handling
(92) broken glass.

5. (Colt, Flea, Flee) bites itch.
(39)

6. There (is, are) two hummingbirds!
(90)

7. Miss Kim reads maps (good, well).
(96)

8. He (has, hasn't) scarcely enough time.
(93)

9. Of all the walkers, I had the (sorer, sorest) feet.
(56)

10. The pronoun *we* is (nominative, objective, possessive)
(64) case.

11. This van is (our's, ours); (their's, theirs) is over there.
(72)

12. Ed is as kind as (her, she). ["is" omitted]
(78)

13. Rita (taked, took) me to the zoo, so I (writed, wrote) her a
(86, 87) thank-you note.

14. Neither of the girls (have, has) made (their, her) lunch.
(83, 91)

15. The brothers or their sister (feed, feeds) the fish.
(89)

16. The baseball team (board, boards) the plane.
(92)

17. Write and underline the words that should be italicized
(84) in the sentence below.

Daniel Defoe wrote the novel Robinson Crusoe.

18. Write the plural form of the singular noun *rosebush.*
(17, 22)

19. Rewrite the sentence below, adding hyphens as needed.
(94)

Twenty two show offs did cartwheels.

20. Write the antecedent of the circled pronoun in the
(62) sentence below.

Nan fixed her old scooter and rode (it) to school.

21. Write whether the circled pronoun in the sentence below
(64) is used as a subject or an object.

He waved at his grandmother and blew (her) a kiss.

22. Write whether the following is a phrase or a clause.
(36)

because eagles have excellent eyesight

23. Rewrite the following, adding capital letters and
(15, 57) punctuation marks as needed:

my uncle asked if i would pick ripe peaches plums and
apricots from his trees

24. For the irregular verb *bite*, write the (a) present participle,
(19, 85) (b) past tense, and (c) past participle.

25. From the sentence below, write the adverb and the word
(95) or phrase that it modifies.

Ed slept peacefully.

26. Rewrite the sentence below, adding capital letters and
(81) punctuation marks as needed.

kim wrote a poem and titled it if we were bats

27. Rewrite the following sentence, adding capital letters and
(57, 67) punctuation marks as needed.

please notice that i have moved to 61 ash lane newtown
iowa

28. Write the three subordinating conjunctions in the
(73) sentence below:

Before I leave, I must tell my parents so that they will
know where I am.

Diagram each word of sentences 29–30.

29. That gigantic shark must have been a megalodon.
(54)

30. Dr. Luz, an oceanographer, gave Nan and me information
(46, 58) about the megamouth.

29.

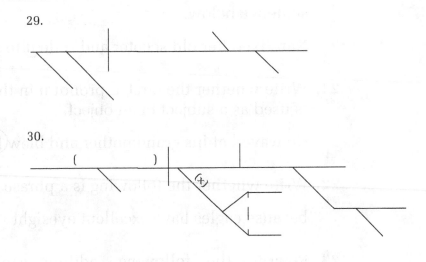

30.

LESSON
97

The Hyphen: Compound Adjectives

Dictation or Journal Entry

Vocabulary:

The Latin *spec-* or *spic-* means "look."

A *species* is a class of individuals or creatures having common characteristics. Sharks belong to the *species* of fish called *Chondrichthyes*.

A *specimen* is a part of something representing the whole. Tooth *specimens* from megaladons are over seven inches long.

We have seen how hyphens are used in compound nouns and with numbers. In this lesson, we will learn more uses for hyphens.

Compound Adjectives Just as we combine words to form compound nouns, we can combine words to form **compound adjectives**. A compound adjective is a group of words that works *as a unit* to modify a noun to express a single thought. It is not a list of adjectives, each modifying a noun in its own way.

COMPOUND ADJECTIVE:	*hand-woven* rug
TWO ADJECTIVES:	*pretty blue* rug

COMPOUND ADJECTIVE:	*waterproof* watch
TWO ADJECTIVES:	*new gold* watch

COMPOUND ADJECTIVE:	*brown and white* shoes
THREE ADJECTIVES:	*old black leather* shoes

As shown above, compound adjectives can be spelled as one word, left as separate words, or hyphenated. How they appear is sometimes a matter of rule but is often a matter of custom or style. The following guidelines will help you form many compound adjectives confidently.

Clarity Our goal is to make our meaning as clear as possible to the reader. When we use hyphens to join two or more words, it helps the reader understand that the words are to be read as a single unit. This prevents confusion. Consider this sentence:

The tailor made vests for boys are handsome.

Grammar and Writing 4

Student Edition
Lesson 97

Seeing a subject (*tailor*), a verb (*made*), and a direct object (*vests*), the reader is likely to misread the sentence. So we hyphenate the compound adjective for greater clarity:

The tailor-made vests for boys are handsome.

Borrowed Phrases and Clauses One of the ways we modify nouns is by borrowing descriptive phrases and clauses and using them as compound adjectives. Hyphens help join words that work as a unit to modify a noun.

Prepositional Phrases When we use a prepositional phrase to modify a noun, it is functioning as a compound adjective. If it comes *before* the noun, it should be hyphenated.

I want an *up-to-date* report.
(The report must be *up to date*.)

I had an *after-dinner* mint.
(I had a mint *after dinner*.)

Words Out of Order When we borrow a descriptive phrase or clause and place it before a noun, we often eliminate or rearrange some of the words. To help them express a single thought, words that are out of their normal order can be held together by hyphens.

She wore *grass-stained* pants.
(Her pants were *stained with grass*.)

Please feed that *hungry-looking* dog.
(The dog *looks hungry*.)

An Exception We *do not* use a hyphen in a compound adjective that begins with an adverb ending in *-ly*.

a *nicely swept* porch, a *securely fastened* gate
the *newly hired* worker, my *painfully swollen* foot

Number + Unit of Measure We use a hyphen when joining a number to a unit of measure to form a compound adjective.

48-foot cable, *ten-mile* run, *thirty-year* loan

We *do not* use a hyphen when the number alone modifies the noun:

48 feet, *ten* miles, *thirty* years

Fractions   We use a hyphen in a fraction that functions as an adjective.

Beth was elected by a *two-thirds* majority.

The tank was *three-fourths* full.

We *do not* use a hyphen if the fraction functions as a noun.

Two thirds of the birds were sparrows.

Three fourths of the students like spinach.

Example 1   Write the words that should be hyphenated in sentences a–e.

(a) She spoke in a high pitched voice.

(b) Ed has above average grades in math.

(c) Look at this mail order catalog.

(d) Ted drew a six inch line on the paper.

(e) Three fifths of the girls had brown hair.

Solution   (a) We hyphenate **high-pitched** because the words work as a unit to modify the noun *voice.*

(b) We hyphenate **above-average** because it is a prepositional phrase that comes before and modifies the noun *grades.*

(c) We hyphenate **mail-order** to help it retain its meaning (a catalog for ordering things through the mail).

(d) We hyphenate **six-inch** because it is a compound adjective formed by a number and a unit of measure.

(e) **None.** We do not hyphenate the fraction *three fifths* because it functions as a noun.

Dictionary Clues   Remember, dictionaries cannot contain all the compound words we can create. If you are faced with an unfamiliar compound, you can search the dictionary for similar compounds and use them as clues.

Other Uses for Hyphens   We use hyphens to avoid confusion or awkward spelling and to join unusual elements.

With Prefixes and Suffixes   If you add a prefix or suffix to a word and the resulting word is misleading or awkward, use a hyphen for clarity.

> Shall I *re-cover* (not *recover*) the sofa with new fabric?

> It had a hard, *shell-like* (not *shelllike*) surface.

Also, use a hyphen to join a prefix to any proper noun.

> pro-American, mid-July, post-World War II

Letter + Word, Number + Number   Hyphens are used to combine unusual elements into single expressions.

When a letter (or group of letters) modifies a word in a compound noun or adjective, a hyphen is often used.

> A-frame, L-shaped, G-rated, U-turn, T-shirt

We can also use a hyphen to join numbers in expressions, such as the following:

> The score at halftime was *27-43*.

> You have a *fifty-fifty* chance of winning.

Example 2   Write the words, if any, that should be hyphenated in sentences a–d. Be prepared to use the dictionary.

(a) Nan must research her room for the lost book.

(b) Are some people antiAmerican?

(c) We must make a U turn here.

(d) We shall split the cost sixty forty.

Solution   (a) We hyphenate **re-search** to avoid misleading the reader.

(b) We hyphenate **anti-American** because we are joining a prefix and a proper noun.

(c) We consult the dictionary and find that **U-turn** is a hyphenated term.

(d) We use a hyphen to form the expression **sixty-forty**.

Practice   Write the words, if any, that should be hyphenated in sentences a–e.

a. Dan built an A frame cabin.

b. I watched the rapidly moving clouds.

c. Let's recover the chair with red velvet.

d. She drank a five ounce glass of juice.

e. My rain soaked gloves need to dry.

For f and g, replace each blank with *species* or *specimen*.

f. The botanist showed us a poison ivy _____, and now we know what plants to avoid as we hike.

g. What _____ is that dog?

Review Set 97

Choose the correct word(s) to complete sentences 1–16.

1. Only skeletons of the ninety-foot (matriarch, megalodon, jester) remain.
(96)

2. The oldest (fraternity, reticent, sage) is a brotherhood founded at Princeton in 1824.
(95)

3. The family's (aviary, aviate, matriarch) started the shortbread tradition.
(94)

4. A compassionate person might (cede, precede, aviate) his or her place in line to an elderly person.
(93)

5. I saw (colts, fillies, fleas) on my white socks.
(39)

6. A pound of grapes (cost, costs) how much?
(90)

7. Eat (good, well) today.
(96)

8. I don't have (no, any) homework.
(93)

9. I have (less, fewer) books than she.
(56)

10. The pronoun *our* is (first, second, third) person (singular, plural).
(64)

11. (Who's, Whose) knocking?
(79)

12. The botanist showed (we, us) hikers a poison ivy specimen.
(78)

13. Ava has (gave, given) me three piano lessons. She has
(86, 87) (teached, taught) me many skills.

14. Someone with horses (have, has) many chores in (their,
(83, 91) his or her) daily routine.

15. Neither Nan nor Ed (sing, sings) like my aunt.
(89)

16. The scissors (was, were) not sharp.
(92)

17. Write and underline the words that should be italicized
(84) in the sentence below.

In the 1800s, Rosa Bonheur painted The Horse Fair.

18. Use a dictionary: (a) The word *osprey* is what part of
(27, 30) speech? (b) Write its pronunciation. (c) Write its
etymology.

19. Rewrite the sentence below, adding hyphens as needed.
(94, 97) I spent twenty five minutes writing two sentences.

20. Write whether the sentence below is simple or compound.
(75)
Mr. Cox cleans and polishes his bugle.

21. Write the nominative case pronoun to complete the
(66) sentence below.

The best buglers are you and (him, he).

22. Write whether the clause below is dependent or
(73) independent.

George Gershwin composed *Rhapsody in Blue*

23. Rewrite the following, adding capital letters and
(80, 88) punctuation marks as needed:

ted asks may i bring some nuts fruit and napkins

24. For the irregular verb *feel*, write the (a) present participle,
(19, 85) (b) past tense, and (c) past participle.

25. From the sentence below, write each adverb and the
(95) word or phrase it modifies.

Martha serves guests joyfully.

26. Rewrite the sentence below, adding capital letters and
(81) punctuation marks as needed.

we read the chapter titled into the forest

27. Rewrite the following sentence, adding capital letters and
(57) punctuation marks as needed.

jen my youngest cousin was born on may 2 2011

28. Write the subordinating conjunction in the sentence
(73) below:

I forgot to lock the door even though you reminded me.

Diagram each word of sentences 29–30.

29. Two thirds of the birds were sparrows.
(45, 51)

30. Entomologist Amy Hart showed Ed and me her
(46, 58) specimens of ticks and fleas.

29.

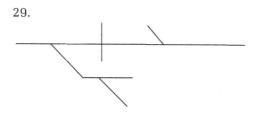

30.

(Amy Hart)

Adverbs That Tell "Where"

Dictation or Journal Entry

Vocabulary:

The Latin *capri* means "goat."

Capricorn is a group of stars that resemble a goat. *Capricorn* is one of the twelve constellations of the zodiac.

To *caper* is to leap playfully. Excited children *caper* like young goats.

We have learned to identify adverbs that tell "how." In this lesson, we will learn to identify adverbs that tell "where." Again, let's think about how Al drives:

Al drives *carefully.*

"Where" Now, let's think about **where** Al drives:

Al drives *everywhere.*

He might also drive *away, up, down, across, nearby, home, here, there,* or *anywhere.*

Here are some common adverbs that tell "where:"

near	anywhere	up	in
far	everywhere	here	out
down	nowhere	there	home
above	somewhere	away	inside
under	around	ahead	outside

We remember that words like *in, out,* and *down* can also be prepositions. But in order to function as a preposition, a word must have an object. When a word like *in, out,* or *down* does not have an object, it is an adverb.

PREPOSITION: She went *out* the door. (object: "door")

ADVERB: She went *out.* (no object)

Example 1 For sentences a–d, write each adverb that tells "where," and identify the verb or verb phrase that it modifies.

(a) Rex capers ahead.

(b) He must stay there.

(c) I searched everywhere for the key.

(d) Everyone was looking up.

Solution (a) The word **ahead** tells "where" *Rex* **capers.**

(b) The word **there** modifies the verb phrase **must stay.** It tells "where" *he* must stay.

(c) The word **everywhere** modifies the verb **searched.** It tells "where" *I* searched.

(d) The word **up** modifies the verb phrase **was looking.** It tells "where" *Everyone* was looking.

Diagramming Adverbs We diagram adverbs just as we do adjectives. We write the adverb on a slanted line under the word it modifies. Here, we diagram this sentence:

Al drives *carefully*.

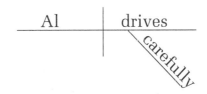

Example 2 Diagram this sentence: Ava walks home.

Solution The adverb *home* tells "where" Ava walks, so we diagram the sentence like this:

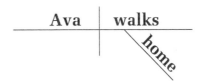

Practice For sentences a–d, write each adverb that tells "where," and identify the verb or verb phrase that it modifies.

a. Rex can sleep anywhere.

b. Meg has come home.

c. They have gone out.

d. Fido jumps around.

Diagram sentences e and f.

e. Ed and Ted work outside.

f. They left the mail inside.

For g and h, replace each blank with *Capricorn* or *caper.*

g. Playful colts and fillies _____ in the pasture.

h. We found the constellation _____ in the night sky.

Review Set
98

Choose the correct word(s) to complete sentences 1–16.

1. Lions belong to the *Panthera leo* (specimen, species,
(97) mirage).

2. The (megamouth, megalodon, mire) is a rare shark with a
(96) large mouth and small teeth.

3. Because Josh and Nate are not identical twins, they are
(95) (maternal, fraternal, aviate) twins.

4. (Maternal, Fraternal, Aviate) instinct prompts an animal
(94) to care for its young.

5. The six-month-old (colt, megalodon, matriarch) trotted
(40) across the meadow.

6. Peep, the finch with black stripes, (cheep, cheeps) loudly.
(90)

7. He had a (good, well) sleep.
(96)

8. They (have, haven't) hardly (any, no) food left.
(93)

9. Fido is the (more, most) docile of the two.
(56)

10. The pronoun *our* is (nominative, objective, possessive)
(66, 69) case.

11. Are these (they're, there, their) jackets?
(72)

12. Dan ran faster than (them, they).
(78)

13. Ed (losed, lost) his map, so he (standed, stood) in the
(86, 87) street, wondering which way to go.

14. (There's, There are) several bats in the attic.
(83, 91)

15. Neither Nan nor her friends (sing, sings) like my aunt.
(89)

16. His pants (is, are) faded.
(92)

17. Write and underline the words that should be italicized
(84) in the sentence below.

Sometimes people write there when they mean their.

18. Write the plural form of the singular noun *water bottle.*
(17, 22)

19. Rewrite the sentence below, adding hyphens as needed.
(94, 97)
Wassim has twenty one goldfish in his thirty gallon
aquarium.

20. Add suffixes:
(33, 34)
(a) try + ed   (b) jog + ed

21. Write whether the circled pronoun in the sentence below
(64) is used as a subject or an object.

Yes, Lucy and (she) can swim.

22. Write whether the following is a phrase or a clause.
(36)
on the collar of the dog with floppy ears

23. Rewrite the following, adding capital letters and
(80, 88) punctuation marks as needed:

i offered the goose a cracker and it bit my finger
exclaimed nan

24. For the irregular verb *fly,* write the (a) present participle,
(19, 85) (b) past tense, and (c) past participle.

25. From the sentence below, write each adverb and the
(95, 98) word or phrase it modifies.

Ed suddenly sat up.

26. Rewrite the sentence below, adding capital letters and
(81) punctuation marks as needed.

my sister sang jingle bells until we arrived in atlanta
georgia

27. Rewrite the following sentence, adding capital letters and
(57, 67) punctuation marks as needed.

on the other hand we could plant tulips violets or pansies

28. Write the subordinating conjunction in the sentence
_(73)_ below:

I have extra time because I came early.

Diagram each word of sentences 29–30.

29. Does the two-liter pitcher of orange juice look full?
_(45, 54)_

30. Entomologist Amy Hart gingerly held up each of the
_(58, 98)_ specimens.

29.

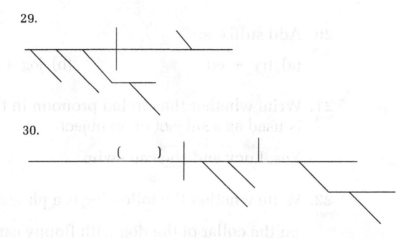

30.

Adverbs That Tell "When"

Dictation or Journal Entry
Vocabulary:
The Greek prefixes *ex-, ec-,* and *e-* mean "out."

An *exit* is a way out. The theater had several *exits*.

An *exodus* is the departure of a group of people. In the Bible, the book of Exodus tells how the Jewish people left Egypt.

We have learned to identify adverbs that tell "how" and "where." In this lesson, we will learn about adverbs that modify a verb to tell "when." Again, let us think about how and where Ed drives:

HOW: Ed drives *carefully*.

WHERE: Ed drives *everywhere*.

"When" Now, we will think about **when** Ed drives:

Ed drives *often*.

He might also drive *daily, weekly, monthly,* or *today*.

Here are some common adverbs that tell "when."

afterward	*daily*	*never*	*then*
again	*early*	*nightly*	*tomorrow*
always	*ever*	*now*	*tonight*
before	*hourly*	*often*	*weekly*
constantly	*late*	*someday*	*yearly*
currently	*monthly*	*soon*	*yesterday*

Adverb Position An adverb usually appears near the verb that it modifies.

Nan will *soon* leave for the library.

Nan will leave *soon* for the library.

However, an adverb can appear almost anywhere in a sentence.

Soon, Nan will leave for the library.

Nan will leave for the library *soon*.

Even though the adverb *soon* modifies the verb *leave* in each of the sentences above, it is not necessarily placed near the verb. Because the placement of the adverb can vary, we must learn to identify adverbs even when they are separated from the verbs that they modify.

Example 1 For each sentence, write the adverb that tells "when" and the verb or verb phrase that it modifies.

   (a) Yesterday, Ava caught two fish.

   (b) Rex sometimes licks my face.

   (c) Why did you come to school early?

Solution (a) The adverb **Yesterday** tells "when" Ava **caught** two fish. *Yesterday* modifies the verb *caught.*

   (b) The adverb **sometimes** modifies the verb **licks.**

   (c) The adverb **early** modifies the verb phrase **did come.**

Example 2 Diagram this sentence: We swam daily.

Solution We place the adverb *daily* under the verb *swam:*

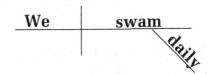

Practice For sentences a–c, write the adverb that tells "when" and the verb or verb phrase it modifies.

   a. Tonight, we shall read stories.

   b. We can climb trees later.

   c. Have you ever written poetry?

Diagram sentences d and e.
   d. Miss Ng tests us weekly.

   e. The bell rang again.

For f and g, replace each blank with *exit* or *exodus.*

   f. Drought and famine might cause an _____ from a country.

   g. When it is time to leave, we shall seek the nearest _____.

Choose the correct word(s) to complete sentences 1–16.

1. A large sign marks the (exodus, exit, species) from the
(99) museum.

2. (Capricorn, Nocturnal, Zephyr) is a group of stars
(98) resembling a goat.

3. Bone (pollination, specimens, species) assist scientists in
(97) identifying animals.

4. The (boar, megalodon, sage) is an extinct shark.
(96)

5. The collie lifts its (foreleg, fetlock, pupa) to "shake
(41) hands."

6. There (was, were) some ice on the road.
(90)

7. The players defend the goal (good, well).
(96)

8. She (has, hasn't) hardly made (no, any) mistakes.
(93)

9. Ed caught (less, fewer) fish than she.
(56)

10. The pronoun *them* is (nominative, objective, possessive)
(66, 69) case.

11. (Your, You're) bags are here; (ours, our's) are not.
(72)

12. She is not as docile as (he, him).
(78)

13. Ed (holded, held) the stack of plates with two hands and
(86, 87) (shut, shutted) the door with his foot.

14. Each of those stories (contain, contains) humor.
(83, 91)

15. Neither the sisters nor their brother (have, has) found the
(89) treasure.

16. A team of teachers (have, has) written the book.
(92)

17. Write and underline the words that should be italicized
(84) in the sentence below.

Have you read The Horse and His Boy?

18. Write the plural form of the singular noun *loaf of bread*.
(17, 22)

19. Rewrite the sentence below, adding hyphens as needed.
(94, 97)

Max has grown forty two ten foot pine trees.

20. From the list below, write the word that is not an adverb.
(98, 99)

now   later   quickly   yellow

21. Write the nominative case pronoun to complete the
(64) sentence below.

Two excellent writers are Juan and (she, her).

22. Write whether the following is a phrase or a clause.
(36)

since Neil Armstrong walked on the moon

23. Rewrite the following, adding capital letters and
(80, 88) punctuation marks as needed:

ed your bike tire is flat exclaims nan

24. For the irregular verb *fight*, write the (a) present
(19, 85) participle, (b) past tense, and (c) past participle.

25. From the sentence below, write each adverb and the
(95, 98) word or phrase it modifies.

Abe boldly steps in.

26. Rewrite the sentence below, adding capital letters and
(81) punctuation marks as needed.

lewis carroll wrote the poem the crocodile

27. Rewrite the following sentence, adding capital letters and
(57, 67) punctuation marks as needed.

he was born on sunday may 5 i believe

28. From the sentence below, write each adverb that tells
(99) "when."

We can always try again.

Diagram each word of sentences 29–30.

29. Has Tom, your ten-year-old brother, grown taller?
(54, 58)

30. I often tell my cousin in Maine stories about my cat.
(46, 99)

29.

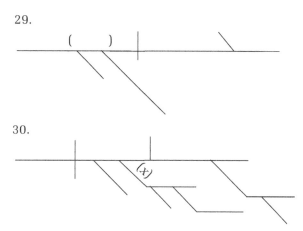

30.

LESSON 100

Adverbs That Tell "How Much"

Dictation or Journal Entry

Vocabulary:

The Latin roots *fa-*, *fam-*, *fan-*, *fat-*, and *fess-* mean "talk or speak."

Affable means "courteous in receiving or responding to conversation." The *affable* docent tries to answer our questions about dinosaurs.

To *confess* is to admit. The docent *confesses* to not knowing everything about dinosaurs.

"How Much" or "To What Extent"

Some adverbs tell "how much" or "to what extent." These adverbs are sometimes called **intensifiers** because they add intensity (either positive or negative) to the words they modify.

Notice how the adverbs in the sentences below add intensity to the words they modify:

He felt *rather* shy.

She laughed *very* hard.

They came *too* late.

You are *most* welcome.

Ed drives *quite* carefully.

This is *just* fine.

Some adverbs that tell "how much" or "to what extent" are easy to identify because they end in *-ly*. However, many others do not. Here are some common intensifiers:

absolutely	*almost*	*altogether*
awfully	*barely*	*completely*
especially	*even*	*extremely*
fully	*hardly*	*highly*
incredibly	*just*	*least*
less	*most*	*not*
partly	*quite*	*rather*
really	*so*	*somewhat*
terribly	*thoroughly*	*too*
totally	*vastly*	*very*

An adverb that tells "how much" or "to what extent" usually modifies an adjective or another adverb. However, it occasionally modifies a verb.

MODIFYING AN ADJECTIVE

They were *so* happy!

The adverb *so* modifies the adjective *happy* and tells "how happy" they were.

MODIFYING ANOTHER ADVERB

Ed drove *rather* slowly.

The adverb *rather* modifies the adverb *slowly* and tells "how slowly" Ed drove.

MODIFYING A VERB

I *completely* agree.

The adverb *completely* modifies the verb *agree* and tells "to what extent" I agree.

Example 1 For each sentence, write the adverb that tells "how much" or "to what extent" and identify the word it modifies.

(a) His mood changed very quickly.

(b) Are we too late?

(c) Has she cleaned her room thoroughly?

(d) Dinner is not ready.

Solution (a) The adverb **very** modifies **quickly**, another adverb.

(b) The adverb **too** modifies the predicate adjective **late.**

(c) The adverb **thoroughly** modifies the verb phrase **Has cleaned.**

(d) The adverb **not** modifies the adjective **ready.**

Diagramming Adverbs That Modify Adjectives or Other Adverbs We have learned to diagram adverbs that modify verbs. Now, we will diagram adverbs that modify adjectives or other adverbs. As shown in the following examples, we place the adverb on a line underneath the adjective or other adverb that is being modified:

Rex barks *quite* loudly.

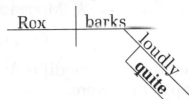

An adverb may be a part of a prepositional phrase, as in the sentence below. The adverb *rather* modifies the adjective *bumpy,* which modifies the noun *road,* which is the object of the preposition *along.*

Ed drove along a *rather* bumpy road.

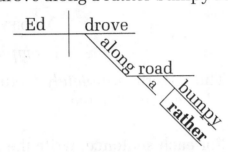

Example 2 Diagram this sentence:

Extremely colorful birds include macaws.

Solution We place the adverb *extremely* underneath the adjective it modifies, *colorful,* which describes *birds.*

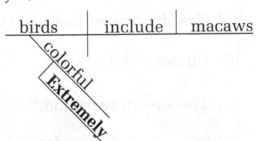

Not Since the word *not* is an adverb, contractions like *couldn't* contain the adverb *not.* When we diagram contractions, we diagram *n't* as an adverb:

I couldn't believe it!

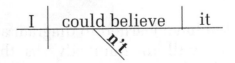

Example 3 Diagram this sentence:

Don't bother him.

Solution We place the adverb *not* (*n't*) under the verb phrase *do bother*.

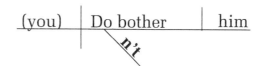

Practice For sentences a–e, write each adverb that tells "how much" or "to what extent" and the word it modifies.

a. My most comfortable shoes have holes.

b. She almost missed the bus.

c. Jake spoke too fast.

d. We couldn't understand him.

e. She appears very cheerful.

For f and g, replace each blank with *affable* or *confess*.

f. I shall _____ my errors.

g. _____ people are easy to talk to.

Diagram sentences h and i.

h. The two artists are altogether different.

i. She paints less boldly.

More Practice See "More Practice Lesson 100" in the Student Workbook.

Review Set 100 Choose the correct word(s) to complete sentences 1–16.

1. The (fraternal, reticent, affable) young bus rider offered
   (100) her seat to an elderly person.

2. The Jewish (exit, quest, exodus) refers to the departure of
   (99) the Jewish people from Egypt.

3. A playful pup might (cede, elapse, caper) in the park.
   (98)

4. What (specimen, species, caper) is that animal?
(97)

5. The horse's (larva, fetlock, hare) was tangled and muddy.
(41)

6. There (was, were) some moths in the closet.
(90)

7. They are (good, well) singers.
(96)

8. There (is, isn't) scarcely (no, any) honey in the jar.
(93)

9. Among the four of us, Juan made the (fewer, fewest) errors.
(56)

10. The pronoun *us* is (first, second, third) person (singular, plural).
(64)

11. (Who's, Whose) dog is howling?
(79)

12. Icy roads slow (we, us) travelers.
(78)

13. I (telled, told) him where she (hided, hid) the clue.
(86, 87)

14. One of the kittens (pounce, pounces) on the catnip.
(83, 91)

15. Either the players or their coach (have, has) turned on the lights.
(89)

16. The microscope lens (have, has) broken.
(92)

17. Rewrite the sentence below, adding a comma to make the meaning clear.
(68)

For Nancy Lee will do his best.

18. Write the plural form of the singular noun *chorus*.
(17, 22)

19. Rewrite the sentence below, adding hyphens as needed.
(94, 97)

Twenty one Spanish speaking students sang in the choir.

20. From this list, write the word that is *not* an adverb:
(98, 99)

not   hardly   almost   ribs

21. Write the objective case pronoun to complete the sentence below.
(69)

I confessed my fear to Miss Moore and (she, her).

22. Write whether the following clause is dependent or independent.
(73)

Abe found the exit

23. Rewrite the following, adding capital letters and punctuation marks as needed:
(80, 88)

students asks miss ng are you affable

24. For the irregular verb *forget*, write the (a) present participle, (b) past tense, and (c) past participle.
(19, 85)

25. From the sentence below, write each adverb and the word or phrase it modifies.
(95, 98)

Ava boldly steps up.

26. Rewrite the sentence below, adding capital letters and punctuation marks as needed.
(60, 81)

the first chapter elusive predators is my favorite

27. Rewrite the following sentence, adding capital letters and punctuation marks as needed.
(57, 67)

yes cora s wise phd teaches math science and latin

28. From the sentence below, write each adverb that tells "when" or "how much."
(99, 100)

The bus came terribly late.

Diagram each word of sentences 29–30.

29. My French poodle, Jazz, has now grown more docile.
(54, 58)

30. We don't feed Jazz tasty treats very often.
(99, 100)

29.

30.

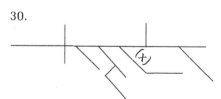

LESSON
101

Comparison Adverbs

Like adjectives, some adverbs can express the three degrees of comparison: positive, comparative, and superlative. Below are examples of the positive, comparative, and superlative forms of some adverbs:

POSITIVE	COMPARATIVE	SUPERLATIVE
soon	sooner	soonest
near	nearer	nearest
quietly	more quietly	most quietly
late	later	latest

Positive The positive form describes an action without comparing it to anything.

Carl came early.

Comparative The comparative form compares the action of **two** people, places, or things.

Carl came earlier than Ed.

Superlative The superlative form compares the action of **three or more** people, places, or things.

Of the three, Carl came earliest.

Example 1 Choose the correct adverb form for each sentence.
(a) Of the two girls, Jen ran (harder, hardest).

(b) Of all the girls, Kate walked (faster, fastest).

Solution (a) Of the two girls, Jen ran **harder.**

(b) Of all the girls, Kate walked **fastest.**

Forming Comparison Adverbs

We form comparison adverbs the same way that we form comparison adjectives. How we create the comparative and superlative forms of an adverb depends on how the adverb appears in its positive form. There are two main categories to remember.

One-Syllable Adverbs

We create the comparative form of most one-syllable adverbs by adding *er* to the end of the word. The superlative form is created by adding *est*.

POSITIVE	COMPARATIVE	SUPERLATIVE
late	later	latest
soon	sooner	soonest
tall	taller	tallest

Two-Syllable Adverbs

Most adverbs with two or more syllables don't have comparative or superlative forms. Instead, we put the word "more" (or "less") in front of the adverb to form the comparative, and the word "most" (or "least") to form the superlative.

POSITIVE	COMPARATIVE	SUPERLATIVE
often	more often	most often
carefully	more carefully	most carefully
happily	less happily	least happily

Since most adverbs are formed by adding the suffix *-ly* to an adjective, the rule above applies to most adverbs.

Irregular Comparison Adverbs

Some adverbs have irregular comparative and superlative forms. We must learn these if we have not already.

POSITIVE	COMPARATIVE	SUPERLATIVE
little	less	least
good, well	better	best
badly	worse	worst
far	farther	farthest
many, much, some	more	most

We check the dictionary if we are unsure how to create the comparative or superlative form of any adverb.

Example 2

Complete the comparison chart by adding the comparative and superlative forms of each adverb.

	POSITIVE	COMPARATIVE	SUPERLATIVE
(a)	far	_____	_____
(b)	well	_____	_____
(c)	joyfully	_____	_____
(d)	quickly	_____	_____

Solution	POSITIVE	COMPARATIVE	SUPERLATIVE
(a)	far	**farther**	**farthest**
(b)	well	**better**	**best**
(c)	joyfully	**more joyfully**	**most joyfully**
(d)	quickly	**more quickly**	**most quickly**

Practice Write the correct adverb form for sentences a–e.

a. The small bears were growling (more ferociously, most ferociously) than the large bears.

b. Of all the students, Ed finishes his work (more quickly, most quickly).

c. I like this picture (better, best) than the other one.

d. Of the three outfielders, Ruth throws the ball (harder, hardest).

e. Max did (worse, worst) than Roy, but I did (worse, worst) of all.

For f and g, replace each blank with *reptant* or *reptile*.

f. A garter snake is a _____.

g. A _____ vine covered the ground.

More Practice Write the correct adverb for each sentence.

1. My brother plays tennis (weller, better) than I.

2. Of all the players, he is (better, best).

3. She drives (farther, farthest) than he.

4. He drives (less, least) than she.

5. Of the four drivers, he drives (less, least).

6. Of the two, Nan walks (slower, slowest).

7. She works (longer, longest) than I.

8. Ed can hit the ball (harder, hardest) than I.

Review Set 101 Choose the correct word(s) to complete sentences 1–16.

1. The (tacit, reticent, reptant) caterpillar edged its way
(101) along the leaf.

2. Did the thief (confess, elapse, collapse) to the crime?
(100)

3. When it is time to leave, we shall find the parking lot
(99) (exodus, exit, famine).

4. (Capricorn, Megalodon, Megamouth) is a constellation.
(98)

5. Next week, hot air balloons will (precede, cede, soar)
(42) over New Mexico.

6. A parrot with bright green and red feathers (was, were)
(90) squawking nearby.

7. My friend Kate listens (good, well).
(96)

8. There (ain't, aren't) (no, any) polar bears here.
(93)

9. Among the six of us, Rob skated (longer, longest).
(101)

10. The pronoun *us* is (nominative, objective, possessive)
(64) case.

11. (Who's, Whose) there?
(79)

12. I think (we, us) poets should publish our poetry.
(78)

13. Have you (shined, shone) your shoes?
(87)

14. Many on their team (is, are) smiling.
(83, 91)

15. Either the baboon or the gorillas (have, has) eaten the fruit.
(89)

16. Measles (was, were) more common when Grandpa was a boy.
(92)

17. From the sentence below, write and underline words that should be italicized.
(84)

Reptile is a noun, but reptant is an adjective.

18. Write the plural form of the singular noun *fruit fly*.
(17, 22)

19. Rewrite the sentence below, adding hyphens as needed.
(94, 97)

They dyed twenty four hard boiled eggs.

20. From this list, write the word that is *not* an adverb:
(98, 99)

soon   reptile   there   here

21. Write the nominative case pronoun to complete the sentence below.
(64)

Ana and (she, her) will thank Mr. Lee.

22. Write whether the following is a phrase or a clause.
(36)

with very long ears and a fluffy tail

23. Rewrite the following, adding capital letters and punctuation marks as needed:
(80, 88)

throw the ball cries coach casey

24. For the irregular verb *flee*, write the (a) present participle, (b) past tense, and (c) past participle.
(19, 85)

25. From the sentence below, write each adverb and the word or phrase it modifies.
(95, 98)

Manny quickly steps forward.

26. Rewrite the sentence below, adding capital letters and
(25, 81) punctuation marks as needed.

nora titled her essay my fish story

27. Rewrite the following sentence, adding capital letters and
(57, 67) punctuation marks as needed.

this essay is due i believe on friday may 4

28. From the sentence below, write each adverb that tells
(99, 100) "when" or "how much."

The dog later became quite friendly.

Diagram each word of sentences 29–30.

29. Soon, the dog on the leash grew more restless.
(45, 54)

30. Almost daily, I make myself a sandwich with pickles and
(46, 99) cheese.

29.

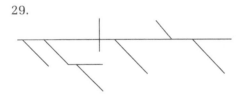

30.

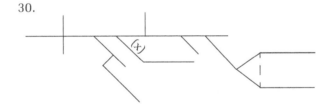

LESSON 102

The Semicolon

Dictation or Journal Entry
Vocabulary:
The Latin *pater* and *patr* mean "father."

Paternal means "fatherly." The *paternal* neighbor kept toddlers out of the street.

A *patriarch* is the father of a family or tribe. Most historians consider George Washington the *patriarch* of the United States.

The **semicolon** (;) is used as a connector. It indicates a pause longer than a comma but shorter than a colon. In this lesson, we will learn how to use the semicolon correctly.

Related Thoughts In a compound sentence, we can use a semicolon instead of a coordinating conjunction (*and, but, or, for, nor, yet, so*) between the two independent clauses. However, these clauses must contain related thoughts.

> YES: Pine trees are evergreens; they stay green through winter. (related thoughts)

> No: Pine trees are evergreens; my sister planted an oak tree. (not related thoughts)

Example 1 Use a semicolon instead of the coordinating conjunction in this sentence:

> She came with a problem, but she left with a solution.

Solution We replace the comma and conjunction with a semicolon:

> She came with a problem; she left with a solution.

Conjunctive Adverbs An adverb used as a conjunction is called a **conjunctive adverb**. Words such as *also, besides, still, however, therefore, consequently, otherwise, moreover, furthermore,* and *nevertheless* are examples of conjunctive adverbs. We place a semicolon before a conjunctive adverb.

> YES: Ray usually plays soccer; *however*, today he played basketball.
>   ↑

Using a comma where a semicolon is needed creates a run-on sentence:

> No: Ray usually plays soccer, *however*, today he played basketball.
>   ↑

Example 2 Place a semicolon where it is needed in this sentence:
His hands had blisters, still, he kept working.

Solution We place a semicolon before the conjunctive adverb *still*:
His hands had blisters; still, he kept working.

With Other Commas If an independent clause contains commas, we can use a semicolon to show where one independent clause ends and another one begins.

UNCLEAR: Kim likes reading, swimming, and drawing, and music, art, and drama are Pat's favorite activities.

CLEAR: Kim likes reading, swimming, and drawing; and music, art, and drama are Pat's favorite activities.

Semicolons can also be used to separate phrases or dependent clauses that contain commas.

I have friends in Sacramento, California; Salem, Oregon; and Olympia, Washington.

He promised to tend the cattle, sheep, and goats; clean the house, barnyard, and stalls; and cook breakfast, lunch, and dinner.

Example 3 Place semicolons where they are needed in sentences a and b.

(a) The bus took us through Boise, Idaho, Denver, Colorado, and Phoenix, Arizona.

(b) She plays the guitar, the banjo, and the bass, and he plays the tuba, the trombone, and the trumpet.

Solution (a) We separate each "city, state" pair of words with a semicolon for clarity:

The bus took us through Boise, Idaho; Denver, Colorado; and Phoenix, Arizona.

(b) Because the independent clauses in this sentence already contain commas, we separate the two clauses with a semicolon:

She plays the guitar, the banjo, and the bass; and he plays the tuba, the trombone, and the trumpet.

Practice Rewrite sentences a–c, replacing commas with semicolons where they are needed.

> **a.** We discussed word pairs such as *bear, bare, main, mane,* and *tail, tale.*

> **b.** We sow in the spring, we reap in the fall.

> **c.** I skinned my knee, moreover, I broke my glasses.

> For d and e, replace each blank with *paternal* or *patriarch.*

> **d.** We call Great Grandfather the _____ of our family.

> **e.** _____ means "fatherly."

More Practice See "More Practice Lesson 102" in the Student Workbook.

Review Set 102 Choose the correct word(s) to complete sentences 1–16.

> **1.** Grandpa's (maternal, matriarch, paternal) leadership held
> *(102)* his family together.

> **2.** The (zephyr, reptant, gale) lizard edged its way toward a
> *(101)* bird.

> **3.** The (affable, reptant, reticent) secretary makes visitors
> *(100)* feel welcome.

> **4.** (Species, Exits, Docents) are marked with lighted signs.
> *(99)*

> **5.** On a windy day, kites (soar, sore, flea).
> *(42)*

> **6.** Here (come, comes) Jim and Ting.
> *(90)*

> **7.** Kate is a (well, good) listener.
> *(96)*

> **8.** Rex (has, hasn't) hardly (no, any) fleas.
> *(93)*

> **9.** Of the two, Rob skated (longer, longest).
> *(101)*

> **10.** The pronoun *we* is (nominative, objective, possessive)
> *(64)* case.

> **11.** (You're, Your) place is here; (our's, ours) is over there.
> *(72)*

12. Ed reads faster than (me, I).
(78)

13. Weeds had (sprang, sprung) up overnight.
(87)

14. Each of the players (is, are) trying hard.
(83, 91)

15. Elle or the neighbors (shovel, shovels) the snow.
(89)

16. The flock of geese (have, has) flown south.
(92)

17. From the sentence below, write and underline words that
(84) should be italicized.

The sailboat Sand Queen sank in the bay.

18. Rewrite the sentence below, replacing commas with
(102) semicolons where they are needed.

I named all the states and their capitals except for Salem, Oregon, Augusta, Maine, and Richmond, Virginia.

19. Rewrite the sentence below, adding hyphens as needed.
(94, 97)

I wear my brother's hand me down T shirts.

20. From this list, write the word that is *not* an adverb:
(95, 99)

swiftly   green   now   later

21. Write the objective case pronoun to complete the
(69) sentence below.

Uncle shows Rex and (me, I) paternal affection.

22. Write whether the following clause is dependent or
(73) independent.

before it rains

23. Rewrite the following, adding capital letters and
(80, 88) punctuation marks as needed:

have you caught any fish asked mr wilson

24. For the irregular verb *burst*, write the (a) present
(19, 85) participle, (b) past tense, and (c) past participle.

25. From the sentence below, write each adverb and the
(95, 98) word or phrase it modifies.

Weeds grow quickly there.

26. Rewrite the sentence below, adding capital letters and
(60, 81) punctuation marks as needed.

elvis presley an american singer sang hound dog

27. Rewrite the following sentence, adding capital letters and
(57, 67) punctuation marks as needed.

the primary colors i believe are red yellow and blue

28. From the sentence below, write each adverb that tells
(99, 100) "when" or "how much."

Sometimes, Ned is too practical.

Diagram each word of sentences 29–30.

29. Today, the waves in the bay aren't very big.
(45, 54)

30. Weekly, the cartoonist would draw five cartoons about
(58, 98) Gomer, a friendly goose.

29.

30.

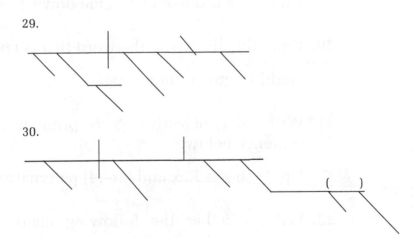

Adverb Usage

Dictation or Journal Entry

Vocabulary:

The Latin *tut-* means "to look after."

A *tutor* is one who instructs someone in an area of learning. The struggling student hired a *tutor* to explain subject-verb agreement.

Tutelage is a noun meaning "guardianship" or "guidance." The prince's manners improved under the king's *tutelage.*

Sure or Surely? The word *sure* is an adjective and not an adverb. *Sure* should not take the place of the adverbs *surely, certainly,* or *really.*

> NO: Kate *sure* helped.
>
> YES: Kate *surely* helped. (modifies verb "helped")

> NO: She's *sure* kind.
>
> YES: She's *really* kind. (modifies predicate adjective "kind")

> NO: You are *sure* welcome.
>
> YES: You are *certainly* welcome. (modifies predicate adjective "welcome")

We remember that *sure* is an adjective, and we use it only as an adjective or predicate adjective, as in the sentences below:

> They were *sure* of their answer. (predicate adjective)

> That is a *sure* solution. (adjective modifying the noun "solution")

> We were *sure* it would snow. (predicate adjective)

Example 1 Choose the correct word to complete sentences a and b.

(a) I (sure, surely) need your help.

(b) Are you (sure, surely) of your answer?

Solution (a) I **surely** need your help. (*Surely* is an adverb. It modifies the verb "need.")

(b) Are you **sure** of your answer? (*Sure* is a predicate adjective. It describes the pronoun "you.")

Real or Really? Like *sure,* the word *real* is an adjective and should not take the place of the adverb *really. Real* modifies a noun or pronoun, while *really* modifies a verb, adjective, or adverb.

> NO: I was *real* sorry.
>
> YES: I was *really* sorry. (modifies predicate adjective "sorry")

NO: That's a *real* big bear.
YES: That's a *really* big bear. (modifies adjective "big")

NO: Ken sings *real* well.
YES: Ken sings *really* well. (modifies adverb "well")

We remember that *real* is an adjective, and we use it only as an adjective or predicate adjective, as in the sentences below:

That toy looks like a *real* cellphone. (adjective modifying the noun "cellphone")

Are those pearls *real* or fake? (predicate adjective)

Example 2 Choose the correct word to complete sentences a and b.

(a) Lily hit the ball (real, really) hard.

(b) Those silk flowers look (real, really).

Solution (a) Lily hit the ball **really** hard. (*Really* is an adverb. It modifies another adverb, "hard.")

(b) Those silk flowers look **real.** (*Real* is a predicate adjective. It describes the noun "flowers.")

Bad or Badly? The word *bad* is an adjective. It describes a noun or pronoun, and often follows linking verbs like *feel, look, seem, taste, smell,* and *is.* The word *badly* is an adverb that tells "how." We do not use *bad* as an adverb.

NO: I did *bad* on the test.
YES: I did *badly* on the test. (adverb that tells "how")

NO: Our team played *bad.*
YES: Our team played *badly.* (adverb that tells "how")

We remember that *bad* is an adjective, and we use it only as an adjective or predicate adjective, as in these sentences:

Roy feels *bad* today. (predicate adjective)

Dirty socks smell *bad.* (predicate adjective)

I earned a *bad* grade. (adjective modifying the noun "grade")

Example 3 Choose the correct word to complete sentences a and b.

(a) My nose froze (bad, badly).

(b) Rotten eggs taste (bad, badly).

Solution (a) My nose froze **badly**. (*Badly* is an adverb that tells "how" my nose froze.)

(b) Rotten eggs taste **bad**. (*Bad* is a predicate adjective. It describes the noun "eggs.")

Practice For a and b, replace each blank with *tutor* or *tutelage*.

a. Under their aunt's _____, the children learned to cook and sew.

b. I asked a _____ to help me with difficult math concepts.

Choose the correct word to complete sentences c–f.

c. Hakeem was (sure, surely) happy today.

d. He laughed (real, really) hard during the comedy.

e. It was (real, really) funny.

f. Did your broken arm hurt (bad, badly)?

More Practice Choose the correct word to complete each sentence.

1. Kenny (sure, surely) swims well now.

2. He (sure, certainly) tries hard.

3. I was (sure, really) sleepy.

4. Rex is (real, really) hungry.

5. He eats (real, really) well.

6. Peg broke her arm (bad, badly).

7. It was a (bad, badly) break.

8. Her arm hurts (bad, badly).

Review Set 103 Choose the correct word(s) to complete sentences 1–16.

1. The teacher suggested that a (patriarch, tutor, capricorn) *(103)* help the struggling student.

2. Many people view God as the (megalodon, megamouth, patriarch) of the human race.
(102)

3. Cold-blooded, scaly lizards are classified as (antennae, centipedes, reptiles).
(101)

4. *To admit* means "to (confess, cede, precede)."
(100)

5. The bumpy dirt (rode, road, fetlock) made travel by car difficult.
(43)

6. The game with my friends (was, were) (real, really) fun.
(90, 103)

7. Aaron (sure, certainly) plays (good, well).
(96, 103)

8. There (ain't, isn't) (nobody, anybody) in the kitchen.
(93)

9. Of the two sisters, Kate writes (more, most).
(101)

10. The pronoun *we* is (first, second, third) person (singular, plural).
(64)

11. (Who, Whom) have they chosen?
(79)

Think: <u>they</u> | <u>have chosen</u> | ?

12. (We, Us) hikers saw some deer!
(78)

13. I (wringed, wrung) out my wet socks and (hanged, hung) them up to dry.
(86, 87)

14. Everyone with earplugs (hear, hears) less noise.
(83, 91)

15. The brothers or sister (collect, collects) plastic bottles.
(89)

16. That pair of slippers (is, are) practical.
(92)

17. From the sentence below, write and underline words that should be italicized.
(84)

Let us ride the last train, Sundown Express.

18. Rewrite the sentence below, replacing a comma with a semicolon where it is needed.
(102)

She remembers the book, however, its title escapes her.

19. Rewrite the sentence below, adding hyphens as needed.
(94, 97)

They have a happy, give and take friendship.

20. From the list below, write the word that is *not* an adverb.
(99)

soon   often   tutor   again

21. Write the nominative case pronoun to complete the
(64)   sentence below.

The tutors were Mrs. Rivas and (him, he).

22. Write whether the following is a phrase or a clause.
(36)

wherever we go

23. Rewrite the following, adding capital letters and
(80, 88)   punctuation marks as needed:

there's a clue shouts ed

24. For the irregular verb *dive*, write the (a) present
(19, 85)   participle, (b) past tense, and (c) past participle.

25. From the sentence below, write each adverb and the
(95, 98)   word or phrase it modifies.

Sue wisely hides the clues there.

26. Rewrite the sentence below, adding capital letters and
(60, 81)   punctuation marks as needed.

one teacher mr dixon sang home on the range

27. Rewrite the following sentence, adding capital letters and
(74, 97)   punctuation marks as needed.

as we sang along mr dixon strummed his old beat up guitar

28. From the sentence below, write each adverb that tells
(99, 100)   "when" or "how much."

Often, they act terribly silly.

Diagram each word of sentences 29–30.

29. Later, some of us became thirsty and rather hungry.
(45, 54)

30. That teacher, Mr. Dixon, certainly could build a home on
(58, 95) the range.

29.

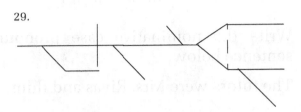

30.

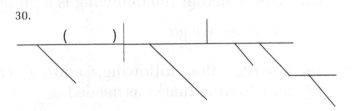

LESSON 104

The Colon

The **colon** (:) signals to the reader that more information is to come. In this lesson, we shall learn to use the colon correctly.

Between Independent Clauses

We have learned that a semicolon can join two independent clauses that contain related thoughts. A colon can join two independent clauses when the first clause introduces the second or the second clause illustrates the first.

On the hike, I learned an important lesson: Always take a compass.

We were lost: We had no idea which way was north.

Example 1 Insert colons where they are needed in these sentences.

(a) There is one sure way to grow stronger Exercise daily.

(b) The musician was amazing She could play two instruments at one time.

Solution (a) The first independent clause introduces the second, so we place a colon between them:

There is one sure way to grow stronger: Exercise daily.

(b) The second independent clause illustrates the first. We place a colon between them:

The musician was amazing: She could play two instruments at one time.

Introducing a List

We use a colon to introduce a list.

We made a grocery list: bananas, milk, bread, and eggs.

He hopes to visit other countries: Mexico, Canada, Peru, and Australia.

Rex knows three commands: sit, stay, and come.

We do not use a colon if the sentence is grammatically correct without it.

> No: You will need: boots, mittens, and sunglasses.
>
> Yes: You will need these things: boots, mittens, and sunglasses.

The Following and As Follows We use a colon with the words *the following* or *as follows* when they introduce a list. Sometimes the list will begin on a separate line.

> Gather *the following* ingredients: flour, sugar, butter, and eggs.
>
> The ingredients are *as follows*:
> 2 eggs
> 1/4 cup milk
> 1 teaspoon sugar

Example 2 Insert colons where they are needed in these sentences.

(a) For the trek, you will need the following a water bottle, a compass, and sturdy shoes.

(b) In the tool shed are shovels, hoes, and rakes.

Solution (a) We use a colon after the words *the following* when they introduce a list:

For the trek, you will need the following: a water bottle, a compass, and sturdy shoes.

(b) We do not use a colon if the sentence is grammatically correct without it. **No colon is needed in this sentence.**

Salutation of a Business Letter We use a colon after a salutation in a business letter.

> Sir:
>
> Dear Mrs. Ogaz:

Time When we write the time of day with digits, we use a colon to separate the hours and minutes.

> Art class begins at 8:30 a.m.

Example 3 Insert colons where they are needed in these sentences.

(a) The show will start at 430 p.m.

(b) Dear Madam
Please send me information...

Solution (a) We place a colon between the hours and minutes when we write the time of day. We write **4:30** p.m.

(b) We use a colon after the salutation in a business letter, so we write **Dear Madam:**

Quotations We can use a colon to introduce a quotation.

Grandpa's autobiography began like this:
The youngest of four children, I was born in Hampton, Virginia...

Aunt Suzi's letter continued: "It rained again yesterday..."

Example 4 Insert colons where they are needed in these sentences.
(a) Nan began her speech like this "Thank you for having me."

(b) Please tell me who said these words "Two wrongs don't make a right."

Solution (a) We can use a colon to introduce a quotation, so we write:

Nan began her speech like this: "Thank you for having me."

(b) Please tell me who said these words: "Two wrongs don't make a right."

Practice Rewrite a–d, inserting colons where they are needed
  a. Let us set the alarm for 600 a.m.

  b. I hope to take the following classes art, chorus, tennis, and science.

  c. Dear Sir

  Please send me your secret recipe for chili.

  d. Abraham Lincoln spoke these words "Be sure you put your feet in the right place, then stand firm."

For e and f, replace each blank with *lunar* or *lunatic*.
  e. The reckless person acted like a _____.

  f. A _____ month is the period of a complete revolution of the moon around the earth.

Review Set 104 Choose the correct word(s) to complete sentences 1–16.

1. Under the (mandible, proboscis, tutelage) of Mr. Wong,
(103) Ed improved in math.

2. The oldest brother showed (reptant, paternal, absent)
(102) concern for his siblings, taking good care of them.

3. (Reptant, Fowl, Mail) red ants carried crumbs across the
(101) floor.

4. Children view Santa Claus as a(n) (lunar, reptant,
(100) affable), elderly gentleman.

5. Shoes that are too small will cause (soar, sore, reptant)
(42) feet.

6. Having sand in my eyes right now (hurt, hurts)(bad, badly).
(90, 103)

7. They (sure, surely) play (good, well) together.
(96, 103)

8. There (ain't, isn't) (nothing, anything) in the oven.
(93)

9. Of all the sisters, Jill smiles (more, most).
(101)

10. The pronoun *our* is (nominative, objective, possessive)
(64) case.

11. (Who, Whom) called?
(79)

12. Did the seal see (we, us) surfers?
(78)

13. They (buyed, bought) Miss Ng flowers.
(85)

14. Some with earplugs (hear, hears) only a little noise.
(83, 91)

15. A duck and a goose (race, races) across the lake.
(89)

16. The first batch of muffins (is, are) ready.
(92)

17. From the sentence below, write and underline words that
(84) should be italicized.

Leonardo da Vinci painted Mona Lisa.

18.
(102) Rewrite the sentence below, replacing a comma with a semicolon where it is needed.

Snow fell, it covered the trail.

19.
(94, 97) Rewrite the sentence below, adding hyphens as needed.

All twenty six hikers wore water repellent boots.

20.
(99) From the list below, write the word that is *not* an adverb.

never   tonight   dream   tomorrow

21.
(69) Write the objective case pronoun to complete the sentence below.

Rex barks at Sam and (me, I).

22.
(104) Rewrite the following business letter, inserting colons where they are needed.

Dear Managers

By 300 p.m., you should have the following your schedules, your timecards, and your keys.

Respectfully,
Ms. Verk

23.
(80, 88) Rewrite the following, adding capital letters and punctuation marks as needed:

ms verk asks was there an earthquake

24.
(57, 67) Rewrite the sentence below, adding capital letters and punctuation marks as needed.

yes he was born on sunday june 2 2011

25.
(95, 98) From the sentence below, write each adverb and the word or phrase it modifies.

Nan happily dances around.

26.
(60, 81) Rewrite the sentence below, adding capital letters and punctuation marks as needed.

jen a fifth grader wrote a story titled too many mice

27. Rewrite the following sentence, adding capital letters and
(74) punctuation marks as needed.

when jen returns she will read us her silly scary story

28. From the sentence below, write each adverb that tells
(99, 100) "when" or "how much."

Jen might write another very silly tale tomorrow.

Diagram each word of sentences 29–30.

29. Without a compass, we might have felt lost and really
(45, 98) worried yesterday.

30. Ron, the oldest hiker, loaned me his compass.
(46, 58)

29.

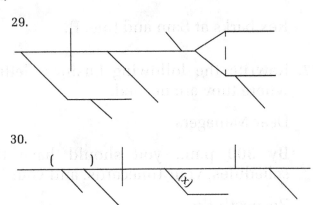

30.

The Prepositional Phrase as an Adverb • Diagramming

Dictation or Journal Entry

Vocabulary:

The Greek word *pathos* means "suffering."

A *pathogen* causes disease. The common word for *pathogens* is "germs."

Pathology is the study of disease, its nature, and its cause. The *pathology* report showed that the child had chickenpox.

Adverb Phrases

We have learned that a prepositional phrase can function as an adjective by modifying a noun or a pronoun. A prepositional phrase can also function as an adverb. A prepositional phrase that modifies a verb, an adjective, or another adverb is called an **adverb phrase**. It answers the question "how," "when," "where," "why," or "to what extent." The italicized adverb phrases below modify the verb "drives."

HOW
Ed drives *like a lunatic.*

WHEN
Ed drives *at night.*

WHERE
Ed drives *in the country.*

WHY
Ed drives *for fun.*

TO WHAT EXTENT
Ed drives *without limits.*

Most adverb phrases modify verbs. However, an adverb phrase can also modify an adjective or another adverb, as in the examples below.

Ed is ready *for dinner.* (modifies predicate adjective "ready")

Ed drives far *from home.* (modifies adverb "far")

Example 1   Write the adverb phrase, and tell which word it modifies.

(a) This road leads to my home.

(b) Water is good for one's health.

(c) I shall wait here on this bench.

Solution   (a) The adverb phrase **to my home** modifies the verb **leads.** It tells "where."

(b) The adverb phrase **for one's health** modifies the predicate adjective **good**.

(c) The adverb phrase **on this bench** modifies the adverb **here**.

Diagramming We diagram a prepositional phrase under the verb, adjective, or adverb it modifies. For example:

Ed drives around the block.

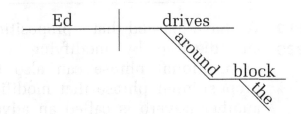

In the sentence above, the adverb phrase *around the block* modifies the verb *drives*. It tells "where" Ed drives.

Example 2 Diagram the three sentences from Example 1.

Solution (a) This road leads to my home.

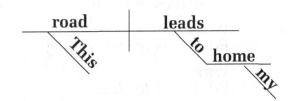

(b) Water is good for one's health.

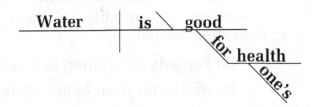

(c) I shall wait here on this bench.

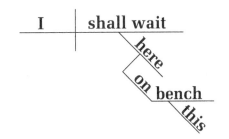

Practice For a–e, write each adverb phrase and tell which word it modifies.

    a. Success comes from hard work.

    b. Rex sleeps under the table.

    c. Lu is nervous about tests.

    d. We are ready for the test.

    e. Are you wise concerning adverbs?

Diagram sentences f and g.

    f. Leave your car with me.

    g. I am sorry about your loss.

For h–j, replace each blank with *pathos, pathology,* or *pathogen.*

    h. The word _____ means "suffering."

    i. A _____ causes disease.

    j. Physicians study _____.

More Practice Diagram sentences 1–5.

    1. She dove into the pool.

    2. Is he sure about the answer?

    3. Is Pat afraid of mice?

    4. Put it in the bag.

    5. Is she hungry for dinner?

Choose the correct word(s) to complete sentences 1–16.

1. The common cold is caused by a (patriarch, lunatic, pathogen).
(105)

2. (Lunatic, Lunar, Paternal) rocks come from the moon's surface.
(104)

3. Sometimes, (tutors, lunatics, specimens) are hired to help children in school.
(103)

4. A (tutelage, paternal, lunatic) trait is inherited from a father.
(102)

5. We (road, rode, mist) the train to San Diego.
(43)

6. The blisters on my foot (sure, really) (sting, stings).
(90, 103)

7. I (sure, certainly) did (bad, badly) in the race.
(103)

8. You don't have (nothing, anything) to lose.
(93)

9. Of the two girls, Grace walks (farther, farthest).
(101)

10. The pronoun *our* is (first, second, third) person (singular, plural).
(64)

11. (Who's, Whose) calling me?
(79)

12. Do seals swim faster than (we, us)?
(78)

13. We (saw, seen) Ed last night.
(86)

14. Anyone with pets (have, has) chores.
(83, 91)

15. Either the servers or the cook (clean, cleans) the kitchen.
(89)

16. Mathematics (is, are) fun.
(92)

17. From the sentence below, write and underline the word that should be italicized.
(84)

Mom reads only one newspaper, the Herald.

18.
(102)
Rewrite the sentence below, replacing a comma with a semicolon where it is needed.

We saw the colt, however, we did not see the mare.

19.
(94, 97)
Rewrite the sentence below, adding hyphens as needed.

I had a two hour appointment with the dentist.

20.
(103)
From this list, write the word that is *not* an adverb:

surely   real   certainly   really

21.
(64)
Write the nominative case pronoun to complete the sentence below.

The most polite are Ana and (he, him).

22.
(104)
Rewrite the following business letter, inserting colons where they are needed.

Dear Club Members

We need to discuss these trail hazards bears, avalanches, and cougars.

Sincerely,
Mr. Cruz

23.
(80, 88)
Rewrite the following, adding capital letters and punctuation marks as needed:

ed shouts happy monday nan

24.
(57, 67)
Rewrite the sentence below, adding capital letters and punctuation marks as needed.

obviously mr cruz fears bears avalanches and cougars

25.
(95, 98)
From the sentence below, write each adverb and the word or phrase it modifies.

They cautiously looked everywhere.

26.
(60, 81)
Rewrite the sentence below, adding capital letters and punctuation marks as needed.

the first singer nan sang the song high hopes

27. Rewrite the following sentence, adding capital letters and
(74) punctuation marks as needed.

while the baby sleeps ed hums a soft sweet lullaby

28. From the sentence below, write each adverb that tells
(99, 100) "when" or "how much."

Tomorrow, I shall tell you a very funny story.

Diagram each word of sentences 29–30.

29. Don't eggs taste bad with too much pepper?
(54, 105)

30. Shall I tell my friend Joe that really funny story?
(37, 46)

29.

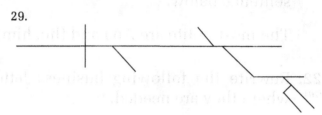

30.

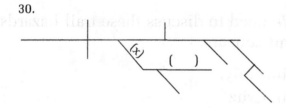

LESSON
106

Preposition or Adverb?
• Preposition Usage

Dictation or Journal Entry

Vocabulary:

The Latin word *tactus* means "touch."

Tact is the ability to speak or act without offending people. Nora used *tact* when talking about my new hairstyle.

Tactile means "of or relating to touch." Our skin receives *tactile* sensations.

Preposition or Adverb? Most prepositions can also be used as adverbs. We remember that an adverb stands alone, but a preposition always has an object.

ADVERB: Ed drives *around*.

PREPOSITION: Ed drives *around the *block*.

ADVERB: Ed drives *past*.

PREPOSITION: Ed drives *past *cattle*.

ADVERB: Ed drives *along*.

PREPOSITION: Ed drives *along the *road*.

Diagramming can help us determine whether a word is being used as an adverb or a preposition. Look at the word "around" in these two sentences:

ADVERB: They kick *around* a ball.

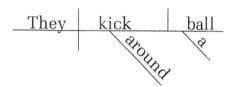

We can see that "ball" is a direct object telling what "They" kick. It is not an object of a preposition.

PREPOSITION: Then, they run *around* the field.

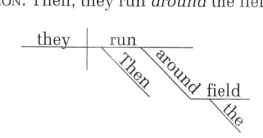

In this sentence, "field" is the object of the preposition "around."

Example 1 Tell whether the italicized word in each sentence is an adverb or a preposition.

(a) Rex barks *outside*.

(b) Nan peeks *inside* the box.

(c) An eagle soars *above* the treetops.

(d) Lambs caper *about*.

Solution (a) *Outside* is an **adverb** that tells where Rex "barks."

(b) *Inside* is a **preposition.** Its object is "box."

(c) *Above* is a **preposition.** Its object is "treetops."

(d) *About* is an **adverb** that tells where lambs "caper."

Preposition Usage Certain pairs of prepositions are frequently misused. In this lesson, we will learn to use these prepositions correctly:

in and *into*

between and *among*

beside and *besides*

In or Into? The preposition *in* refers to position but not to movement.

Ed is *in* the car.

I am *in* the room.

The preposition *into* refers to moving from the outside to the inside.

Ed climbs *into* the car.

I step *into* the room.

Between or Among? We use *between* when referring to two people, places, or things.

Nan and Ed divided the nuts *between* themselves.

There is not much difference *between* you and me.

We use *among* when referring to three or more people, places, or things.

> He is one *among* many good students.

> She is *among* the greatest poets in our school.

> Which is tallest *among* the four trees?

Beside or Besides? The preposition *beside* means "at the side of."

> The sister stands *beside* her brother.

> Ed parks *beside* the curb.

Besides means "in addition to" or "as well as."

> *Besides* cotton, they grow corn and peanuts.

> Who *besides* me likes squash?

Example 2 Choose the correct preposition for each sentence.
(a) They jump (in, into) the pool.

(b) Rex walks (beside, besides) Nan.

(c) Pat was (among, between) the four shortest players.

Solution (a) They jump **into** the pool.

(b) Rex walks **beside** Nan.

(c) Pat was **among** the four shortest players.

Practice For sentences a–d, write whether the italicized word is an adverb or a preposition.
a. A gull flew *by*.

b. I climbed *aboard* the bus.

c. Elle hurries *across* the street.

d. You may come *along*.

For e–g, choose the correct preposition.
e. He tosses the wrapper (in, into) a trash can.

f. (Among, Between) two oaks, we built a fort.

g. Does anyone (beside, besides) Josh like spinach?

For h and i, replace each blank with *tact* or *tactile*.

h. Thoughtful people use _____ __ when they speak with their friends.

i. A cat's whiskers are _____ organs.

Review Set 106

Choose the correct word to complete sentences 1–16.

1. When we study (ichthyology, pathology, entomology), we
(105) learn about disease-caused changes in cells.

2. King David pretended to be a (quest, docent, lunatic) to
(104) make his enemies believe that he was insane.

3. Under their father's (tutelage, tail, tale), the children
(103) learned to respect differences in others.

4. (Maternal, Fraternal, Paternal) instincts of fathers lead
(102) them to provide for and protect their offspring.

5. Mountainous (rodes, creaks, roads) connected the two
(43) cabins.

6. There (go, goes) some (real, really) young geese!
(90, 103)

7. They (sure, surely) fly (good, well).
(96, 103)

8. Jesse doesn't want (no, any) soda.
(93)

9. Of all the girls, Grace walks (farther, farthest).
(101)

10. Jen, Ken, and Sid sneak (in, into) the pantry and divide
(107) the pretzels (between, among) themselves.

11. (Your's, Yours) is here, but (theirs, their's) is not.
(72)

12. Seals watch (we, us) surfers.
(78)

13. Have you (saw, seen) the whale?
(86)

14. Some in the class (has, have) more work to do.
(83, 91)

15. Either the cook or the servers (clean, cleans) the kitchen.
(89)

16. This pair of boots (fit, fits) well.
(92)

17. From the sentence below, write and underline words that
(84) should be italicized.

In Spanish, we say perro instead of dog.

18. Rewrite the sentence below, replacing commas with
(102) semicolons where they are needed.

We stopped in Denver, Colorado, Lincoln, Nebraska, and
Helena, Montana.

19. Rewrite the sentence below, adding hyphens as needed.
(94, 97)

The thirty two singers did an out of this world
performance.

20. From this list, write the word that is *not* an adverb:
(99)

now   never   often   skate

21. Write the objective case pronoun to complete the
(69) sentence below.

Have you seen Nan and (he, him)?

22. Rewrite the following business letter, inserting colons
(104) where they are needed.

Dear Dr. Bone

Please examine these animals the horses, the chickens,
and the goat.

Sincerely,
Miss Lee

23. Rewrite the following, adding capital letters and
(80, 88) punctuation marks as needed:

have nate and josh gone home asked elle

24. Rewrite the sentence below, adding capital letters and
(57, 67) punctuation marks as needed.

they have gone i believe to juneau alaska

25. From the sentence below, write whether the circled word
(106) is an adverb or a preposition.

We wrote (down) our ideas.

26. Rewrite the sentence below, adding capital letters and
(60, 81) punctuation marks as needed.

i liked the fourth chapter turkish delight

27. Rewrite the following sentence, adding capital letters and
(74) punctuation marks as needed.

as the sun rises a big old rooster crows

28. From the sentence below, write each adverb that tells
(99, 100) "when" or "how much."

We always thoroughly wash our hands.

Diagram each word of sentences 29–30.

29. Eggs shouldn't taste so peppery.
(54)

30. Now, I shall help my friend Ann with the chores.
(99, 105)

29.

30.

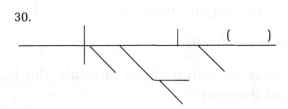

LESSON 107

The Apostrophe: Possessives

> **Dictation or Journal Entry**
> **Vocabulary:**
> The Latin *sol* means "sun."
>
> *Solar* means "relating to the sun." *Solar* batteries convert the sun's energy to electricity.
>
> A *solstice* is one of the two times during the year when the sun appears farthest from the equator. In the Northern Hemisphere, summer *solstice* occurs on or about June 21.

We use the apostrophe to show possession.

Singular Possessive Nouns

To give a singular noun ownership, we add an apostrophe and an *s* (*'s*). The noun then becomes a **singular possessive noun**, as in the examples below.

SINGULAR NOUN	SINGULAR POSSESSIVE NOUN
trumpet	trumpet's sound
Lucy	Lucy's tooth
truck	truck's horn
fox	fox's tail
Mrs. Bass	Mrs. Bass's voice

In a compound noun, possession is formed by adding *'s* to the last word.

sister-in-law	sister-in-law's plan
middle school	middle school's playground
grandson	grandson's shoes

Shared or Separate Possession

When more than one noun shares possession of something, we add *'s* to the last noun.

Dan, Roy, and Ed's basketball game

When the nouns each possess something separately, we add *'s* to each noun.

Ann's and Nan's jackets

Example 1

Use *'s* to make each singular noun possessive.

(a) Kenny   (b) Luis

(c) brother-in-law   (d) Rex

(e) Luz and Dan (home)

Solution (a) **Kenny's**   (b) **Luis's**

(c) **brother-in-law's**   (d) **Rex's**

(e) **Luz and Dan's** (home)

Plural Possessive Nouns

To give a regular plural noun ownership, we add only an apostrophe. The noun then becomes a **plural possessive noun**, as in the examples below.

PLURAL NOUN	PLURAL POSSESSIVE NOUN
hens	hens' beaks
boys	boys' names
the Curtises	the Curtises' kindness

In a compound noun, possession is formed by adding *'s* to the last word.

editors in chief's comments

sisters-in-law's ideas

Irregular Plurals

To give an irregular plural noun ownership, add *'s*.

children	children's games
men	men's suits
mice	mice's nest
oxen	oxen's strength

Many people make errors when forming plural possessive nouns. To avoid this, form the plural noun first. Then, apply the guidelines above to make it possessive.

Example 2 Use the apostrophe to form a plural possessive noun from each plural noun.

(a) geese   (b) doctors

(c) flies   (d) cattle

(e) sons-in-law

Solution (a) **geese's**   (b) **doctors'**

(c) **flies'**   (d) **cattle's**

(e) **sons-in-law's**

Practice For a and b, replace each blank with *solar* or *solstice*.

    a. In the Northern Hemisphere, winter _____ occurs in December.

    b. _____ power depends upon the sun.

For c–h, add an apostrophe to each word that requires an apostrophe to show possession.

    c. My two sisters-in-laws cars look alike.

    d. Jen, Ken, and Eds job is to set up tables.

    e. All the puppies tails were wagging.

    f. I need my two friends help.

    g. Miss Ng knows each childs name.

    h. Has the buss door closed?

More Practice For 1–8, make each singular noun possessive.

    1. goose   **2.** story   **3.** tutor   **4.** aviary

    5. aunt   **6.** insect   **7.** daisy   **8.** matriarch

For 9–16, make each plural noun possessive.

    9. fish   **10.** idols   **11.** colts   **12.** deer

    13. boys   **14.** sheep   **15.** fillies   **16.** women

Review Set 107 Choose the correct word(s) to complete sentences 1–16.

    1. Ed used (elapse, collapse, tact) and spoke politely.
    (106)

    2. Some pesticides are considered (pathogens, patriarchs, *(105)* matriarchs).

    3. Few people have experienced a (lunatic, lunar, tutelage) *(104)* landing.

    4. Sometimes a (pathogen, tutor, lunatic) helps a student to *(103)* learn.

    5. The children dug (roads, sages, elapses) in the sand.
    (43)

6. Every one of you (have, has) (real, really) good ideas.
(90, 103)

7. They (sure, surely) play (good, well).
(96, 103)

8. There (was, wasn't) nothing in the cupboard; it was
(93) empty.

9. Of the two lamps, this one is the (brighter, brightest).
(101)

10. We sat (beside, besides) each other.
(106)

11. (Whose, Who's) bicycle is that?
(72)

12. (We, Us) surfers were watching seals.
(78)

13. I (saw, seen) her this morning.
(86)

14. Many in the class (has, have) more work to do.
(83, 91)

15. The servers and the cook (clean, cleans) the kitchen.
(89)

16. This pair of shoes (fit, fits) well.
(92)

17. From the sentence below, write and underline words that
(84) should be italicized.

Ted sailed a small boat, Star of Hope.

18. Rewrite the sentence below, replacing a comma with a
(102) semicolon where it is needed.

I wanted to swim, however, the water was too cold.

19. Rewrite the sentence below, adding hyphens as needed.
(97)

Look at the snow covered fields!

20. From the list below, write the word that is *not* an adverb.
(96)

good   happily   tomorrow   there

21. Write the nominative case pronoun to complete the
(66) sentence below.

Will Ed and (she, her) make tacos?

22. Rewrite the following business letter, inserting colons
(104) where they are needed.

Dear Mr. Hill

Please provide these items brooms, mops, soap.

Sincerely,
Ann Goot

23. Rewrite the following, adding capital letters and
(80, 88) punctuation marks as needed:

ann shouts it's a huge cockroach

24. For a–c, write the possessive form of each noun.
(107)
(a) mares   (b) Carlos   (c) boss

25. From the sentence below, write whether the circled word
(106) is an adverb or a preposition.

They walked (down) the path.

26. Rewrite the sentence below, adding capital letters and
(81) punctuation marks as needed.

ann will title her poem the mature insect

27. Rewrite the following sentence, adding capital letters and
(74) punctuation marks as needed.

when the gale grew stronger a large heavy bough fell on
my roof

28. From the sentence below, write each adverb that tells
(99, 100) "when" or "how much."

Next, Ann almost screamed.

Diagram each word of sentences 29–30.

29. Couldn't you become a really helpful tutor someday?
(54)

30. During the summer, we campers viewed the awesome
(99, 105) beauty of Half Dome from different places in the valley.

29.

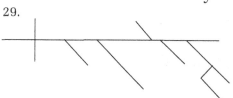

30.

LESSON 108

The Apostrophe: Contractions and Omitting Digits and Letters

Dictation or Journal Entry

Vocabulary:

The Latin *somnus* means "sleep."

To *somnambulate* is to walk while asleep. I am not aware that I sometimes *somnambulate*.

Somnolence is sleepiness or drowsiness. Because of my *somnolence*, it was difficult to pay attention in class.

Contractions When we combine two words and shorten one of them, we form a **contraction.** We insert an apostrophe to take the place of the letter or letters taken out.

Sometimes a verb is shortened, as in the examples below.

I have	⟶	I've
we are	⟶	we're
she will	⟶	she'll
he would	⟶	he'd
it is	⟶	it's

Other times we combine the verb and the word *not*. We shorten the word *not*, and insert an apostrophe where the letter *o* is missing.

do not	⟶	don't
is not	⟶	isn't
are not	⟶	aren't
were not	⟶	weren't
could not	⟶	couldn't

Note: The contraction *won't* (will not) is spelled irregularly.

Example 1 Use an apostrophe to write the contractions of a–d.

(a) you are   (b) they are

(c) would not   (d) did not

Solution (a) **you're**   (b) **they're**

(c) **wouldn't**   (d) **didn't**

Omitted Digits We use an apostrophe when the first two digits are omitted from the year.

2009	⟶	'09
1997	⟶	'97
1923	⟶	'23

Omitted Letters We use an apostrophe to show that we have taken letters out of a word. In informal writing, we can leave out letters to indicate the way we imagine the words being spoken.

good morning	⟶	good mornin'
best of luck	⟶	best o' luck
until then	⟶	'til then
let them go	⟶	let 'em go

Example 2 Rewrite sentences a and b, inserting apostrophes where they are needed.

(a) Tim was born in 07.

(b) Lem hollered, "Good mornin, Sam!"

Solution (a) **Tim was born in '07.**

(b) **Lem hollered, "Good mornin', Sam!"**

Practice For sentences a–c, add an apostrophe to each word that needs an apostrophe.

a. I havent much time.

b. She said, "Im singin in the rain."

c. They bought the house in 49 and sold it in 09.

Make contractions of d and e.

d. should not   **e.** he would

For f and g, replace each blank with *somnambulate* or *somnolence*.

f. Their _____ caused them to make many errors.

g. It might be dangerous to _____ near the edge of a cliff.

Review Set 108   Choose the correct word(s) to complete sentences 1–16.

1. (Lunar, Solar, Paternal) rays cause sunburn.
   (107)

2. Some people learn by touching things; they are (tactile,
   (106) solar, lunar) learners.

3. The medical doctor took a (tutelage, lunar, pathology)
   (105) class.

4. Some authors create insane characters who are obviously
   (104) (lunatics, lunars, pathogens).

5. My (deer, dear, soar) horse faithfully carried me on her
   (44) back up the mountain.

6. Every one of you (have, has) (real, really) creative ideas.
   (90, 103)

7. This pipe leaks (real, really) (bad, badly).
   (96, 103)

8. There (was, wasn't) nobody at the desk.
   (93)

9. Of all the lamps, this one is the (brighter, brightest).
   (101)

10. No one (beside, besides) Ted had a compass.
    (106)

11. (Who, Whom) wants to play checkers?
    (79)

12. Nan reads faster than (me, I).
    (78)

13. I (saw, seen) Nan at the library.
    (86)

14. Someone with keys (has, have) opened the doors.
    (83, 91)

15. (Your, You're) next in line.
    (108)

16. That pair of scissors (cut, cuts) (good, well).
    (92, 96)

17. From the sentence below, write and underline words that
    (84) should be italicized.

    Next, we shall read the book The Silver Chair.

18. Rewrite the sentence below, replacing a comma with a
(102) semicolon where it is needed.

It's late, nevertheless, I shall read another page.

19. Rewrite the sentence below, adding hyphens as needed.
(94, 97)
I bought a half pound apple for ninety nine cents.

20. From the list below, write the word that is *not* an adverb.
(99)
always   tonight   someday   sleeping

21. Make contractions of a and b.
(108)
(a) should not   (b) they are

22. Rewrite the following business letter, inserting colons
(104) where they are needed.

Dear Sir or Madam

I expect the delivery before 500 p.m.

Your customer,
Mr. Hill

23. Rewrite the following, adding capital letters and
(80, 88) punctuation marks as needed:

ted asked have you seen my compass

24. For a–c, write the possessive form of each noun.
(107)
(a) sisters   (b) James   (c) fly

25. From the sentence below, write whether the circled word
(106) is an adverb or a preposition.

They giggled (throughout) the story.

26. Rewrite the sentence below, adding capital letters and
(60, 81) punctuation marks as needed.

our teacher mr cox sang america

27. Rewrite the following sentence, adding capital letters and
(74) punctuation marks as needed.

when it rains the field looks like a deep muddy lake

28. From the sentence below, write each adverb that tells (99, 100) "when" or "how much."

Tonight, I felt terribly somnolent.

Diagram each word of sentences 29–30.

29. Shouldn't we remain completely silent throughout a (54, 105) symphony?

30. After the symphony, my brother Ed can give us his own (45, 105) concert with banjo and harmonica.

29.

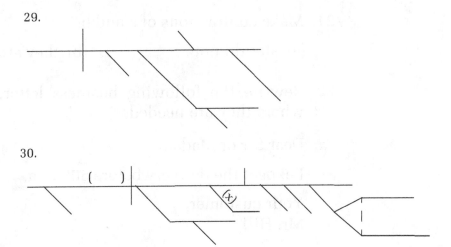

30.

LESSON 109

The Complex Sentence

Dictation or Journal Entry

Vocabulary:

The Latin word *sonare* means "to make a noise."

A *sonata* is an instrumental composition often written for piano. I played a *sonata* by Haydn.

Sonorous means "producing a deep, full, or rich sound." Uncle Jay has a *sonorous* voice.

We have learned how to join two simple sentences, or independent clauses, with a coordinating conjunction to form a compound sentence.

<u>Ben plays the flute well</u>, **and** <u>he plays it every day</u>.

In a compound sentence, each of the independent clauses can stand alone. They are equal grammatical parts.

Ben plays the flute well. = He plays it every day.

Subordinate Clauses   Not all sentences are composed of equal parts. Sometimes, a dependent clause is connected to an independent clause. We remember that we can turn an independent clause into a dependent clause, or **subordinate clause**, by adding a subordinating conjunction, such as *after, although, because, even though, if, since,* or *unless.*

<u>Ben plays the flute well</u> ***because*** *he plays it every day*.

The subordinate clause "because he plays it every day" cannot stand alone; it is dependent on the main clause, "Ben plays the flute well."

Complex Sentence   A **complex sentence** contains one independent clause and one or more dependent, or subordinate, clauses. In the sentences below, we have underlined the independent (main) clause and italicized the subordinating conjunction that introduces the dependent clause.

He feels <u>lonely</u> *after* his friends leave.

When it rains, <u>the field floods.</u>

Example For a–c, tell whether each sentence is simple, compound, or complex.

(a) Sam has read many books about reptiles, amphibians, and other creatures.

(b) As we wait, time passes slowly.

(c) I read the lessons, and I understand them.

Solution (a) This is a **simple** sentence. It is one independent clause.

(b) This sentence is **complex.** It has one independent clause ("time passes slowly") and one dependent clause ("As we wait").

(c) This is a **compound** sentence—two independent clauses joined by the coordinating conjunction "and."

Practice For a–c, tell whether each sentence is simple, compound, or complex.

a. A large, curious pelican pokes its beak into my lunchbox.

b. This road becomes slippery and dangerous when it rains.

c. Cattle eat plants, for they are herbivores.

For d and e, replace each blank with *sonata* or *sonorous*.

d. The angry bear gave a _____ growl.

e. She composed a _____ for the piano.

More Practice Write whether the sentence is simple, compound, or complex.

1. Mr. Ling corrected me because I made an error.

2. His foot is sore, so he limps.

3. Do you know the story about the tortoise and the hare?

4. When I fell, I skinned my knee.

Choose the correct word(s) to complete sentences 1–16.

1. Some people (somnolence, somnambulate, cede) right
(108) out the front door!

2. June 21, the summer (solar, solstice, tutelage), marks the
(107) longest day of the year.

3. The (tactile, lunar, lunatic) sensation of burlap is rough
(106) and uneven.

4. Bacterial (pathology, ichthyology, pathogens) cause smallpox.
(105)

5. The letter began, "(Deer, Dear, You're) Sir, ..."
(44)

6. Rex's fur (was, were) (real, really) muddy.
(90, 103)

7. This tool (sure, surely) works (well, good).
(96, 103)

8. There isn't (nobody, anybody) at the desk.
(93)

9. Ed is the (more, most) serious of the two.
(101)

10. He stepped (in, into) the closet.
(106)

11. (Who's, Whose) in the closet?
(79, 108)

12. Is Nan as old as (him, he)?
(78)

13. Has Nan (saw, seen) Ed?
(86)

14. Everyone with broken tools (has, have) time to fix them.
(83, 91)

15. (Their, There, They're) coming soon.
(108)

16. This bag of onions (smell, smells) (bad, badly).
(92, 96)

17. From the sentence below, write and underline words that
(81) should be italicized.

Sonata is a noun, and sonorous is an adjective.

18. Rewrite the sentence below, replacing a comma with a
(102) semicolon where it is needed.

The shelves are dusty, therefore, I shall dust them.

19. Rewrite the sentence below, adding hyphens as needed.
(94, 97)

My ten year old brother took a two day trip to Kansas.

20. From the list below, write the word that is *not* an adverb.
(99)

real   now   then   never   again

21. Make contractions of a and b.
(108)

(a) cannot   (b) you are

22. Rewrite the following business letter, inserting colons
(104) where they are needed.

Dear Sir or Madam

I have enclosed my payment of $1.00.

Your customer,
Mr. Hill

23. Rewrite the following, adding capital letters and
(80, 88) punctuation marks as needed:

at monday's ball game ed yelled run nan

24. For a–c, write the possessive form of each noun.
(107)

(a) Sandy   (b) players   (c) Chris

25. From the sentence below, write whether the circled word
(106) is an adverb or a preposition.

Nate sat (down) beside Josh.

26. Rewrite the sentence below, adding capital letters and
(60, 81) punctuation marks as needed.

aaron wrote the poem fox tails

27. Write whether the sentence below is simple, compound,
(109) or complex.

He will herd the sheep if you will shear them.

28. From the sentence below, write each adverb that tells
(99, 100) "when" or "how much."

Soon, the dusty shelves will look much better.

Diagram each word of sentences 29–30.

29. Very soon, the dusty shelves will look much better.
(99, 100)

30. Today, my cousin Meg gave me a book about the most
(99, 105) courageous person!

29.

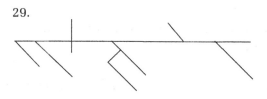

30.

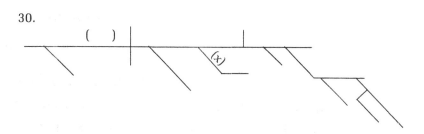

Active or Passive Voice

Dictation or Journal Entry
Vocabulary:
Tho Greek *nomas* means "wandering."

A *nomad* is a person who wanders from place to place. A *nomad* has no permanent home.

Nomadic is an adjective meaning "wandering." *Nomadic* shepherds moved to greener pastures.

A transitive verb can be either **active** or **passive.** When the subject acts, the verb is **active.**

I <u>saw</u> nomads.

When the subject is acted upon, the verb is **passive.**

Nomads <u>were seen</u> by me.

Passive verbs usually contain a form of "to be." Often, the sentence contains a prepositional phrase beginning with "by." The subject *receives* the action; it does not *do* the action.

PASSIVE: The *garden* <u>was weeded</u> by Mary.

ACTIVE: *Mary* <u>weeded</u> the garden.

Active Voice Writing is more exciting and powerful in the active voice. We try to use the active voice as much as possible.

WEAK PASSIVE:
Rex <u>had been followed</u> by a puppy.

STRONG ACTIVE:
A *puppy* <u>had followed</u> Rex.

WORDY PASSIVE:
Sheep <u>were led</u> to green pastures by shepherds.

CONCISE ACTIVE:
Shepherds <u>led</u> sheep to green pastures.

INDIRECT PASSIVE:
Sandwiches <u>were taken</u> by Ed to the picnic.

DIRECT ACTIVE:
Ed <u>took</u> sandwiches to the picnic.

Passive Voice We see that the passive voice can be wordy and indirect. It can confuse the reader and tends to be dull. However, the passive voice does have a purpose. We use the passive voice in order to leave something unsaid. When the doer is unimportant or unknown, or when we want to emphasize the receiver of the action, we use the passive voice.

The whole *class* <u>was</u> very <u>confused</u>.

Many *homes* <u>were destroyed</u> during the storm.

The *work* <u>had been finished</u>.

Example Tell whether the verb in each sentence is active or passive voice.

(a) A young woman rode the gray mare.

(b) The gray mare was ridden by a young woman.

(c) A bald eagle was seen by the birdwatcher.

(d) The birdwatcher saw a bald eagle.

Solution (a) The verb is **active.** The subject (woman) acts.

(b) The verb is **passive.** The subject (mare) is acted upon.

(c) The verb is **passive.** The subject (eagle) is acted upon.

(d) The verb is **active.** The subject (birdwatcher) acts.

Practice For sentences a–d, write whether the verb is active or passive voice.

a. The house was built by Uncle Tim.

b. Uncle Tim built the house.

c. A home run was hit by me.

d. I hit a home run.

For e and f, replace each blank with *nomad* or *nomadic.*

e. A _____ person has no permanent home.

f. A _____ moves from place to place.

Review Set 110 Choose the correct word(s) to complete sentences 1–16.

1. Unlike a *cantada* that is sung, a (sonorous, sonata, (109) solstice) is played.

2. Sunglasses protect the eyes from (tactile, solstice, solar)
(107) rays.

3. People use (tactile, tact, solstice) so that they do not
(100) offend others.

4. (*Affable, Reptant, Tactile*) means "courteous in conversation."
(100)

5. (Dear, Deer, Wails) grow new antlers each year.
(44)

6. One of the paths (lead, leads) to a (real, really) green
(90, 103) meadow.

7. Ben (sure, surely) plays drums (well, good).
(96, 103)

8. She didn't give (no, a) hint.
(93)

9. Ed was the (more, most) serious of all.
(101)

10. Ana climbs (in, into) the attic.
(106)

11. (Who's, Whose) boots are these?
(72, 108)

12. Nan is older than (I, me).
(78)

13. We (saw, seen) pelicans on the pier.
(86)

14. Some on the team (have, has) sore muscles.
(83, 91)

15. (You're, Your) very kind.
(108)

16. Her brown pants (fit, fits) (good, well).
(92, 96)

17. From the sentence below, write and underline words that
(84) should be italicized.

They read about crustaceans in a magazine, The
Smithsonian.

18. Rewrite the sentence below, replacing commas with
(102) semicolons where they are needed.

Ed drove through Columbus, Ohio, Albany, New York,
and Trenton, New Jersey.

19. Rewrite the sentence below, adding hyphens as needed.
(94, 97)

My brother in law caught a ten pound fish.

20. From the list below, write the word that is *not* an adverb.
(99)

sure   surely   afterward   constantly

21. Make contractions of a and b.
(108)

(a) have not   (b) they will

22. Rewrite the following sentence, inserting a colon where it
(104) is needed.

Please study the following parts of speech verbs, nouns, and adjectives.

23. Rewrite the following, adding capital letters and
(80, 88) punctuation marks as needed:

are you from texas asked amy

24. For a–c, write the possessive form of each noun.
(107)

(a) eagles   (b) James   (c) Amy

25. From the sentence below, write whether the circled word
(106) is an adverb or a preposition.

I am running (behind) today.

26. Rewrite the sentence below, adding capital letters and
(60, 81) punctuation marks as needed.

let us learn the song getting to know you

27. Write whether the sentence below is simple, compound,
(109) or complex.

Beth plants wildflowers because they attract butterflies.

28. From the sentence below, write each adverb that tells
(99, 100) "when" or "how much."

Later, she gave a more helpful hint.

Diagram each word of sentences 29–30.

29. Can you explain this very difficult lesson to me after
(99, 100) school?

30. Have we almost finished the very last lesson in this book?
(45)

29.

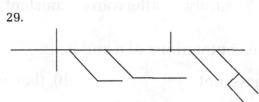

30.

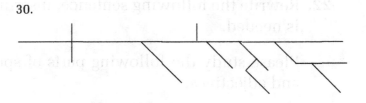

LESSON 111

Interjections

Interjections   A word or short phrase used to show strong emotion is called an **interjection.** An interjection is one of the eight parts of speech. It can express excitement, happiness, joy, rage, surprise, pain, or relief. Interjections are italicized below.

Aha! I understand now.

Ouch! The soup is hot.

Whoops, I dropped my spoon.

Oh my, this tastes good.

An interjection is not a sentence and has no relationship with the words around it. For this reason, it is usually set apart from the rest of the sentence by some sort of punctuation. Generally, an exclamation point follows an interjection, but if the emotion is not very intense, a comma follows the interjection.

INTENSE: *Wow!* Did you see that whale?

NOT INTENSE: *Okay,* I shall do my best.

Below is a list of common interjections. Notice that sounds can be interjections, too.

ah	*oh dear*	*ugh*	*man*
aha	*oh my*	*uh-oh*	*drat*
bam	*oh yes*	*well*	*oops*
boy	*far out*	*yippee*	*bravo*
oh no	*whee*	*good grief*	*okay*
whoops	*goodness*	*ouch*	*wow*
hey	*ow*	*yikes*	*hooray*
phew	*yuck*	*hurrah*	*pow*
boo	*oh*	*shh*	*whew*

We must not overuse interjections. They lose their effectiveness when used too frequently.

Example 1   Write each interjection that you find in a–d.

(a) Shh. People are sleeping.

(b) Hey, where were you?

(c) Whew! I passed the test.

(d) Yippee! My friend is coming.

Solution   (a) **Shh**   (b) **Hey**

(c) **Whew**   (d) **Yippee**

Diagramming   We diagram an interjection by placing it on a line apart from
the rest of the sentence.

Bravo! You finished the job.

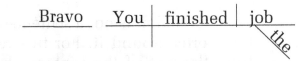

Example 2   Diagram this sentence:

Ugh, this work is hard.

Solution   We place the interjection on a line apart from the rest of the
sentence.

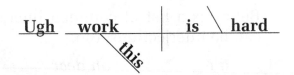

Practice   Write the interjection that you find in a–d.

a. Oops, I made a mistake.

b. Well, what do you think?

c. Hurrah! They won the game.

d. Yuck! The food is moldy.

Diagram e and f.

e. Yikes! That is scary.

f. Shh, students are studying.

For g and h, replace each blank with *omnipotent* or *omniscient.*

g. One who knows everything is _____.

h. One who is all-powerful is _____.

Review Set
111

Choose the correct word(s) to complete sentences 1–16.

1. C. S. Lewis defines (*omnipotent, nomadic, sonorous*) as
(111) "having power to do the impossible."

2. A tuba can make a (lunar, tactile, sonorous) sound.
(109)

3. In short stories, the (omnipotent, omniscient, sonorous)
(111) narrator knows everything.

4. (*Paternal, Maternal, Nomadic*) means "wandering."
(110)

5. Following their herds of sheep, shepherds are
(110) (omnipotent, omniscient, nomads).

6. One of the cubs (has, have) (real, really) thick fur.
(90, 103)

7. Pat (sure, surely) paints (well, good).
(96, 103)

8. The lizard didn't have (no, a) tail.
(93)

9. Ben is the (more, most) affable of the two.
(101)

10. Hank jumps (in, into) the swimming pool.
(106)

11. (Who's, Whose) baggage is this?
(72, 108)

12. Ed is taller than (I, me).
(78)

13. I (saw, seen) Nan and him yesterday.
(86)

14. Some in our group (have, has) caught fish.
(83, 91)

15. (You're, Your) poem is beautiful.
(108)

16. That pair of scissors (cut, cuts) (good, well).
(92, 96)

17. Write whether the sentence below uses active or passive voice.
(110)

The rabbit was startled by a coyote.

18. Rewrite the sentence below, replacing commas with semicolons where they are needed.
(102)

Our plane passed over Denver, Colorado, Cheyenne, Wyoming, and Helena, Montana.

19. Rewrite the sentence below, adding hyphens as needed.
(94, 97)

Al has a ten foot rowboat.

20. From the list below, write the word that is *not* an adverb.
(99)

often   tonight   real   really   soon

21. Make contractions of a and b.
(108)

(a) they are   (b) you are

22. Rewrite the following sentence, inserting a colon where it is needed.
(104)

The following people are tutors Lin Yu, Mike García, and John Cohen.

23. Rewrite the following, adding capital letters and punctuation marks as needed:
(80, 88)

have you seen my keys asked al

24. For a–c, write the possessive form of each noun.
(107)

(a) states   (b) Ms. Loomis   (c) Jerry

25. From the sentence below, write whether the circled word is an adverb or a preposition.
(106)

Chad was running (behind) Dan.

26. Rewrite the sentence below, adding capital letters and punctuation marks as needed.
(60, 81)

the band will play america the beautiful

27. Write whether the sentence below is simple, compound, or complex.

(75, 109)

He is flying to India, for his brother lives there.

28. From the sentence below, write each adverb that tells "when" or "how much."

(99, 100)

Then, I found the most helpful clue.

Diagram each word of sentences 29–30.

29. Tomorrow, we shall write a story about our vacation.

(45, 99)

30. Ah, we have finally finished the very last diagram in this grammar book.

(100, 111)

29.

30.

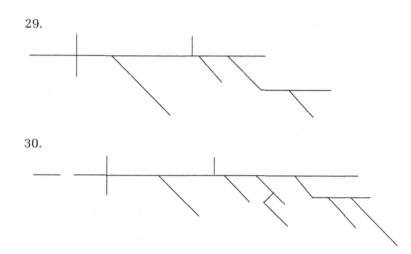

Appendix

Dictations

At the beginning of class each Monday, students will copy their dictation to study and prepare for a test on Friday.

Week 1 The American bison is another name for the American buffalo. It has two coats: a heavier, dark brown winter coat and a lighter, light brown summer coat.

Week 2 Bison graze on prairie grasses in the morning and the evening. They rest during the middle of the day. They can stand over six feet tall and weigh more than two thousand pounds.

Week 3 In the United States, the largest member of the deer family is called a moose. The second largest member is called an elk. In Europe, both animals are called elk.

Week 4 Male moose have antlers shaped like the palm of a hand. These are called palmate antlers. After the mating season, male moose drop their antlers. New ones grow in the spring.

Week 5 The second largest member of the deer family is called an elk or a wapiti. The males are called bulls, and the females are called cows. Elk eat grasses, plants, leaves, and bark.

Week 6 Only the male elk have twig-like antlers. These are shed once a year and are made of bone. The antlers can grow up to one inch per day!

Week 7 The grizzly bear is also known as the silvertip bear. It is a member of the brown bear family. The grizzly bear gets its name from the "grizzled" or gray hair in its fur.

Week 8 Grizzly bears live in the uplands of western North America. They usually live alone. Sometimes, grizzly bears gather together along the edges of streams to catch salmon.

Week 9 Over the shoulders of the grizzly bear is a large hump. This is a muscle mass. The front legs receive their digging power from this hump.

Week 10 The hind legs of the grizzly bear are even more powerful than the front ones. The strong muscles in the back legs allow the bear to stand up and walk.

Week 11 The pronghorn is an ungulate mammal. Ungulates have paws or hooves and use their toes to run. The pronghorn lives in grasslands and deserts of the Americas.

Week 12 The pronghorn is a very fast mammal. In fact, it is the fastest land animal in the Americas. Only the cheetah is faster. The pronghorn can run up to seventy miles per hour.

Week 13 The grey wolf, or gray wolf, is also called a timber wolf or just a wolf. Some believe that wolves are closely related to dogs. Others argue that they are quite different.

Week 14 Wolves have powerful teeth, bushy tails, and bulky coats consisting of two layers. The first layer repels water and dirt. The second layer insulates the wolf against cold weather.

Week 15 Searching for food in winter, wolves usually travel in packs of two to twenty members. The most common pack consists of eight wolves: a male, a female, and their offspring. This is called a nuclear family.

Week 16 The wolf's den, or lair, may be a cave, a hollow tree trunk, or a thicket. Wolves breed in the spring, and the female has a litter of three to nine cubs. The cubs stay with their parents until they are about two years of age.

Week 17 Bighorns are wild sheep of the Rocky Mountains with large, curving horns. This is why they are named "bighorn" sheep. These horns can weigh up to thirty pounds.

Week 18   Bighorn sheep graze on grasses and get their minerals from natural salt licks. They can climb very steep mountains to avoid predators. Bighorn sheep live in herds.

Week 19   Because bighorn sheep were becoming scarce in the Arizona mountains, Major Frederick Burnham began conservation efforts. He enlisted the help of the Boy Scouts.

Week 20   The Arizona Boy Scouts led a very successful campaign to save the bighorn sheep. Now, the beautiful animal is no longer endangered.

Week 21   Coyotes are cousins of the gray wolves. They are also called prairie wolves. Coyotes live in Central and North America.

Week 22   Coyotes travel in packs that are smaller than wolf packs. Typically, the coyote pack consists of six closely related adults, yearlings, and young.

Week 23   Most people hear coyotes rather than see them. The call of coyotes is high pitched. It has been described as a yip, bark, or yelp.

Week 24   Raccoons are native to North America. They are a medium-sized mammal with very sensitive front paws and a facial mask.

Week 25   In captivity, raccoons wash or douse their food in water. However, raccoons do not wash their food in the wild.

Week 26   Another mammal native to the Americas is the cougar. There are many other names for the cougar, such as mountain lion, puma, catamount, and panther.

Week 27   The cougar is a large, solitary cat. It is the second heaviest cat in the Americas. Only the jaguar is heavier. The cougar is the fourth heaviest cat in the world.

Week 28   The cougar is a slender, agile cat with huge paws and large hind legs. These characteristics give the cougar great leaping and sprinting ability.

Week 29   The American black bear lives throughout North America. In fact, it lives in forty-one of the fifty states in the United States. The black bear is generally smaller than the brown bear and lacks the shoulder hump.

Week 30

"The Panther"
OGDEN NASH

The panther is like a leopard,

Except it hasn't been peppered.

Should you behold a panther crouch,

Prepare to say Ouch.

Better yet, if called by a panther,

Don't anther.

Journal Topics

Someone who wants to become a better piano player plays the piano every day, and someone who wants to become a better painter paints every day. In the same way, a person who wants to become a better writer should write every day.

Just as a pianist enjoys playing the piano and a painter enjoys painting, we should enjoy writing without worrying about whether or not someone is going to correct our writing. We should write for fun and pleasure, knowing that practice will make us better writers.

A good way to practice your writing every day is to write in a journal—a notebook with blank paper. When you write in your journal, do not worry about anyone correcting your writing. This is a time for you to have fun putting your thoughts on paper.

Example   Write at least three sentences on the following topic:

Describe yourself.

In your journal, you might write something like the following:

> I am a skinny nine-year-old boy with straight dark brown hair and brown eyes. My skin is brown except for the pink scars on my knees that I got when I crashed my bike. I am wearing blue jeans and a red shirt.

At the beginning of class on Tuesday, Wednesday, and Thursday, you will spend five minutes writing in your journal. Each entry should be at least three sentences long. The following are suggested topics.

Topic # 1.   Write about what you like to do after school.

2.   Describe the place where you are now.

3.   Write about something for which you are thankful.

4.   Write about somewhere you would like to go.

5.   Write about how you once helped someone.

6.   Write about something that you can do now that you could not do when you were small.

7. Describe an animal that you like.

8. Write about something that you would like to learn to do.

9. Describe what you like to do outdoors.

10. Describe what you like to do indoors.

11. Describe a friend whom you admire.

12. Write about someone in your family.

13. Some people like to swim in the ocean. Others do not. Write your opinion about swimming in the ocean.

14. Write about an ocean creature.

15. Write about one of your favorite teachers.

16. Do you like snow? Why or why not?

17. What makes you laugh? Explain.

18. Write about someone for whom you are thankful.

19. What can you do to help someone at home?

20. Write about a time when you were surprised.

21. Write about an animal that you think is dangerous.

22. What makes you happy? Explain.

23. Imagine that you had a pet alligator. What would you name it and feed it? How would you care for it?

24. Write about a gift that you once received.

25. What would you like to do when you grow up? Why?

26. If you could plant some seeds, what kind would you plant? Why?

27. What is your favorite book? Why?

28. Write two or more things that you like about yourself, and explain.

29. What is your favorite game? Why?

30. Describe one of your friends.

31. If you could live anywhere in the world, where would you like to live? Why?

32. Would you like to travel to the moon? Why or why not?

33. If you had five dollars to spend at a grocery store, what would you buy? Why?

34. Do you like rain? Why or why not?

35. Write about what you can do to have a healthy body.

36. What school subject do you enjoy most? Why?

37. If you were to make dinner for your teacher, what would you make and how would you make it?

38. Would you rather spend a day in the mountains or at the ocean? Explain.

39. Describe an animal that you think is beautiful.

40. Explain how you think ice cream is made.

41. How can you show friendship to someone?

42. How should friends treat each other?

43. Write about what you can do to take care of your teeth.

44. Write about a holiday that you enjoy.

45. Describe an animal that lives in a tree.

46. Write about something that you would like to make or build someday.

47. If you were to write a book someday, what kind of book would it be? Explain.

48. For what would you like people to remember you someday?

49. Write about why it is important to tell the truth.

50. Would you rather travel by bus or by airplane? Write reasons for your answer.

51. What can you do to make your home cleaner and more orderly?

52. Kay would like to go deep sea fishing someday. Would you? Why or why not?

53. What can you do to make your home a more cheerful place?

54. If you were to plant a garden, what would you plant? Why?

55. Write about something funny that once happened to you or to someone you know.

56. Write about a time when you were injured or ill.

57. If you could paint a room where you live, which room would you paint, and what color would you paint it? Write reasons for your answer.

58. Miss Ng believes her students should do an hour of homework each day even on weekends. How do you feel about homework?

59. Write what you know about owls.

60. Explain how you think lemonade is made.

61. Tom wants to be a teacher when he grows up. Would you like to become a teacher? Why or why not?

62. Kim cleans her house every Saturday. What do you usually do on Saturdays?

63. Write about something that you do well.

64. Write about something that you wish you could do better.

65. Write about someone who helps you.

66. Write about a story or movie that you enjoyed.

67. Write about a time when you lost something.

68. Describe a special toy that you liked when you were small.

69. Ann wants to become a veterinarian. Would you like to become a veterinarian? Why or why not?

70. Write about someone you know who might make a good U.S. President someday. Explain.

71. What is your favorite season—spring, summer, fall, or winter? Why?

72. Describe winter where you live.

73. Write about what you usually do on Mondays.

74. Which is your favorite day of the week? Why?

75. If you could be any animal for a day, what animal would you like to be? Why?

76. If you could have a grown-up's job for a day, which job would you choose? Why?

77. Write about someone whom you trust.

78. Write about what you can do to prevent sickness.

79. If you could be a super hero, what name and talents would you have? Why?

80. If you could fly like a bird or a super hero, where would you go, and what would you do?

81. Would you like to sail around the world? Why or why not?

82. Write about a gift that you would like to give someone someday.

83. How would your life be different if you were a tortoise?

84. Would you rather read a mystery story or a book about nature? Why?

85. Write about an insect or bug that you think is a pest.

86. Explain how you might groom a very dirty, shaggy dog.

87. What would you do if you found a mouse eating your food?

88. If you lived near the North Pole, what would you do to keep warm?

89. Write what you know about bees.

90. On a bunk bed, would you rather sleep on the top or on the bottom? Explain your answer.

91. Everybody makes mistakes. Write about a time when you made a mistake.

92. If you could go to the zoo today, what animals would you like to see? Write what you know about them.

93. Some people enjoy diagramming sentences. Others do not. How do you feel about diagramming sentences?

94. Write about what you can do to save electricity.

95. Explain how you think french fries are made.

96. Bill likes Mexican food, and Jill likes Italian food, but Rob prefers Chinese food. What kind of food do you like best? Describe it.

97. If you could dress up in a costume for fun, how would you dress? Why?

98. Write about a time when you were brave.

99. Would you like to spend a month in a submarine? Why or why not?

100. Why is it important to obey traffic laws?

Index

But (conjunction), 221

C

Canine, (L12)
Caper, (L98)
Capitalization, 57, 103, 107, 168, 184, 194
    abbreviations and initials, 168
    areas of country, 184
    family words, 168
    first word in line of poetry, 57
    first word of direct quotation, 107
    first word of sentence, 57
    greetings and closings, 185
    I, 57
    literary and music titles, 103
    outlines, 107
    proper adjectives, 189
    proper nouns, 27
    religions, *Bible*, deity, 184
    school subjects, 168
    seasons of the year, 195
    titles of persons (family words), 168
Capri, (L98)
Capricorn, (L98)
Case
    nominative, 243, 324
    nominative pronoun, 324
    objective, 248, 340
    objective pronoun, 340
    personal pronoun, 347
    possessive, 358
Cede, (L93)
Cedere, (L93)
Cent, (L61)
Centimeter, (L78)
Centipede, (L78)
Centum, (L78)
Cheap, (L33)
Cheep, (L33)
Cirrus, (L52)
Clarity, 336
Clause, 158
    dependent, 364, 371, 573
    independent, 364, 371
    subordinate, 364, 371, 573
Clause, (L62)
Claws, (L62)
Close, (L51)
Clothes, (L51)
Collapse, (L86)
Collective noun, 40
    subject-verb agreement, 476
Colon, 545

Colt, (L40)
Comma
    after dependent clauses, 371
    after introductory words, 330
    and appositives, 289
    before conjunction, 382
    in addresses, 274
    in compound sentence, 382
    in dates, 273
    in direct address, 284
    in direct quotation, 383
    in letter, 306
    in parts of an address, 274
    in titles or academic degrees, 285
    reversed names, 306
    separating descriptive adjectives, 370
    words in a series, 275
    words out of natural order, 331
Common noun, 27
Comparative degree, 259, 267, 529
Comparison adjectives, 259, 267
Comparison adverbs, 528–529
Comparisons using pronouns, 396
Complete sentence, 17
Complex sentence, 573–574
Compound adjective, 505
Compound forms, hyphen in, 489, 505
Compound nouns, forming plurals, 90
Compound parts of sentence, 226
    diagramming, 226
    subjects and verbs, 226
Compound relative pronouns, 389
Compound sentence, 375
    diagramming, 375
Compound subject, with singular or plural
    verb, 459
Concrete noun, 39
Confess, (L100)
Conjunction(s), defined, 221, 365
    coordinating, 221
    in compound parts of a sentence, 221
    in compound sentence, 376
    subordinating, 365
        list of, 365
Conjunctive adverb, 534
Contraction(s), 568
    apostrophe in, 568
    list of common, 568
    subject-verb agreement with, 471
    verb, a part of, 568
Coordinating conjunction(s), 221, 376
    list of, 221, 376

Cow, (L29)
Creak, (L35)
Creek, (L35)
Cumulus, (L52)

D

Molt, (L28)
Morning, (L25)
Mourning, (L25)

N

Negatives, 481
    avoiding double, 482
    in contractions, 481
New, (L17)
No and *yes*, comma after, 330
Nocturnal, (L18)
Nomad, (L110)
Nomadic, (L110)
Nomas, (L110)
Nominative case, 243, 324
Nominative pronoun, 324, 347
Nonessential, (L60)
Nor (conjunction), 221
Not (adverb), 481
Noun(s), defined, 39
    abstract, 39
    as antecedents, 299
    as appositives, 279
    collective, 40
    common, 27
    compound, 48
    concrete, 39
    diagramming, 138, 164, 205, 211, 226,
        238–239
    direct address, 284
    direct object, 163
    forming plurals of, 62, 66, 90
    indirect object, 210
    kinds of, 27, 39, 48–49
    modifiers, 173, 178, 189, 204
    object of preposition, 199
    possessive, 49
        as adjective, 179
    predicate nominative, 237
    proper, 27
    singular, 48
    special, 90

O

Object(s), 163, 199, 210, 340
    direct, 163
        diagramming, 164
    indirect, 210
    of preposition, 199
        correct use of pronouns as, 340
        diagramming, 205
Objective case, 248, 340, 347
    pronouns in, 340, 347
Offensive, (L13)

Omni, (L111)
Omnipotent, (L111)
Omniscient, (L111)
Optic, (L56)
Or (conjunction), 221, 376
Outline, 107, 216
    capitalization in, 107
    punctuation in, 216

P

Passive voice, 578
Past participle, 76, 318, 436–438, 442–443,
    447–448
Past tense, 35–36, 76, 318, 436–437, 442–443,
    447–448
Pater, patr, (L102)
Paternal, (L102)
Pathogen, (L105)
Pathology, (L105)
Pathos, (L105)
Patriarch, (L102)
Pause, (L2)
Paws, (L2)
Ped-, pedi-, (L64)
Period, 216, 231
    in outlines, 216
    rules for use of, 216, 231
Person, 311, 324, 347
Personal pronoun case forms, 347
    list of, 347
    plural, 347
    singular, 347
Phrase, 158, 199–200, 551–552
    diagramming, 199–200, 551–552
Pinniped, (L64)
Plural(s), formation of, 48, 62, 66, 90
Pollen, (L34)
Pollination, (L38)
Possessive adjective, 358
Possessive noun, 48
    diagramming, 178
Possessive pronoun, 358
    distinguishing from contractions, 359
Posterior, (L23)
Pre-, (L92)
Prearrange, (L92)
Precaution, (L92)
Precede, (L93)
Predator, (L3)
Predicate, 2, 10–11, 14, 138, 226
    compound, 226
    diagramming, 138, 226
    simple, 11

compound, 375
declarative, 6
diagramming, 138, 164, 205, 211, 226,
            238, 254, 280, 353, 523–524, 552
exclamatory, 6
fragment, 17, 21
imperative, 6
interrogative, 6
punctuation of, 216, 273, 284, 289,
            330–331, 336, 370–371, 382–383,
            408–409, 413, 453, 534–535,
            545–547
run-on, 94, 99
simple, 375
Series, commas in, 275
Silent letters, 117, 122
Simple predicate, 11
Simple preposition, 81, 86
Simple sentence, 375
Simple subject, 10
Singular, 48, 347
Soar, (L42)
Sol, (L107)
Solar, (L107)
Solstice, (L107)
Somnambulate, (L108)
Somnolence, (L108)
Somnus, (L108)
Sonare, (L109)
Sonata, (L109)
Sonorous, (L109)
Sore, (L42)
Sow, (L31)
Spec-, spic-, (L97)
Species, (L97)
Specimen, (L97)
Spelling, 62, 66, 90, 117, 122, 142–143, 149, 154
    adding suffixes, 142, 149
        to words ending in consonants, 149
        to words ending in silent *e*, 142
        to words ending in *y*, 143
    plural forms, 62, 66, 90
    possessives, 564
    words with *ie* and *ei*, 154
    words with silent letters, 117, 122
Spider, (L19)
Split predicate, 14
Stamen, (L34)
Stern, (L73)
Subject of a sentence, 2, 10, 14, 138, 226, 324
    agreement with verb, 458–459, 464–465,
        470–471, 476–477
    complete, 10

compound, 226
diagramming, 138, 226, 375
    of imperative and interrogative
        sentences, 17
    pronoun as, 324
    simple, 10
    understood, 17
Subject-verb agreement, 458–459, 464–465,
        470–471, 476–477
Subordinating conjunction, 365
Sufficient, (L21)
Suffixes, 142–143, 149
Superlative degree, 259, 267, 528
Sure or *surely*, 539

T
Tace-, tacit-, (L89)
Tacit, (L89)
Tact, (L106)
Tactile, (L106)
Tactus, (L106)
Tail, (L6)
Tale, (L6)
Than, (L54)
That or *which*, 387
Their, (L8)
Then, (L54)
There, (L8)
Thorax, (L67)
Titles, 103, 414, 430
Troublesome verbs, 71, 318–319, 436–437,
        442–443, 447–448
Tut-, (L103)
Tutelage, (L103)
Tutor, (L103)

U
Underline or italics, 430

V
Vad-, (L80)
Verb(s), defined, 24, 44, 132
    action, 24
    active voice, 578
    agreement with subject, 458–459, 464–465
        470–471, 476–477
    compound, 226
    diagramming, 138, 226, 375
    helping (auxiliary), 44
        list of, 44
    irregular, 71, 318–319, 436–437, 442–443,
        447–448
    linking, 132
    passive voice, 578

principal parts of, 76
regular, 31, 35
tense, 35
Vertebrate, (L15)
Vertical, (L24)

W
Wail, (L27)
Weak, (L65)
Week, (L65)
Well and *good*, 500
Whale, (L27)
Which or *that*, 387
Who and *whom*, 401–402
Who's, (L10)
Whose, (L10)

Y
Yes and *no*, comma after, 330
You understood, 17
Your, (L11)
You're, (L11)

Z
Zephyr, (L46)